Heretics

Heretics

The Other Side of Early Christianity

Gerd Lüdemann

SCM PRESS LTD

Translated by John Bowden from the German
Ketzer. Die andere Seite des fr hen Christentums,
published 1995 by Radius Verlag, Stuttgart, with
additions and corrections by the author.

0 334 02616 4

First British edition published 1996
by SCM Press Ltd,
9–17 St Albans Place, London N1 0NX

Typeset by Regent Typesetting,
and printed in Great Britain by
Biddles Ltd, Guildford and King's Lynn

For David K. Wilson of Nashville, who since 1979 has listened to much of the material and has discussed it over lunch with me several times. Thank you for your friendship over the years, Pat!

Contents

Preface

The 'Explanation to my Readers' and Chapter 1 explain the layout of this book and the need for it. I recommend reading the 'Ten Golden Words' of the Epilogue as a way into it. They do not completely sum up the content of the book, but they always underlie the explanations and draw conclusions for the present from the historical reconstruction.

This work is on the one hand deliberately intended to be a specialist work and therefore contains extensive notes, which include an account of the state of research on various issues. On the other hand I have written the text in such a way that interested lay people can also follow the argument. The sources quoted in the text and in the appendixes, translated by me, are meant to encourage curiosity about early Christianity. If this book can arouse new interest in the time of Christian origins, which is decisive for Christian culture, then it will have fulfilled its main purpose.

Again I have to thank many helpers. The main burden has been borne by my secretary Silke Röthke, Christina Abel and Frank Schleritt. Dr Jürgen Wehnert read through the whole manuscript critically. I am also indebted to Matthias Günther and Andreas Technow for valuable references. Martina Janssen helped in specialized Coptic and Matthias Wellstein in specialized Latin questions. Arnold Betz was helpful in Nashville. Dean Joseph Hough granted me the status of a Visiting Scholar at the Vanderbilt Divinity School between 1992 and 1996. I am grateful to my wife Elke and our daughters Amrei, Eyke, Marei and Reiga for their love and care on both sides of the Atlantic. Last but not least, I thank my Vanderbilt colleague and friend Eugene TeSelle for a final look at the manuscript and my friend Dr John Bowden for his great care and the creative empathy with which he translated the present book. Since I have added considerable material to it and corrected some mistakes, this book, which is being published simultaneously by SCM Press and Westminster John Knox Press, is a new edition of the German original.

Where they are not immediately obvious, the abbreviations follow the list in the *Theologische Realenzyklopädie*.

Göttingen, May 1995   Gerd Lüdemann

An Explanation to my Readers

The subject of this book has occupied me since my very first work in 1975 on Simon Magus,[1] first mentioned in Acts 8, who is traditionally regarded as the first Christian heretic. Since then I have gone more deeply into the topic in several monographs and articles.[2] Some chapters came into being during my involvement in the McMaster research project on 'Normative Self-Definition in Early Christianity and Judaism' in Hamilton, Ontario between 1977 and 1979; others formed the basis for lectures in the June Ramsey Sunday School Class of the First Presbyterian Church in Nashville and were later developed into lectures and seminars at Vanderbilt Divinity School and in Göttingen.

The sometimes vigorous controversies in the church and theology and in public over my book on the resurrection published last year[3] are the internal context in which I am now presenting this book. This controversy made clear an abysmal ignorance[4] of critics in the historical sphere,[5] and at the same time a splitting apart of piety and scholarship which amounts to schizophrenia. Therefore it seemed necessary in the interest both of historical truth and of Christianity itself to make a critical examination of another pillar of church and theology, namely holy scripture and its authority. The starting point of this investigation is the insight already developed by Gotthold Ephraim Lessing in his dispute with the chief pastor of Hamburg, Johann Melchior Goeze, that the Christian faith and the Christian church already existed before there was a holy scripture of the New Testament.[6] As he put it succinctly, the New Testament is 'a work of the Catholic church, and the appeal to the writings of the New Testament as intrinsically binding on the faith is a dogma of the Catholic church. From this fact ... anyone may draw the conclusion he thinks to be good and right.'[7]

However, one can get the impression that while this has been confessed in the church and theology, its consequences have not been recognized, and in public silence has prevailed. To make the point once again: holy scripture is the word of man (and not the word of God), collected by people at a time when Christianity had already left its beginnings behind it. It is the collection of the victorious party, which, following a well-tried recipe, excluded and suppressed the documents of the groups that it had overcome, and finally also exterminated their defenders. Precisely from this perspective the striking finds in Nag Hammadi in Egypt in 1945, which have been overshadowed by the most recent discussion of the Dead Sea Scrolls,[8] and have only been accessible in their entirety in English translation for two brief decades,[9] are an indispensable corrective for gaining an unpartisan view of the beginnings of Christianity, at the same time taking into account sources which were previously already in existence. Whereas before the Nag Hammadi find scholars had to content themselves almost completely with inferring the doctrines contested by the church fathers from their own polemical treatises, now the situation has fundamentally changed. The 'heretics' speak for themselves, and we have the occasion, indeed the obligation, to examine and correct our views of Christian origins.[10] One might almost follow Friedrich Nietzsche in saying that as a result of this find we are again in the youth of science where the history of earliest Christianity is concerned and can investigate the truth like a beautiful fairy which almost bewitches us: 'What a different attraction this exerts compared to that time when everything essential has been found and there only remains for the seeker a scanty gleaning (which sensation may be learnt in several historical disciplines).'[11]

However, I have also written this book to direct attention once again to Jesus, out of the conviction that the Christianity of all times *must* be able to take up a relationship to Jesus of Nazareth if it is to be credible. This is true of the beginnings of the Christian religion, which, along with all later developments, have to be measured by Jesus. However, *today* this appeal to Jesus cannot take place without pain and consequences; after decades of the massive influence of kerygmatic or dialectical theology, it requires changes in theology and in the church.[12] So the pages which follow also describe another, unknown, side of Christianity. I would like once again to show curious Christians their Christianity as something strange, in order to direct their attention to what is really Christian, to Jesus as hardly anyone still knows him today.

I

Introduction. Method and Interests

The history of primitive Christianity[13] sets out to depict the historical course of the first two Christian centuries, or, more precisely, it deals with the first phase of church history which was inaugurated by the appearance of Jesus. It ends[14] where the process of the consolidation of the early Christian groups has been completed. At this stage dogmatic and ethical norms had been developed over what was right and wrong, good and bad; the canon had been formed; with the rise of the monarchical episcopate the early Christian communities or their bishops had established a power base over against their opponents, and it was also possible to implement sanctions externally.[15] There is further historical justification for this demarcation in the fact that towards the end of the second century oral traditions genetically connected with Jesus came to an end, and academic Christian theology – if it is more than mere reconstruction of the past – has to[16] safeguard its origins by constant reference back to Jesus.[17] That is true even given the discovery that a good deal of early Christian literature, e.g. the letters of Ignatius of Antioch, [18] get by without having recourse to the historical Jesus, since from a historical perspective Jesus remains the decisive catalyst of the Christian movement.[19]

This first phase of early Christianity is the period in which the direction is set for what is later to be regarded as Christian. In it Christianity emerged as a separate phenomenon. What Johann Salomo Semler (1725–1791) first discovered, [20] and Gotthold Ephraim Lessing (1729–1781) branded on the conscience of every honest person, is true of this time, namely that in it there was already Christian faith and a Christian church before a New Testament existed.[21] To this degree the history of earliest Christianity retains a significance which towers above subsequent eras. In it we can recognize fundamental Christian principles, and only in this phase of Christianity are there traditions of Jesus which were not handed down exclusively in literary form (e.g. through the Gospels). This early period of Christianity needs to be investigated in purely historical terms – one could almost say that it is our primary Bible – since as a result of the dissolution of the dogma of inspiration the scriptural principle[22] has once and for all become a historical entity for academic theology.

This can be explained by referring to an article written by Wolfhart Pannenberg in 1962.[23] Appealing to the clear exegetical sense of scripture, Luther joined battle with the papal magisterium, in the conviction that his own exegetical results were *identical* with the '"essential content" of Scripture as this was concentrated in the person and history of Jesus Christ and unfolded in the dogmas of the church' (5). This certainty was the basis for his hermeneutical principle that scripture is clear or self-evident.[24] 'The doctrine of the clarity of Scripture necessarily led to the demand that each theological statement should be based on the historical-critical exposition of scripture' (6). Nevertheless, historical-critical research into scripture conjured up the fundamental crisis which we face today. If for Luther the literal sense of the scriptures was still identical with their historical content, for us by contrast the two have moved apart: 'The picture of Jesus and his history which the various New Testament writers give us cannot, without further qualification, be regarded as identical with the actual course of events ... Luther could still identify his own doctrine with the content of the biblical writings, literally understood. For us, on the contrary, it is impossible to overlook the historical distance between every possible theology today and the primitive Christian period. This distance has become the source of our most vexing theological problems' (6). Or to put it another way: the gulf between historical fact and its significance, between history and proclamation, between the history of Jesus and the varied picture of his history in the New Testament[25] makes it impossible for us to continue to offer a serious defence of the inspiration of the writings of the New Testament or even to identify Word of God and holy scriptures.[26]

Demarcations and positive construction

These insights lead to three ways in which the approach of the present book polemically stands apart, and the consequences which they entail. First, it stands apart from a Word of God theology according to which 'an authoritative revelation which can be ascertained methodologically provides an objective basis for the presentation of Christian teaching'.[27] Here there is a presumption of dogmatic content vertically from above which is no longer accessible to historical questioning, so that any historical investigation sees itself demoted to being an ancillary discipline. At the same time I should point out that such an objectifying theology sooner or later falls under the spell of supranaturalism and thus by-passes both the historicity of the people of antiquity who composed the biblical writings and present-day contemporaries who are perceiving the word of that time. For such dogmatic theology the glimmering, flickering life which the historical approach attempts to grasp is merely colourless and insignificant.

Secondly, it stands apart from a kerygmatic theology[28] according to which theology is essentially the exegesis of scripture.[29] The representatives of this theology refuse to speak at any point of the history *behind* the texts[30] in which the proclamation of the New Testament is rooted. They say that while this may perhaps be historically interesting, it is theologically illegitimate, since 'all the reconstruction which investigates behind the text is justified only as long as it subordinates itself without compromise to interpretation that respects the text'.[31] Instead of devoting themselves to the task of a historical reconstruction they deliberately want to devote themselves to the address and claim of the New Testament witnesses and derive the criterion for distinguishing between theology and history from this.[32] It is no coincidence that this trend, too, has not produced any history of earliest Christianity.[33]

Thirdly, it stands apart from a trend in scholarship which seeks to combine historical-critical work with a salvation-historical view. Thus e.g. Leonhard Goppelt[34] presupposes that only the 'salvation-historical' view can appropriately take account of the relationship between Christianity and Judaism. But although Goppelt's work is also historical in its arrangement and gives an instructive picture of 'the development of the relationship between Christianity and Judaism up to the formation of the catholic church at the end of the second century' (15), its author postulates a salvation-historical continuity, a fulfilling of the old covenant in the work of Christ (319), and thus a very primitive theory of restitution. For example, Goppelt says: 'In fact the repudiation of the gospel by Israel as a

3

community of people is the last decisive turning point in its history and the ... ultimate cause of the destruction of the second temple' (311). But such a view, which is shattering for all Jews of the subsequent period, is only a dogmatic-triumphalistic postulate of Christian theology and *in no way* the result of historical scholarship, though we have to recognize that here at least, in contrast to kergyma theology, the investigation of the history of the first two centuries is recognized as a task and there is a move beyond the limits of the canon.[35]

Besides, despite all attempts at differentiation (e.g. the 'canon in the canon'), in practice the principle of the canon[36] leads to the writings included in the canon being given a higher status (cf. the number of commentaries written on the individual writings of the canon by comparison with those on non-canonical writings) and history being made a history of the victors. In this respect Gustav Krüger is right:

'The existence of a New Testament science or a science of the New Testament as a special theological historical discipline is a main hindrance, first to a fruitful investigation of earliest Christianity and indeed the New Testament itself, which leads to assured and generally recognized results, and secondly to a healthy theological and academic education.'[37]

For it is quite simply a requirement of historical justice that initially all the extant writing from the initial phase of Christianity should be accorded the same rights, and that historical understanding should not be hindered or limited *a priori* by the dogmatic positing of a holy scripture. However, that is unfortunately the case today, since contemporary theological literature is to a considerable degree partisan, i.e. has an ecclesiastical or clerical orientation.[38]

This clericalization is favoured by the fact, first, that with a few exceptions, ancient historians and philologists do not generally involve themselves in exegesis, and secondly, that access to a theological career at a German university is closed to those who have not been baptized. In addition it should be noted that those who do not have a baptismal certificate may not take the state (!) examination for a theological diploma in the theological faculties, and e.g.

Jews cannot get a theological doctorate on a New Testament subject in a German theological faculty.

Thirdly, it is often presupposed that theology is a discipline of the church.[39] This widespread view has hindered research more than it has helped it.[40] Here a statement applies which at first sounds brutal: 'A science of Christian faith is no more Christian than the science of criminology is criminal.'[41] For theology as a discipline is primarily un-ecclesiastical,[42] in that it is in search of the truth. However, it must immediately be added that Protestant Christianity whole-heartedly endorses the radical quest for truth, and 'people in all the church parties of Protestant Christianity know that it has an end where fear of the truth begins to prevail. A church which closes off the way to the quest for the truth for the sake of blessedness may be deeply grounded in human nature, but it will not be grounded in Jesus Christ. It is not a Christian church at all.'[43]

Fourthly, most exegetical contributions today are artificially focussed on the theological meaning, the scope, of the New Testament texts. The question of the canon remains tacitly outside the discussion, as though its significance could be determined even without solid historical foundations. These contributions often presuppose unconsciously that reason is to be instructed and limited by revelation or the kerygma. 'In practice that then means nothing other than clericalism. For reason is valid either wholly or not at all.'[44] In this connection it is often emphasized that exegesis is a matter of obedience.[45] But once the language of preaching infiltrates, then I would prefer to say that exegesis is 'first and above all a matter of love which makes any person and any text speak and seeks to understand what it means, without going beyond it'.[46]

It is a fact that many works of present-day exegesis seem bloodless, and by seeking out the intention of the text, comparing individual Gospels and carefully separating redaction and tradition, lead us to forget that the early Christian writings derive from a movement which was so brimming over with vitality that it had virtually conquered the whole of the Roman empire within 150 years. An atmosphere of unreality thus surrounds most works on the New Testament.[47] Often people prefer to use vague religious abstractions instead of giving concrete historical details.[48] So one can hardly avoid the impression that the method traditionally applied sometimes literally robs the texts of their power. On the other hand we need to ask whether 'the widespread frightful lameness and staleness of the church's message, its powerlessness to speak to people of today, and likewise the lack of credibility that attaches to the church as such are not very largely connected with its fear of letting the work of critical historical theology bear fruit in the proper way'.[49] Here we need not bring the affirmation of the historical-critical method into such a close intrinsic connection with the doctrine of justification as Ebeling does, but we must regard it as an already profane and even more Christian requirement of truthfulness or what Friedrich Albert Lange has called the 'morality of thought'.

In its account of earliest Christian history my work deliberately begins 'below'; in other words, my concern is to humanize the history of earliest Christianity so that present-day contemporaries can recognize themselves in the violent process of the earliest history of Christianity – in the conflicts, anxieties, longings and dreams of the people of the time. Interestingly enough, the first Chancellor of the University of Göttingen, Johann Lorenz von Mosheim (1694–1755), thought of the task of writing church history in a similar way.[50] For example, this 'father of modern church historiography' regards the conversion of many from paganism to Christianity not as a consequence of the miracles – as supernatural church historiography of his time sought to do – but as a consequence of the fear of punishment and hope for a life of bliss in the beyond. The pragmatic method which Mosheim used in this way resulted in a tremendous humanization of the process of church history. Such a quasi-anthropological approach to church history also formally meant a Copernican shift for the history of earliest Christianity, [51] since from now on, here too recourse to the Holy Spirit or the exalted Christ as supernatural entities was made impossible.[52] That was all the more the case since 'as Mosheim understood it ... church history is more a pragmatic series of events which take place within the world and to this degree can be seen through'.[53]

However, a church historiography understood in this way[54] does not reckon with a special intervention of God at individual points in history. I regard the objection which can so often be heard in this

6

context, [55] that every historiography has its presuppositions, so that theological church historiography presupposes that God intervenes in the course of the history, as quite simply outrageous. Of course all historiography has a subjective colouring. But from that we are merely to derive the requirement that one should be aware of this presupposition with the aim of producing research which is as objective as possible, [56] and not take refuge in an underhand way almost in a *deus ex machina*.

Anyone who investigates the history of Christianity is also often required to be a believer. But such a demand closes its eyes to what really happened in history. The historian who constantly puts a dogmatic weight in the scales in order to weigh his historical object lacks any real historical understanding. This seeks above all to investigate, discover, detect, examine and understand, and if it evaluates at all, it does so only at a secondary stage. For example, the condemnations of the church fathers according to a particular dogmatic criterion seem more like tinkering with things at a later stage, an activity which seems no more significant than, say, that of a doctor today who wants to cure the ancient Greeks and Roman of the illnesses from which they died. Such an enterprise can only be described as a model example of paper scholarship. [57] Genuine historical research seeks above all to do justice to its subject, to describe it in a living way instead of judging it by criteria derived from outside. But that does not exclude the description of intrinsic problems, the internal tensions of what is being considered.

Scholarship lives in and by its methods, but that does not mean that it is exhausted in these methods and that 'of themselves they give it its value. For there are good and bad methods, and only the critical ones are good, above all those to the preference of which scholarship owes its self-criticism.' [58] There is no universally valid method which fits every source. That cannot even be expected in historiography, since it does not approach the material with a prior view but grows out of the object itself and constantly checks whether it is doing justice to the object. Moreover, methodological reflection always follows methods which work organically. [59]

All our lives we must fight against a reluctance to keep going back into the real sources. Nothing is so paralysing for historical criticism than seeking the solution of historical problems outside it or even in a divine intervention. The natural methodological principle must be to infer the unknown primarily from the known. In other words, it is important to begin with completely clear facts[60] and from there to argue back to what is less certain.[61]

My idea of a secular church history, developed in connection with the thinking of Franz Overbeck, [62] issues in the requirement that the process of church history should be pursued 'in pure worldliness and, as the literal translation of the word "profane" has it, in a "nefarious" way', [63] deconsecrated and purged of all special ecclesiastical and theological regulations and privileges of knowledge. Such a statement has not yet said anything about the truth or untruth, the reality or the unreality, of the object to be described. 'Profane church history is not based on the assumption that human religious life is an error, but it does presuppose that it must be investigated as far as possible without prejudices.'[64] However, I think that if God is revealed to human beings in Jesus of Nazareth, profane church historiography, too, indeed profane church historiography in particular, cannot come out against the truth. If it is an honest quest for the truth, it will not oppose its object. In showing that the claim is experienced as true, [65] it may ultimately bring out its truth as a possibility, or, to put it another way, following Erich Seeberg: 'I would think that historical work is capable of producing a historical picture of Christianity which to some degree has the same productive effect as an original itself.'[66]

Now it is clear that if the enormous amount of historical and literary material – even in the first two Christian centuries – is to be tamed, over and above the definition of a history of earliest Christianity which has already been given, the task has to be meaningfully pursued on the basis of a certain set of questions. Thus the guiding perspective could be the cult or worship or the liturgy, [67] or it could be theology, [68] or the history-of-religions question how in the first two centuries the Hellenization of Christianity as an originally Jewish religion took place (Adolf Harnack).[69] At the same time, attention should be drawn to the importance of local early histories (Rome, [70] Corinth, [71] Ephesus, [72] Philippi, [73] Antioch, [74] Alexandria, [75] etc.).

However, I want to choose as my guiding perspective the aspect of heresy or the heretic.[76] The term 'heresy' today denotes deviations 'from a view or norm of behaviour which is generally declared to be valid', [77] and is therefore well suited to be a guiding perspective for an account which aims to interest the general reader.[78] The last history of heresy[79] in earliest Christianity was written in 1884 by the Jena professor Adolf Hilgenfeld, [80] and is to some degree the offshoot of a great many histories of heresy, though these in part cover the whole of church history.[81] Hilgenfeld's work is orientated on the question of which groups of the Catholic church can be seen as heretics, and after a survey of the anti-heretical writings of the first century he begins with Simon; then follow Menander, Satornilus, Basilides, etc.[82] However, I shall not strive to imitate this approach, which in some respect corresponds to that of Hilgenfeld's predecessors. Here I shall go more by the questions raised by the Göttingen patristic and New Testament scholar Walter Bauer, who in 1934 produced a truly memorable work *Orthodoxy and Heresy in Earliest Christianity*.[83] In the introduction to this book, written with passion, [84] he states:

'In our day and age there is no longer any debate that in terms of a scientific approach to history, the New Testament writings cannot be understood properly if one now looks back on them from the end of the process of canonization as sacred books, and prizes them as constituent parts of the celestial charter of salvation, with all the attendant characteristics. We have long since become accustomed to understanding them in terms of their own time – the gospels as more or less successful attempts to relate the life of Jesus; the Pauline letters as occasional writings, connected with specific and unrepeatable situations, and having spatial as well as temporal limitations to their sphere of authority. We must also approach the "heretics" in the same way. We need to understand them also in terms of their own time, and not to evaluate them by means of ecclesiastical doctrine which was developing, or which later became a ready-made norm ...

In order to exclude from the outset all modern impressions and judgments, I will proceed from the view concerning the heretics and their doctrines which was cherished already in the second century by the ancient church, and will test its defensibility in hopes of discovering, by means of such a critical procedure, a route to the goal. The ecclesiastical position includes roughly the following main points:

1. Jesus reveals the pure doctrine to his apostles, partly before his death, and partly in the forty days before his ascension.

2. After Jesus' final departure, the apostles apportion the world among themselves, and each takes the unadulterated gospel to the land which has been allotted him.

3. Even after the death of the disciples the gospel branches out further. But now obstacles to it spring up within Christianity itself. The devil cannot resist sowing weeds in the divine wheatfield – and he is successful at it. True Christians blinded by him abandon the pure doctrine. This development takes place in the following sequence: unbelief, right belief, wrong belief. There is scarcely the faintest notion anywhere that unbelief might be changed directly into what the church calls false belief. No, where there is heresy, orthodoxy must have preceded. For example, Origen puts it like this: "All heretics at first are believers; then later they swerve from the rule of faith."

4. Of course, right belief is invincible. In spite of all the efforts of Satan and his instruments, it repels unbelief and false belief, and extends its victorious sway ever further.

Scholarship has not found it difficult to criticize these convictions. It knows that ecclesiastical doctrine was not yet present with Jesus; likewise, that the twelve apostles by no means played the role assigned to them out of consideration for the purity and revealed nature of ecclesiastical dogma. Further, historical thinking that is worthy of this name refuseso to employ here the correlatives "true" and "untrue", "bad" and "good". It is not easily convinced of the moral inferiority attributed to the heretics ...

Sooner or later, however, a point is reached at which criticism bogs down ... It all too easily submits to the ecclesiastical opinion as to what is early and late, original and dependent, essential and unimportant for the earliest history of Christianity. If my impression is correct, even today the overwhelmingly dominant view still is that for the period of Christian origins, ecclesiastical doctrine (of course, only as this pertains to a certain stage in its development) already represents what is primary, while heresies, on the other hand, somehow are a deviation from the genuine. I do not mean to say that this point of view must be false, but neither can I regard it as self-evident, or even as demonstrated and clearly established. Rather, we are confronted here with a problem that merits our attention.[85]

Bauer's method is wholly rooted in historicism, which is shaped by the emergence of the autonomy of historical consciousness.[86] It presupposes the validity of historical facts and is not afraid of setting the insights of scholarship critically against the assertions of the church.[87] Accordingly, Bauer is similarly the representative of a profane church historiography, [88] the topicality and fruitfulness I shall be going on to demonstrate.

The fact that I have taken over his approach does not mean that I always agree with the individual results of his work. Thus at the end of the second century the heretical doctrines, or what the official church regarded as heretical, were not necessarily identical with what certain circles regarded as heretical a century earlier.[89] Moreover, the theology of those groups which branded others as heretics at the end of the second century cannot automatically be identified with the theology of those who did the same thing at the end of the first century. Rather, several points should be made. First, Bauer's approach, which, starting from the end of the second century, begins by using the expressions 'heresy' and 'orthodoxy' purely formally for the early period, represents a fruitful heuristic perspective for doing justice to the multiplicity of 'Christianities' in the first two centuries and the battles between them. Used for the early period, 'orthodoxy' then simply means the claim to possess the right faith, which denies it to others who deviate and even accuses them of heresy. Secondly, beyond question, in some areas what was later called heresy preceded 'orthodoxy'. This insight of Bauer's proves itself in particular in connection with the earliest Jewish Christian community of Jerusalem, the descendants of which were declared heretics. But it may also apply to other Christian groups. Thirdly, Bauer's work leaves the task of describing how despite, or precisely because of, the plurality of Christian groups in the early period, at a later date an 'orthodox' Catholic church developed with fixed forms and institutions from which 'heresy' was finally excluded. However, as since the publication of the second edition of his work (in 1964), the whole manuscript find from Nag Hammadi has been made accessible, [90] more attention is being paid to the so-called New Testament Apocrypha[91] and the interest of scholars in the second century generally has deepened, [92] a new reconstruction of the origins of early Christianity makes sense, all the more so since the development of what is known as the New Testament took place in this second century.[93] In other words, this period – and not already the first century – saw the emergence of the basic decision as to what was to form the holy scripture of catholic Christians, a decision which had far-reaching consequences for the non-Catholic groups. To put it pointedly: *in the period from the first Christian generations to the end of the second century, more important decisions were made for the whole of Christianity than were made from the end of the second century to the present day.*

The structure of the present book

The following chapter deals with two works which disputed with heretics at the end of the second or the beginning of the third century, the five books 'Against the Heresies' of Bishop Irenaeus of Lyons, and the 'Prosecution Speech against the Heretics' from the pen of Tertullian of Carthage. Both works made an essential contribution to the 'refutation' of the heresies excluded by the Catholic church, and with their historical picture of orthodoxy always preceding heresy misled Christian theology for almost two thousand years, deterring critical scholarship from reconstructing Christian origins as they really were. By closely examining the methods of these two influential opponents of heresy and showing their limitations, I hope to lift some of the veil which still lies over the first two Christian centuries and arouse a desire for a new approach to Christianity during this period.

Chapter 3 is about the Jewish Christians of Jerusalem in the first two centuries. The title is 'How the Heresiologists Became Heretics.' It centres on the fact that the earliest visible battle against those who thought otherwise was started by the first Christians in Jerusalem. *They* were the ones who in fact introduced the concept of heresy into the church, in opposition to Paul, whereas Paul was distinguished by a relatively great openness towards Christians who thought otherwise. 'Paul's as yet quite rudimentary organization of thought patterns, in combination with an apostolic openness that leads him to become everything to everyone so as to win all, allows him to display a spirit of toleration which scarcely knows what a heretic might be.'[94] Of the apostles before him Paul writes: 'Whether then it was I or they, so we preach and so you believed' (I Cor. 15.11). At the same time, he shows himself conciliatory towards adversaries and remarks:

'Some indeed preach Christ from envy and rivalry, but others from
good will. The latter do it out of love, knowing that I am put here
for the defence of the gospel; the former proclaim Christ out of
partisanship, not sincerely but thinking to afflict me in my imprisonment. What then? Only that in every way, whether in pretence or in
truth, Christ is proclaimed, and in that I rejoice' (Phil. 1.15–18a).

Paul even attempts to convince those who deny the resurrection in
Corinth (I Cor. 15.12) without excluding them from the community. His condemnation is sweeping only of such a severe offence as
sexual intercourse between stepson and stepmother (I Cor. 5.1ff.)
and of Jewish-Christian adversaries who had found their way into
his Gentile Christian communities. In the latter case he speaks of a
conditional judgment of condemnation (Gal. 1.8f.; cf. Phil. 3.2) as
a reaction[95] to the way in which they have vilified him, and in the
former case 'the handing over to Satan' is qualified by an explicit
statement of deliverance in the last judgment.[96] Chapter 4 is therefore devoted to Paul as the sole heretic of the earliest period.

After what has been said about heresy as the perspective governing this account, the other chapter headings follow almost automatically. Chapter 5 describes the heirs of Paul, who in fact
divided into two wings: both appealed explicitly to the apostle and
composed or forged letters in his name; one wing accused the other
of heresy (but not *vice versa*).

For reasons dictated by the subject matter, Chapter 6 turns
directly from this to Marcion, the great reformer of the second
century, who compiled the first canon of the New Testament, consisting of the Gospel of Luke and letters of Paul (both in their
'original' content); however, he was soon vilified as the firstborn of
Satan.

Chapter 7 discusses the heresies in the Johannine circle, though
these come chronologically *before* Marcion; here special attention
is paid to the split in this circle which by a stroke of luck has been
documented in II and III John.

After the spotlight has been directed, through such concrete
persons and situations, on the 'heresies' in earliest Christianity, and
their history has been related, Chapter 8 turns to the question of
the origin of the Apostles' Creed and Chapter 9 to the problem of
the formation of the New Testament canon. In this way we again

reach the historical starting point of the book, the catholic stand-point of Irenaeus and Tertullian. At the same time this represents a contribution to the origin of the catholic church in the two over-lapping questions of the creed and the canon. From here, in Chapter 10 we look back at the beginnings, at Jesus of Nazareth, to clarify for the present day the relationship between his teaching, his actions and his hopes and what came after him.

2

Irenaeus of Lyons and Tertullian of Carthage. The Most Important Heresiologists in the Early Christian Period

I. Irenaeus[97]

Irenaeus came from Asia Minor; he was born there before 142 CE. In his youth he listened to Bishop Polycarp of Smyrna (for Polycarp see 160, 176 below). Later he became a presbyter in Lugdunum (Lyons); in 177 CE he brought a letter about Montanism from his community to Rome and after 178 was appointed Bishop of Lyons as successor to Pothinus. Two of his works have survived in translation: the 'Demonstration of the Apostolic Preaching', [98] a work of his old age discovered at the beginning of this century (in Armenian), and a Latin version from the end of the fourth century of his five-volume work on heretics, 'Unmasking and Refutation of the Gnosis Falsely So Called' (= *Haer*).[99] The Greek original of the latter work can be recovered in numerous places, [100] since not only the church historian Eusebius of Caesarea, but also later heresiologists like Hippolytus, [101] Epiphanius, [102] Theodoret[103] and the church historian Eusebius of Caesarea[104] make extensive literal quotations from it.

The lay-out of Irenaeus' work 'Against the Heresies'

The first book sets out to bring the doctrines of the heretics to light and contains much valuable material from the tradition (for this see further below, 18ff.). In the second book Irenaeus sets himself the aim 'of refuting their whole system by means of lengthened treatment' (Preface 2): for example, he discusses God the creator (II1–3) while at the same time repudiating Gnostic doctrines which differ.

The third book again sets out to refute the heretics on the basis of the traditional writings of the church and first discusses the four Gospels (III 1) and the teaching of the apostles (III 12f.); thematic excursuses are continually inserted (e.g. III 8 on Matt. 6.24; III 10: Luke and Mark on the God of the Old Testament). The fourth book turns to the discourses of Jesus and the fifth mainly to the letters of Paul, holding out the prospect of the new earth or the end of the world (V 28–36). In the prefaces to the five books and in individual transitional passages and retrospects Irenaeus links together what he says. But the whole work is fairly difficult to follow. One gets the impression that the bishop has taken over much material which had already been shaped, including interpretations of the Old Testament by his predecessors.

Irenaeus' interest

Irenaeus' theology is that of a churchman. He wages his war on the heretics on the one hand to defend the Creator God and on the other to protect the simple Christians of the church. Some passages in which the bishop himself speaks may make that clear.

'Certain men have set the truth aside and bring in lying words and vain genealogies which, as the apostle says, "promote speculations (*zeteseis*) rather than the divine training that is in faith" (I Tim. 1.4). By means of their craftily-constructed plausibilities they draw away the minds of the inexperienced and take them captive. These men falsify the oracles of God and prove themselves evil interpreters of the good word of revelation. They also overthrow the faith of many, by drawing them away under the pretence of superior knowledge, from him who founded and adorned the universe, as if they had something more excellent and sublime to reveal than that God who created the heaven and the earth and all things in them (Ex. 20.11; Ps. 146.6, LXX 145.6; Acts 4.24; 14.15). By means of specious and plausible words, they cunningly allure the simple-minded to inquire into their system; but they nevertheless clumsily destroy them, while they initiate them into their blasphemous and impious opinions respecting the Demiurge; and these simple ones are unable, even in such a matter, to distinguish falsehood from truth' (*Haer* I, Preface 1).[105]

'For this is the subterfuge of false persons, evil seducers and hypocrites, as they act who are from Valentinus. These men discourse to the multitude about those who belong to the church, whom they themselves call "vulgar" and "ecclesiastical". By these words they entrap the more simple, and entice them, imitating our phraseology, so that these may listen to them the oftener; and then these are asked regarding us, how it is that when they hold doctrines similar to ours, we without cause keep ourselves aloof from their company; and when they say the same things, and hold the same doctrine, we call them heretics?' (*Haer* III 15, 2).[106]

Thus Irenaeus sees the flock entrusted to him as an episcopal pastor threatened by heretical agitation in his own community. He insists on rigorous separation because, despite assertions to the contrary, the heretics were teaching something quite different from the church.

The following polemic against Marcus, a Gnostic Christian teacher from the middle of the second century, vividly attests how the contact between 'heretics' and 'believers' came about. Irenaeus reports:

'A sad example occurred in the case of a certain Asian, one of our deacons, who had received him (viz. Marcus) into his house. His wife, a women of remarkable beauty, fell a victim both in mind and body to this magician, and for a long time travelled about with him. At last, when with no small difficulty the brethren had converted her, she spent her whole time in the exercise of public confession, weeping over and lamenting the defilement which she had received from this magician' (*Haer* I 13, 5).

This polemic with its sexual undertones is as typical as it is unjust, but at the same time it illuminates the range of influence of the chief heretic Marcus whom Irenaeus is attacking.[107]

At this point Irenaeus continues his polemic by again using the almost automatic conclusiveness of a sexual accusation:

'Some of his disciples too, addicting themselves to the same practices, have deceived many silly women and defiled them. They proclaim that they are "perfect", so that no one can be compared to them with respect of the immensity of their knowledge, not even were you to mention Paul or Peter, or any other of the apostles. They assert that they themselves know more than all others, and that they alone have imbibed the greatness of the knowledge of that power which is unspeakable. They also maintain that they have attained to a height above all power, and that therefore they are free in every respect to act as they please, having no one to fear in anything ... Such are the words and deeds by which, in our own district of the Rhone, they have deluded many women, who have their consciences seared as with a hot iron (cf. I Tim. 4.2). Some of them, indeed, make a public confession of their sins; but others of them are ashamed to do this, and in a tacit kind of way, despairing of the life of God (cf. Eph. 1.18), have apostatized altogether; while others hesitate between the two courses and incur what is implied in the proverb "neither without nor within"' (*Haer* I 13, 6f.)

When those who were attacked read this and other remarks on liturgical rites and formulae of redemption (cf. *Haer* I 21), they protested vigorously, as Hippolytus reports around twenty years later:[108]

For also the blessed presbyter Irenaeus, having approached the subject of a refutation in a more unconstrained spirit, has explained such washings and redemptions (viz. of their teacher Marcus, like the spiritual wedding and anointing the dying with olive oil), describing their action at length. And when some of them read it, they denied having received such doctrines. Indeed they are always taught to deny' (*Ref* VI 37).[109]

It is important to recognize that Irenaeus and his successors are polemicists in the grand style and treat their opponents unjustly. Irenaeus' work is a typical 'example of an unorganized and tiresome attack on heretics which, lacking spiritual superiority, seizes upon any argument with which it will disparage, cast suspicion on and caricature the enemy'.[110]

For Irenaeus, 'Gnosis falsely so called' is a portmanteau name for a series of groups which are in many respects opposed to one another.[111] Thus in the preface to *Haer* II he writes that in Book I he has first demonstrated the falsehood of the inventions of the Valentinians (and here in particular the Ptolemaeans). The other heretics are in effect their forebears, and all derive from Simon

Magus. In attacking the Valentinians, Irenaeus thinks that he can get at the others at the same time. Cf. further *Haer* II 31, 1: 'Since those who are of the school of Valentinus have been refuted, the whole multitude of heretics are in fact also overthrown.'

In his first book he had evidently assimilated an earlier work against the heretics which derives all heresies from Simon Magus (cf. *Haer* I 23, 1: Simon, 'from whom all heresies derive'). In the work by his predecessor which Irenaeus uses, Simon is followed by his pupil Menander, then Saturninus, Basilides, Carpocrates, Cerinthus, the Ebionites, the Nicolaitans, Cerdo and Marcion. As the Apologist Justin around 150 CE in I Apology 26 refers to a work against the heretics that has not been preserved in which the sequence Simon – Menander – Marcion appears, Justin's lost work is often regarded as the basis for Irenaeus, *Haer* I 23ff. However, by way of qualification it must immediately be remarked that in no way could the Ebionites have been part of a work of Justin's against the heretics, since most of them were not yet heretics for this Apologist, who was born in Palestine (Neapolis: *Dial.* 46f.; for this text see below, 53f.). Moreover, the Nicolaitans might be a secondary addition, since contrary to the 'heading' of the work against the heretics which preceded Irenaeus, they are not derived from Simon but from Nicolaos: 'The Nicolaitans are the followers of Nicolaos [and thus not Simon] who was one of the seven first appointed deacon by the apostles' (*Haer* I 26, 3).

The section against the heretics in Irenaeus *Haer* I 23–28 is structured in such a way that most heretics put forward at least one detail of what Simon had already taught.[112] The agreements are particularly striking between Simon Magus (I 23, 1–4) and the Basilidians (I 24, 3–7) and Carpocratians (I 25, 1–6).[113]

1. Creation of the world by rebellious angels (I 23, 5; 24, 1f.; 25, 3);
2. Lack of a single creator;
3. Ignorance of the primal being by the hostile powers (cf. also I 26, 1);
4. Migration of souls;
5. War motif;
6. Pseudo-crucifixion (cf. also I 26, 1);
7. Prophets as the emissaries of the angels;
8. Pauline-Cyrenaean doctrine of the law;

9. Libertinism (cf. additionally I 26, 3; 27, 3 [?]; 28, 2 – further I 6, 3; 13, 6f.; 31, 2);

10. Magic and idolatry (cf. additionally I 13, 5);

11. Identification of the followers with the master.

In this way it is formally 'proved' historically that they are really descended from Simon. If that is the case, then the questionable doctrines can already be seen to be heresies from the fact that Simon was rebuked by Peter. This is shown indubitably in the account in the canonical Acts of the Apostles (ch. 8), which Irenaeus transcribes even before the catalogue of heretics (*Haer* I 23, 1), though without mentioning Simon's request to the apostles to pray for him, Acts 8.24: 'Pray for me to the Lord, that nothing of what you have said may come upon me.'

The author of Acts was therefore rather milder towards the archheretic Simon than Irenaeus was a century later. The reason for this lies above all in the different church-historical situation. Irenaeus strictly presupposes the division between orthodoxy and heresy, whereas for the author of Acts the situation is not yet so fixed. He is carrying on a limited dialogue with rival syncretistic groups. This is evident not only from the Simon pericope (Acts 8) but also from the relatively open way in which the sections on Elymas (Acts 13.6–12) and the sons of Sceva (Acts 19.13–17) are shaped. Elymas' blindness is only limited (13.11), and the sons of Sceva fled naked (19.16), which gives more of a comic effect. The author 'is able ... to carry through the criticism of syncretism without already in principle abandoning its representatives'.[114]

Irenaeus describes the dependence of the various heretics on one another with a terminology which can be called technical. Simon has a successor in Menander; Marcion is successor to Cerdo. All the Gnostics reported on, who are also called Simonians (*Haer* I 29,1), are pupils and followers of Simon (*Haer* I 27,4). The preface to Book II states: 'I have shown the doctrine of Simon Magus of Samaria, their progenitor, and of all those who succeeded him.' From the occurrence of this technical terminology Norbert Brox has concluded that there was 'a fixed idea of doctrinal tradition'[115] among the Gnostics. By contrast with this, however, we must reckon that these forms of expression are to be understood in terms of the struggle by Irenaeus or his predecessors against 'Gnosis falsely so-called'. They transferred their own principle of tradition to their opponents and, as with all their own church doctrines, also derived all Gnostic phenomena from persons in the apostolic age. Thus they found the origin of the teachings of their opponents in the preaching of Simon Magus attested in Acts 8, and the contemporary conflict could be taken to have been settled long ago in the normative period of the apostles, since Peter the prince of the apostles had repudiated that Simon.

The theology of Irenaeus

Irenaeus's theology, which is strongly stamped by his fight against heretics, can be summed up in the following points:

First, the Creator of the world and the Father of Jesus Christ are one and the same.

Secondly, Christ sums up the 'universe', human beings and all that goes with them. He 'recapitulates' it, takes up the whole history of disaster and thus makes it invalid. In this way the ultimate union of creation and redemption is secured.

Thirdly, the bishops and teachers of the church have preserved the connection with the apostles in a straight line.

> 'We have learned the plan of our salvation from no others than those through whom the gospel has come down to us. At one time they proclaimed it in public and, at a later period, by the will of God, handed it down to us in scriptures, to be the "ground and pillar" (I Tim. 3.15) of our faith' (*Haer* III 1, 1).

Fourthly, alongside scripture, the preaching of the apostles as the 'rule of truth' is also the norm of exegesis (cf. *Haer* II 35, 4). Here the concept of the canon stands in a dialectical relationship to the canon of scripture itself. Theoretically, it would even be the case that 'had the apostles themselves not left us writings, it would be necessary to follow the course of the tradition which they handed down to those whom they set over the churches' (*Haer* III 4, 1).[116]

According to the witness of Jerome (*Vir.ill.* 53), Tertullian was a presbyter in Carthage, but the accuracy of this note is doubtful. The years of his birth and death are unknown and cannot even be determined approximately. However, some works indicate the time of their origin and therefore allow us to limit Tertullian's activity as a writer to the period between 196 and 220 and to put his writings in sequence. He became a Montanist[118] at the latest in 207. Conflicts with the church and especially with the bishop of Rome were almost pre-programmed, but his writings from all the periods of his life found an interested readership at that time, with the result that a large number of them have been preserved down to modern times, so powerfully did the fire burn in them. We do not know when, where and why Tertullian became a Christian; however, he himself attests that he was formerly a pagan.[119]

Tertullian's attack upon the heretics; his personal character

In his 'Prosecution Speech against the Heretics' (*De praescriptione haereticorum*), the Roman Tertullian with his legal training transferred the legal process of the trial, disputing the rights of his opponent by objections, into the theological sphere. 'By this he understands establishing the validity of formal law, laying down the conditions of the dispute before discussing its substance.'[120] According to him, scripture is the legal possession of the church. The heretics are not authorized to use it; they must *a priori* be declared to be illegitimate because the catholic church received directly from the apostles both their teaching and holy scripture, at a time when there were as yet no heretics. Here Tertullian writes:

'As they are heretics, they cannot be true Christians, because it is not from Christ that they get what they pursue of their own choice, and from the pursuit incur and admit the name of heretics. Thus, not being Christians, they have acquired no right to the Christian scriptures; and it may very fairly be said to them, "Who are you? When and whence did you come? As you are none of mine, what have you to do with what is mine? Indeed, Marcion, by what right do you hew my wood? By whose permission, Valentinus, are you diverting the streams of my fountain? By what power, Apelles, are you removing my landmarks? This is my property. Why are you, the rest, sowing and feeding here at your own pleasure? This is my property. I have long possessed it; I possessed it before you. I hold sure title deeds from the original owners themselves to whom the estate belongs. I am the heir of the apostles"' (*Praescr* 37).

On reading such sentences, the present-day reader gets the feeling that here is someone who wants to uphold the law at any price; the means justifies the end, and objective accuracy is not striven for. Here speaks Tertullian, the legally trained Christian, who wants to win the case, but has somehow lost the truth because he thinks that he possesses it firmly. He is no longer concerned with a quest for truth, and any religious quest[121] on the part of the heretics which was based, for example, on Jesus' saying in Matt. 7.7/Luke 11.9 ('Ask and it shall be given to you; seek and you will find; knock and it will be opened to you') would be an abomination to him. He writes:

'Once for all I would say, No man seeks, except him who either never possessed something or else has lost it. The old woman (viz. in the Gospel) had lost one of her ten pieces of silver (Luke 15.8f.), and therefore she sought it; but as soon as she found it, she stopped looking for it. The neighbour was without bread (Luke 11.5-8), and therefore he knocked; but as soon as the door was opened to him and he was given the bread, he stopped knocking. The widow kept asking to be heard by the judge (Luke 18.1-8), because she was not admitted; but when her suit was heard, she no longer pestered him. *So there is a limit both to seeking, and to knocking and to asking*' (*Praescr* 11).
'Since Jesus Christ we need no more searching nor investigation, now that the gospel has been proclaimed. With our faith we desire no further belief. For that is the first thing that we believe, and there is nothing that we ought to believe besides' (*Praescr* 16).

No wonder that according to Tertullian, the dispute with the heretics produces 'no other effect than to help to upset either the stomach or the brain' (*Praescr* 16).
But Tertullian did not content himself with the argument of the prosecuting speech; he was also concerned to provide an extremely

precise, extensive refutation of the Monarchians, Marcionites and the common species of Gnosticism which cannot be described in more detail here.[122]

Karl Holl has described Tertullian's way of working against the heretics like this:

> 'For every opinion he finds a contrast to make it ridiculous. He also openly confessed this technique: "If one laughs there, one will only do justice to the matter here. Some things are worth refuting in this way, so that one does not do them the honour of serious treatment."'[123]

So it is no coincidence that this character, when he was a Montanist and was fighting against the Roman church, vilified the church love feasts which he once praised so highly (*Apol* 39, 16–21).[124] And when the Roman bishop Calixtus in principle confirmed the right of bishops to grant forgiveness to those who had committed mortal sins (i.e. sins of unchastity), this unleashed an avalanche of protest from Tertullian.[125] Given his character, it is not surprising that in the end Tertullian left even the Montanists and founded a party of his own.[126]

III. What Irenaeus and Tertullian have in common and what distinguishes them

Whereas Tertullian disputes the right of the heretics to use scripture, Irenaeus accepts the Gnostics as disputants over scripture, since their conversion cannot be excluded. For example, he writes: 'I want to adduce the words of the Lord, if through means of the very instruction of Christ I may succeed in persuading them' (*Haer* III 25, 7). Irenaeus wants to be victorious with scripture alone; Tertullian explicitly rejects this. For him, an 'authority above scripture and exegesis is decisive. Accordingly, scripture is left out of the dispute, and the Gnostics are not allowed to appeal to it.'[127]

In the case of both church fathers, perspectives from outside theology must be brought into play which may have shaped the way in which they wrote their polemic. Without them we would not understand what was really happening at that time.[128]

The far-reaching lack of institutional differentiation among the Gnostic Christians seemed particularly suspect to Tertullian. Of it he wrote:

'I must not omit an account of the conduct of the heretics also – how frivolous it is, how merely human, without seriousness, without authority, without discipline, as suits their creed. To begin with, it is doubtful who is a catechumen and who a believer; they all have access alike, they hear alike, they pray alike – even heathens, if any such happen to come among them. "That which is holy they will cast to the dogs, and their pearls, " although to be sure they are not real ones, "they will fling to the swine." Simplicity they believe to consist in the overthrow of discipline, attention to which on our part they call lip-service. As for peace, they observe it with everyone, observing no distinctions. Nor is there any distinction between them, although they hold different doctrines, since they have sworn to join together in fighting against the one truth. All are puffed up, all offer you knowledge. The catechumens are perfect before they are fully taught' (*Praescr* 41).

The heretical women were a particular scandal. He goes on immediately to write of them:

'The very women of these heretics, how wanton they are! For they are bold enough to teach, to dispute, to perform exorcisms, to undertake cures – it may be even to baptize' (ibid.).

Another point which provoked his special resistance was the way in which the Gnostics dealt with authority and especially the office of bishop.[129] Of this he writes: 'And so it happens that today one man is their bishop, tomorrow another; today someone is a deacon and tomorrow a reader; today someone is a presbyter who tomorrow is a layman. For even on laymen, too, they impose the functions of priesthood' (*Praescr* 41).

Such a view was also intolerable to Irenaeus, who had been bishop of the community of Lyons and Vienne since 178 CE. There may also have been political reasons for his strict insistence that the Father of Jesus Christ and the Creator of the world are identical. The pre-eminence of an ordered structure in the community and an ordered structure in heaven corresponded. Had there been room for an unknown God in heaven, it would have represented a danger that the community could become unstable. And a democratic church of the kind of which there were the beginnings among the heretics went completely against the notion of a patriarchal God, all the more so since Irenaeus understood his role as bishop in the categories of ruler, teacher and judge, transferred to the church from the legal situation of the state.

Finally, both heresiologists emphatically advocated the resurrection of the flesh, Irenaeus even in its chiliastic variant.[130] They justified this in extended exegesis of I Cor. 15 and in so doing vainly relativized I Cor. 15.50 ('flesh and blood cannot inherit the kingdom of God')[131] in order to take the wind out of the sails of the Gnostic disciples of Paul against whom they were fighting. Didn't this penetrating insistence on the fleshly resurrection of Jesus and believers, along with (and we must not forget this) unbelievers to the judgment of condemnation, [132] also have a political dimension? This first served towards creating a clerical authority.

Now it would certainly be a mistake to derive theological principles directly from political convictions. Religious reality is more complicated, and it is too simplistic to assume that theology is directly conditioned by society. But the reference to the consequences of theology for politics sheds light on a dimension which was also an issue in the dispute between Tertullian and Irenaeus on the one hand and the Gnostic heretics on the other. At the same time we can see here how and why the Catholic church in the making could have a much easier time with the state (and *vice versa*) than the heretics, who put everything in question, and who in their religious quest and curiosity represented a constant danger to the *closed* system of Irenaeus and Tertullian.

3

How the Heresiologists became Heretics, or, The Jewish Christians of Jerusalem in the First Two Centuries[133]

Historical demarcations. The problem of continuity

Externally, it is possible to distinguish two phases of Christianity in Jerusalem, the period before the Jewish War from 67 to 70 CE and the time afterwards, when the Christians of Jerusalem could not continue to live in the Jewish metropolis because with the destruction of the temple by pagans the holy place had been permanently desecrated and thus there was an unbridgeable break with the past.

There is dispute as to how the Jerusalem Christians left the holy city of the Jews. The church father Eusebius in the fourth century gives a dogmatically motivated answer. This is what he writes in his *Church History* (*HE*) III 5, 2f. (the relevant biblical verses which Eusebius has in mind have been put in brackets):

'2 But to resume. After the ascension of our Saviour (Acts 1.9), the Jews, in addition to their crime against him (i.e., their guilt for his death: I Thess. 2.15; Mark 15.6-15), had devised innumerable plots also against his apostles: first they put Stephen to death by stoning (Acts 7.58f.); and then, after him, James who was the son of Zebedee and the brother of John, was beheaded (Acts 12.2); and finally James, who was the first, after the ascension of our Saviour, to receive the throne of the episcopate there, departed this life in the manner we mentioned above.[134] As for the other apostles, countless plots were laid against their lives, and they were banished from the land of Judaea; but they journeyed to all the nations to teach the message, in the power of the Christ who said to them, "Go and make disciples of all the nations in my name" (Matt. 28.19).

3 Moreover, the people of the church of Jerusalem, in accordance with a certain oracle that was vouchsafed by way of revelation to approved men there, had been commanded to depart from the city before the war, and to inhabit a certain city of Peraea. They called it Pella. And when those who believed in Christ had removed from Jerusalem, as if holy men had utterly deserted both the royal metropolis of the Jews itself and the whole land of Judaea, the justice of God then visited upon them all their acts of violence to Christ and his apostles, by destroying that generation of wicked persons root and branch from among men.'

The wider context is the *theological* statement that the destruction of Jerusalem was a divine punishment for the many wicked acts of the unbelieving Jews against Jesus and his apostles.[135] Into it Eusebius inserts the isolated report which goes back to tradition, [136] that the Christians had a prophecy before the war that they should leave Jerusalem and go to live in Pella. Thus a clean division is achieved between the good who have so far prevented a catastrophe, and the wicked who remain in the city. Now that the holy men have left, Jerusalem and indeed the whole of Judaea can be punished.

But here, as elsewhere in the story, such a clear solution arouses the mistrust of those asking critical questions. The following questions immediately arise:

1. How old is the tradition of the exodus of the earliest community to Pella and where does it come from? *Answer*: it may go back to Aristo of Pella (beginning of the second century, cf. Eusebius, *HE* IV, 6, 3f.) and presupposes that the community remained in Pella and did not return to Jerusalem.

2. Are there also rival traditions? That is beyond doubt the case. The Jewish Christian Hegesippus, who was born in Palestine, composed a five-volume *Hypomnemata* in the second half of the second century. Extensive fragments of it have been preserved in Eusebius's *Church History*. Hegesippus clearly assumes that there was a continuity of the Jerusalem community (cf. n. 660 below).

3. Is it imaginable that the whole of the Jerusalem community could have fled so shortly before the war? The question must surely be answered in the negative. Those who defend the historicity of the Pella report are therefore compelled to predate the exodus, e.g. to 62, immediately after the murder of James.

4. If Pella was recognized as a Gentile city, is it conceivable that a Jewish Christian group could have taken refuge there? The answer to this question must be no.

I have discussed these questions in more detail elsewhere, [137] and have come to the conclusion that the tradition of an exodus of the earliest community to Pella is unhistorical and is the foundation legend of the church of Pella, which by it derived itself from the Jerusalem community. I would now like to enlarge this thesis to the effect that the immediate occasion of the origin of this tradition may have been the narrative of some Jewish Christians from Jerusalem who indeed left Jerusalem shortly before the war, as did also other Jews (cf. Josephus *Antt*. XX 256/ *BJ* II 279: at the end of 64, on the accession to office of Gessius Florus, Jews left Jerusalem).[138] These Christians would then later have found a permanent home in Pella.

In one way or another the destruction of the temple marked a deep break for the Jerusalem community of the time (and similarly for the 'non-Christian' Jews). Subsequently their descendants lived divided between various places: in Pella, Cochaba, Nazareth and Syrian Beroea. Some of the earliest members of the Jerusalem community and sections of Palestinian Christianity may have moved to Asia Minor (cf. the daughters of Philip [Acts 21.8f.], whose stay in Ephesus or Hierapolis is reported by later writers [Polycrates of Ephesus in Eusebius *HE* III 31, 3 and Papias of Hierapolis, *HE* III 39, 9]. And finally, we cannot completely exclude the possibility that groups representing remnants of the Jewish Christians of Jerusalem settled in Jerusalem again after some time).

Eusebius' report that fifteen bishops had followed one another in succession in Jerusalem up to the subjection of the Jews under Hadrian and that all were Hebrews by birth should not be used to support the last possibility mentioned, since this tradition is to be doubted for two reasons. First, allegedly Simeon, the successor to James and second bishop, occupied the episcopal throne until 115 CE.[139] But in that case it is improbable that thirteen bishops reigned in the remaining time up to the revolt under Hadrian, i.e. twenty years. Secondly, in the same breath Eusebius says that he has 'quite failed to find their dates preserved in writing' (*HE* IV, 5, 1). This robs the whole list of bishops of credibility. Presumably it comes from the Gentile Christian bishop Narcissus at the beginning of the third century, or from his followers, [140] since for the second period up to him, in an artificial schematism, [141] Eusebius similarly lists fifteen Gentile Christian bishops (IV 5.1–4; V 12).

The leading role of the kinsfolk of Jesus. The fate of the Jewish Christians

James the brother of the Lord was the authority in the later phase of the Jerusalem community. After his murder in 62 (see below, 49f.), a cousin of Jesus, Simeon, was leader of the 'Jerusalem' alliance of communities until the time of Trajan (98–117). However, it is not very clear whether he had his seat in Jerusalem. Hegesippus certainly presupposes this (in Eusebius, *HE* IV, 22, 4), because he is interested in the continuity of those who held office on the episcopal throne of Jerusalem, [142] but on historical grounds generally that is improbable. We only know that after the murder of James, at a certain point in time Simeon became his successor, because he was related to Jesus. Hegesippus (in Eusebius, *HE* III 32, 3) reports that Simeon suffered martyrdom under Trajan at the age of 120. So he must have been a well-known figure in Palestine. The same is true of the grandsons of Jude, who was a brother of Jesus. According to Hegesippus (in Eusebius, *HE* III 20, 1–6), they were taken before the emperor Domitian, but were set free because they were of no account. At the end of the narrative we read: 'And when released they ruled the churches, in as much as they were both martyrs and of the Lord's family; and when peace was established, remained alive until the time of Trajan' (20.6).

Finally, we have a further piece of evidence about the esteem for the relatives of Jesus in Palestine, when Eusebius, *HE* I 7, 14 (in an excerpt from Julius Africanus), says: 'When they went out from the Jewish villages of Nazareth and Cochaba, they travelled to other parts of the land ...'[143] We can hardly think it a coincidence that the home of the kinsfolk of the Lord, Cochaba, and the place where numerous Jewish Christians (Ebionites [for this identification see 52f. below]) lived, had the same name.[144] Rather, it indicates a union of the two groups, which is in any case probable, as James the brother of the Lord was leader of the (Jewish Christian) community of Jerusalem.

Separated from the other (Gentile) Christians, the Ebionites and relatives of the Lord were also parted from their Jewish brethren and thus as it were fell between the stools of a church which was becoming increasingly Gentile Christian and the Jewish synagogue alliance which was newly forming.

As a result of the destruction of Jerusalem, the young Gentile Christian churches had lost their centre, which had been formed by Jesus and the Jerusalem community(!); a new one established itself with the Roman community, which looking back to Peter and Paul (I Clem. 5) soon made a claim to leadership which it consolidated within a century. Only in the second half of the second century did individual Gentile Christians rediscover the Holy Land (Bishop Melito of Sardes visited Jerusalem around 160 [cf. Eusebius, *HE* IV 26, 14]),[145] but that was already too late for a rehabilitation of the Jerusalem Christians; they had become Ebionite heretics. Nor did they fare any better in their relationship with their Jewish brethren. If for example they wanted to take part in synagogue worship, they would fear that in the recitation of the Eighteen Benedictions they were applying the saying against the heretics to themselves.[146]

Part I : The Jewish Christians of Jerusalem before the Jewish War

In what follows I shall attempt to outline the dramatic *prehistory* of the development.[147]

The activity of Jesus had come to an end with his bloody execution. The Roman prefect Pilate executed Jesus because he regarded him as a political agitator who had to be done away with. The inscription 'The King of the Jews' on the cross (Mark 15.26) shows that Jesus' activity could be understood in political terms. Yet a special reason was needed for the Jewish authorities to hand Jesus over to the Romans. This may have been found in Jesus' attitude to the temple.[148] In the Synoptic Gospels in the New Testament, the appearance of Jesus in the temple (Mark 11.15–19) is directly connected with his later execution. Certainly it is not immediately clear what Jesus wanted to achieve with his action – assuming its historicity. (*a*) Was it intended as a *purification* of the temple? But who could regard someone who drove out the merchants and sellers and overthrew the tables of the money-changers and those who dealt in doves in such a way? (*b*) Was it to be interpreted as *reform* of the temple? But that does not fit, since it did not affect the whole temple, but only a small area. (*c*) Jesus' action in the temple may have been more of a symbolic action pointing towards something else (cf. the symbolic actions of the Old Testament prophets[149]). Jesus attempted symbolically to do away with the temple cult. 'However, this abolition was not to reform the temple cult or to stop its (further) profanation, but to make room for a completely new *temple*, the eschatological temple, and thus one expected from God.'[150] The presupposition of this understanding is twofold: 1. Jesus understood literally the overthrow (cf. Mark 11.15) aimed at the whole temple; 2. with this he combined the hope of a new temple of the kind that can be found in Judaism in various forms (Isa. 60.13; Micah 4.1–2; Hag. 2.6–9; Tobit 14.7; I Enoch 90.28f.).

We find a further reflection of Jesus' criticism of the temple in the account of his trial. Cf. Mark 14.58: 'We heard him say, "I will destroy this temple that is made with hands and in three days I will build another, not made with hands."' It is very probable that this saying about the temple originates with Jesus, all the more so as Mark 14.57 explicitly presents it as false witness (cf. Acts 6.13, to which it has been transposed by the author of Acts – to tone it down?) and thus robs the radical quality of Jesus' preaching of its point here. Furthermore Jesus' expectation of the heavenly temple is also understandable in view of the fact that the earliest Jerusalem community identified itself with the temple. Its members were constantly in the temple (Acts 2.46; 3.1ff.; 21.26) and here in accord with Jesus expected the end of time.

As an analogy to Jesus' saying about the temple and the reaction of the Jewish and Roman authorities, reference might be made to the example of Jesus, son of Ananus. The Jewish historian Josephus writes this about him in a report which so far has not been sufficiently evaluated:[151]

'Four years before the war began, and at a time when the city was in very great peace and prosperity, a certain Jesus the son of Ananus, a plebeian and an husbandman, came to that feast whereon it is our custom for everyone to make tabernacles to God. and began all of a sudden to cry aloud and in the temple, "A voice from the east, a voice from the west, a voice from the four winds, a voice against Jerusalem and the holy house, a voice against the bridegrooms and the brides, and a voice against the whole people!" This was his cry, as he went about by day and by night, in all the lanes of the city. However, certain of the most eminent among the populace had great indignation at this dire cry of his, and took up the man, and gave him a great number of severe stripes; yet did not he either say anything for himself or anything peculiar to those that chastized him, but still went on with the same words which he cried before. Hereupon our rulers, supposing, as the case proved to be, that this was a sort of divine fury in the man, brought him to the Roman procurator, when he was whipped till his bones were laid bare: yet he did not make any supplication for himself, nor shed any tears, but tuning his voice to the most lamentable tone possible, at every stroke of the whip his answer was, "Woe, woe to Jerusalem!" And when Albinus (for he was then our procurator) asked him, "Who he was? and whence he came? and why he uttered such words?" he made no manner of reply to what he said, but still did not leave off his melancholy ditty, till Albinus took him to be a madman, and dismissed him. Now, during all the time that passed before the war began, this man did not go near any citizens, nor was seen talking to them; but he every day uttered these lamentable words, as if it were his premeditated vow, "Woe, woe to Jerusalem!" Nor did he give ill words to any of those that beat him every day, nor good words to those that gave him food; but this was his reply to all men, and indeed no other than a melancholy presage of what was to come. This cry of his was the loudest at the festivals; and he continued this ditty for seven years and five months, without growing hoarse, or being tired therewith, until the very time when he saw his presage in earnest fulfilled in our siege when it ceased; for, as he was going round upon the wall, he cried out with his utmost force, "Woe, woe to the city again, and to the people, and to the holy house!" And just as he added at the last, "Woe, woe to myself also!" there came a stone out of one of the engines, and smote him, and killed him immediately; and as he as uttering the very same presages, he gave up the ghost' (BJ VI, 300–9).[152]

Back to Jesus of Nazareth: the group of male disciples who had come up with him to Jerusalem from Galilee for the feast of the Passover had fled and abandoned him before or at his arrest – even, after initial hesitation, Simon Peter, who had a position of pre-eminence among them. By contrast, women friends of Jesus, who had similarly travelled with him from Galilee to Jerusalem for the Passover, remained longer with their master. But even they could not avert his fate. They certainly included Mary from the Galilean fishing town of Magdala, who had been healed by Jesus from a severe illness.

So if Good Friday ended like a great riddle and thus everything seemed to be at an end, not long after the death of Jesus on the gallows of the cross and the flight of the disciples to Galilee, a new spring dawned unhoped-for. Precisely when that happened we will never know. But not long after the Friday on which Jesus died, Peter saw him alive in a vision, and this event led to an unparalleled chain reaction.[153] The fact that Peter had seen and heard Jesus determined the content of the visions and auditions of the others. The news spread like lightning that God had not left Jesus in death, indeed had exalted him to himself, and that Jesus would soon come again as Son of Man on the clouds of heaven. This created a new situation, and the Jesus movement experienced an explosive new beginning. Now his friends could go to Jerusalem once again and take up the work which their master had left incomplete there, calling on both the people and their leaders to repent. Perhaps the present was understood as the very last reprieve that God had given. The circle of the Twelve which had been called into being by Jesus during his lifetime (Matt. 19.28)[154] was caught up with Peter, and similarly saw Jesus (I Cor. 15.5). And probably at the Feast of Weeks (= Pentecost) which followed the Passover at which Jesus died, an appearance took place before a considerable crowd of people which were reckoned at more than 500 (I Cor. 15.6). Women were now among those who saw Jesus. Indeed, when opponents objected from the Jewish side and asked where the body of Jesus was, it was immediately reported that women had found the tomb empty and later that Jesus had even appeared to the women there.[155]

We must imagine that the initial dynamic[156] was highly explosive, all the more so if we are to take into account an ecstatic disposition on the part of those who had been left behind by Jesus (C. Colpe). The beginning was not marked, as Ernst Haenchen still thought in his influential commentary on Acts, by a pietistic quietism, [157] but by a disconcerting experience which has been domesticated by

34

Luke.[158] The physical brothers of Jesus were also caught up into the maelstrom and went to Jerusalem; James even had a vision of his own (I Cor. 15.7) – that James who in Jesus' lifetime had not thought much of his brother (Mark 3.20f.).

We should estimate little more than a year for these events. Much will have taken place contemporaneously. In addition to the experience of the 'Risen Christ' in visions and auditions we can ascertain the following historical elements in the development:

1. In the breaking of bread by the assembled community, communion with the executed Messiah Jesus who was now alive became immediately present.

2. The recollection of Jesus' activity and his word were directly present.

3. Jesus' imminent expectation was taken over without a break, and the new temple predicted by Jesus was replaced by the community as the temple, which was supported by the apostles as pillars.

4. Certain psalms, like Ps.110, were soon related to the exalted Messiah/Son of Man Jesus.

The movement reached a new stage when Greek-speaking Jews joined it in Jerusalem.[159] This may already have happened at the Feast of Weeks (= Pentecost) following the Passover at which Jesus died, when people were in Jerusalem from all countries and heard of Jesus. Jesus' saying about the temple had an electrifying effect on them, but now in such a way that it issued in criticism of the law (Acts 6.13). Forced out of Jerusalem, they spread the message of Jesus in the areas outside Jerusalem (for the details see 38f. below) and attracted the attention of the Pharisee Saul. He decided to act, and suppressed the new preaching until he was similarly overwhelmed by Jesus and saw and heard him. With this event a conclusion to the earliest Easter faith seems to have been reached. Indeed, for the earliest community in Jerusalem the appearance of Jesus to Paul already lay outside the period of the Easter events. The tradition in I Cor. 15.7 explicitly says that Christ appeared to all the apostles. In nevertheless claiming to have received an appearance of Christ and then describing himself as 'one born out of due time' (I Cor. 15.78) by comparison with the earliest apostles, Paul endorses this view of the earliest community.[160]

Ecstatic experiences framed as a vision of Christ were also had in Jerusalem even later and continued with Paul. Thus Acts 7.55f. reports of Stephen:[161]

> 'But he, full of the Holy Spirit, gazed into heaven and saw the glory of God, and Jesus standing on the right hand of God; and he said, "Behold, I see the heavens opened, and the Son of man standing at the right hand of God."'[162]

And under the heading 'visions and revelations' provoked by the accusations of his opponents, in II Cor. 12 Paul feels forced to give his own account of a transportation or journey to heaven:

v. 2	v. 3f.
I know a man	And I know that this
in Christ who fourteen years ago	man
whether in the body	whether in the body
I do not know	
or out of the body	or out of the body
I do not know,	I do not know,
God knows,	God knows,
that this man was caught up	that he was caught up
into the third heaven.	into paradise.

However, these experiences did not take on the normative significance of those mentioned earlier. The first *shared* experience of the crowd in Jerusalem, which was probably identical with the appearance of Jesus to more than 500 (I Cor. 15.6), had a kind of initiatory character, and its significance is the same as that of the first vision of Peter in Galilee. Just as Peter's real call took place in this vision, so too the Pentecost event was constitutive for the formation of a new group within the Jews of Jerusalem. It gave the Jesus community powerful influence and fundamentally changed their situation from that before the execution of Jesus.

The first institutionalizations and formation of parties[163]

The reconstitution of the group of Twelve brought about by Peter in Galilee already bears the mark of an institutionalization, but this evidently had an eschatological-symbolic character and was wholly stamped by enthusiasm. For 'it only made sense if, as with Jesus, twelve tribes of Israel were to be fully represented at the dawn of the kingdom of God',[164] and this presupposed an almost intoxicated expectation of the end. By contrast, after the ebbing away of the experience of Pentecost, there was the need for a greater realism, all the more so since the prophecy of a new temple and a new age expected by Jesus, preceded by a world catastrophe, and its productive further development in the earliest community, had not been fulfilled. Life went on. The institutionalizations which now followed were orientated on a continuation of the present age – not on its end; here individual elements of the teaching and expectation of Jesus were taken up and developed further productively.[165]

The first and most significant institutionalization with a new character consisted in the introduction of baptism,[166] which from the beginning was administered for the forgiveness of sins and was connected with the bestowing of the Holy Spirit by the laying on of hands. The real reason for this action may have been simply the baptism of Jesus by John ('for the forgiveness of sins'[167]). After Jesus became the centre of the new cult, the view probably arose that he himself had also baptized (cf. John 3.26 [Jesus 'baptizes and all come to him']), but this was immediately corrected (cf. John 4.2 ['Jesus did not himself baptize, but his disciples']).

The second equally significant institutionalization was that of the 'day of the Lord' (thus literally in Rev. 1.10), on which the Lord's supper was celebrated. The 'day of the Lord' was the day after the sabbath, on which according to earliest Christian faith Jesus had been raised from the dead (I Cor. 15.4b). The early community probably also observed the sabbath with the Jews, but the celebration of the Lord's Supper on Sunday which similarly took place every week already strongly emphasized its identity.

A third institutionalization is sometimes seen in the care of widows depicted in Acts 6.1ff. as a diaconate or a serving of tables.[168] However, it is difficult to accept this thesis, since by writing of the care of widows in Acts 6 Luke is evidently covering over another conflict.[169] Nevertheless, the Seven (like the Twelve) may have had an institutional task. Perhaps the Seven were formed in contrast to the Twelve, the representatives of the people of the twelve tribes hitherto. However, as yet we know nothing of their function.[170]

In any case the Seven indicates the formation of a party, for the seven men (Stephen, Philip, Prochorus, Nicanor, Timon, Parmenas and Nicolaos) all bear Greek names. They were evidently representatives of a Greek-speaking community, to be differentiated from the Aramaic-speaking followers of Jesus. This community recruited Jews from the Diaspora and, as Acts 6–7 reports, with reference to Jesus (Acts 6.13f.) criticized the law more freely than the 'Hebrews'.[171]

It thus needs to be noted that almost from the beginning two different kinds of Christianity are assembled in the Holy City, one Aramaic-speaking and maintaining Jewish customs, the other Greek-speaking with a latent antinomian tendency. So there is plurality at the beginning of the earliest community, which already contained within itself many of the later conflicts which broke out. But to begin with they all kept together.

The historical development: from the beginnings to the Apostolic Council

The first phase is to be seen as the eschatological gathering under the leadership of Peter. During this time the Greek-speaking party of Christianity, the Hellenists, were forced out of Jerusalem and Stephen, one of the Seven, was killed in a riot (Acts 7.58). Here, in contrast to the trial of Jesus in which the Romans intervened, those involved were Jerusalem Jews, who stoned Stephen. The other party of Christianity remained undisturbed in the Jewish metropolis. 'The eschatological institutionalization was the work of Peter ... He led the assembly for God and to this degree was its theocratic representative. As such he could only be a sole individual.'[172] It is not by chance that Paul sought to make Peter's acquaintance soon (three years) after his conversion (Gal. 1.18).

In the subsequent period two other men, James and John (the sons of Zebedee), along with Peter, formed a theocratic governing body and were given the honorific title 'the pillars'. Along with Peter, they had been Jesus' closest confidants during his lifetime.[173] When James the son of Zebedee became the victim of a persecution (Acts 12.1f.), his namesake James, the brother of Jesus, took his place, probably not primarily because he was a disciple but above all because of his relationship to the family.[174] At any rate, fourteen years after his second visit to Jerusalem (Gal. 2.1), Paul was dealing with a governing body which was composed of this second James, Peter, and John the other son of Zebedee (Gal. 2.9).

In the meantime the Hellenists who had been driven out of Jerusalem had not remained inactive. They spread the new faith around Jerusalem and as far as Damascus, Antioch and Phoenicia (Acts 11.19–22). Their preaching, filled with the Spirit (Acts 6.10), now no longer excluded Gentiles; indeed both Jewish and Gentile Christians soon formed one community.

In Antioch the remarkable new group made up of Jews and non-Jews received the name by which they were to be known from then on: their members were called 'Christians' (Acts 11.26). This does not derive from the programme of the group concerned but is a designation given to it by political authorities seeking to classify it, or by rival groups who marked it off in this way.[175] This name was very soon taken over by the Christians, probably also because it was an apt term for their concern. Already two generations later Bishop Ignatius, from Antioch where this designation first arose, could speak of 'Christianismos' almost as a matter of course and triumphantly proclaim: 'For Christianity did not base its faith on Judaism, but Judaism on Christianity' (Magn. 10.3, etc.).

The Jerusalem community may have watched this development in Antioch with great scepticism and anxiety. It dwelt on the threshold of salvation, Jerusalem, and saw itself as the community which rested on the pillars Peter, James and John. While it might have some offshoots outside Jerusalem, in Antioch there was a new type of church. This was not founded on Peter and the other pillars but on Christ himself (cf. I Cor. 1.12), and in practice was explicitly demolishing the barriers between Jews and Gentiles. One vivid example of this is the description which Paul gives in Gal. 2.12 of the way in which Jewish and Gentile Christians ate together (see below, 43f.).

Another feature which distinguished the two types of church was the title 'apostle'. While those in Jerusalem understood it in connection with the apostolate of those to whom the risen Lord had appeared, which was chronologically limited, the Antiochene community could use it for its delegates, and evidently knew no kind of chronological limitations (cf. Acts 14.4, 14; Didache 11.4). Here we have a pneumatic-charismatic itinerant apostolate.

Thus theoretically we may say that in Jerusalem and Antioch there were two different types of church.[176] However, this was true only in theory, since in historical reality types are realized only to a certain degree, and Paul, from whose works the characteristics given above have been largely derived, is not free of contradictions where his understanding of the church is concerned. He did not push the independence of his understanding of the church too far, and could occasionally have been understood to be indicating that Jerusalem was in fact the centre of Christianity (see below, 214).[177] We find a similar combination of ideas in his understanding of his apostolate. While Paul once asserts that this is in accord with the Jerusalem apostolate and related to the appearances of the Risen Christ (I Cor. 15.8), he is in fact an itinerant apostle.

Given the way in which the Christian groups were drifting apart in the early period, conflicts were pre-programmed. For the Aramaic-speaking community which remained in Jerusalem, the Torah was still valid. Anyone who was baptized in the name of Jesus – whether Jew or Gentile – was not free to dispense with the law. Jesus had come to fulfil the law, not to destroy it (Matt. 5.17).[178]

The so-called Apostolic Council, reported by Paul in Gal. 2 and Luke in Acts 15, was a crucial attempt to resolve this crisis. We shall keep to Paul's account, since he himself was crucially involved in crisis management.[179]

Here the discussion was over the requirement that Gentile Christians should be circumcised in order to be able to become members of the Christian community (Gal. 2.3). It was directed against the practice of accepting Gentiles into the community without circumcision, a decision not just made at the time of the council, but previously, specifically in the community of Antioch, into which those whom Paul calls 'false brethren' had crept in, in order to 'spy out'[180] the freedom of the Christians there.

Immediately after that, Paul goes up to Jerusalem with Barnabas and in a provocative act also takes with him the Gentile Christian Titus, in order to obtain in principle the assent of the Jerusalem community to his own practice, which is free of the law.

Two different sets of negotiations can be distinguished in Paul's account in Galatians: one takes place within the framework of an assembly of the community (Gal. 2.2a), the other with the 'pillars' in a small group (Gal. 2.2b, 6ff.). The chronological relationship between the discussions is unclear.

After tough discussions and excited arguments, which at the

latest were rekindled in the disputes at the time of Galatians, Paul is able to wring out of the 'pillars' an agreement that the Gentile Christians need not be circumcised. At any rate, Paul's companion, the Greek Titus, was not forced to be circumcised (Gal. 2.3; cf. 2.14; 6.12).[181] Nevertheless, the agreement was fiercely fought for, and indeed it even had to be accepted that the 'false brethren', at least initially, had considerable support in the Jerusalem community for their demand that Titus should be circumcised. They probably also continued to have the 'pillars' on their side, at least in part.

Nevertheless, Paul in principle had the assent of the Jerusalem community to his mission to the Gentiles without circumcision.[182] The reason for the agreement sealed with a solemn handshake as a sign of their equality was evidently its *success*, to which the Jerusalem Christians could not close their eyes, and also the readiness of the Gentile Christian communities or their representatives, Paul and Barnabas, to seal their agreement with a gift of money.

The Christians from Jerusalem probably adopted an ambiguous attitude to Paul: on the one hand his action was obviously inadequate, since those who had been converted by him did not observe the Torah, and even dangerous, since their example constantly prompted Jews to transgress the law. On the other hand, it was better than nothing, since Christ was being preached and centres were being founded in which the work could be continued and corrected by delegates from Jerusalem. Assuming that these reflections are true, the generous gesture of Paul was perhaps the point which won them over – at least for the moment – to this strange person from Tarsus born out of due time – all the more so, if they could infer certain legal requirements from the gift. Certainly Paul is restrained in this respect in his account of the conference. He asserts: 'Those, I say, who were of no repute added nothing to me' (Gal. 2.6). But then follows another clause, 'only they would have us remember the poor, [183] which very thing I was eager to do' (Gal. 2.10). 'Therefore the most important resolution of the conference was the least apparent: the collection for the Jerusalem community; and Paul's further efforts for this collection were among the most important of his activity.'[184]

Scholars have puzzled a great deal over this collection. One tendency understands it in analogy to the temple tax, [185] while another points out that with it the promise of the pilgrimage of the nations is fulfilled.[186] Finally, it is claimed that the collection had been insisted on in Jerusalem and made in the Pauline communities so that these 'could adopt the traditional status of the group of the "godfearers"'.[187] As we have no primary sources for the view of the Jerusalem community, all this remains hypothetical. However, one thing seems to be certain: the negotiating partners from Jerusalem and Paul seem to have understood the collection in different ways, [188] or, to put it more cautiously, the agreement allowed them to interpret the collection in different ways. Here the Jerusalem community in all probability inferred legal requirements from the 'agreement', [189] but Paul disguised the legal character of the constant support. Cf. Rom. 15.25f.: 'At present, however, I am going to Jerusalem with aid for the saints. For Macedonia and Achaia have been pleased to make some contribution for the poor among the saints at Jerusalem.' But at other points it emerges that 'poor'[190] and 'elect' (Rom. 8.33; Col. 3.12) and 'saints' were honorific titles for the Jerusalem community.[191]

At any rate, even during the conference, considerable tensions remained between Paul and the leaders of the Jerusalem community from whom he was able to extract an agreement. At the same time, despite the concordat with the apostle to the Gentiles, the 'false brethren' continued to belong to the Jerusalem community, and will have contested the agreement as much as they could. At all events, their open hostility to Paul is to be presupposed as a normative factor at the council and afterwards, when the Jerusalem church under the leadership of James intervened actively in the Pauline communities.

If these reflections are not too far from the historical truth, we may also assume that the 'false brethren' indirectly influenced details of the results of the negotiations, despite their defeat over the question of circumcision. This assumption is confirmed by a close examination of the formula of agreement in Gal. 2.9, which displays a *legal* character: 'We to the Gentiles, they ... to the Jews.' The mission field is divided. From now on the mission to the Gentiles is the task of Paul and Barnabas, and the mission to the Jews that of James, Cephas and John, based in Jerusalem. The very wording of the phrases 'to the Gentiles' or 'to the Jews' allows only an exclusive understanding of the groups defined by them. From this we are therefore to infer that each time only Gentiles or *exclusively* Jews are the focal point of the mission. But that means that the apostolic agreement on a *union* was at the same time an agreement on a *division* of the two churches, one loyal to the law and one free from it. The union formula mentioned above certainly assured Paul the unqualified right to engage in mission to the Gentiles. But at the same time it could also be used to reverse a mission to Gentiles *and* Jews. Therefore the regulation did not exclude the possibility that in future Jews who lived in a Gentile Christian community without observing the law could be obliged to observe the Jewish law. Here we find a development which is by no means rare in history, namely that too deep a concern for unity, almost at any price and therefore really of no use, revives the opposed forces which first sparked off the conflict.

Another event of which we have an eye-witness report provides abundant material to demonstrate this.[192]

In the newly founded community of Antioch, Christians who had been born Jews and Christians who had been born Gentiles regularly ate together. Paul had taken part in these meals when he had been in Antioch, and so had Peter. When 'some people from James', i.e. messengers sent by him, arrived in Antioch, all this suddenly changed. Peter, Barnabas and the other Jewish Christians who were present withdrew out of fear of the 'people from the circumcision' and in so doing excited the wrath of Paul. In his view Peter was in this way compelling the Gentile Christians, who had been left alone, to be circumcised in order to restore the table fellowship between Jewish and Gentile Christians. Indeed, Paul further aggravates the situation by saying that previously Peter had lived as a Gentile (Gal. 2.14).

The question arises as to just how 'Gentile' the life-style was of the members of the community who were present? Had roast pork, donkey or hare come to the table?[193] Did people even drink Gentile wine, which had been offered to the gods? Were there foods on which the tithe had not been paid?[194] Or did people eat meat which had originally been sacrificed to the gods? To raise these questions is on the one hand to show how little we really know about the interlude in Antioch. On the other hand, we know Paul's attitude about meat offered to idols from I Cor. 8–10. In general he had no hesitations about eating it (I Cor. 10.25–27). But if anyone's attention was drawn to the origin of the meat, he advised against eating it – for the sake of the members of the community who were weak in the faith (I Cor. 10.28f.). So if Paul personally was very free about eating meat offered to idols, that may have not been the case with Barnabas and the other Jewish Christians; otherwise they would not have retreated so quickly in Antioch. For *this* reason it is improbable that the extreme possibilities mentioned above applied. Rather, the Torah will have been observed to a minimal degree; only James himself insisted on strict observance and evidently had good reason for that, because the Jewish Christians in Jerusalem were no longer to be compromised. In other words, here too there is a division – as at the council of Jerusalem. Only when this had come about could there be reflections on interim solutions.[195]

Paul saw Peter's behaviour as a false understanding of the righteousness before God in which he had been at one with him (v. 25), but then exaggerates in remarking that previously Peter had lived in Gentile fashion. However, immediately the general question arose as to what validity the law was still to have for the young church generally. At any rate the charge made against Paul both previously and later could not be rejected, namely that in painting things so much in black and white, culminating in an either-or, he had dealt the Jewish law a decisive blow, even if he claimed the opposite (see below, 93f.).

The historical development (continued): from the Apostolic Council to the rejection of Paul's collection and the execution of James

In the period between Paul's visit to Jerusalem for the Council and his last visit there, the community under the leadership of James increasingly adopted an attitude which was hostile to him. Indeed it formally stylized Paul as a heretic. The reaction to that was increasing bitterness on the part of Paul to those sent out by Jerusalem. He had conditionally cursed the Judaizers in Galatia (Gal. 1.6ff.) and made similar comments on the people from Jerusalem who had infiltrated the community in Philippi (Phil. 3.2ff.). (In the next chapter we shall be pursuing the history of this hostility to Paul further.) The report in Acts (ch. 21) confirms the opposition to the Jerusalem community.

Between his second and third visits to Jerusalem Paul was concerned to meet the requirements of the additional formula in the Jerusalem concordat and make a collection in his communities for the poor in Jerusalem. He dropped his original plan to sent delegates with this collection to Jerusalem (cf. I Cor. 16.3: 'And when I arrive [viz., with you in Corinth] I will send those whom you accredit by letter to carry your gift to Jerusalem') and planned to take the collection there himself (Rom. 15.25; 'At present, however, I am going to Jerusalem with aid for the saints') – he had already considered this as a possibility at a previous time (I Cor. 16.4: 'If it seems advisable that I should go also [to Jerusalem], they [the delegates of the community] will accompany me'). The only explanation for this change in strategy (foreseeable since II Cor. 9.4) seems to be that Paul wanted to, indeed had to, meet the Jewish Christian opposition on the spot. The collection formally crystallized into a symbol of the unity of the church of Jewish Christians and Gentile Christians, on the outcome of which its future would be decided. For Paul, everything depended on the communion of Gentile Christians and Jewish Christians. Precisely for that reason, in accordance with the agreement made a few years previously, he *had to* bring the collection which had been agreed to Jerusalem and at the same time settle the dispute which had been caused in his communities by emissaries from Jerusalem. These are not 'untenable assumptions', as the great Danish New Testament scholar Johannes Munck thought, [196] but statements which are orientated on the complex and contradictory situation of Pauline communities in the first century.

Granted, we do not have any testimony from Paul himself about his last stay in Jerusalem, but the report in Acts 21 contains valuable, ancient textual material, even if the first person plural account is fictitious and only meant to give the impression of an eye-witness.[197]

Paul travels with some companions from Miletus through Caesarea to Jerusalem. In Caesarea he receives hospitality from the Hellenist Philip and in Jerusalem from the Hellenist Mnason. In the Jerusalem community, which lives in fidelity to the law and which is presided over by James, his person is highly controversial, since rumours are rife: Paul is said to be an apostate from the law and to be against the circumcision of Jewish boys. So James says to Paul that many thousands of believers among the Jews 'have been told about you that you teach all the Jews who are among the Gentiles to forsake Moses (*apostasia apo Moyseos*), telling them not to circumcise their children or to observe the customs' (Acts 21.21). Paul counters this by accepting responsibility for absolving the vows of four Nazirites (Acts 21.26). Such an act, which in Jerusalem was regarded as a pious work, consisted in making a gift of money to the temple: this marked the end of the Nazirites' vows. He himself therefore goes to the temple in order to make atonement as one who has been among Gentiles.

The question has been asked whether the narrative sequence obtained on the basis of the tradition in Acts can have any claim to historical probability. This is emphatically to be affirmed, as other sources confirm the individual elements of the tradition that can be extracted.

(a) Other sources[198] endorse the leading position of James and the nomistic character of the community in the fifties of the first century.

(b) The participation of the apostle in a cultic act is quite conceivable, given Paul's understanding of freedom. Thus in general terms he writes in I Cor. 9.19–21:

19 For though I am free from all men, I have made myself a slave to all, that I might win the more. 20 To the Jews I became as a Jew, in order to win Jews, to those under the law I became as one under the law – though not being myself under the law ... 21 To those outside the law I became as one outside the law ...

(c) Because of Paul's earlier close connection with the Hellenist circles, it is probable that he found lodging with a Hellenist. Indeed he was instructed in Christianity by these groups which he once persecuted (see 67f. below).

(d) Finally, the charge against Paul expressed in Acts 21.21 may be historical, and aptly indicate the reservations which Jerusalem Christians raised about Paul. It says that Paul teaches 'all the Jews who are among the Gentiles to forsake Moses, telling them not to circumcise their children or observe the (Jewish) customs'. Such a

charge seems surprising in connection with what is reported of Paul in Acts. Luke had described Paul as a practising Jew who, for example, circumcised Timothy (Acts 16.2f.) and later gave himself out as a Pharisee faithful to the law (Acts 23.1–9). So the charge mentioned certainly goes back to a pre-Lukan tradition. Historically it found support in what *really* happened in Pauline communities. Certainly Paul preached the gospel predominantly to the Gentiles, in accordance with the agreements at the Council and in keeping with his calling. Nor does the kind of statement imputed to him in Acts 21.21 appear in any one of his extant letters. But the apostle expected those who had been born Jews at least in part to ignore the dietary laws in their dealings with Gentile Christians (cf. Gal. 2.11ff.), and in his letters often emphasized how unimportant the law was compared with the new creation in Christ. A principle which could quickly become a battle slogan ran: 'For neither circumcision counts for anything nor uncircumcision but keeping the commandments of God' (I Cor. 7.19), and another: 'For neither circumcision counts for anything nor uncircumcision but a new creation' (Gal. 6.15).[199] Could it not happen that as a consequence of such a practice, those who had been born Jews were alienated from the law and no longer circumcised their children?

Therefore Acts 21.21 quite definitely gives historically reliable information about the consequences of Paul's preaching and his practice among Jews, and about the strong reservations, not to say the hostility, of the Jerusalem community towards him. Certainly Paul suffered in Jerusalem for a cause which was not his own, namely the total detachment of Christianity from Judaism. But the Jewish Christians were right: *in the last resort Paul's activity destroyed Jewish customs and put an end to the law of Moses.*

Now if it is certain that Paul's last journey to Jerusalem had the sole purpose of delivering the collection, why is there nothing about this in Acts 21? That seems all the more astonishing, since Acts 21 essentially contains historical elements. Precisely for that reason, it seems that we must rule out the possibility that the source used in Acts 21 contained *no* reference to the collection. This provokes the question: why does Luke *delete* any reference to the collection in that chapter? The urgency of an answer to the question is increased if Acts 24.17 (Paul in Jerusalem: 'Now after some years I came to bring to my nations alms and offerings') conceals a displaced note about the significance of Paul's last journey to Jerusalem.[200] The only possible answer to the question raised therefore has to be that in Acts 21 Luke deliberately avoids the topic of the collection because the source he used reported either a failure to hand it over or its rejection. Had the source described its acceptance, Luke would have accepted this information (at this point!), since he is particularly concerned to demonstrate the good relationship between Paul and the Jerusalem community. Instead of this he shifts the topic of the collection, which he anxiously avoided in ch.21, and introduces it in Acts 11.27ff., where with the use of individual traditions he constructs a 'model visit'[201] and has Barnabas and Paul bringing a collection to Jerusalem. (However, even there it is not explicitly said that the collection is accepted!).

Now of course one can attempt historically to connect the redemption of the vows of the four Nazirites with the collection, and conjecture that Paul might have used part of the collection money for this.[202] But even if that were the case, the absence of any mention of the collection needs explaining, and the thesis that it was 'apparently as it were simply handed over and received with whispers in a side room'[203] is a desperate expedient, since it begins from a presupposition which is not further investigated, namely that the Jerusalem community wanted at all costs to avoid a break with Paul. But that is precisely the question, all the more so since a few years previously in Jerusalem Paul had had some difficulty in presenting things in his favour.

This inference that the collection was refused, [204] which is, granted, a radical one, has often not been drawn in this way by scholars. For example, Jürgen Becker writes: 'There must have been ... people among the Jewish Christians in Jerusalem who argued that the collection should be rejected.' But he then goes on immediately to qualify this: 'It is highly probable that James as not one of these.'[205] However, the main reason for this is not clear, since in a situation of conflict which is taking shape and simmering, it is quite conceivable 'that James could have gone back on his recognition of Gentile Christianity at the Apostolic Council ... by official rejection of the Gentile collection, in practice in the form of a public rebuff'.[206]

But in that case, one might ask, how could a collection no longer

48

have been welcome to the Jewish Christians of Jerusalem when they had *accepted* one some years before? Many possible reasons suggest themselves. On the one hand, the tension between Paul and the Jerusalem Christians had intensified to an almost intolerable degree. The apostle had written words against the law which had come to the ears of the Jerusalem Christians. They had sent spies into the Pauline communities. There they had observed abominations against the law involving people who had been born Jews: Jewish Christians no longer circumcised their children and ate with Gentile Christians. And on the other hand, the situation in Jerusalem had become more difficult for the community there, because influential groups in Jerusalem had become more radical in the run-up to the Jewish War. And perhaps the collection was not even called for at the conference, but was first brought into play by Paul, in order to achieve some success in negotiations.

The eighteen halakhot (cf. MShab 1, 4–9), which some Jews had resolved on before the destruction of Jerusalem in 70 CE, included a prohibition against accepting gifts from Gentiles.[207] One might see here a parallel to the attitude of the Jerusalem community towards the gift of the Gentile Christian churches: what had once been acceptable had now become intolerable for the Jerusalem community, as a result of developments in Jerusalem and in Pauline mission territory; indeed it had become a 'poisoned chalice'.[208]

Paul evidently expected the worst, since shortly before his fateful journey to Rome he asked the Romans for support in prayer, 'that I may be delivered from the unbelievers (= Jews) in Judaea, and that my service (= the collection) for the saints (= the community in Jerusalem) may be acceptable' (Rom. 15.31). In other words, he knows the indignation of the (unbelieving) Jews in Jerusalem, but also the reservations of the community there towards his person and the collection.

The Jewish historian Josephus on the execution of James

Josephus, *Antiquities* XX 199–203:

'The younger Annas, who, as we have said, had been appointed to the high priesthood, was rash in his temper and unusually daring. He followed the school of the Sadducees, who are indeed more heartless than any of the other Jews, as I have already explained, when they sit in judgment. Possessed of such a character, Annas thought that he had a favourable opportunity because Festus was dead and Albinus was still on the way. And so he convened the judges of the Sanhedrin and brought before them a man named James, the brother of Jesus who was called the Christ, and certain others. He accused them of having transgressed the law and delivered them up to be stoned. Those of the inhabitants of the city who were considered the most fair-minded and who were strict in observance of the law were offended at this. They therefore secretly sent to the king (viz. Agrippa) requesting him to require Annas in writing to desist from any further such actions, since this was not the first time that he had not acted justly.'[209]

The narrative by the Jewish historian Flavius Josephus 'is an authentic account by the Jerusalem priest and eye-witness and is certainly reliable, not a later Christian interpolation'.[210] At the time of the execution of James around 62 CE Josephus was a priest in Jerusalem and was around twenty-five years old (*Vita*, 12f.). The interest of the narrative relates to the Sadducean high priest Annas, who has incurred blame for an illegitimate execution, not that of James. For this reason, too, the theory that there is a later Christian insertion here fails.

> By way of contrast , in emphasizing the cruelty of the Sadducean Annas Josephus is evidently looking back on an incident under John Hyrcanus (*Antt.* XIII 293–6) which attested the mildness of the Pharisees before the court.

The text of Josephus quoted above allows the following conclusions:[211]

1. At the instigation of the high priest Annas, James, along with some others who are probably to be identified as Jewish Christians, was condemned to death by stoning before the supreme council. This happened between the death of the procurator Festus and the arrival of the new procurator Albinus, around 62.

2. A group which included the most zealous observers of the law, i.e. Pharisees, protested most sharply against Annas' action, and this led to his deposition. Here we may leave it open whether the Pharisees were protesting against the right of the high priest to

convene the supreme council in a capital trial without the consent of the procurator, or were objecting to the death penalty, or to both.[212] In any event the Pharisees were protesting both against the accusation and against the outcome of the proceedings. *The accusation that James and his followers were lawbreakers was therefore unjust.*

We must now see James's position as being so prominent that the group which he represented was no longer regarded as standing within the Jewish community but alongside it. He was regarded as 'the Just' (cf. Hegesippus in Eusebius, *HE* II 23, 7). According to Martin Hengel, the 'nickname "the Just" ... here has similar "ecclesiological" significance to that of "Cephas" for Simon; indeed, for Jewish Christianity it far surpassed the latter in importance. At the same time the function of James as *saddiq* explains his designation as "protective wall". His very existence keeps disaster from his people; his intercession penetrates to God and has the function of bringing about atonement, since the just transform God's penal righteousness into mercy.'[213] James' exemplary obedience to the Torah was evidently also recognized outside the Jerusalem community.

His office may have been felt to be a rival one by the high priest. The power of his person, and the traditional mistrust of innovations by the Sadducees, who usually provided the high priest, will have been an additional factor. So the high priest Annas could also have counted James among his opponents, against whom he carried through death sentences in the supreme court. James was stoned, but in truth he did not die as a 'lawbreaker', as even Martin Hengel writes in a way which is open to misunderstanding, [214] but out of a personal rivalry the theological background to which is now impossible to judge.[215] If anywhere, then here, James's unblemished way of life in Judaism is clear.

Nevertheless, the execution of James created enormous tensions within Judaism which led to a break between two communities, one of which would not continue to belong to Jewish society for much longer. *An unplanned historical development led to a result which no one could have guessed at previously and which – from a historical perspective – was unfair to the Jerusalem community under James.*

However, it would be going too far to assume that the followers of James did not take part in the Jewish revolt against Rome. Certainly the majority refused to rebel against the Romans. Even the high priest Annas who had James stoned belonged to the moderate party which rejected a war against the Romans. But it by no means follows from that that the Jerusalem community left the capital, all the less so since a majority of the so-called 'peace party' did not flee from Jerusalem either. Rather, we must take seriously the possibility that part of the Christian community, and the Pharisees and Sadducees who wanted peace, perished in the Jewish War in solidarity with their people. Another part had already left Jerusalem previously, and other Jewish Christians may have fled before the advancing army from Galilee and Samaria into Transjordan.

Part II: The Jewish Christians of Jerusalem after the Jewish War

The report in Irenaeus

There is a summary report of the Jewish Christians in Irenaeus, *Haer* I 26, 2:

> 'Those who are called Ebionites agree (with us) that the world was made by God; but their opinions with respect to the Lord are similar to those of Cerinthus and Carpocrates. They use the Gospel according to Matthew only, and repudiate the Apostle Paul, maintaining that he was an apostate from the law. As to the prophetic writings, they endeavour to expound them in a somewhat singular manner: they practise circumcision, persevere in the observance of those customs which are enjoined by the law, and are so Judaic in their style of life that they even adore Jerusalem as if it were the house of God.'[216]

Since there is a good century between the end of the Jerusalem community and the writing down of the report quoted above, of course reasons must be given why the group of Ebionites should be seen as an offshoot of the Jerusalem community. The following considerations tell in favour of the historical plausibility of this:

1. The name 'Ebionites' might be the term this group used to denote themselves. Irenaeus or his source in fact uses it without further commentary – probably because there was nothing more that they could say about it. The name derives from the Hebrew *ebyonim*. This predicate may take up a Jewish honorific designation (cf. Pss. 86.1f.; 132.15f.; Isa. 61.1ff.); in all probability, however, the group was adopting a title of the earliest Jerusalem community, 'the poor'.[217]

2. Hostility to Paul in the Christian sphere before 70 is attested above all in groups which come from Jerusalem. Cf. the verbal agreement between the anti-Pauline charge in Acts 21.21 (*apostasia apo Moyseos*) and the present text (*apostates tou nomou*).

3. The same is true of observance of the law culminating in circumcision.

4. The direction of prayer (*qibla*) towards Jerusalem makes the derivation of the Ebionites from there probable.

The conclusion must be that Irenaeus' report contains valuable testimony about the offshoot of the earliest Jerusalem community. Here, however, we must assume that Irenaeus has brought together several groups in this report.

Justin's report[218]

A generation before Irenaeus, the apologist Justin describes Jewish groups in his *Dialogue with Trypho*, 46f. Because of its importance, [219] extracts from the relatively extensive text are printed at the end of the book in an English translation.[220]

Justin lists the following characteristics of the Christians he describes: they observe the sabbath, practise circumcision, observe months and practise baptisms or baths of purification (cf. Dial. 46.2).[221] That shows that they are Jewish Christians. In addition they may be said to be predominantly to be Jews in the ethnic sense. Justin certainly presupposes that a Gentile Christian could become a Jewish Christian or even a Jew. But these are special cases, the exceptions which prove the rule, namely that in Dial. 46f. Justin is discussing Christians who were born Jews and their relation to Gentile Christians.

According to Justin's account, the Jewish Christians adopted varied attitudes to their Gentile brothers in faith. They differed

over whether they should require Gentile Christians also to observe
the law which they practised. One part rejected fellowship with the
Gentile Christians if these did not similarly live a Jewish life (47.3).
The other part argued for fellowship with them without such a
demand (47.2).

What kind of fellowship is envisaged? In 47.2 Justin speaks of
living together, i.e. of social intercourse and eating together.

The problem was acute for travelling Christians who sought
lodging in Christian houses and depended on the help of their
Christian brothers and sisters. Justin, who by his own account
comes from Flavia Neapolis in Palestine (*I Apol.* 1, 1) and later
stayed in Ephesus and Rome, was aware of the importance of such
a question by virtue of his own biography. Since he came to know
Jewish Christians personally, at least in Palestine, he had an
understanding of their particular characteristics. Other Gentile
Christians did not show this tolerance and in general rejected
fellowship with Jewish Christians.

Thus Justin seems to be familiar with Jewish Christians of *both*
kinds, so that his report has special value. Since the only controversial issue between them seems to have been what attitude to
adopt to the Gentile Christians, we may begin by assuming that
they did not belong to different communities but were united in a
single community. A parallel is provided by the Jewish Christian
church in Jerusalem before 70 CE, which formed one community
despite a difference in attitudes to Gentile Christianity. 'It is easy to
recognize here (viz., in Justin's report) the two positions from the
Jewish Christian side in Jerusalem which were represented at the
Apostolic Council, whatever the historical context may have
been.'[222]

Unfortunately Justin does not say anything about the geographical location of the Jewish Christians. We should probably think of
Palestine (but perhaps also of Asia Minor): Justin spent a considerable time in both areas.

Now it is possible to demonstrate that Justin's Jewish Christians
were probably hostile to Paul, although Justin does not say so
explicitly.

As a presupposition we may introduce the assumption that Paul
was well known in both Eastern and Western Christianity in the
first half of the second century. Certainly we cannot presuppose the

use of his letters and/or knowledge of his person in every Gentile Christian community, but we can do so in the centres of Antioch, Asia Minor, Greece and of course Rome.

Only one class of Justin's Jewish Christians made rigorist demands of Gentile Christians and rejected fellowship with them because they did not observe the law. This presupposes that the Jewish Christians were informed about Gentile Christians, including their estimation of the apostle to the Gentiles. Therefore in many cases a rejection of fellowship with the Gentile Christians was *necessarily* bound up with a repudiation of Paul.

The question whether Justin knew and used letters of Paul is *certainly* to be answered in the affirmative. Thus in *Dial.* 27.3 he uses the same quotations from the Psalms and Isaiah as Rom. 3.12 – Ps. 14.3; 5.10; 140.4; Isa. 59.7f., in the same order – and in *Dial.* 39.1f. he reproduces 'Elijah's lament against Israel and God's answer (cf. I Kings 19.10/17) in a way which in several details corresponds with Rom. 11.2/5 against the LXX version'.[223] Moreover we should recall that in Rome before the end of the first century Peter and Paul were an established pair and at least Romans and I Corinthians were available. One might compare with this the letter of the Roman church to the Corinthian community composed at the end of the first century, I Clem. 5.1–11:

'1 But, to cease from the examples of old time, let us come to those who contended in the days nearest to us; let us take the noble examples of our own generation. 2 Through jealousy and envy the greatest and most righteous pillars of the church were persecuted and contended unto death. 3 Let us set before our eyes the good apostles: 4 Peter, who because of unrighteous jealousy suffered not one or two but many trials, and having thus given his testimony went to the glorious place which was his due. 5 Through jealousy and strife Paul showed the way to the prize of endurance; 6 seven times he was in bonds, he was exiled, he was stoned, he was a herald both in the East and in the West, he gained the noble fame of his faith, 7 he taught righteousness to all the world, and when he had reached the limits of the West he gave his testimony before the rulers, and thus passed from the world and was taken up into the Holy Place – the greatest example of endurance.'

Some scholars conclude from the fact that Justin does *not* explicitly mention Paul, along with other arguments, that he was hostile to Paul – beyond question wrongly, since Justin does not attack him at all. Andreas Lindemann has explained this situation in a different way: 'The fact that he does not mention Paul is a consequence of his theological principle: the truth of Christianity is demonstrated from the Old Testament; alongside that, only sayings of Jesus which are given in the "Memorials of the Apostles", i.e. the Gospels, are significant.'[224] But that immediately raises the question why Justin uses letters of Paul. So Lindemann's solution is improbable.

Instead of this, we may interpret the above evidence as follows: Justin is standing between two fronts. On the one hand, he attacks Marcion and develops a distinctive doctrine of the law against him,[225] in order to guarantee the continuity of the Old Testament and New Testament revelation. On the other hand, he is engaged in a dialogue with Judaism, however much of a monologue this may prove to be. Now the fatal aspect of the situation was that the Christian heretic Marcion, whom Justin had explicitly challenged in an earlier work (see above, 19), had emblazoned Paul on his shield, and on the other hand the same Paul was tabu to the Jews. To have mentioned the apostle to the Gentiles would therefore at the same time both have put Justin too near to Marcion and made dialogue with the Jews difficult. The 'deliberate mention of the apostle and the explicit reference to him as an orthodox interpreter of Old Testament typology would not have been helpful in a city in which at the same time Marcion was active and using Paul to fight against the Old Testament'.[226]

All this has consequences for our assessment of *Dial.* 46 f. For if Paul had *deliberately* been omitted by Justin for the reasons given, it automatically followed that the rejection of Paul by Jewish Christians was not to be mentioned either. Justin was then compelled to pass over the anti-Paulinism of the Jewish Christians about whom he reported.

In view of what has just been said, therefore, it seems that we should conclude that Justin's Jewish Christians are a historical connecting link between the Jewish Christianity of Jerusalem before the year 70 and the Jewish Christian communities summed up in Irenaeus' account of the heretics.

Offshoots of the Jewish Christianity of Jerusalem can be demonstrated down to the fourth century, scattered over Palestine,
Transjordan and Syria. This follows from an analysis of the reports
in the church fathers Hippolytus, Eusebius and Epiphanius which
will not be entered into here.[228] Today the Pseudo-Clementines,
which were once highly valued for the knowledge they offer of
earlier Jewish Christianity, have almost been forgotten – in my
view wrongly, as some soundings of their hostility to Paul will
make clear.

In their latest (fourth-century) version the Pseudo-Clementines
are a 'recognition romance', allegedly composed by Clement of
Rome, who in them reports the loss of his family and their happy
reunion. Different source writings have been inserted into them,
the earliest strata of which date from the second century. They
contain vigorous polemic against Paul, which sometimes seems like
pamphleteering, and 'the whole argument culminates in a coarse
repudiation of the legitimacy of his apostolate'.[229] In a disputation
in Laodicea, the tradition of which points to the second century,
Peter explains once and for all, in a way typical of an opponent of
Paul in Jerusalem, that Paul cannot on any account have seen the
risen Christ. The reason for this is as simple as it is illuminating:
only the eyewitnesses to the historical Jesus can be considered for
apostolic office. (A similar argument had already been used in Acts
1.21f. [cf. below, 104f.].) Compared with this, the visions of the
Lord which Paul received according to II Cor. 12.1 have no validity; moreover they are revelations, rather, of an evil demon or lying
spirit. Only personal converse with the historical Jesus and instruction by him could give certainty; the vision, which could also come
from a demonic spirit, leaves things uncertain. Granted, visions
sent by God do not lie. 'But it is uncertain whether the seer saw a
dream that was sent by God' (Hom. XVII 15, 2).

Following this Peter cites a series of biblical visions or dreams
(XVII 17, 1–4) and then emphasizes immediately that the pious
person did not need this sort of thing:

'For what is true springs up in the understanding of the pious, which
is innate and pure – not striven for in a dream, but given to the good

through insight. For in this way to me, too, the Son has been revealed by the Father. From this I know what the essence of revelation is, as I have experienced this in myself. For the moment that the Lord asked what people called him and I heard that each person called him a different name, it arose in my heart; and I said – I truly do not know how I came to do so – "You are the Son of the living God" (Matt. 16.16). And after he had called me blessed, he told me that it was the Father who had revealed it to me. And since then I have known that revelation is knowledge without instruction, without appearance and dreams' (Hom XVII 17, 5–18, 2).

The polemical application of this to Paul then runs:

'If our Jesus really appeared to you in a vision and made himself known to you, then he has become angry with you as with an adversary; that is why he spoke through visions or dreams or even through revelations which are from outside. Can anyone be made skilful in teaching on the basis of an appearance? And if you say, "It is possible", why then did the teacher remain and spend a whole year with those who were awake? But how can we believe you, even if you say that he has appeared to you? How can he also have appeared to you if what you think is contradictory to his teaching? But if you have been visited by him for an hour and instructed and thereupon become an apostle, then proclaim his words, expound his teaching, love his apostles. Do not fight with me, his disciple, for you are hostile to me, firm rock that I am, the foundation stone of the church. If you were not an adversary, you would not shame me by calumniating my preaching, so that people do not believe me when I say what I heard personally from the Lord, as if I had been condemned without dispute and you had a good reputation. But if you say that I am "condemned", you are accusing God, who revealed Christ to me, and disparaging the one who called me blessed on the basis of revelation. Now if you truly want to further the truth, then learn first from us what we learned from him, and if you are a disciple of the truth, then come and work with us' (Hom. XVII 19, 1–7).

This speech of Peter's is sensational. It seems authentic and gives the impression of containing the most important arguments of Paul's Jewish Christian adversaries against him. Formally it has a parallel in Paul's speech to Peter in Antioch, and is steeped in the bitter taste that this left behind in Peter. Peter's remark at another point in the Pseudo-Clementines, that Paul gave a false account of the incident in Antioch, stands on the same level. The letter from Peter to James which prefaces the Homilies says:

'For some of those who are of the Gentiles have rejected the preaching of the law proclaimed by me and followed the foolish teaching of the enemy (= Paul) which is outside the law. Moreover, though I am still alive, some have attempted with some shimmering interpretations to distort my words in the direction of a dissolution of the law, as though I myself thought in this way but did not preach it honestly. Far be it from me!' (2.3f.).

On the other hand, despite the seeming authenticity of the style of Peter's speech, this or the tradition which is handed down in it comes from the second century at the latest, and cannot be attributed directly to Paul's adversaries. That is also impossible because the historical Peter was relatively close to Paul and the real opposition goes back to the circles around James or to James himself. Nevertheless, we might be justified in assuming that in the Pseudo-Clementines the 'old arguments of the Jewish Christians of Jerusalem against Paul ... have been utilized and preserved'.[230]

The uncompromising resistance of the Jewish Christians to Paul was kindled when he used his Damascus vision (a) to demonstrate that he was on a level with the Jerusalem apostles, and (b) to derive from it his justification to preach among the Gentiles 'without the law'. Those who had had personal dealings with Jesus could never have allowed that.

Among these Jewish Christians Paul was even regarded as 'the enemy'. In the letter from Peter to James quoted above they attack his false gospel and abhor his doctrine, which ignores the law. By contrast, Peter and James present a preaching 'of the law' which is addressed to Jews but also to Gentiles. A gospel is said to have come from the heretic Paul. Then, after the destruction of Jerusalem, 'a true gospel was secretly sent out to correct the coming heresies' (Hom. II 17, 4). Evidently the Jewish Christians teachers who stand behind this tradition had replaced circumcision with baptism as an act of initiation. Were they not aware that they were now engaged in mission to the Gentiles in the same way as their enemy, and were thus dispensing with the requirement of circumcision in the same way? Did they not notice that they had come some way towards meeting Paul without intending to? This would not be the first time in church history that the opposing side took over decisive points from the heretical front against which it was fighting. But now it was too late for a real accommodation between these Jewish Christians and Paul.

In addition, it is an irony of fate that the Jerusalem Jewish Christians or their descendants continued to engage vigorously in polemic against Paul at a time when his person and influence were already advancing in the catholic church. Walter Bauer has described the irony of this process which took place over one hundred and fifty years in the following words:

'Thus, if one may be allowed to speak rather pointedly, the apostle Paul was the only heresiarch known to the apostolic age – the only one who was so considered in that period, at least from one particular perspective. It could be said that the Jewish Christians in their opposition to Paul introduced the notion of "heresy" into the Christian consciousness. The arrow quickly flew back at the archer.'[231]

This earliest heretic of the apostolic age will be the subject of the next chapter.

4

The Only Heretic of the Earliest Period, or, A Human Paul[232]

The sources

Paul is the only person from the beginnings of Christianity who encounters us as a human being with all his weaknesses and strong points. In contrast to all the other figures of earliest Christianity, the sources about him are extraordinarily rich. We only have third-person accounts of Jesus. They are not composed in his Aramaic mother tongue, nor do they come from eye-witnesses. Moreover the narratives about him are often contradictory. By contrast, we possess original documents in the truest sense of the word from Paul: in his letters we hear his own voice in his mother tongue, free from all background noise, accessible to all who do not shrink from the trouble of reading him.

Now it would be presumptuous to believe that these letters illuminate the whole of Paul's life, or reproduce his thought completely. They are just the tip of an iceberg. However, early Christian collectors of letters of Paul made quite a good selection, so that the letters of Paul which we know give us plenty of information about his theological views and tell us a good deal about his eventful life. Scholars generally agree that of the thirteen extant letters, seven are authentic (Romans, I and II Corinthians, Galatians, Philippians, I Thessalonians and Philemon), whereas the rest have been composed by later disciples in the apostle's name.[233] Sometimes one or other letter which is not regarded as authentic is again attributed to the apostle (Colossians, II Thessalonians, more rarely Ephesians).[234] However, that does not alter what is now a happily wide consensus on the authenticity of the letters.

The letters are supplemented by the Acts of the Apostles; while this work was not written by an eyewitness, it is based on numerous old and reliable traditions which have to be extracted carefully from the text of Acts and then can be cautiously used in a description.[235] It can be taken as a rule of thumb that the chronological framework of Acts is usually incorrect and has to be corrected by the letters of Paul, [236] whereas the individual reports may be accurate, where they do not betray a clear Lukan bias.[237] On the other hand, Acts is documentation of how a theologian at the end of the first century dealt with conflicts at the beginning: he harmonized them, ordered them or kept quiet about them, and all is so to speak purged in the literal sense by the course of salvation history.[238] The distortion of historical facts which is made necessary by these aims goes so far that in Acts Paul himself is not an apostle;[239] in effect he belongs to the post-apostolic age, and as the thirteenth witness[240] guarantees the continuity between the time of the beginning and the time of the author of Luke-Acts. Moreover the theology attributed to him in the speeches – with some exceptions – has little to do with the Paul of the authentic letters.[241] However, that does not alter the basic significance of Acts, above all for Paul's history (for the picture of Paul in Acts cf. further below, 104f.).

Some narratives about Paul from various Christian groups come from an even later time (second and third centuries), but none of them tells us much about the real Paul. Thus opponents of Paul, of whom there have been large numbers at all times, invented stories, for example, about how Paul had originally been a Greek and later went over to Judaism in Jerusalem because he wanted to marry the high priest's daughter. When she turned him down, he was offended, and in his wrath wrote against circumcision, the sabbath and the law.[242]

By contrast, Paul's supporters heightened the miracle-working and missionary success of the apostle immeasurably, and even reported how he made friends with a wild lion in the arena.[243] Finally, we are even given a description of him. Thus it is said of him that he is 'a man small of stature, with a bald head and crooked legs, in a good state of body, with eyebrows meeting and nose somewhat hooked, full of friendliness; for now he appeared like a man, and now he had the face of an angel'.[244]

These examples may suffice to document how unusable such sources are historically.[245] But they again show that in both early and later Christianity Paul had a living influence, and this was exercised in a very human way: the interpreters mentioned (and others not cited here) each read their own views into Paul – an indication that our own presuppositions, too, always need critical examination.

The pre-Christian Paul[246]

First, we can claim with confidence that Paul is an urban man, [247] since the images in which people speak faithfully reflect their surroundings. By contrast, Jesus' preaching reflects the village. One might compare the world of his parables: Jesus knows the sower in the field (Mark 4.3–8), the mustard plant in the garden (Mark 4–30–32); he sees the shepherd with his flock (Mark 6.34) and the birds under the heavens (Matt. 6.26), the lilies in the field (Matt. 6.28) and so on. Paul also uses images from nature. He speaks of the grain of wheat and its shooting up as an image of the resurrection (I Cor. 15.37), of the stars and their shining bodies (I Cor. 15.40f.), the anxious waiting of creation for the revelation of the children of God (Rom. 8.19–23). This last saying shows how sensitive the apostle was to the longing of nature. But at the same time it reflects the distance between him and Jesus, since he echoes the feelings with which a person experiences the hard work of the weary and tormented animals of a large city, whereas for the village dweller even the sparrow who falls to the ground (Matt. 10.29) suggests the omnipotent activity of God rather than universal transitoriness. At all events, the majority of Paul's images are drawn from city life. He uses the image of building extraordinarily often: cf. I Cor. 3.12: 'Now if any one builds on the foundation with gold, silver, precious stones, wood, hay, stubble.' He knows these houses, from the palaces of gold and silver to the straw huts of the workers in the suburbs. The mirror on the wall (I Cor. 13.12; II Cor. 3.18) and the letter on the table (II Cor. 3.2) become images in his talk. His letters show life in the city with its shops (II Cor. 2.17) past which the slave responsible for looking after children (Gal. 3.24f.) takes his protégés to school, holding them by the hand; the street down which the ceremonial triumphal procession moves (cf. II Cor. 2.14). He often derives his imagery from the life of soldiers (II Cor. 10.3–5), and even their trumpets (I Cor. 14.8) serve as a comparison for him; similarly, he draws parallels from the practice of law (Gal. 3.17), indeed even from the theatre (I Cor. 4.9) and from athletic competitions (I Cor. 9.24ff.). The relative frequency and naturalness with which Paul uses this imagery makes it probable that it was part of his acculturation. Similarly, the fact that the Christian Paul 'virtually visited only Hellenistic Roman cities is probably a reflection of his socialization in an urban Hellenistic atmosphere'.[248]

In which city did Paul grow up? He himself does not give an answer to this question, but Luke does in Acts 22.3: 'I am a Jew, born at Tarsus in Cilicia' (cf.9.30; 21.39). On the assumption that this piece of information is based on reliable tradition, it has a high degree of probability.[249] It is confirmed to some extent by the fact that three years after his conversion, without any other motive, Paul retreated to this city in Cilicia which was far away from his abode at that time (Gal. 1.21; Acts 9.30). Here he will have spent his childhood and youth.

We do not know how long Paul was in Tarsus. At any rate he may have gone to a school there and received the general education of his time. This included above all a stylistic training in rhetoric and some knowledge of the most important Greek literature and mythology. One could compare the verse of the Greek writer of comedies, Menander, which Paul quotes in I Cor. 15.33: 'Do not be deceived, "Bad company ruins good morals."' At the same time his father, from whom he may have inherited Roman citizenship (cf. Acts 22.27), will have introduced him to the basic elements of the Bible and perhaps also taught him Hebrew or Aramaic. Here we may take it for granted that Paul regularly shared in the worship of the Jewish synagogue and was instructed in the special character of his own people.

By his own account Paul was circumcised on the eighth day (Phil. 3.5). Every Jew has an obligation to circumcise his son (according to Gen. 17.12 on the eighth day). Usually this was followed by the giving of a name (cf. Luke 1.59; 2.21). Paul was given the Hebrew name 'Saul' after his famous royal ancestor of the tribe of Benjamin, to which he belonged (Phil. 3.5), whereas 'Paul' was a word play on Saul and his Roman name (every Roman citizen had the duty and the right to bear a Roman name).

Paul also calls himself a 'Hebrew of the Hebrews' (Phil. 3.5).

This is occasionally taken as proof that he spoke Aramaic. But 'Hebrew' can also denote the nationality of the Jews as opposed to that of the Gentiles. At all events, Paul's mother tongue was Greek,[250] as also clearly emerges from his use of the Greek translation of the Old Testament (the Septuagint)[251] in his letters. However, we cannot completely rule out the possibility that his family was bilingual.

Moreover, Paul sees himself in Phil. 3.5 as a 'Pharisee according to the law'. In its Aramaic root the word Pharisee, which probably arose as a term given to the group by others (= 'the separated ones') but was then adopted by those to whom it was applied as a description, emphasized the Pharisees[252] as the holy ones. The goal of the Pharisees was the sanctification of everyday life by adopting the way of life to which the priests in the service of the temple were subject. They sought to achieve sanctification by segregation. Thus the regulations of the Torah which applied to priests and related to the temple cult became a matter for individual Jews. One might remember Lev. 19.2: 'You shall be holy, for I the Lord you God am holy.' However, this holiness 'in the everyday life of the world', which sounds almost modern – so to speak a priesthood of all believers – was possible outside the temple only by reinterpretation. The Pharisaic ideal therefore called for the collaboration of scribes, who are not necessarily identical with Pharisees. The Pharisees thus developed the religion of Israel further, while methodically keeping to the letter of the Old Testament. For example, unlike the Sadducees (cf. Mark 12.18: 'The Sadducees ... teach that there is no resurrection'), they also put forward a doctrine of the resurrection, which appears only on the periphery of the Old Testament.[253]

The Pharisees organized themselves in communities. There was probably a probationary period, a set of regulations and a disciplinary law. Therefore one of their most important features was their fellowship, as a contemporary, the Pharisee Josephus, [254] reports: 'The Pharisees are friendly to one another, and are for the exercise of concord, and regard for the public' (*BJ* II, 166). This fellowship was expressed in shared meals, especially every Friday evening on the dawn of the sabbath. Any (male) Jew could become a member. Granted, the leadership was usually exercised by Pharisaic scribes, but the learning of the 'normal' Pharisee should not be underestimated. As a historical illustration of this one might refer to Josephus' own account:

> At the beginning of the war Josephus had the supreme command in Galilee. But his sworn enemy John, son of Levi, gained the leadership in Jerusalem against him. Therefore four men were to challenge the competence of Josephus in Galilee: 'Two of them were from the lower ranks and adherents of the Pharisees, Jonathan and Ananias; the third, Joazar, also a Pharisee, came from a priestly family. The youngest, Simon, was descended from high priests' (*Life*, 196f.).

Regulations about purity played a major role in the precepts of the Pharisees;[255] they primarily represented separation from the other Jews and Gentiles. The New Testament Gospels also mention good works (Matt. 6.2), prayer (Matt. 6.5) and fasting (Luke 18.12: twice a week). The separation of written and oral law was also important for the Pharisees; Paul alludes to this in Gal. 1.14 when he speaks of the traditions of the elders. At the time of Paul, according to Josephus there were more than 6,000 Pharisees (*Antt.* XVII 42). They were mainly to be found in the homeland of Judaea.[256] In Jerusalem, Paul will have joined a Pharisaic community and received special training in scripture.

Paul's emphatic statement that he was superior to many of his contemporaries in observing the law (Gal. 1.14) is not only a reflection of the Pharisaic sense of superiority, but also has a basis in his character; as a Christian he would later say of himself that he worked more than all the other apostles (I Cor. 15.10),[257] or spoke in tongues more than all the Corinthians put together (I Cor. 14.18). It is easy to see from this how difficult he must have been at times as a person. 'He was like a ruler to his communities, was accustomed to get his way and impose himself on others ... he was always right, and readily showed his rough side to those who were less compliant.'[258] He could not take a middle course – he was too direct for that; his desire for an absolute faith was too deep and his experience near Damascus too overwhelming. One could be certain that as a disciple of Jesus he would show the same fiery zeal that he showed as a persecutor. As a Christian, his fanaticism had merely changed its focus.[259]

His activity as a tentmaker (Acts 18.3) probably derives from the rabbinic custom of learning a trade (cf. I Thess. 2.9; I Cor. 4.12;

9.6–18, etc.). It is also clear from his letters that Paul went through a Jewish school. Thus he is familiar with the rules for interpreting the Old Testament then current. To mention and cite the two most important ones: (*a*) The procedure of inference from the smaller to the greater can be found e.g. in the contrast between Adam and Christ (Rom. 5.15, 17); (*b*) the use of analogy, i.e. the process of relating to each other two biblical passages containing terms which sound or mean the same, is used by Paul in Rom. 4.3–8 to interpret the imputing of faith as righteousness (Gen. 15.6). Paul learned these and other rules in his pre-Christian period; in other words, he was already a theologian before he became a Christian.

Given Paul's scribal training, it is surprising that he was evidently not married, as were most of the Jewish teachers of the law known to us.[260] Only of one scholar, the mystic Simon Ben Azzai (beginning of the second century), is it reported that he remained unmarried. When asked why, he gave the following reason: 'What should I do? My soul hangs on the Torah; let the world be maintained by others.'[261] We may presuppose the same thing for Paul: his soul in fact hung on the Torah, which led him, indeed formally drove him, to persecute Christians (cf. Phil. 3.6; I Cor. 15.9; Gal. 1.23f.). It was his zeal which moved him more than most of his contemporaries to be active in matters of the law where it was transgressed. Here his gaze fell upon the followers of Jesus, who claimed that a crucified man was Messiah. For an expert in the law that was impossible, simply because 'cursed is the one who hangs on the cross' (Gal. 3.13/Deut. 21.23).

And there was a second factor: in Jerusalem and a little later Paul had come to know Christians who became brothers and sisters in Christ with Gentiles, and at baptismal celebrations cried out in joy: 'Here is neither Jew nor Greek; here is neither slave nor free; here is neither male nor female; for you are all one in Christ Jesus' (Gal. 3.28). That might not be, because it put the purity of the Jews at risk: the fellowship between Jews and Gentiles polluted this purity and did away with the Jewish identity.

For Paul, it was the command of the hour to fight against this dangerous movement which was opposed to the law. To do that he did not need to be authorized by the supreme council in Jerusalem and be sent to Damascus with letters, as Luke romantically writes in Acts 9.[262] As an ambitious upstart he took things into his own hands. A fire burned in his soul; the desire pricked him to surpass his contemporaries. And he knew how to hate, as only believers can hate those of other faiths.

At first glance it might seem that the explanation of this hatred could be that Paul's fanaticism sprang from an authoritative belief that the teaching of the Christ whom he persecuted sullied God's honour and destroyed the divinely willed purity of the Jewish community, and therefore had to be exterminated.[263] But such a view makes it difficult to understand the sudden change from persecutor to preacher (unless one simply reckons with a miracle, in which case there would be an end to any effort to arrive at a historical understanding).

What is more probable is that the basic elements of the preaching of Christians were sub-consciously a strong influence on Paul. In that case he would have become a persecutor of Christians in order to silence his own self-accusations. His encounter with Christians, with their preaching and practice, took place not only at a cognitive level but at the same time and above all at an emotional and unconscious level – which is probably true of all social and religious experiences. The interpretation suggests itself that Paul's vehement rejection of Christians and his aggressive attitude towards them was based on an inner tension in his person, of the kind that numerous studies in depth psychology have identified in other cases as a motivation for aggressive behaviour. Is it too much to assume that the basic elements of Christian preaching and practice unconsciously attracted Paul? However, for fear of his unconscious strivings in this direction, he projected them on to Christians so that he could attack them there all the more intemperately.

Fanatics often suppress doubts about their own view of life and practice. A strongly normative consciousness comes up against not only the heterodoxy of others but also unavoidable individual elements of its own inner inadequacy in the face of a norm which is so decisive. If that is the case with Paul, his religious zeal was a kind of thermometer of his inner tension, which was formally resolved in the event at Damascus. Thus we can say with Carl Gustav Jung that Saul was already unconsciously a Christian before his conversion, that Saul's Christianity was an unconscious complex for him.[264]

The strongest argument for the correctness of the assumption that already during his time as a persecutor Paul had 'seethed' within is the apostle's own testimony, in Romans 7. This chapter is formulated in retrospect and describes the unconscious conflict which Paul had endured before his conversion. 'Romans 7 is the result of a long retrospective bringing to consciousness of a conflict that had once been unconscious.'[265]

However, the almost unanimous consensus of present-day exegesis is that Rom. 7 may not be applied to the biography of Paul. Three objections have been made to a biographical understanding of the 'I' in Rom. 7 since the classic 1929 work of Werner Georg Kümmel:[266]

1. The 'I' which speaks is a stylistic form, as e.g. in the Old Testament Psalms:

2. Romans 7 is to be understood in the context of the whole of Romans: in retrospective form it gives a theological, not a historical, description of the pre-Christian 'I';

3. In other passages like Phil. 3.6, where he emphasizes his blameless righteousness in fulfilling the law, Paul indicates nothing of a split in his life before he became a Christian.

However, in criticism of the first two arguments it has to be objected that they certainly do not rule out a biographical understanding. Indeed, a reference to the theological form of this retrospect does not by itself do away with the historical question as to how far this theological interpretation of Paul's own biography corresponds to a historical nucleus.

The third argument may be rejected through a critical discussion of Martin Hengel's major book on the pre-Christian Paul.[267] According to Hengel, Phil. 3.6 ('as to zeal a persecutor of the church, as to righteousness under the law blameless') expresses a quite solid self-confidence in the pre-Christian Paul. 'No one who is afflicted by depressions talks like that. This unique confession shows that the young scribe Paul believed that he could live up to the high demands of perfect observance of the Torah of a Pharisaic kind, without any qualifications' (79). But a really historical understanding, which is precisely what Hengel is concerned for in all his works, cannot be content with this. Hengel's reference to Phil. 3.6 takes too little account of the argumentative character of the text, in which the apostle was concerned to emphasize his perfection in the fulfilment of the law. Moreover one can be proud in awareness of one's nomistic achievements and at the same time unconsciously be coping with a conflict.

My thesis is that the conflict depicted in Rom. 7 is too authentic, too 'loaded with experience', 'too alive', for Paul to have been able to develop it purely theoretically, e.g. in retrospect on Jewish existence. Granted, Rudolf Bultmann argued that 'just as little as Rom. 7 is a confession of Paul, but rather a description of Jewish existence generally, so for that very reason it must also apply to Paul's life as a Jew'.[268] But that immediately raises the question: if by deduction Romans 7 can be applied to Paul, why should not this text also have arisen by induction from his personal experiences?[269] Here an exegesis exclusively orientated on existential analysis, which has lost sight of the aspect of experience on the one hand and the task of historical reconstruction on the other, takes its revenge. It cannot be shown plausibly why Rom. 7 should not be applied to a historical reconstruction of this period of Paul's life if it is a description of his Jewish existence.

Now if Kümmel's three reasons mentioned above are not proof that Paul's argument in Rom. 7 is purely theoretical, Rom. 7.7–25 has to be analysed once again:[270]

Structure

vv. 7–12: The primal history of the 'I' (told in the past tense).
v. 13: The particular sinfulness of sin.
vv. 14–25: The conflict in the 'I' (described in the present).

Argument

The opening in v. 7 ('What then shall we say?') matches the beginning already chosen in Rom. 6.1. With 'You shall not covet', Paul is citing the Decalogue commandment Ex. 20.17; Deut. 5.21 (cf. Rom. 13.9), with the omission of the object. Here Paul sees 'the Decalogue commandment with the prohibition in Gen. 2.16f. and the story of the "knowledge" of sin alongside the story of the fall in Gen. 3'.[271] The statement: 'I should not have known what it is to covet if the law had not said, "You shall not covet"' is based on the psychological insight: 'The more he is admonished, the more the tendency opposed to the admonitions is goaded on.'[272]

[8] For the parenthesis 'apart from the law sin lies dead', cf. Rom.

5.13b ('but sin is not counted where there is no law'). However, that in no way changes the actual existence of sin.

[9] The coming of the law already leads to the revival of sin. In other words, it is not just the failure to observe the commandment but its presence which is threatening.

[10] 'Commandment' is a reference to the specific commandment to Adam in paradise. It aimed at life (cf. Rom. 10.5; Gal. 3.12), but in fact brought death in its train. The reason for this is given in the next verse.

[11] Sin achieved this through deception.

[12] Therefore the holiness of the law (= Sinai Torah) and the holiness, righteousness and goodness of the commandment (given in Paradise to Adam) are safeguarded.

[13] This discusses the question whether the law, which has proved itself to be good, nevertheless destroys people. The argument here should possibly be termed unfortunate. For what is the meaning of the answer 'that sin might become sinful beyond measure'?[273]

The third section begins in v. 14:

[14] 'The law is spiritual' recalls what is said in v. 12; the reason for 'sold under sin' was given in vv. 7–12, 13.

[15] This explains why the 'I' is sold under the power of sin: v. 15b explains v. 15a and in this way radicalizes the conflict between willing and (real) doing, for which Medea provides the model in antiquity.[274]

[16] 'I do not want' is identical to 'I hate' (v. 15). The conflict demonstrated in v. 15 shows that the side which is not expressed in the 'I' certifies that the law is good. 'Good' as a designation of the law takes up 'spiritual' (v. 14) and v. 12 generally.

[17] Mentions positively the power which determines human actions: sin.

[18] This is a kind of resumé of vv. 15–17. The beginning is perhaps modelled on the beginning of v. 14. It is important that a conceptual distinction is made for the first time between 'I' and 'flesh'. As v. 18 is a resumé, it is not surprising that

[19] repeats[275] or develops v. 15b and

[20] reproduces vv. 16 and 17, omitting 'I agree that the law is good'.

[21] This explains the conflict that has been described by inserting the twofold concept of the *nomos*; 'law' here certainly does not mean the Old Testament law.

[22] refers back to v. 16, [23] to v. 17.

[24] A lament is succeeded by [25] thanksgiving to God; the basis of the thought is explained in ch.8.

The 'I' in Rom. 7

It is striking that the section comprising vv. 7–12 does not speak specifically of laws, sins, etc. but of the encounter of 'the' law with 'the' 'I' and the revival of sin with the definite article. So Paul is not relating the primal history of the 'I' in strongly generalized terms, though this does not necessarily exclude a biographical reference. For the moment, it is certain only that Paul is not speaking about the conflict in the Christian 'I', because what is said in Rom. 8, where the life in the Spirit is described, tells against this (cf. esp. vv. 12–14). Therefore it is generally assumed that vv. 7–12 refer to the I standing under the law, in such a way that it has become visible from the viewpoint of the person freed from the law.[276] Verse 7, with its statement 'if it had not been for the law, I should not have known sin', is used to argue against the assumption of an unconscious conflict. How can there be an unconscious conflict if the law brings about a *consciousness* of sin? However, the decisive question here is *when* the consciousness begins. In fact the sentence referred to is formulated didactically in retrospect, and the story of the primal history of the 'I' (vv. 8–11) contains no cognitive elements. In other words, the hypothesis of an unconscious conflict and thus an element of Paul's biography behind vv. 8–11 remains a possibility. Verse 13 would then indicate a growing awareness of sin.[277]

The real decision is made in vv. 14–25: the conflict here embraces both the consciousness *and* the unconscious.[278] On the one hand, the split between willing and doing is an ethical conflict taking place in the human consciousness. On the other hand, the conflict lies deeper than the consciousness and is to be put in the unconscious, since the 'do' (v. 15) refers not only to the empirical act of transgression but above all to the result of the action, to death. (It becomes an ethical-moral conflict only where v. 15 is taken further by v. 19.) And the 'I' knows nothing of this (in the consciousness).

What is the relationship between the unconscious and the conscious conflict in vv. 14–25? The direction of the text points towards an increasingly sharp awareness of the conflict. The 'I' of

vv. 21ff. sees through its dividedness, and in comparison with vv. 7–12, too, greater insight into the growing awareness of the conflict can be recognized. According to v. 11 the 'I' is deceived; in vv. 21ff. it recognizes this deception, although it cannot free itself from it. But when it is freed, in retrospect the knowledge of a conflict takes hold, which according to Rom. 7 was a conflict with the Jewish law. (That cannot in any way change the fact that v. 21 contains a twofold concept of *nomos*.) What was called a Christ complex above, using Jung's term, first had to do with the law, as Rom. 7 shows. In practice this conflict could have been provoked, secondly, by the preaching of the crucified Christ (a crucified man could not be the messiah), thirdly by the universalist tendencies of the Christians persecuted by Paul, and fourthly by Jesus' preaching of love as handed down by the Hellenists. Oskar Pfister suggested that Paul was a hysteric with a strong gift of love for other people.[279] He had a feeling of anxiety, of the kind that is very frequent among hysterics, 'which in religious natures amalgamates with the guilt feeling and heightens the pressure of sin' (276). 'Jesus and the Christians called for love and only love. As a true hysteric, before his conversion Paul could not love completely, and that was what caused him suffering' (277). 'When Paul approached Damascus, the catastrophic breakthrough of his long-suppressed longing took place ... Paul took flight from his painful situation into the other world of hallucination' (279f.).

The crucial point here is that what he had longed for uncon-sciously had become reality in a human being. Paul's ideal of Christ, which first broke through in the preaching of the person whom he had persecuted, had a parallel in the activity of Jesus. What Paul longed for for himself through a 'blameless life accord-ing to the law' had become reality in a despised, crucified man who could not (and did not want to) hold a candle to him where correct Jewish observance of the law was concerned. The persecution of the followers of Jesus increasingly confronted Paul with the failure of his efforts. Thus the historical cross of Jesus gave Paul's picture of Christ at the same time a previously unknown dimension, especially as the idea of a crucified Messiah was something new, and its consequences first had to be thought through by the former Pharisee. This split in Paul between his efforts, which he felt to be a failure, and the followers of Jesus, standing so openly before his eyes and embodying his own longing, finally discharged itself in the so-called Damascus event.

The Damascus event

The career of the Pharisaic zealot came to an abrupt end. Paul is one of those people whose life is cut into two halves by a single inner catastrophe. His person breaks apart. He almost literally plunges into Christ, and once for all escapes the disastrous connection between death, law and sin (cf. I Cor. 15.56), standing in life, illuminated by eternity, warmed by the experience of the love of God. Here he has the tremendous discovery of receiving a new self, and gains a fundamental guideline for his thought in the subsequent period. Paul had hated Jesus as a false messiah and had fought against his followers. But on the way to Damascus, in the middle of a bloody persecution which he himself had started, he saw this Jesus in heavenly light and was irresistibly seized by a conviction which overturned his former life: the one who had been crucified was alive, so he was the messiah. This moment was decisive for his life.

Psychologically, this event may have been a vision (cf. esp. I Cor. 9.1: Paul has seen the Lord).[280] That is often disputed in Protestant biblical research, and the story of the prejudice against visions (and auditions), indeed the failure to understand them, has still to be written. For Paul, visions were not limited to the 'Damascus event';[281] in a later period, too, his life was accompanied by visionary experiences (cf. Gal. 2.2; Acts 16.9) which he often had to pay for with an illness.[282]

Visions are something that happens in the human mind, products of human powers of imagination, though visionaries regularly tell things differently: they claim to perceive images and hear sounds from outside. So too Paul certainly never doubted that he had seen Jesus at that time (and also later), and the vision had just as much influence on him as an objective fact would have had.[283] However, the objectivity of the mode of expression cannot be played off against the fact that this is a religious expression of the subject.[284]

The vision is a primary phenomenon, a religious experience which does away with the limitations of space and time and the

74

subject-object relationship, and takes place in a non-rational sphere. That cannot be otherwise. However, visions have become alien to us present-day men and women. They are experiences but not respected, and are often identified with hallucinations (of the sick), without it being noted that they derive from a way of thinking in primal images and symbols which transcends – indeed already precedes – the understanding and is peculiar to all human beings. Nowadays this 'thinking' has often wandered off from theology and the church into art and poetry; it flashes out in everyday life where we first begin to understand properly someone we love, in an event which discloses them to us, when we 'see' them. Furthermore, there is a parallel in some dreams which generally spring from the same world of experience as visions. Full, authentic life is probably possible only if we correspond to these images in ourselves. To this degree it can also be said that Paul encountered his image of Christ before Damascus.

Theologically, through the Damascus event Paul gained the insight that the crucified Christ is the Messiah.[285] This recognition runs like a scarlet thread through the letters, and the term 'cross' can be found more frequently in Paul's letters than in the other writings of the New Testament and early Christianity. Cf. what he says about the 'cross of Christ' in I Cor. 1.17 (' ... lest the cross of Christ be emptied of its power'); Gal. 6.14 ('But far be it from me to glory except in the cross of our Lord Jesus Christ, by which the world has been crucified to me and I to the world'); Phil. 3.18 ('For many, of whom I have often told you and now tell you even with tears, live as enemies of the cross of Christ'); the remarks about the 'word of the cross' in I Cor. 1.8, the scandal of the cross in I Cor. 1.23; Gal. 5.11 and finally the emphasis that Jesus suffered death on the cross (Phil. 2.8 ['obedient to death, death on the cross']). Cf. further how Paul presents the crucified Christ: 1 Cor. 1.23 ('But we preach Christ crucified, a stumbling block to Jews and folly to Gentiles'); 2.2 ('For I decided to know nothing among you except Jesus Christ and him crucified'), or the recognition that Christians are crucified with Christ (cf. Gal. 2.18; Rom. 6.6) . 'Crucified with' here denotes a present relationship to the crucified Christ. *So in what he says about the cross, Paul presupposes the historical crucifixion, but always so that the cross and the crucified Christ have an immediate effect on the present.*[286]

From this insight which he gained in the Damascus event, that the crucified Jesus is the messiah, Paul also derives his contrast between law and Christ, namely that by the death of the messiah on the cross God has contradicted the law at a decisive point, and from now on life, for which the law was originally given (Rom. 7.10), is present in Christ. From that it follows for the educated theologian Paul that his task is to put law and Christ in a new relationship. He expresses this new insight in retrospect in Gal. 2.16:

'Because we know that a man is not justified by works of the law but through faith in Jesus Christ, even we have believed in Christ Jesus, in order to be justified by faith in Christ, and not by works of the law, because by works of the law shall no one be justified.'

Here it is relatively unimportant whether Paul had already found these formulations at the time of the Damascus event or not; at all events it is clear that the doctrine of justification is contained in the Damascus event and from the beginning represents the structure of Pauline theology, even where it is linguistically expressed by different images, e.g. in the images of ransom (I Cor. 6.20), atonement (Rom. 3.25), reconciliation (II Cor. 5.18), coming of age (Gal. 4), being transformed (II Cor. 3.18–4.6) or union (I Cor. 6.15–17).

With the Damascus event the second part of Paul's life begins, stamped with restless activity and thoughtfulness.

Chronology

At his conversion Paul was around thirty years old, since in the letter to Philemon (v. 9), written towards the middle of the 50s, he calls himself an old man (between fifty and fifty-six).

The Christian period in Paul's life can be divided into two phases: from his conversion (c.32) to the Jerusalem conference (c.48), and from the conference to his imprisonment in Rome (c.57). Until recently it was thought that all the authentic Pauline letters came from the second period, but recently more and more scholars have suggested that I Thess., which is generally regarded as the earliest extant letter of Paul, could come from the first period.[287] Whereas the proponents of the former thesis point out that according to Acts the communities of Greece were founded only after the Jerusalem conference (Acts 15/Gal. 2), the defenders of the latter use as a criterion for dating the information about the collection, obtainable only on the basis of Paul's letters, which according to Gal. 2.10 was agreed upon at the Jerusalem conference. The letters are then dated according to the phase of development of the collection. The explanation of the lack of any mention of the collection in I Thess. and Phil. (and Philemon) would be that the work of collection was not going on when these letters were written: *not yet* at the time of I Thess. – hence the composition of this letter before the conference – and *no longer* at the time of Philippians, because this letter was written in prison in Rome after the collection had been completed. Furthermore, those who defend an early dating of I Thess. point out that it would have been very strange if at the conference Paul had promised to raise a collection from communities which did not yet exist at that time. Moreover, it would be hard to reconcile with Paul's consciousness of himself as apostle to the Gentiles (Rom. 11.13) had he begun the mission in Europe only towards the end of his life.

That results in the following conjectural dates for Paul's life:

33	Conversion
35	First visit to Jerusalem (Gal. 1.8); around three years after his conversion
35–48	Mission in Syria, Cilicia (Gal. 1.21), possible also in Asia Minor and Greece (in that case I Thess. was written around 40)
48	Jerusalem conference (Gal. 2.1); around fourteen years after the first visit to Jerusalem
48–53	Journey to the Pauline communities in Asia Minor and Greece; I Cor., II Cor., Gal. and Rom. were written at this time.
53	Journey to Jerusalem to take the collection
56	Journey to Rome

When Paul changed from persecuting to preaching the gospel, he joined a movement which was stamped by a strong expectation of an imminent end and anticipated the coming of Jesus from heaven virtually at any hour.[288] Only towards the end of the last century was this recognition was seen to be of *decisive* significance for a historical understanding of early Christianity. But Paul cannot be understood without it. So, first, here is a brief survey.

In 1892 Johannes Weiss (1863–1914),[289] *extraordinarius* professor of New Testament at Göttingen, wrote a powerful short book only sixty-seven pages long[290] which provoked a moderate earthquake in the theological and ecclesiastical world. What disturbed him was that the notion of the kingdom of God as a cultural force which was put forward in the culture Protestantism[291] of his day was something very different from the idea of the kingdom of God in the preaching of Jesus.

At no point, he argued, does Jesus identify the kingdom of God with the circle of disciples, as the culture Protestants of his time thought. Furthermore, in particular the second petition of the Our Father ('Thy kingdom come') excluded the notion of a growth of the kingdom of God within the world: 'The meaning is not "may thy Kingdom grow", "may thy Kingdom be perfected", but rather, "may thy Kingdom *come*".'[292] In other words, the kingdom is not yet there even in its beginnings. In this connection Weiss refers to Matt. 12.28 (Luke 11.20): 'But if it is by the finger of God that I cast out demons, then the kingdom of God has come upon you, ' in order to express the special manner of the presence of the kingdom of God with Jesus. He argued that this saying was to be understood against the background of Jewish-eschatological thought, according to which everything that happens on earth has its parallel or prehistory in heaven. 'Thus an event which on earth is only just beginning to take place may not merely be determined, but even already enacted in heaven.'[293]

Weiss argued that the widespread designation of Jesus as the founder and inaugurator of the kingdom of God was also to be rejected, since Jesus imagined the establishment of the kingdom of God coming about through a supernatural divine intervention.[294] Initially he had hoped to experience the establishment of the kingdom, but gradually he became certain that he would die before this, and would have to contribute towards the establishment of the kingdom in Israel through his death. Then he would 'return upon the clouds of heaven at the establishment of the kingdom, and do so within the lifetime of the generation which had rejected him'.[295]

Thus at a stroke the theological foundation of the culture Protestantism of the time, according to which the kingdom of God and culture were to be closely related to each other, was severely damaged. By contrast, the recognition remained harsh and inexorable that the immediate beginnings of earliest Christianity had an eschatological stamp and were dominated by a strong expectation of an imminent end. This expectation of an imminent end meant that the first generation of Christians after Jesus' death and resurrection (visions) as a rule thought that they would not have to die, because the advent of the Son of Man or the kingdom of God was imminent. *In other words, the earliest members of the community regarded themselves not only as the first Christians but above all as the very last Christians.*

To recognize that more clearly, we might first look at the earliest document of the New Testament, I Thessalonians. This extremely interesting letter, which truly deserves the name 'fiery', was probably written around 40 (see 76 f. above).

In I Thess. 4.13–17[296] Paul makes the following remark about his expectations of the future: 'For this we declare to you by the word of the Lord, that we who are alive, who are left until the coming of the Lord, shall not precede those who have fallen asleep' (v. 15). He then goes on to elaborate the cosmic-dramatic event: the Lord will come with a cry of command, with the call of an archangel and the sound of the trumpet of God from heaven; the few who have fallen asleep will arise, and the majority, who have survived, including Paul, will be caught up in the air together with those who have been raised, to meet the Lord.

The statements 'we who are left until the coming of the Lord' (v. 15) and 'we who are alive, together with them will be ...' (v. 17) are important for assessing the text.

For centuries, readers of I Thess. related the 'we' to themselves and understood the passage to mean that the Lord would come in their own lifetimes. Even today, not a few fundamentalist or evangelical Christians read the text as a statement for the present, and that is really only consistent, if the Bible is regarded as an absolutely inerrant authority. For like the other prophets, with his crystal-clear foresight Paul would have been speaking about the truly last time. But such a view does not respect Paul, the human being and letter writer who is at first strange to us. It recklessly and heedlessly commandeers him, whereas he was writing to the historical community in Thessalonica, and was writing about himself.

It must immediately be granted that a fundamentalist reading of the letters of Paul has some degree of justification, for present-day Christians encounter I Thess. not as a letter of Paul from the first century, but as a foundation document of the holy scripture of the New Testament. In other words, between Paul and today's readers lies canonization, which among other things sanctioned I Thess. as an ingredient of the Bible. This canonization in fact first made such a timeless (but therefore unhistorical) understanding of the 'we' in I Thess. 4.17 possible. *It follows from this that formally, a canonical understanding and a historical understanding are mutually exclusive. Moreover I am not interpreting I Thess. within the framework of the canon,* [297] *but want to understand Paul himself, who at the time of I Thess. neither was an ingredient of the canon nor had canonized himself.* [298]

From a historical perspective, of course the 'we' is to be related to Paul and the recipients of the letter – and only to them. But in that case we also have to say that Paul thought that along with the Christians of Thessalonica he would experience the advent of Jesus from heaven with the voice of an archangel and the trumpet of God. There is no clearer picture anywhere in the New Testament of what the expectation of an imminent end means than this statement. So an expectation of an imminent end means that the coming of Jesus is immediately ahead; it will take place with cosmic signs within the lifetime of the first Christian generations.

Now of course in view of individual deaths as in Thessalonica one can ask how many people will die before the advent of Jesus. The answer is that since Paul says 'we who are left behind', and includes himself with the Thessalonians in the 'we', we are to conclude that Paul apparently presupposes that although some have died, no more will do so (or at least very few). [299] So not only will Jesus' coming on the clouds of heaven take place within the lifetime of the first generation, but even death itself will be an exception.

As is generally recognized, this expectation came to grief. Time went on, and as it did so more and more people died, until finally the majority of the first generation were dead. So we may ask: what then happened to Paul's expectation of an imminent end? What was the apostle's attitude to this manifest failure?

The next of the extant letters of Paul that we have is I Corinthians.[300] In I Cor. 15.51f. he is again concerned with the question how many Christians will survive until the coming of Jesus. He writes:

'Lo! I tell you a mystery. We shall not all sleep, but we shall all be changed, in a moment, in the twinkling of an eye, at the last trumpet. For the trumpet will sound, and the dead will be raised imperishable, and we shall be changed.'

First of all it should be emphasized here that the expectation of Jesus' coming (= parousia) has remained constant, and similarly that Paul continued to assume the survival of Christians to that point. But precisely what does the statement 'we shall not all sleep' mean? The following answer seems to me to be probable: although not all will die, most of those who are alive now will.[301] Therefore in I Cor. 15 survival might represent the exception, whereas in I Thess. 4 it was the rule. In other words, in I Cor. 15 death before the parousia of Jesus is the norm, but it is not in I Thess. 4. But in that case it seems likely that I Cor. 15 reflects a delay in the parousia and a first shifting of the expectation of an imminent end. However, at the same time it should be emphasized that this is only a slight shift, since the expectation of the coming of Jesus on the clouds of heaven in the time of the present generation remains constant. At the parousia of Jesus in this not too distant future, the Christians who have died and those who survive will be changed and clothed with a resurrection body. The Paul who writes these lines evidently is not yet reflecting on the interim state between the death of the individual and the coming of Jesus, or – to put it more cautiously – he does not express himself on the question.[302]

It is similarly uncertain whether at the time of I Corinthians Paul reckons himself among those who will be alive at the parousia. How this question is decided depends on whether the 'we' in 'we shall be changed' (I Cor. 15.52) refers exclusively to those alive at the time of the parousia or includes the dead who are rising incorruptible. However, as 'incorruptible' already presupposes a transformation (cf. I Cor. 15.42, 53), the former possibility may be the case, so that at the time of I Cor. 15, too, Paul counted himself among those who would experience the parousia and then be changed.[303]

Around two years later, when Paul dictated II Cor. 5.1–10, [304] things had evidently changed: v. 1 with the reference to putting off the earthly tent refers to the moment of death and to what happens at it ('For we know that if the earthly tent is destroyed, we have a building from God, a house not made with hands, eternal in the heavens'). At any rate this understanding is the most obvious one, unless for other reasons it is regarded as unthinkable that the apostle could have changed his views. Paul evidently no longer thinks, as in I Cor. 15, that the Christians will all be changed together at the parousia of Jesus. Rather, he is now discussing the question what will happen to them as individuals at the time of their deaths, and expects at the moment of death the transformation which according to I Cor. 15 he had evidently thought to be reserved for the coming of Jesus on the clouds of heaven. That seems to be a real step beyond the position of I Cor. and reflects the consciousness of an increasing delay in the coming of Jesus.

The shift in the statements about the future of Christians may also have been caused by events which Paul indicates in II Cor. 1.8f. There he writes: 'For we do not want you to be ignorant, brethren, of the affliction we experienced in Asia; for we were so utterly, unbearably crushed that we despaired of life itself.'[305]

It should be emphasized that here and also later (cf. esp. Rom. 13.11)[306] Paul does not give up the hope of Jesus' speedy coming, though it was in fact delayed. However, also as a result of the delay of the parousia, he develops a two-stage solution: every Christian will receive a transformed body at the time of death, and Jesus will return in a future which is further postponed. The combination of these two expectations can be found in II Cor. 5. Verses 1 and 8 ('We are of good courage and we would rather be away from the body and at home with the Lord') speak of the union of Christians with Christ immediately after death, and v. 10 speaks of the judgment which takes place after Christ's coming from heaven: 'For we must all appear before the judgment seat of Christ.'

As confirmation of these conclusions, reference might be made to Phil. 1.23: 'My desire is to depart and be with Christ.' Here Paul is thinking of the union of the believer with Christ immediately after death, but in his letter at the same time (following tradition[307]) he teaches the coming of Jesus as the saviour from heaven in the future (Phil. 3.20f.) – an example of how fluid the various ideas in early Christianity still were.

There are no counter-arguments from chronological or source-critical perspectives against the use of Philippians in this connection. Chronologically the letter was written either at the same time as II Corinthians (or its parts) in Ephesus, or a few years later in Rome. In the latter case Paul would have reintroduced the structure underlying II Cor. 5. In terms of source criticism, although it has often been disputed, Philippians is likely to be a unity, and Phil. 1.23 and 3.20f. seem to belong to the same letter.[308]

One thing in particular may spring into view in our consideration of the statements about the future in the various letters of Paul. The Paul of I Thess. 4 and I Cor. 15 is to be distinguished (on this point) from the Paul of II Corinthians and Philippians. Jesus' parousia was in fact delayed, and the 'two-stage model' of II Corinthians and Philippians which reckoned with the death of most of Paul's contemporaries replaced both the early Pauline 'solution' in I Thess., according to which only a minority will fall asleep, and its modification in I Cor. 15, according to which a minority will survive while the majority dies.

How was Paul in a position to reconcile his earlier conviction with the death of an increasing number of Christians? What presuppositions made the reinterpretations or revisions described above possible, along with the acceptance of a disappointing, unexpected development of reality?

One possibility for a *theological* explanation is as follows: the reason for Paul's capacity to come to terms with the harsh fact of death was evidently the increasing significance of the person of Jesus Christ for him. *If at an early point the coming Lord determines the present, so from a certain point in time onwards the Lord who is experienced in the present increasingly determines the future.* The figure of Jesus is evidently what remains the same in the differing expectations of the future. Though the former belief as belief in Jesus Christ was still framed by the parousia – faith is faith in the coming Christ – , as a living faith it developed a dynamic of its own and overtook notions of time. For Paul, the real issue had already always (!) been the indestructible communion of Christians with Christ.[309] To this degree it is in keeping with religious language generally, which always means more than it says.

This principle can be referred to the present example: Paul *said*, 'I will be united with Jesus at his parousia'; what he really *meant* was, 'We shall be united with Jesus regardless of whether this takes place at the coming of Jesus or at my own death.'

The reason for such a bold statement was that Jesus was present and increasingly made a breakthrough in Paul after Damascus. From then on Paul experienced this Christ as grace, spirit and life. So in a bold leap of thought, but at the same time as a consequence of the Damascus event, he can also put the indestructibility of this life which has been given him into words. Therefore one can follow Fritz Buri in describing this process as a drive towards a complete fulfilment of life.[310] According to Paul, real life is possible only in and with Christ. That is Paul's concern: that others should feel with him that through Jesus a veil has been removed from human eyes and that the golden sun of God's dawn is warming their hearts.

Paul the apostle to the Gentiles

Paul understood the vision before Damascus, which amounted to a breakthrough in his life, as a call to take the gospel into the Gentile world (Gal. 1.15f.). Here the increasing delay of the coming of Jesus from heaven possibly intensified his missionary activity – as has happened in millennial groups in the present day.[311] From the beginning it had been addressed to Gentiles. Granted, occasionally scholars wonder, with reference to Gal. 5.11 ('But if I still preach circumcision, why am I still persecuted?'),[312] whether initially Paul also engaged in a mission to the Jews. However, there is no clear evidence of this.[313] Paul's own testimonies (cf. only Rom. 11.13: 'Now I am speaking to you Gentiles. Inasmuch as I am an apostle to the Gentiles, I magnify my ministry'; 15.16: '... to be a minister of Christ Jesus to the Gentiles in the priestly service of God, so that the offering of the Gentiles may be acceptable, sanctified by the Holy Spirit') virtually exclude a deliberate mission to the Jews on his part, [314] as does the fact that we know only of predominantly Gentile Christian Pauline communities (Galatia, Philippi, Thessalonica, Corinth).[315] There are also other pieces of evidence in support of this, like the note from the protocol of the Jerusalem conference (Gal. 2.9), that Paul and Barnabas are to go to the Gentiles (and the Jerusalem Christians, James, Cephas and John, to the Jews).

So Paul preached the gospel to the Gentiles within the framework of a missionary undertaking supported by many colleagues, [316] and formulated it along the same lines as the community which he persecuted.[317] At one point the apostle himself points out that he handed on to the Corinthians the gospel as he had received it, 'that Christ died for our sins in accordance with the scriptures, that he was buried, that he was raised on the third day in accordance with the scriptures, and that he appeared to Cephas, then to the twelve' (I Cor. 15.3–5).

There were other doctrines which came from the traditional Jewish preaching to Gentiles: turning away from idols to the one God (I Thess. 1.9f.), and ethical traditions orientated on the Decalogue (Rom. 13.8–10) and especially on the commandment to love (Gal. 5.14).

In his earliest letter (I Thess.), Paul reminds his converts of the instruction they were given when the community was founded:

'4.2 For you know what instructions we gave you through the Lord Jesus. 3 For this is the will of God, your sanctification: that you abstain from immorality; 4 that each of you know how to take a wife for himself in holiness and honour, 5 not in the passion of lust like heathen who do not know God; 6 that no man transgress, and wrong his brother in this matter, because the Lord is an avenger in all these things, as we solemnly forewarned you. 7 For God has not called us for uncleanness, but in holiness.'

Two things are striking in this passage: (a) the emphasis on holiness (which is mentioned three times), and (b) turning away from unchastity (porneia) as the achievement of holiness.

Here Paul stands in the tradition of an ethic with a Jewish stamp, in which unchastity has a central position in the pagan transgressions which are to be fought against.[318] This can be further illustrated from the catalogues of vices in Paul's letters, in which sometimes unchastity has the key position (Gal. 5.19). According to I Cor. 6.13, 15 the alternative for the body consists in belonging either to Christ or to unchastity. Peter Brown has given the following sensitive description of the ethical sensibility of even the Christian Paul:

> 'Paul was a Jew, burning to make pagans into children of the true God. He looked out with undisguised disgust at the tedious prospect of the sins of the Gentile world. In that dark landscape, sexual sins cluttered the foreground. By committing the supreme anomaly of worshipping created things rather than their Creator, pagans had brought upon themselves every kind of sexual anomaly. All boundaries had collapsed before their ignorant pride and lust.'[319]

Paul did not make his own unmarried state the norm in his communities, but he thought it really worth striving for, since 'the unmarried man is anxious about the affairs of the Lord, how to please the Lord' (I Cor. 7.32). To marry was only the second best Christian possibility in the fight against unchastity, but at any rate it was safer than an unconsidered unmarried state. (Cf. I Cor. 7.2: 'But because of the temptation to immorality [!], each man should have his own wife and each woman her own husband'). Those who were married had divided hearts, because they were anxious about the things of the world, how to please their spouses (I Cor. 7.34). But at any rate marriage was legitimate, and there was no question of divorce between Christians. Even if a spouse was a pagan, the Christian partner should not practise divorce, since the children were automatically sanctified by the marriage. 'For the unbelieving husband is consecrated through his wife, and the unbelieving wife is consecrated through her husband' (I Cor. 7.14).

Paul and women

According to a widespread verdict Paul is regarded as a misogynist (George Bernard Shaw called him the 'eternal enemy of women'). In support of this his critics refer to I Cor. 14.33b–35, which says:

'As in all the churches of the saints, 34 the women should keep silence in the churches. For they are not permitted to speak, but should be subordinate, as even the law says. 35 If there is anything they desire to know, let them ask their husbands at home. For it is shameful for a woman to speak in church.'

The suspicion immediately arises that this passage (plus v. 36) is an addition from the pen of 'orthodox' disciples of Paul who have introduced the views of a later time into I Corinthians. For (a) v. 33b begins abruptly, whereas v. 37 takes up the interrupted argument again (v. 37 refers back to vv. 29–32, the theme of which is prophecy); (b) there are tensions in content with I Cor. 11.5, where it is presupposed that women prophesy in worship.

If the thesis that I Cor. 14.33b–36 is a later addition is highly probable, the question inevitably arises: did Paul in his life maintain the equality of men and women which is presupposed in the baptismal cry of Gal. 3.28? There we read: 'There is neither Jew nor Greek, there is neither slave nor free, there is neither male nor female; for you are all one in Christ Jesus.' But Paul was not as modern as we would like. That emerges beyond any question from other texts.

I Corinthians 11.2–6 shows the apostle formally involved in a living thought-process. The starting point is that in worship the man has nothing on his head (v. 4), but the woman covers her head. If she does not cover it, 'she dishonours her head – it is the same as if her head were shaven' (v. 5). Paul goes on to defend this custom against the criticism of Corinthian women. He advances four arguments for maintaining it. (a) It is an ordinance of creation (v. 6–10); cf. esp. v. 7: 'For a man ought not to cover his head, since he is the image and glory of God; but woman is the glory of man.' (b) The general power of judgment among the Corinthians confirms the legitimacy of the custom (vv. 11–13). (c) Nature does the same thing (v. 14f.). The next argument (d) shows that Paul does not really trust in any of the reasons previously given.[320] He writes: 'If anyone is disposed to be contentious, we recognize no other practice, nor do the churches of God' (v. 16). A powerful statement by the apostle brings the debate to an abrupt end.

Wolfgang Schrage has spoken of perplexity on Paul's part and observes: 'It is clearly not all that easy to accept the consequences of "emancipation" if Gal. 3.28 is taken seriously.'[321] It is almost treacherous that when Paul repeats the baptismal cry of Gal. 3.28 in I Corinthians, he omits the pair 'male and female'. Now it simply runs: 'For by one Spirit we were all baptized into one body – Jews or Greeks, slaves or free – and all were made to drink of one Spirit' (I Cor. 12.13).

But embarrassing expedients which ultimately have their foundation in a split consciousness[322] do not yet make Paul an enemy of women. Rather, throughout his writings the apostle displays a remarkably open relationship with the other sex.

This is evident first from his language, which may almost be called inclusive. Thus he uses the metaphors 'father' (I Cor. 4.15; Phil. 2.22; Philemon 10), but also 'mother' (cf. Gal. 4.19)[323] and indeed 'nurse' (I Thess. 2.7), to describe his relationship with the communities which he has founded. Cf. also II Cor. 11.3, where the *whole* community consisting of men and women is compared with Eve, who was deceived by the serpent. By contrast, the author of I Timothy puts Adam and Eve side by side in 2.13ff., 'but it is stressed that Adam was created first, while Eve was created after him. Adam was not deceived, but Eve was deceived and became a transgressor. This passage thus explicitly restricts the image of Adam to men and Eve to women in order to stress the priority and fidelity of men over against women.'[324] By contrast, in II Cor. 11.3 the interest of the historical Paul is not aimed at identifying Eve with women. On the other hand, Paul is not a man of the twentieth century, but one of the first century. Thus for example his remarks on the role of circumcision for young Christianity are beyond question written from a male perspective (cf. Gal. 5.2f.), and he did not arrive at the insight that with the abolition of circumcision and its replacement by baptism women would be put on the same level as men. (This had not been possible previously, since women were not circumcised.[325])

Secondly, women play a predominant role in Paul's mission strategy: Phoebe has supported many people, including Paul himself (Rom. 16.2); Prisca is named before her husband as having risked her (their) neck(s) for the life of the apostle (Rom. 16.4).

Thirdly, Paul in fact opened up a leading role for women in the communities, even if in cases of conflict he restricted their rights again, as is indicated by the example from I Cor. 11 cited above.[326]

So if anything becomes clear from what Paul says about the relationship between male and female, it is that it is amazingly open and that by contrast this fundamental living openness of the author is deliberately withdrawn by the author of the Pastorals (see also below, 106).

Love, the greatest commandment[327]

If Paul's remarks about the other gender and about sexuality showed considerable, time-conditioned limitations, in what he writes about love he achieves a level reached by few. In a timeless way he remains topical, encouraging and generous. However, by way of qualification, first of all it must be emphasized that for Paul love was a social attitude within the community, while the spheres outside the community came into view at best on the periphery. Nevertheless, the commandment to love points beyond the framework of the community. 'This self-sacrificing love for others is not only the heart and core but also the fundamental criterion of Pauline ethics' (212).

Here are some samples: 'Let all that you do be done in love' (I Cor. 16.14). 'Owe no one anything, except to love one another; for one who loves one's neighbour has fulfilled the law. The commandments, "You shall not commit adultery, You shall not kill, You shall not steal, You shall not covet, " and any other commandment, are summed up in this sentence, "You shall love your neighbour as yourself." Love does no wrong to a neighbour; therefore love is the fulfilling of the law' (Rom. 13.8–10). At the same time, love is the way which leads beyond all other ways:

'1 If I speak in the tongues of men and of angels, but have not love, I am a noisy gong or a clanging cymbal. 2 And if I have prophetic powers, and understand all mysteries and all knowledge, and if I have all faith, so as to remove mountains, but have not love, I am nothing. 3 If I give away all I have, and if I deliver my body to be burned, but have not love, I gain nothing.

4 Love is patient and kind; love is not jealous or boastful; it is not arrogant or rude. 5 Love does not insist on its own way; it is not irritable or resentful; 6 it does not rejoice at wrong, but rejoices in

the right. 7 Love bears all things, believes all things, hopes all things, endures all things' (I Cor. 13.1–7).

Certainly this passage from I Cor. 13 is not a systematic treatise by Paul on love, but goes back to tradition.[328] The section has its fixed place in the context of the argument of I Cor. 12–14 and is a commentary on I Cor. 12.4–31, where the variety and unity of the gifts of the Spirit are being discussed. Love 'alone prevents Christians from losing sight of others even when exercising spiritual gifts such as glossolalia in worship' (213). But that really cannot limit what Paul has written in I Cor. 13. He truly means what he writes and writes what he means. *Therefore it remains the case that with his message of love Paul is in continuity with Jesus himself* (212f.).

The short way to faith

Paul thought that circumcision was unnecessary for Gentiles to be able to become Christians and members of the people of God – through faith alone. Gentile Christians did not need to become Jews in order to be able to become Christians. At the same time he spoke out against Jews denying their Jewish origin and especially reversing their circumcision in order to be Christians. Cf. I Cor. 7.17f.: 'Only, let every one lead the life which the Lord has assigned to him, and in which God has called him. This is my rule in all the churches. Was anyone at the time of his call already circumcised? Let him not seek to remove the marks of circumcision. Was anyone at the time of his call uncircumcised? Let him not seek circumcision.'

But for the most part these noble principles were pure theory and hardly practicable, because the mission to the Gentiles was never limited to them. The situation became most acute because everywhere there were Jewish as well as Gentile believers. Both parts were to form one community. But what could it look like in practice for different Gentile and Jewish life-styles to be brought together in one community? Wasn't the consequence inevitably that the members of the minority either separated from the others or gave up their own identity by joining the majority? In other words, Paul's insistence on the unity of the church made up of

Gentiles and Jews was from the beginning more wish than fact, as the previous chapter on the history of the Jerusalem community (36–60) vividly demonstrated.

Paul and his opponents

Paul was facing two fronts: both Gentile Christian and Jewish Christian opponents. The term 'opponents' does not really fit the former. They were basically over-converted followers of Paul. As born Gentiles they had zealously listened to Paul and, for example in Corinth, enthusiastically agreed with his preaching.

They referred what Paul wrote about wisdom and the Spirit to themselves, without further ado:

> 'The unspiritual person does not receive the gifts of the Spirit of God, for they are folly to him, and he is not able to understand them because they are spiritually discerned. The spiritual person judges all things, but is himself to be judged by no one' (I Cor. 2.14f.).
> 'But we impart a secret and hidden wisdom of God, which God decreed before the ages for our glorification. None of the rulers of this age understood this .... but God has revealed it to us through the Spirit' (I Cor. 2.7–10).

Paul is speaking here as a pneumatic, [329] who has access to a supernatural wisdom. He has also given his friends glimpses of it. This wisdom included speaking in tongues, in which he surpassed all the Corinthians (I Cor. 14.25), but also the visions and revelations which he cites in II Cor. 12.1. At any rate we should not deny the apostle this important experiential complex of Pauline theology and piety and attribute it, e.g., to Apollos, [330] since in that case the remarks of Paul which I have just quoted would hardly be comprehensible.

The effect on the Gentile-Christian Corinthians must have been enormous. Paul's preaching sparked off in them an enthusiastic faith in which they already felt removed from the world and its conditions by participating in the divine Spirit. Had not their great exemplar himself said that in Christ all social distinctions are done away with (I Cor. 12.13; Gal. 3.28)? Hadn't he expressly confirmed their own formulation in a letter, namely that 'we all have know-ledge' (I Cor. 8.1)? And finally, didn't the Pauline preaching of the death and resurrection of Jesus (I Cor. 14.3–5), which was transferred to believers in baptism (cf. Rom. 6.4: 'We were buried therefore with him by baptism into his death ... so that we too might walk in newness of life'), speak of a resurrection of individual Christians which had already taken place?

Some Gentile Christian followers of Paul reacted enthusiastically to the preaching of the great apostle in this or a similar way, and in Corinth even founded a Pauline party (I Cor. 1.12: 'I belong to Paul'). But Paul felt that he had been misunderstood. He rated such wisdom folly, and he censured his Corinthians for their pride, their arrogance and their certainty of salvation: 'Already you are filled! Already you have become rich! Without us you have become kings! And would that you did reign, so that we might share the rule with you!' (I Cor. 4.8). Instead, he taught that Christians are exposed to tribulation.

'4 But as servants of God we commend ourselves in every way: through great endurance in afflictions, hardships, calamities, 5 beatings, imprisonments, tumults, labours, watching, hunger, 6 by purity, knowledge, forbearance, kindness, the Holy Spirit, genuine love, 7 truthful speech, and the power of God; with the weapons of righteousness for the right hand and for the left; 8 in honour and dishonour, in ill repute and good repute. We are treated as impostors, and yet are true; 9 as unknown, and yet well known; as dying, and behold we live; as punished, and yet not killed; 10 as sorrowful, yet always rejoicing; as poor, yet making many rich; as having nothing, and yet possessing everything' (II Cor. 6.4–10).[331]

As such, they walk by faith, not by sight (II Cor. 5.7), and first know only in part: 'For now we see in a mirror dimly, but then face to face. Now I know in part; then I shall understand fully, even as I have been fully understood' (I Cor. 13.12). Later Paul even interprets weakness as spiritual strength, and writes: 'When I am weak, then I am strong' (II Cor. 12.10). And finally he advanced – almost dogmatically – the eschatological proviso against his disciples who already asserted their own resurrection in the present, in parallel to Christ's resurrection. This says that the final rising with Christ will take place only in the future. Nevertheless the future resurrection is already reflected in the new way of life (Rom. 6.4).

In the context of this controversy with the Corinthians Paul formulated insights which lasted for centuries and have remained topical and challenging. With them he formulated a hard core of indispensable truths which, like love as the great commandment, in fact corresponds to the message of Jesus.[332]

The Jewish Christian opposition

If a dialogue was possible with these over-converted Paulinists, the same cannot be said of the Jewish Christian opposition. As the previous chapter showed, after the conference a counter-mission was undertaken in the Pauline communities by Jewish Christian fellow-countrymen of Paul. This had unpleasant aspects, and destroys once for all the idea that circumstances in earliest Christianity were pure and ideal. Polemic between the two sides reached such a pitch that sometimes it is no longer even clear what the substantive or theological issues were. Paul was accused of being vacillating and double-tongued; it was said that he only spoke great words from a distance, exclusively praised himself and wanted to rob the community.[333] Paul countered with biting irony, with disparagement and sarcasm, and repaid his opponents in the same coin.[334] Christians threatened to tear one another limb from limb, caught up in a mishmash of mutual misunderstanding, violence but also self-assertion.

Here I shall once again summarize the substantive issues and look at them from a different perspective from that in Chapter 3.

Paul's Jewish Christian opponents first accused him of being a defective apostle. This was correct in so far as Paul did not belong to the circle of apostles whose original home was in Jerusalem. We can detect this weak spot in Paul when he himself speaks of his call to be an apostle as a 'birth out of due time' (I Cor. 15.8). Secondly, the opposition made the accusation that Paul's preaching destroyed the law and thus the identity of Jewish Christians. In the view of his opponents, Paul taught his communities to do evil that good might come (Rom. 3.8).[335] The polemic was sparked off by Paul's statement that justification and salvation came about only through faith in Christ and not through the law. What was more natural than to think that the denial of the law was the criterion for faith, and therefore that the greater the transgression of the law, the more abundant the grace? Over against this Paul insists that the law is holy, just and good (Rom. 7.12), and that necessarily the fruits of the Spirit, i.e. good deeds, proceed from the reception of salvation (Gal. 5.22).

Now the criticism by Paul's opponents at this point is certainly malicious. But the eye of the enemy often sees more sharply than that of the friend or the blind admirer, even if it is clouded by hatred. Paul's opponents really had found a weak point in his theology. For it was in fact difficult on the one hand to unhinge the law through Christ and at the same time to use it at another point as a criterion for conduct (cf. Gal. 5.14; Rom. 13.8–10) and a testimony to Christ (Rom. 3.21; 4 etc.). A conflict was brewing here which burst out on Paul's last visit to Jerusalem, when the community there under the supreme leadership of James rejected the apostle and the collection which he had brought with him – and more. Thus many looked on inactively when Paul was arrested by the Romans – that is, if the Jewish Christians did not inflame the masses generally against the apostle.

The grandiose concept of a church consisting of Gentiles and Jews had finally come to nothing over the rejection of the collection in Jerusalem. From then on the Jerusalem church and Paul's communities went their separate ways. It took only a century for the Jewish Christians of Jerusalem who followed James' line to be condemned along with other heresies as Ebionites by the church which canonized the letters of Paul, and for the unbelieving Jews to be regarded as murderers of God.[336]

What would Paul have said to this vilification of the Jerusalem community? Given his own rejection in Jerusalem, would he have reacted with satisfaction? And how would he have regarded the complete replacement of Israel by the church?[337] But had not he himself written in this direction?

Paul and Israel[338]

We shall now go on to ask what position Paul occupies in the line of development of early Christianity, which – in retrospect – almost necessarily led to an increasing alienation of the church from its Jewish roots.

The polemic in I Thessalonians

The earliest extant letter of Paul contains very sharp polemic against the Jews. I Thessalonians 2.14–16[339] reads:

> '14 For you, brethren, became imitators of the churches of God in Christ Jesus which are in Judaea; for you suffered the same things from your countrymen as they did from the Jews, 15 who killed both the Lord Jesus and the prophets, and drove us out and displease God and oppose all men 16 by hindering us from speaking to the Gentiles that they may be saved – so as always to fill up the measure of their sins. But God's wrath has come upon them at last.'

Scholars have long recognized that at this point Paul is drawing on older models. The statement that the Jews displease God and are hostile to all men can already be found in the polemic of pagan authors against the Jews. Thus for example the Roman historian Tacitus writes that the Jews of his time have become increasingly powerful and

> 'rigidly insist upon loyalty and faith ..., whereas they adopt a spiteful and hostile attitude to all non-Jews ... Those who go over to their religion observe the same customs, and the first thing to be inculcated into them is the precept to despise the gods, to deny their fatherland and their parents and to regard children and kinsfolk as worthless things ...' (*Histories*, V 5).

The accusation that the Jews killed the prophets corresponds to the Old Testament-Jewish view of the violent end of the prophets, which is mainly a theologically interpretative (not a historical) statement.[340] Israel and Judaism had long ago formulated it against themselves, cf. Neh. 9.26: 'They were disobedient and rebelled against you and cast your law behind their back and killed your

95

prophets, who had warned them in order to turn them back to you, and they committed great blasphemies.'

For the statement that the Jews killed Jesus, reference could be made to the passion narratives written later in the Gospels, according to which the Jewish authorities initiate proceedings against Jesus, condemn him to death (!) and hand him over to the Romans.[341]

Paul has taken up the traditions cited, which go back to an already formed piece of tradition, and added the comment 'hindering us from speaking to the Gentiles that they may be saved' (I Thess. 2.16). This thesis is based on the observation that the passage mentioned displays features of Pauline language and that similar comments on traditions also appear elsewhere in Paul without the apostle specifically noting the fact.[342]

Thus the direction of the text in Paul is clear: the unbelieving Jews who are hindering Paul from preaching to the Gentiles have finally fallen victim to God's wrathful judgment. Paul's view of a church made up of Jews and Gentiles is the positive parallel to the negative verdict on unbelieving Judaism. The Gentile Christians from Thessalonica have become imitators of the Jewish Christian communities of Judaea. Their fellowship is one in suffering and in Christ. At the beginning of I Thess., Paul reminds his Gentile community of their election (I Thess. 1.4), but this equally applies to the Jewish Christian churches in Judaea.

So we can say that with the calling of the Gentiles, of whom Paul is the apostle, the election has gone over to the church made up of Jews and Gentiles. For the unbelieving Jews who are hindering the mission to the Gentiles, there is no alternative to judgment.

Could Paul persist in this clear verdict? In this assertion of the rejection of the Jews is he thinking only of those Jews who are preventing him from preaching to the Gentiles, and does he for example leave some room for the salvation of the remainder of Israel which, while unbelieving, is not hindering his preaching? Is the harsh statement in I Thess. 2 to be explained from the effusive, fiery character of I Thess.? What would Paul say if the Jews rejected the gospel not only as individuals, but as a majority? We should remember that I Thess. is Paul's earliest letter, in which such a development could not yet be foreseen.

In almost every letter Paul says something about the unbelieving Jews, but nowhere at such length as in Romans. So we must turn to this, and especially to Rom. 9–11.

The beginning of Rom. 9 can only be said to be extremely abrupt. Here Paul turns to his fellow-countrymen, on whose behalf he feels great pain (v. 2); indeed, he wishes himself accursed for them and to be cut off from Christ (v. 3).

This wish stands in stark contrast to Rom. 8.39, where the apostle had still emphatically asserted that nothing could separate him from the love of Christ. However, this wish is also unreal and incapable of fulfilment: Paul would give up everything, indeed even his own bond with Christ, if he could save his unbelieving brethren by doing so. But he knows that this is impossible. The reason for this wish, which Paul does not really give here (but cf. Rom. 10.16), is that the predominant majority of the Jews have not accepted the gospel – despite the gifts (listed in vv. 4f.) by which God has bound himself to them and which culminate in the promises to the fathers.

But what is the status of the promises to Israel which are contained in the list in Rom. 9.4f.? Does what God once promised still hold? Can one no longer rely on God?

In the following passage three questions are inseparably intertwined and overlap: first, the meaning of the history of Israel; secondly, the validity of the promise; and thirdly, the loyalty and truthfulness of God. It is decisive for Paul that the middle one stands at the centre. So doesn't the (overwhelming) repudiation of the gospel by the Jews endanger the validity of the promises? And does the gospel remain a power of God for all believers if God has not kept his word to the original recipients of the promises?

That is the internal connection between Paul's reflections in Rom. 9–11, which already began in Rom. 3.1–8, but were then dropped again.

For understandable reasons, it is impossible to give a detailed exposition of the three chapters. Instead, we shall investigate how Paul describes the relationship between the Jews and the Gentile Christians in these chapters when he is tackling the questions listed above. In my view the apostle gives three different answers.

The first answer: Rom. 9.6–29

The first answer is contained in Rom. 9.6–29 and begins with the statement: 'But it is not as though the word of God had failed. For not all who are descended from Israel belong to Israel.' In other words, the promise does not relate to physical Israel but to spiritual Israel, as the subsequent example of Abraham demonstrates. God's promise *a priori* relates to those who are elected by God's free grace. Here God has mercy on whomever he wills to have mercy (v. 15). Verse 22 refers to the unbelieving Jews of his time and v. 23 to the Christians (moreover cf. especially v. 24). As 'vessels of wrath' (v. 22), human beings are already prepared for destruction. In the manifestation of wrath, this predestination is realized in final destruction (cf. I Thess. 2.16b). Here, in an eschatological perspective, God's patience is not aimed at salvation, but rather at damnation. The fact that we know from ch. 11 that this is not Paul's last word the problem of Israel and salvation history must not be a reason for toning down the sharpness of Paul's argumentation in an interpretation of 9.22f., or doing away it in a dialectical fashion. So God has fulfilled his word of promise as it was intended right from the beginning, in the church made up of Jews and Gentiles (v. 24).

The second answer: Rom. 9.30–11.10

This second answer can be found in 9.30–11.10: Israel has heard the preaching of the gospel (Rom. 10.18) but wants to become righteous through works (Rom. 10.3), whereas by contrast the Gentiles have attained righteousness by faith (9.30). Israel has stumbled over the stumbling stone (9.32b). Nevertheless, it would be wrong to conclude that God has rejected his people (11.1). Granted, the majority of them have become stubborn, but a remnant has remained (11.5). So Paul demonstrates the realization of the promises by a reference to those Jewish Christians who in fact exist.

The third answer: Rom. 11.11–36

[11] Paul begins with the question whether Israel has stumbled so as to fall (completely; cf. 11.1, 'Has God rejected his people?'). Paul rejects such a conclusion and points out the positive con-

sequence of Israel's 'false step': because the (majority of) Jews did not accept the gospel, salvation has also come to the Gentiles. The whole section is addressed as a warning to the latter, the predominantly Gentile Christian readers of the letter in Rome.

[12] If the refusal of Israel and its rejection (v. 15) already mean 'riches' (= salvation) and reconciliation for the world and the Gentiles, so even more does their inclusion again when the 'full number is redeemed'. Accordingly, their 'full number' denotes Israel as a whole, i.e. the filling up of the present remnant (= the Jewish Christians) with the stubborn majority in order to make up the full number of Israel. Thus 'their trespass' must mean the diminution of this full number which has come about through the fall of the unbelieving Jews. But how is the redemption of the full number to be possible despite the fall of the majority? The statement in Rom. 11.25f. already indicates this: the recovery of the unbelievers will be none other than 'life from the dead' (v. 15).

[13–14] Thus Paul sees his office as apostle to the Gentiles as consisting, he hopes, in making some Jews jealous (cf. 10.19; 11.1), in order to save them.

[16] With an image, Paul seeks to explain to the Gentile Christians their relationship to the Jews: 'If the dough offered as first fruits is holy, so is the whole lump; and if the root is holy, so are the branches.' This 'holy root' is a reference to the patriarch Abraham chosen by God (or to the patriarchs generally, see v. 28).

[17–24] The image of the olive tree now shows God's [paradoxical] action: through their unbelief the Jews are 'cut off' from the olive tree, and God has instead 'grafted in' the Gentiles, thus making them children of Israel. But the Gentiles who have now been called to salvation are not to be arrogant towards Israel, since God who has rejected Israel and given the Gentiles a share in the promise to Abraham in its place can equally well again pull out the Gentiles who have been grafted into the olive as wild shoots, just as he has the power to accept Israel again (vv. 23f.).

[25–36] The idea of the acceptance back of unbelieving Israel, of its being grafted back into the olive tree, permeates the whole section from v. 11 on and is summarized here. Paul communicates a mystery to the Roman Christians, again with the warning that they should not be wise among themselves. The apostle begins the passage with the phrase, 'I do not want to leave you in ignorance.'

In Paul's writings this formula always introduces something new: thus in I Thess. 4.13 the teaching that despite their death those who have died will participate in fellowship with Christ; in II Cor. 1.8 the report of the deadly danger to Paul in Asia; and in Rom. 1.13 the fact that Paul has often wanted to come to Rome (cf. further I Cor. 10.1; 12.1).

But after the previous verses there is nothing that is really new at this point: the hardening of Israel which affects only part of it had already been mentioned in 11.7; that all Israel, i.e. the Jews as a people, will finally be saved was already emerging in vv. 11f., 15, 23f. The only motif which has not appeared previously is the statement that the hardening of Israel will last until 'the full number of Gentiles determined by God' has come in. The whole statement of v. 25 is substantiated in vv. 26b–27a by a mixed quotation from the Old Testament.

Paul does not say anything here about how Israel will be saved. A dispute has flared up over this in most recent discussion. Some exegetes speak of a special way for Israel to salvation which does not include the acceptance of the gospel but does rest on the principle of grace. By contrast, reference can be made to v. 23, in which Paul presupposes that only the acceptance of the gospel can ensure belonging to the olive tree. Furthermore, talk of arousing the jealousy of the Jews makes sense only if it is hoped that they will accept the gospel. Cf. especially vv. 13f. 'Now I am speaking to you Gentiles. Inasmuch then as I am an apostle to the Gentiles, I magnify my ministry in order to make my fellow Jews jealous, and thus to save some of them.' But in these verses Paul is speaking only of the immediate present in which some Jews may accept the gospel. It cannot be demonstrated conclusively on the basis of this that in Rom. 11.25f. Paul presupposes the conversion of all Jews, all the less so since here the apostle is speaking of the historical Israel, and thus so to speak infers salvation in the future from its election in the past (cf. 11.28ff.). So a decision on the question touched on here has to be left open.

At what point in time does Paul envisage the salvation of all Israel in Rom. 11?

In Rom. 11.15 he had explained that the acceptance of Israel once again was like life from the dead. Furthermore, he grounded his statement about the salvation of all Israel in scripture (Rom.

11.26f.: 'The deliverer will come from Zion, he will banish ungodliness from Jacob'; 'and this will be my covenant with them when I take away their sins'). Now the coming of the deliverer probably means the parousia of Jesus, and the expression 'life from the dead' similarly focusses on the end-event. Therefore it seems likely that Paul is transferring the salvation of all Israel to the end of history, where the resurrection of the dead takes place with the coming of Jesus.

In the following verses (vv. 28–36), Paul once again thinks through comprehensively the basis and purpose of God's action towards Israel. Because of its repudiation of the gospel, Israel is hated by God, and therefore salvation can also come to the Gentiles; but as Israel is the elect people, it is God's beloved for the sake of the patriarchs (v. 28), since the gifts of grace entrusted to Israel (cf. Rom. 9.4f.) and the call by God are irrevocable (v. 29). The Gentiles who were once disobedient to God have come to have a share in salvation as a result of the present disobedience of Israel (towards the gospel); in precisely the same way, God will also show mercy to Israel in the future (vv. 30f.); indeed, despite its disobedience in the present, God's mercy is extended to Israel in the present.

Verse 32 sums up vv. 30f.: God has included both the Gentiles in the past and the Jews in the present in disobedience, in order finally to have mercy on them all, both the Jews and the Gentiles who have been called.

Paul's remarks on Israel culminate in a hymn of praise to God's wisdom (vv. 33–36).

The relationship of the third answer in Rom. 9–11 to the first two answers, and to the answer in I Thess. 2.14–16

What is the relationship of the third answer in Rom. 9–11 to the first two and to the answer in I Thess. 2.14–16? A series of motifs from the first two answers also recurs in 11.11–36, including the rejection of Israel (v. 15) and its guilt (v. 20, cf. Ch. 10). However, the marked emphasis on the ultimate salvation of all Israel clearly stands apart from what is said in chs. 9 and 10 and is in marked tension with it. And in fact there is a direct contradiction between Rom. 11.25f. and I Thess. 2.14–16.

Evidently towards the end of his life Paul arrives at a statement about Israel which is in tension with what he said earlier, indeed contradicts it. The basis for it is Paul's renewed reflection on God's saving action to Israel in view of his experience of the *de facto* failure of the mission to the Jews. Here the statements in I Thess. 2.14ff. and Rom. 11.24f., the wording of which is so contradictory, may nevertheless stem from a unitary starting point, once we note how they are conditioned by their situation. In I Thess. 2.14ff. the mission to the Gentiles is in danger; Rom. 11.25f. reflects the possible loss of Jewish Christianity. *Both* letters are based on the indispensable presupposition that the church must consist of both Jews *and* Gentiles at the same time.

However, at this point the reality of earliest Christianity at the same time presents a contradiction. It shows us that the exalted notion of a church consisting of Jews and Gentiles remained wishful thinking in the first century – and not only then. The historical reality underlying this judgment was as shocking as the actual failure of Jesus to return. Nevertheless, even here Paul did not seem to be at his wits' end. Evidently he intimated that very soon the Jewish Christian part of the church would be lost, and for that reason warned the Gentile Christians in Rome not to lord it over the Jewish Christians. Indeed, it almost seems that with his prophecy of the salvation of all Israel in Rom. 11, Paul wanted to make up for going off the rails in his hostility to the Jews in I Thess., so that later Gentile Christians could not appeal to him in their battle against the (unbelieving) Jews. Thus Paul leaves behind, almost as a legacy, an abiding reference to the roots of the church in Israel, whether or not it now consists entirely of Gentile Christians.

Hermeneutical reflections

All those who want to be in harmony with Paul would do well to note his idea of a church of Jews and Gentiles. I would like to raise as a question: how is the forgetfulness of Israel in present-day biblical exegesis, theology and preaching to be countered? Certainly not by a 'mission to the Jews', of the kind that it is still advocated as a matter of course even in the sphere of academic theology, [343] and supported by the scriptural principle. [344] Rather, this must happen by Christians and Jews working out a common heritage and soberly recognizing their differences through meeting and struggling with the truth. However, working things out in this way calls for a total renunciation of epistemological privileges of any kind. *But what has happened to the faithful workers in the tremendous harvest?*

A thoroughgoing investigation of the early Christian sources has led to the fundamental insight that what seems historically to have been the inevitable direction of the history of early Christianity towards a purely Gentile church which formally denied the Jews the theological right to existence was not in keeping with Paul's views, however much his words and actions set off an avalanche in this direction. To this degree Paul's theology is not a closed system. Granted, on the basis of all Paul's letters, E. P. Sanders has rediscovered a unitary structure and has remarked that 'it seems reasonable to call this way of thinking participationist eschatology'.[345] But this 'system', too, opens up specifically on eschatology, namely on the question of the future of Israel.

However, the historian must add something else. Outwardly, Paul's life and work – like that of Jesus – ended in a fiasco. His further plans to extend his mission to Spain were thwarted by Jewish Christian 'brothers'. He left behind almost nothing that lasted, [346] and had not Luke painted an impressive portrait of him in Acts, and had not his various letters been kept from destruction by unknown helpers, the apostle to the Gentiles would have had no further history. Granted, these letters were not to have an immediate effect, though they did have very soon. Still, for the moment Paul remained a heretic.

5

Heresies over the Legacy of Paul

This chapter is divided into six sub-sections. It is concerned, first with the picture of Paul in the Acts of the Apostles; secondly, with the fate of I Thessalonians as 'interpreted' by II Thessalonians; thirdly, with the reception of Pauline theology by Colossians and Ephesians; and fourthly, with the way in which that theology is developed by the Nag Hammadi Letter to Rheginos. Fifthly, it depicts the anti-Gnostic 'rescue' of Paul by the Pastorals, and sixthly, the Paul of III Corinthians as an anti-Gnostic defender of the Catholic confession of faith. As has already been indicated above, all the so-called 'Pauline' letters just mentioned have false attributions; in other words, they are documents which cannot have been composed by the historical Paul. Therefore in a separate section, before the individual letters are discussed, we need to clarify the phenomenon of false attributions, so-called 'pseudepigraphy', also called 'forgery' by some. But first we must discuss:

Paul in the Acts of the Apostles

The picture of Paul in Acts has already been touched on several times in the account so far. The following features emerged. Paul is not one of the twelve apostles, since he does not meet the criteria of an apostle. These consist in having been with Jesus during his lifetime and having seen him as the Risen Christ (cf. Acts 1.21f., where these are the requirements for an apostle at the election of Matthias in place of the traitor Judas, who has disappeared). Rather, one may term Paul the thirteenth witness.[347] He is the connecting link between the Jerusalem community and Luke's community. Therefore at the same time he is the decisive figure who legitimates Lukan Christianity; in other words, the right interpretation of him is what discerns the spirits.

Now Luke makes Paul himself say (in his speech to the elders of

Ephesus in Miletus) that after him wolves will come in sheep's clothing (Acts 20.29), from their midst (20.30), who will say perverse things (in I John, in an analogous way, reference is made to a break within one and the same community). In all probability the teachers who are attacked in v. 29 put forward their own interpretation of Paul and claimed to have a secret doctrine which was accessible only to the perfect. Verses 20 and 27 then oppose this with their statement that in his preaching of the gospel Paul did not fall short in anything. But that means that a Christian community with a Pauline stamp in Asia Minor had fallen apart. Luke is the representative of one Pauline party, which is in hopeless opposition to that of the Christian 'wolves' (we do not know what the latter thought of Luke and his supporters). A dispute has begun over Paul, which is played out in places where the apostle himself had worked.

The authenticity of what Luke reports is merely confirmed by the report in the first person plural which is the framework for the Miletus speech, since the 'we' suggests to the readers that a real speech of Paul is being handed down. Thus they are being given precise information about what Paul *really* said in Miletus to the presbyters of Ephesus by a disciple of Paul himself. Now it is the irrefutable finding of critical research into Acts that the 'we' is fictitious and that it only gives the impression of the presence of a companion of Paul (Acts 16.10–17; 20.5–15; 21.1–18; 27.1–28.16).[348] So here we come upon a phenomenon which in a way corresponds to the false attribution of letters to Paul and which urgently needs prior clarification in the interest of the historical truth.

False attributions of authorship in early Christianity[349]

The seriousness of the problem of false attribution in the Bible may first be illustrated by an episode related by Friedrich Delitzsch (1850–1922), looking back on his student days. He writes:

'As a young student I heard a series of lectures given by a celebrated liberal Old Testament theologian on "Old Testament Introduction" and there one day learned that the so-called Fifth Book of Moses, Deuteronomy, had not been written by Moses, although throughout it claims to have been spoken and indeed written down by Moses. Rather, it had only been composed seven centuries later for a quite specific purpose. Since I came from a strictly orthodox Lutheran family, I was deeply moved by what I heard, in particular because it convinced me. So the same day I sought out my teacher during his office hours, and in connection with the origin of Deuteronomy let slip the remark: "So is the Fifth Book of Moses what might be called a forgery?" His answer was, "For God's sake! It may well be, but you can't say things like that."[350]

Even today, theologians have reservations about making statements about the phenomenon of false attribution in the Bible, especially in the New Testament. These reservations in extreme cases lead to a refusal to accept any example of false attribution in the New Testament.[351] Others accept e.g. the broad consensus of scholars that of the thirteen letters of Paul in the New Testament, only seven can be proved to be 'genuine', while all the others are in all probability pseudepigraphical.[352]

However, here the most recent Introduction to the New Testament[353] attributes the following positive significance to the false attributions: 'New Testament pseudepigraphy was ... bound up with a quite specific historical situation, and must be regarded as a successful attempt by the third generation of earliest Christianity to cope with central problems' (326). 'A theological assessment must not start from the moral categories of falsification or deception, but must reflect on the intrinsic connection between the historical situation of the time and New Testament pseudepigraphy. In the last third of the first Christian century[354] the literary form of pseudepigraphy was the most effective form of solving the problems which had newly arisen from the perspective of the authors of the pseudepigrapha, along the lines of the authorities to which in each case they appealed ... Here the perspective of the whole church is characteristic of the pseudepigraphical writings; they came into being out of an ecumenical responsibility' (327f.). – This flight into theology is as typical as it is academically inappropriate. For early Christian (not New Testament) pseudepigraphy calls for both literary and historical clarification.

The recognized state of research into false attribution in antiquity is shown in this comment by Norbert Brox:[355]

Antiquity was 'neither blind nor tolerant nor unscrupulous' about intellectual deception, falsification and criteria of authenticity, 'though it did not know the modern consequences of an appropriate justification or the modern sharpness of the scientific critique of authenticity' (316). 'On the other hand, the quantity of ancient forgeries indicates the innocence, the credulity, the uncritical attitude, indeed the widespread readiness to accept religious pseudepigrapha in particular, and that too must be taken into account' (316). 'The literary disguise was certainly not something which could be taken for granted and accepted without further ado; however, it was also not generally what would be described in modern terms as a reprehensible moral failing. In this respect, too, assessment therefore remains difficult, not least because for example ancient authors could be critics and forgers in the same person, and above all because even in late antiquity there was not only criticism and indignation, but support, or at least pertinent justification, for incorrect indications of authorship' (316f.), particularly where 'the teacher-pupil relationship recognized in piety was seen reflected in the pseudepigraphy' (317 n.12).[356]

Referred to the sphere of early Christianity, that means that every single pseudepigraphical writing has to be investigated individually, and that both the function and the derivation of the false attribution has to be defined. Here at the same time we must remember that early Christian pseudepigraphy formed part of a movement which for the most part was still within the framework of a Jewish horizon of thought. The judgment of Martin Hengel, that 'in the Jewish-Hellenistic sphere ... the awareness of intellectual property and the writer's individuality was underdeveloped compared with the Graeco-Roman world',[357] applies here, and the same goes for a sense of historical reality and truth.

At the same time, we need to reflect on Norbert Brox's critical questions about this view of Hengel's. Brox comments:

'The perplexity which people are caused by the phenomena can also be put like this: What is an "underdeveloped sense of historical reality and truth" (M. Hengel), where quite often there are pseudepigraphical assertions of truthfulness and refined (not just naive) fictions of authenticity? ... If the exegesis of the literature of the early church has to be interested in an assessment of literary forgery which is appropriate on literary, psychological, moral, etc. grounds, the question of the appropriate criteria remains, and to my mind this is still unresolved. That the aim of the author who gave a false name justified his means is not sufficiently illuminating as a conjecture or statement, in so far as ancient criticism already repudiated such "generosity" and thus is not always attested as a naive component of the awareness of the time.'[358]

So in what follows the task is to investigate each of the pseud-epigraphical writings mentioned individually, and to define its historical context and characteristics separately. 'Research into pseudepigraphy has to be carried on neither out of delight in possible unmasking nor as doing one's duty in relieving apologetic of a burden.'[359]

The fate of I Thessalonians in its interpretation by II Thessalonians

More than sixty years ago, Walter Bauer conjectured that from the beginning, Macedonia was to be reckoned as one of those regions touched by Christianity in which after the death of Paul 'heresy' was predominant.[360] In this connection he referred to the Paul of the Pastorals, with his ecclesiastical disposition, according to whom 'Demas, in love with this present world, has deserted me (= Paul) and gone to Thessalonica' (II Tim. 4.10). That indicates that between the composition of I Thessalonians and the writing of II Timothy, people like Demas were living in Thessalonica, to whom the orthodox Paul of the Pastorals could not be well disposed and who evidently had another view of Paul than that of the author of the Pastorals.

Another consideration which is based on the remarkable relationship between I Thess. and II Thess. points in a similar direction. It had become clear, as I said above, that as a 'fiery letter', I Thess. is filled with a glowing expectation of an imminent end. Therefore the question necessarily arises: what happened to this writing when the normative power of what actually happened had refuted this faith, which was expressed so unambiguously?

To understand the issue better I want to look briefly at the way in which other early Christian communities coped with such expectations that had gone wrong.

Excursus: other cases of coping with the delay of the parousia in early Christianity

First example: John 21.23a reports an expectation expressed in a saying of Jesus that the Beloved Disciple would live until the parousia ('This disciple will not die'). Then he died nevertheless, and nothing happened. The following solution was devised in his community: Jesus did not say, 'He will not die', but, 'If it is my will that he remain until I come, what is that to you?' (John 21.22, 23b). In other words, the error is corrected by a *reinterpretation* of the relevant saying of Jesus, though the interpreters may not have been clear about it. As always in living religions, the dogma – in this case the view that Jesus could not have erred – precedes the brutal reality.

Second example: In II Peter 3,[361] the question of the mockers, 'Where is the promise of his return?' (v. 4),[362] based on the fact of the imminent expectation of the parousia,[363] is 'answered' as follows:

Two arguments disqualify the opponents from the start:

1. Those who ask this kind of question are following their own desires (v. 3).

2. In the plan of salvation it is said that such mockers will appear in the last time (v. 3).

Then the author introduces three reasons to the contrary:

1. For the Lord, a day is as a thousand years (v. 8).

2. The postponement has been given by way of forbearance (cf. v. 15), so that all could still be converted (v. 9).

3. The day of the Lord comes like a thief in the night (v. 10).

The author then admonishes his readers to 'lives of holiness and godliness' (v. 11) and inculcates the expectation of the end as the day of God (v. 12f.). The ending of the letter shows that the problem of the delay of the parousia which is discussed by the author stands in the context of a dispute over Paul. In vv. 15f. he goes on to speak directly of the apostle and writes:

'15 And count the forbearance of our Lord as salvation. So also our beloved brother Paul wrote to you according to the wisdom given him, 16 speaking of this as he does in all his letters. There are some things in them which are hard to understand, which the ignorant and unstable twist to their own destruction, as they do the other scriptures.'

Many things are worth noting in this passage. First, the author has a very positive picture of Paul. Secondly, there is evidently already a collection of Paul's letters, otherwise it would not have been said that in *all* his letters[364] Paul spoke of the forbearance of God. Thirdly, the 'forbearance' refers to the eschatological statements in the letters of Paul, i.e. to the picture of the future which underlies them. Here the author attributes to Paul his own idea, which he has developed in vv. 3–10. In other words, he knows Paul only as someone who no longer has any expectation of an imminent parousia, which could have given occasion for the mockery in v. 4. Fourthly, it is all the more amazing that the author refers to 'things that are hard to understand' (v. 16) in Paul. This suggests that the opponents whom he is attacking could explain precisely these passages in the letters of Paul that were hard to understand and, hand in hand with this, put forward a different interpretation of the eschatological statements from that of the author of II Peter.[365]

After these early Christian examples of the way in which the delay in the parousia was assimilated, we return to I Thessalonians and its relationship to II Thessalonians.

The relationship between I Thessalonians and II Thessalonians[366]

The similarities between the two letters in structure and vocabulary, which had always been striking, were collected by William Wrede in 1903[367] and acutely and thoroughly investigated. The result was the view that the authenticity of II Thess. cannot be maintained if it is supposed to have been sent to the same community shortly after I Thess. Now this is (and was) generally accepted by the defenders of the authenticity of II Thess.,[368] in order to give a plausible explanation of the agreements between the two letters.

In fact no expedient can get round the recognition that II Thess.

has used I Thess. as a model (this is the use hypothesis). This follows both from the similar construction of the two letters[369] – thus the most striking formal characteristic of I Thess., namely a second thanksgiving (2.13), also appears in II Thess. (2.13) – and from the numerous verbal agreements:

Prescript

I Thess 1.1.	II Thess. 1.1f.
Paul, Silvanus and	Paul, Silvanus and
Timothy, to the church	Timothy, to the church
of the Thessalonians in God	of the Thessalonians in God
the Father and the Lord	our Father and the
Jesus Christ:	Lord Jesus Christ:
Grace to you and	Grace to you and
peace.	peace from God our
	Father and the Lord
	Jesus Christ.

Transition to paraenesis

I Thess. 3.11	II Thess. 2.16
Now may our God	Now may our Lord
and Father himself and our	Jesus Christ and God
Lord Jesus	our Father ...

Ending

I Thess 5.23	II Thess. 3.16
May the God of	Now may the Lord of
peace himself ...	peace himself ...

I Thess. 5.28	II Thess. 3.18
The grace of our Lord	The grace of our Lord
Jesus Christ be with you.	Jesus Christ be with you all.

However, the contradiction between what is said in the two letters to the Thessalonians about the beginning of the end should be noted. According to I Thess. (4.13–17), the parousia will come in the imminent future; according to II Thess. the day of the Lord is not immediately imminent, for first must come the rebellion, and the man of lawlessness must be revealed, 'the son of perdition who opposes and exalts himself against every so-called god or object of worship, so that he takes his seat in the temple of God, proclaiming himself to be God' (II Thess. 2.3f.). This, too, tells against the authenticity of II Thess.

Two attempts to disprove the thesis that II Thess. uses I Thess. do not get us any further: first, that II Thess. is earlier than I Thess.;[370] and secondly, that I Thess. with its lack of explicit scriptural quotations, is addressed to the Gentile Christian part of the Thessalonian community, while II Thess., which often cites the Old Testament, is addressed to the Jewish-Christian part.[371] For the latter thesis is contradicted by the fact that Paul's predominantly Gentile Christian communities were instructed in scripture *from the beginning*.[372] The former view again does not explain the difficulty of the different expectations of the parousia, which remains. Moreover it is faced with the clear evidence that I Thess. 2.1–3.5 is looking back at Paul's stay on which he founded the community, which is quite recent. How then can there be room for a letter in the meantime?

But if II Thess. was not written by Paul, and I Thess. remains the earliest extant letter, then the question arises when, by whom and why II Thess. was written.

The thesis predominantly put forward today, which goes back to William Wrede, runs: II Thess. seeks to correct the future expectation of I Thess., which has been refuted in the meantime. It is so to speak a commentary on the right way to understand I Thess. In that case we could see in the relationship of II Thess. to I Thess. a similar phenomenon to that in John 21.23 and II Peter 3.8–10 in respect of the original expectations (of the future) which are corrected there.

Now – to quote William Wrede freely – reality is sometimes more radical than we commonly believe.[373] With reference to the two letters to the Thessalonians, this means that today we have peacefully standing there in the Bible something that was not intended either by the author of II Thess. or by the historical Paul.

Thus a thesis which was already argued for in the nineteenth century seems unavoidable, namely that II Thess. was not meant to comment on I Thess. but to *displace* it,[374] because its author could only see the future expectation of I Thess. as heresy. Because of this he declared it out of hand as inauthentic. But even measured by the criteria of antiquity, he is the one who deliberately produced a *forgery*.[375] Here – if the displacement thesis is true – the reference to another understanding of reality or the different nature of the early Christian period is no longer enough to excuse the author of such a falsification or at least to make his forgery psychologically plausible. In fact the author of II Thess. offers in a highly personal way proof that for him there was even a 'conscience' in these things,[376] since he himself warns against a forged letter of Paul (II Thess. 2.2). *How grotesque that II Thess. draws attention to itself as a counter-forgery!*

This verdict that II Thess. is a counter-forgery, which is surprising above all because of its importance for the canon, will now be justified further.

An analysis of II Thess. 2.1–17

II Thess. 2.1 designates the theme of the next section: the parousia of the Lord Jesus and the union of the faithful with him. In II Thess. 2.2 it is said that the community is not to allow itself to be confused over the parousia, 'either by spirit (= an exclamation in the Spirit) or by word, or by letter[377] purporting[378] to come from us, to the effect that the day of the Lord is imminent/is here'.[379] After this follows the correct teaching about the end: it will only come (in the indefinite future) when the adversary has revealed himself (2.3–12). To this is attached (on the basis of I Thess 2.13) the second thanksgiving (II Thess. 2.13a), and II Thess. 2.13b–14 formulates the state of salvation in the community (referring back to I Thess. 4.7 and 5.9) as a positive counterpart to II Thess. 2.10, 12. II Thess 2.15 takes up II Thess. 2.2 antithetically and summarizes it: 'So then, brethren, stand firm and hold to the traditions which you were taught by us, either by word of mouth or by letter from us.'

To what does the 'letter from us' in v. 15 refer? Wolfgang Trilling argues that 'letter' in the framework of the fictional letter could refer to I Thess., but here the idea of a letter of Paul more generally as a vehicle of the tradition is likelier.[380] According to Wrede, II Thess. 2.15 'almost certainly refers to the first letter'.[381] Therefore the author of II Thess. cannot be describing I Thess. as inauthentic (ibid.).

However, beyond doubt in the context II Thess. 2.15 is to be referred to II Thess., 'whose doctrine the Christians are to observe'[382] and which is antithetically dissociated from a forged letter. This letter mentioned in II Thess. 2.2 is probably identical with I Thess. (for the reason see the next section).[383] So the recipients of II Thess. are to maintain the valid traditions about the end which have been communicated to them by word of mouth[384] or by the present II Thess.

A special problem: the origin of the forged letter of Paul in II Thess. 2.2

Willi Marxsen observes: the slogan 'the day of the Lord is here/ imminent' in II Thess. is repudiated 'with a reference to the *preaching* of the apostles in Thessalonica (2.5!), the content of which is recalled in 2.3b–4. So the refutation so to speak passes over I Thess. Now if the slogan really came through a letter, this must be a forged letter.'[385]

To what does the slogan that the day of the Lord is here or imminent refer? Of what forged letter which contains such a statement is the author thinking?

Now it is *a priori* likely that this letter is I Thess., since our author knows this letter and imitates it. So does I Thess. state that the day of the Lord is here or imminent?

As became clear above, the most striking characteristic of I Thess. is an ardent expectation of the coming of Jesus from heaven in the very near future (I Thess. 4.15, 17). To this degree it comes very near to the slogan which is rejected by the author of II Thess.

On the other hand, the slogan 'the day of the Lord is here/ is imminent' does not appear in so many words in I Thess. But if we reflect on the time that has passed, a reading of I Thess. *would have to* lead irrefutably to the position summarized in the slogan.[386]

Two indications from the time of Hippolytus (end of the second century) give us an idea of what the appropriation of I Thess. may have looked like or how the expectation of an imminent end may have been expressed in practice.

In his *Commentary on Daniel* (IV 18, 1ff.), Hippolytus writes: 'I can also relate something which happened recently in Syria. For a certain leader of the church in Syria ... was himself deceived and deceived others ... he deceived many of the brethren so that they went out into the wilderness with women and children to meet (*eis synantesin*)[387] with Christ. These also wandered around in vain in the mountains, so that they would almost have been seized by a centurion as robbers and executed, had not his wife, who was a believer, asked him to desist from his anger so that all were not persecuted for their sake.'[388]

Immediately after that (IV 19, 1ff.), Hippolytus gives another example:

'Similarly, another man in Pontus, who was also a leader of the church, a pious and humble man, but one who did not hold fast to scripture; rather, he believed more the faces which he himself saw ... And then he once spoke in his error and said, "Know, brothers, that the judgment will take place after a year." They heard him saying that the day of the Lord was imminent (*enesteken he hemera tou kyriou*),[389] and prayed to the Lord with weeping and laments day and night, having the coming day of judgment before their eyes. And he led the brethren astray into such great anxiety and fearfulness that they left their lands and fields desolate and most of them sold their possessions. And he said to them, "If what I have said does not happen, then no longer believe scripture, but let each of you do what he wills." So they waited for what was to come. And when a year was past, but nothing of what he had said had happened, he himself was ashamed that he had lied, but the scriptures seemed truthful. But the brethren took offence, so that they married their virgins and their men went to work on the land. However, those who had sold their property in vain were found begging bread.'[390]

The two examples cited attest two concrete instances of an imminent expectation and the way in which it was disappointed; here the vocabulary coincides word for word with I Thess. 4.17 and II Thess. 2.2. However, II Thess. contains no *refutation* of the imminent expectation. Therefore the question whether the opponents were apocalyptists who still expected the day of the Lord in the imminent future, or Gnostics who began from the assumption that the end had taken place or interpreted this spiritually, is difficult to answer (cf. further below, 118).

The Paulinist of II Thess. cannot accept such an appropriation of I Thess. and 'refutes' a corresponding appeal to Paul by describing I Thess. tersely as a forgery. Instead of it, he puts the 'authentic' letter to the Thessalonians into circulation (or introduces it to the community). In that case II Thess. 2.2 and 2.15 are to be understood as follows: those who are confusing the community (in Thessalonica) 'by spirit and word' are basing themselves on a *false* document, I Thess. Rather, the correct tradition about the end-time lies in II Thess; moreover, the content of the whole letter forms the basis for Christian faith and applies unconditionally. Therefore the author remarks: 'If anyone refuses to obey what we say in this letter, note that man, and have nothing to do with him, that he may be ashamed' (3.14). In other words, the right way to approach Paul is through obedience to II Thess.[391]

The next question, of course, is: how could the author of II Thess. come to regard I Thess., which had been known and handed down for decades, as a forgery? Was he also *subjectively* convinced of this? By what criterion for criticizing authenticity did he work? Evidently the author began by assuming that I Thess. in its present form does not come from Paul. That followed for him from the false teaching of his opponents, who had linked their theology closely to it. And because he had arrived at this conviction on dogmatic grounds, the end sanctified the means; he turned to forgery, which may have been his deliberate intent from the beginning. But probably memory soon played a trick on him. '"I did that," says my memory. "I could not have done that," says my pride, and remains inexorable. Eventually the memory yields.'[392]

Now of course it can be asked, conversely, whether the close connection between II Thess. and I Thess. does not suggest that 'the author of II Thess. was convinced of the authenticity of the first letter, which he had before him'.[393]

This way of thinking is probably too modern, since in II Thess. 2.2 the author had already declared I Thess. to be a forgery. On the other hand the author needed I Thess., because he did not want to give up the apostle Paul. So he had to change the letter in such a way that his opponents could no longer appeal to it.[394]

How audaciously the forger acted is shown by the conclusion of the letter with its 'sign of authenticity' (3.17): 'I, Paul, write this greeting with my own hand. This is the mark in every (!) letter of mine; it is the way I write.' Here the author is even over-trumping the Paul of I Thess., which has no such sign of authenticity, and formally sealing the inauthenticity for his readers who knew it. At the same time he commended II Thess. by its echoes of I Thess. In this brilliant ploy he was possibly guided by the sign of authenticity in I Cor. 16.21 and Gal. 6.11, two passages in which Paul adds something in his own hand.

However, the following objection is sometimes made to the harsh judgment that II Thess. is a forgery: 'We may not approach such a phenomenon with our own criteria of authors' rights and intellectual property. Thus in his own eyes, and also in the eyes of many of his readers, the author of II Thess. is not perpetrating any deception when he writes in the name of Paul. He feels that he is preserving the Pauline tradition. There are other New Testament writings in which the situation is the same: thus in all probability the letters to the Ephesians and the Colossians are likewise letters from the tradition of the disciples of Paul, and not from the apostle's own hand.'[395]

The first part of this judgment does not hold, for the reasons already given, and the reference to Colossians/Ephesians as a substantive parallel to II Thess. is clumsy, since Colossians/Ephesians productively take Pauline theology *further* in a recognized way, whereas II Thess. would not be itself without the intention of deceiving. This is not to deny that Colossians/Ephesians are also pseudepigraphical writings. But the two kinds of pseudepigraphy must be kept separate (for Colossians/Ephesians see 120–35 below).

The observations on the relationship of II Thess. to I Thess. and the conclusions which followed from it shed light on a conflict among the followers of Paul in Macedonia, a battle between orthodoxy and heresy. (Chronologically we may think of the end of the first century, but a later date is also possible.)

One trend appropriated the Pauline legacy of I Thess. (and presumably other letters of Paul – see below) in such a way as to take up indisputable statements by Paul about the nearness of the end.[396] That could, first, have taken place in the same way as the two examples from Hippolytus quoted above. In that case we would have a flaring up of the expectation of an imminent end: the day of the Lord is immediately at hand. (However, the fact that there is no mention of their mistake tells against this.) The other and more probable possibility is that the Paulinists attacked in II Thess. in fact taught that salvation and the end were present: the day of the Lord had already dawned. They would later have to be termed Gnostics or enthusiasts.[397] In this case the statement *enesteken he hemera tou kyriou* (cf. n.379) is to be understood in the present, and here we cannot completely rule out the possibility that the linguistic formulation derives from the author of II Thess. (Similarly, this statement in the second of Hippolytus' examples may have been formulated by Hippolytus himself.)

The other trend, personified in the author of II Thess., contests these Paulinists and even resorts to falsification in order to destroy the foundation in a letter or the ideological basis of the rivals whom they are vilifying (we do not know what those who were attacked thought about this). Here he is also writing for a 'wider circle of readers for whom the geographical and historical recollections of the first readers did not exist,[398] and for a later generation which was no longer served by such a short perspective on the future (viz., as that in I Thess.)'.[399]

Andreas Lindemann, whose 1977 article[400] has been so fruitful for present discussion on II Thess., energetically disputes at another point that 'a controversy between "orthodoxy" and "heresy" is emerging'[401] behind II Thess.; he argues (contrary to Philipp Vielhauer) that one cannot say that II Thess. was written with the intention of 'snatching Paul from the enthusiasts, interpreting him in accord with the time and thus keeping him useful for the church'.[402] He continues:

'Basically, II Thess. has no polemical features at all. The letter rather gives the impression that its author simply wants to warn the Christians he is addressing against taking I Thess. 4.15 literally. At most one could conclude from II Thess. 2.3 that there are "false teachers" who are using I Thess. for their special purposes; however, it is more probable that the *tis* (= someone) cited in 2.3 is the author of I Thess. – and thus *de facto* Paul himself, whom the author of II Thess. presents as a "forger". This does not endanger Paul's reputation: in fact, according to the author of II Thess., I Thess. does not even come from him.'[403]

These remarks suffer from a failure to translate source-critical research into history. For if the exegetical situation worked out above on the basis of Lindemann's work is correct, namely that II Thess. is seeking to replace I Thess. and is designating it a forgery, then from a historical perspective II Thess. is highly polemical. Lindemann stops at the point where real historical reflections have to begin.

From a theological perspective, there is a radical change in the Pauline heritage in II Thess. Its author 'proves' this by holding fast literally to the assertion that the end will come in the future, whereas for Paul himself eschatology always clarifies the state of salvation of the community in the present.[404]

Whether one defines the theological level of II Thess. as high or low is more a matter of taste. At all events, the author 'rescues' the legacy of Paul by copying a model, making a decisive correction in it and attempting to destroy it with the assertion that it is a forgery. Here it seems most likely that we have a churchman who adopts such draconian measures in the face of a concern to care for and develop the legacy of Paul in a scholarly way, but also in the face of the threat of confusion to ordinary people (cf. the later example of Irenaeus).

At any rate, the opponents declared to be heretics are formally right and have I Thess. on their side. In this connection we do not need to come to a decision on the question whether we should vote theologically for II Thess. or the Paulinists against whom it is fighting,[405] for a lie remains *a lie, even if it is part of a holy scripture.*

However, the forger could hardly have imagined any more than the author of I Thess., Paul himself, that the detailed work he did on II Thess. would one day stand in the New Testament canon alongside I Thess., a work that he felt to be a threat and therefore to be excluded.[406] So the vilification of the apostle progresses, although at the same time a process of 'resurrection' and rescue of Paul is beginning. Indeed the apostle is claimed by the forger for himself and partly saved, i.e. at least in fragments.

However, the forger of II Thess. was not Paul's only heir.

A essential precondition for understanding the two letters is the source-critical observation that there is a genetic relation between them. Consider the following synopsis, in which the identical sequence of themes in Col. 3.18–4.1/Eph. 5.21–26; 6.1–9 is particularly striking. The terms which are word for word the same have been underlined.

Col. 1.1f.:	Eph. 1.1f.:
<u>Paul, an apostle of Christ Jesus by the will of God</u>, and Timothy our brother, to the <u>saints and faithful</u> brethren in Christ at Colossae: <u>Grace to you and peace from God our Father.</u>	<u>Paul, an apostle of Christ Jesus by the will of God</u>. To <u>the saints</u> who are also faithful in Christ Jesus: <u>Grace to you and peace from God our Father</u> and the Lord Jesus Christ.

Col. 3.18–4.1:	Eph. 5.21–26; 6.1–9
	Be subject to one another out of reverence for Christ.
<u>Wives, be subject to your husbands</u>, as is fitting in the <u>Lord</u>.	<u>Wives, be subject to your husbands</u>, as to the <u>Lord</u>. For the husband is the head of the wife as Christ is the head of the church, his body, and is himself its Saviour. As the church is subject to Christ, so let wives also be subject in everything to their husbands.
<u>Husbands, love your wives</u>, and do not be harsh with them.	<u>Husbands, love your wives</u>, as Christ loved the church and gave himself up for her, that he might sanctify her, having cleansed her by the washing of water with the word ...
<u>Children, obey your parents</u> in everything, <u>for this</u> pleases <u>the Lord.</u>	<u>Children, obey your parents in the Lord, for this</u> is right. 'Honour your father and mother'

(this is the first commandment with a promise), 'that it may be well with you and that you may live long on the earth.'

Fathers, do not provoke your children, lest they become discouraged.

Slaves, obey in everything those who are your earthly masters, not with eye-service, as men-pleasers, but in singleness of heart, fearing the Lord. Whatever your task, work heartily, as serving the Lord and not men, knowing that from the Lord you will receive the inheritance as your reward; you are serving the Lord Christ. For the wrongdoer will be paid back for the wrong he has done, and there is no partiality.

Masters, treat your slaves justly and fairly, knowing that you also have a Master in heaven.

Fathers, do not provoke your children to anger, but bring them up in the discipline and instruction of the Lord.

Slaves, be obedient to those who are your earthly masters, with fear and trembling, in singleness of heart, as to Christ; not in the way of eye-service, as men-pleasers, but as servants of Christ, doing the will of God from the heart, rendering service with a good will as to the Lord and not to men, knowing that whatever good anyone does, he will receive the same again from the Lord, whether he is a slave or free.

Masters, do the same to them, and forbear threatening, knowing that he who is both their Master and yours is in heaven, and that there is no partiality with him.

Col. 4.7f.:

Tychicus will tell you all about my affairs; he is a beloved brother and faithful minister and fellow-servant in the Lord. I have sent him to you for this very purpose, that you may know how we are and that he may encourage your hearts.

Eph. 6.21:

Now that you also may know how I am and what I am doing, Tychicus the beloved brother and faithful minister in the Lord will tell you everything. I have sent him to you for this very purpose, that you may know how we are, and that he may encourage your hearts.

Today the answer given to the question of priority is usually that Ephesians presupposes Colossians, i.e. is an expanded and revised version of Colossians. That follows:

(*a*) for formal reasons – the filling out and supplementation of Colossians by Ephesians is easier to understand than *vice versa*; the assumption that the author of Ephesians has undertaken to tone down and generalize the polemical statements of Colossians is more probable than the thesis that the author of Colossians related the treatise-like Ephesians to the controversies over a particular heresy,[408] and

(*b*) from observations on the theology of Ephesians, which is understandable as a further development of that of Colossians. Thus in Ephesians the term 'church' means the universal church, whereas in Colossians – as in the historical Paul – the church is still understood as a concrete community. Moroevoer in contrast to Ephesians, Colossians still knows the expectation of an imminent end (Col. 3.4: 'When Christ who is our life appears, then you also will appear with him in glory').

Colossians

According to the address, the destination of the letter is Colossae (1.2), but *a priori* a wider but more concrete circle of readers and hearers is to be presupposed. Thus for example Colossians is also to be read aloud in the community of Laodicea (4.16). Historically correct traditions from the Colossian community, as being founded by Epaphras (Col. 1.7), may underlie the letter. The author used them, and here, by incorporating the list of greetings from Philemon (23f.; cf. Col. 4.10), gives the impression that Colossians is a letter written at the same time as Philemon.[409]

As the earliest deutero-Pauline writing, Colossians is at the same time the first pseudepigraphical document of early Christianity, thus establishing in it a form of literature which was of decisive significance for further developments. A distinction needs to be made between pseudepigraphy and forgery, even if the borderline is fluid. In any case, for the reasons given above, II Thess. (like II Peter)[410] is a forgery, whereas as a pseudepigraphon Colossians takes Pauline theology further and claims the reputation of the apostle to make theological statements along Paul's lines in current controversies. If – as is probable – its author comes from the immediate circle of Paul's disciples, the difference in the false attribution of authorship from that of II Thess. becomes still clearer. Here an immediate disciple of Paul is writing, whereas in the other case someone has appropriated a Pauline writing to some extent from outside in the fight against Paul. Of course we are not to expect to find explicit references to Pauline letters or even literal quotations in a pseudo-Pauline letter, since 'Paul' is writing it himself. Nevertheless it is certain that the author of Colossians knew letters of Paul, especially as the formulae and structure resemble the Pauline model.

The treatment of a Pauline theme is visible in Col. 2.12. The author writes: with Christ 'you were buried in baptism, in which you were also raised with him through faith in the working of God, who raised him from the dead'. This passage manifestly takes up Rom. 6.4: 'We were buried therefore with him by baptism into death so that as Christ was raised from the dead by the glory of the Father, we too might walk in newness of life.' (I shall not discuss here the other possibility, that the two texts go back independently of one another to pre-Pauline material.)

The difference between the two passages is that the author of Colossians speaks unguardedly of a having-been-raised which has already taken place, whereas the historical Paul has a proviso: certainly Christians are buried with Christ, but the rising with him comes about in the present only in a new way of life. However, the author of Colossians corrects his presentist eschatology and writes: 'For you have died, and your life is hid with Christ in God' (Col. 3.3), i.e. the uncovering is still to come. Cf. in connection with this Col. 3.4: 'When Christ who is our life appears, then you will also appear in glory.' On this Hans Conzelmann aptly comments: 'But there is nothing to say that this manifestation will take place *soon* ... Christ is now our life (cf. Phil. 1.21). The prospect of the parousia is in fact without significance for the theology of the epistle.'[411] So again in Col. 3.3, the close connection with Rom. 6 is striking, though this follows less from the linguistic formulation than from the theological concern to introduce the eschatological proviso.

There are also differences from or developments of what Paul says in christology. The christology of Colossians has a cosmic stamp: one need only look at Col. 1.15–17: '15 He is the image of the invisible God, the first-born of all creation; 16 for in him all things were created, in heaven and on earth, visible and invisible, whether thrones or dominions or principalities or authorities – all things were created through him and for him. 17 He is before all things and in him all things hold together', and Col. 2.9f.: 'For in him (Christ) the whole fullness of deity dwells bodily, and you have come to fullness of life in him, who is the head of all rule and authority' (cf. v. 15).

Granted, in Paul too Christ is involved both in creation and also in redemption (I Cor. 8.6); II Cor. 4.4 calls him the 'image of God', and according to Phil. 2.9f. he was raised by God 'that in the name of Jesus every knee should bow, in heaven and on earth and under the earth'. According to I Cor. 2.8, none of the rulers of this age recognized Christ. But these statements can only be found occasionally in Paul. Whereas the cosmic significance appears in the background in his writing, as a subsidiary motive, in Colossians it has the utmost relevance. Here it is an element in a rounded thought which can hardly be explained by a development of his own position by the historical Paul. Rather, in Colossians, another, theologically creative, author is writing.[412]

The author of Colossians also differs from the historical Paul in what he says about the apostolate, above all when he speaks of the suffering of the apostle: 'Now I rejoice in my sufferings for your sake, and in my flesh I complete what is lacking in Christ's afflictions for the sake of his body, that is, the church' (Col. 1.24). Thus according to Colossians, the afflictions of Christ, i.e. his suffering and dying as a work of salvation, are incomplete and have to be supplemented by the apostle (!). Such a notion stands in sharp contrast to Paul's theology of the cross, and it is impossible that it goes back to this.

The place of Colossians in the history of theology can be specified by the controversy with its opponents:[413] the opponents are Christians who are convinced that they embody true Christianity. They understand their teaching as 'philosophy' (2.8), and in so doing are evidently referring to a secret knowledge based on tradition (2.8) which above all gives redemption. Three characteristics of this 'philosophy' can be reconstructed:

1. The 'elements of the world' (2.8, 20) are evidently a basic concept. These are powers and authorities (2.10, 15), and angels (2.18).

2. The elements of the world require 'worship'. This takes place in the observance of particular precepts, which expresses humility

towards the powers (2.18, 23).[414] They include asceticism over food or the practice of fasting (cf.2.16a with 2.21), but also the observance of particular times (feast days, new moons, sabbaths [2.16b]).[415]

3. The opponents are organized within the framework of a mystery cult, but hardly anything can be said about its precise form. However, it is certain that Col. 2.18 ('what he/she has seen [at the initiation]') alludes to a rite of initiation and to a 'seeing' of the angelic powers (= a visionary experience).[416]

The author of Colossians writes as a pupil of Paul in the name of his teacher. In particular, it must be emphasized that he has maintained and reinstated the relationship between the indicative and the imperative in Paul (cf. the transition from Col. 3.1a to 1b). At the same time, however, he has probably also partly succumbed to some of the tendencies of the Colossian 'heresy' against which he is fighting. First, christology and ecclesiology have in part lost their reference to history. Christ is a cosmic power, but here too the correction remains to be noted. Since Christ is the head of the elements (Col. 2.9f.), these are subordinated to him and thus robbed of their power or their divinity. Secondly, while the future expectation is not completely abandoned, it stands in a tension which is not completely resolved with the statements that *Christians are already raised with Christ*. According to Philipp Vielhauer,

'Colossians is a significant witness to the theological battle against Christian Gnosis within the church. In terms of the history of theology it occupies a middle position: with its recourse to the normative concepts of the liturgy and the apostolate, on the one hand it takes up Pauline motifs and develops them; on the other hand, in so doing it prepares for two quite different elaborations of Paulinism, first the speculative ecclesiology of Ephesians which develops the christology of Colossians, and then the orthodox nature of the church of the Pastorals which is based on office and tradition, excluding the speculative element of Colossians.'[417]

However, the *normative* concept of the liturgy is hardly the basis for the citing of hymns to Christ, and Paul's apostolate was similarly claimed by the Gnostic opponents for themselves. Rather, after what has been said, we may see the adoption of a genuinely

Pauline legacy in two other areas: *(a)* in the priority of the indicative over the imperative (cf. the transition from Col. 3.1a to b), and *(b)* in the critical function of the christology (cf. Col. 2.9f. and 1.20). To take up once again the view of Philipp Vielhauer which has already been quoted: Colossians has already *itself* taken a step in the direction of Ephesians and Christian Gnosticism.[418]

For this reason, the author of the Pastorals could no longer link up positively with Colossians, nor did he want to. Moreover, his retreat to Paul and the Pauline tradition is different, simply because the historical starting point was quite different. Colossians is concerned with a concrete situation, whereas the Pastorals are addressed to the whole church, to bring the Pauline legacy into it (see below, 135).[419]

Ephesians[420]

Ephesians comes 'from a disciple of Paul ... in whom the legacy of the master is alive with unusual force'.[421] It does not argue with specific opponents, nor is it a real letter. For that, a recipient would have to be identified, and this is absent from the earliest manuscripts.[422]

The form of address 'in Ephesus' was only added later, when the collectors of Paul's letter were looking for an appropriate community. Of course they noticed that no letter to the Ephesians had survived, although Paul had spent several years there (cf. also I Cor. 16.8, 'I will stay in Ephesus until Pentecost'). That suggested that this community should be the recipients. Or possibly the address came into being even more simply, as Philipp Vielhauer (following Martin Dibelius) suggests: 'It seemed possible to supply the missing information about a place by combining the note about Tychicus in 6.21f. with the other in II Tim. 4.12 ("Tychicus I have sent to Ephesus"); in this way Ephesus got a letter from Paul and the church got "Ephesians".'[423]

Ephesians – which is based on Colossians (see the synopsis on 120ff. above) – is a kind of treatise, an attempt at an independent synthesis which uses all (!) the other letters of Paul apart from the Pastorals. This suggests that these letters were already in a collection (or were put in a collection by the author of Ephesians).[424] Of course Ephesians was written in a particular historical situation.

However, we can hardly arrive at this through direct references in the letter (unfortunately they are absent!), but only on the basis of historical considerations (which will be discussed later).

Right at the beginning, reference should be made to a fascinating hypothesis which would solve (almost) all the difficulties of Ephesians.

Referring to an idea of Adolf Jülicher's,[425] the North American Edgar J. Goodspeed proposed that Ephesians was composed as the introduction to a collection of the letters of Paul which was planned by its author.[426] Here Goodspeed referred among other things to a point which has already been made, namely that in Ephesians there are parallels to all the extant letters of Paul (with the exception of the Pastorals), and that there is no form of address in the earliest manuscripts. Furthermore, unlike the other writings of Paul, Ephesians is a treatise and not a real letter. Goodspeed and his school supported this attractive hypothesis with further reflections as to *why* the author of Ephesians should have collected and edited the collection of Paul's letters. Their answer was that the publication of Acts had aroused the interest of the (later) author of Ephesians in collecting Paul's teaching.[427]

The immediate influence of the first collection of Paul's letters is also explained by a bold hypothesis. Under the impact of their publication, the author of the Revelation of John put at the beginning of his work a corpus of letters to seven specific communities (Acts 2f.), and prefaced them with a prescript to the whole church (1.4f.), corresponding to the bipartite Pauline prescript (address, greeting: 'Grace be to you and peace from ...').[428]

Unfortunately there is no *external* evidence whatsoever for Goodspeed's brilliant idea.[429] In other words, no list of the canon known to us puts Ephesians at the head of a collection of letters of Paul. Similarly, there is no *internal* support. 'The work itself does not contain even the most discreet indication of such an origin.'[430] So the interpretation of Ephesians must start without this thesis.

Summing up and developing what has been stated earlier (122) about the relationship between Ephesians and Colossians, the following may be said:

The difference between Colossians and Ephesians consists in the fact that ethically the call for a heavenly way of life on earth (cf. Col. 3.1f., 5, 'Seek the things that are above ... put to death what

127

earthly') has become the call for a confrontation with the non-Christian environment (cf. Eph. 4.17–19: no longer live as the Gentiles; 5.3–14: walk as children of the light set apart from the barren works of darkness).[431]

Furthermore, Colossians still knows the expectation of the coming of Christ (Col. 3.4: 'When Christ who is our life appears, then you also will appear with him in glory'), whereas Ephesians gives it up completely. Here eschatology is always in the present and is completely swallowed up by cosmology. Spatial notions are fundamental to Ephesians. The world consists of spheres, with the surface of the earth as the innermost and the sphere of heaven itself as its upper realm. There is no longer an underworld or a subterranean hell. Rather, the devil lives in the air between heaven and earth (Eph. 2.2). Christians no longer look forwards, but upwards.[432] By contrast, there has been a concern to understand the present in Ephesians as strictly eschatological, with a reference to the statements about the future in Ephesians (4.30; 5.16; 6.13).[433] But what are alleged to be specific statements about the future in Ephesians prove in reality to be statements about the present:

Eph. 4.30: 'And do not grieve the Holy Spirit of God, in whom you are sealed for the day of redemption.' Now the 'day of redemption' is beyond question an apocalyptic concept. Being sealed with the Holy Spirit corresponds to Eph. 1.13: Christians *have been* sealed in Christ with the Holy Spirit. Here redemption is understood exclusively in the present.[434] The basis of Eph. 4.30 is merely traditional language which does not have any special theological function.

Eph. 5.16: 'Making the most of the time, because the days are evil.' This is based on Col. 4.5: 'Conduct yourselves wisely toward outsiders, making the most of the time.' The addition 'evil days' in Ephesians could be understood as a reference to the future, which is to be understood in terms of the last time. But the author is manifestly referring to the present, in which the devil has to be resisted. According to Eph. 2.6, the church is already in heaven, and therefore it fights as it were from above.

Eph. 6.13: 'Therefore take the whole armour of God, that you may be able to stand in the evil day, and having done all, to stand.' Again, this is based on apocalyptic language. The reference is to the battle which has to be waged now and which is already decided, since Christians are in heaven (2.6). 'The situation of 2.7 is evidently presupposed: the Christians have been transported in Christ to heaven, and from there are fighting against the aeons, the powers hostile to God ... The victory is certain for those Christians who have been saved and are in heaven; it is only on the basis of this certainty that the battle is taking place at all.'[435]

The difference between Colossians and Ephesians also extends to the shift from christology to ecclesiology. Thus in Ephesians the Colossian Christ hymn (1.26f.) becomes the mystery of the church composed of Jews and Gentiles (Eph. 3.14ff.), and in Ephesians the concept of fullness which in Colossians is related to Christ (1.19: 'For in him all the fullness of God was please to dwell'; 2.9: 'In him [Christ] the whole fullness of deity dwells bodily') has been transferred to the church: the church is the body of Christ, 'the fullness of him who fills all in all' (Eph. 1.23).[436]

Beyond question *ecclesiology* stands at the centre of Ephesians. It has become almost unhistorical, since there is no reference back to the people of God of the Old Testament, any more than there is any perspective on the future,[437] in which the historical Paul still hoped for the acceptance of Israel back. Here his church is more at home in heaven than on earth. But at the same time we must note the persistent concern to find a link with Paul himself. Therefore the author keeps inserting key Pauline statements (2.6–8.16); he refers to biographical facts from Paul's life and takes over individual views from Pauline ethics.

Thus along with Colossians, Ephesians belongs in one particular line of development of Paulinism in which theological theses of Pauline theology are developed and radicalized in a creative way and thus markedly bent into a relationship with the historical Paul. How could it have been otherwise? What is attractive about the enterprise is the honest intention to keep to Paul and to go on thinking in close connection with him. What had been arrived at Colossians is formulated in a straightforward way in Ephesians. It is taken further and developed – one might almost say, necessarily – into an ontology of the church, whose members from now on had a clear identity. 'Paul' once again addressed his words to them and summed up in a systematic way what the historical Paul had already said to all the individual communities.

So the *reason for writing* Ephesians must not be defined

separately, without looking at the other Pauline letters. In other words, Ephesians could indeed have been composed as an introduction to the Pauline corpus. There need have been no other reason for this than that there was a Christian community which was in danger of splitting and which needed an interpretation of the Pauline legacy. Just as the Lukan Paul emphasizes that the cause of Christ did not take place in a corner (Acts 26.26), so the author of Ephesians emphasized the universality of the church. So the letter is far more than an introduction to the Pauline corpus.[438] At the same time it presents the fruit of Pauline doctrine.

'The nucleus of the argument of the letter is ... an attempt to establish emphatically that the church is not merely local, conditioned by its time and place, but universal and unlimited. The church belongs more to heaven than to earth. It is a metaphysical entity. It is not just a society in the history of the world which has recently been invented. Its message is addressed to all generations (Eph. 3.21); the Creator had had its coming in mind from eternity (Eph. 3.9, 11), and he called it into existence "in the fullness of time" (Eph. 1.10).'[439]

An important argument which has been advanced against Goodspeed's hypothesis, namely the lack of any external attestation to Ephesians at the head of the corpus (see 127 above), perhaps proves to be an argument in favour of it. The order of Marcion's collection of letters of Paul was: Galatians, I and II Corinthians, Romans, I and II Thessalonians, Laodiceans (= Ephesians), Colossians, Philippians, Philemon. The reason why Galatians comes first is that by reading it Marcion gained his new knowledge. Marcion may have arranged the other letters by length.[440] However, it is striking that I and II Thessalonians come before Ephesians, although the latter is longer. If we assume that Marcion exchanged Galatians for Ephesians from the collection which he knew, there is a smooth sequence of Pauline letters by length with Ephesians at the head of the collection (Galatians is shorter than I/II Thessalonians!). As we must assume that Marcion kept to the collection which had already been made in the churches of Asia Minor, the collection with Ephesians at the head is also brought into the realm of the possible (no more!) by what Marcion says about the letters of Paul.

The further development of Ephesians in the Letter to Rheginos[441]

The Letter to Rheginos was unknown before the discovery of the manuscripts of Nag Hammadi.[442] In this writing from Nag Hammadi Codex I (Jung Codex), which is preserved only in a Coptic translation and certainly goes back to a Greek original with the probably secondary title 'Treatise on the Resurrection', an unknown author who is close to Valentinian Gnosis[443] instructs his son Rheginos on the resurrection. It is generally thought that the letter comes from around the middle or the end of the second century.

The Letter to Rheginos is the committed writing of a teacher who is concerned that his remarks should be understood and handed down. So in conclusion he remarks:

> 'These things I have received from the generosity of my Lord, Jesus, the Christ. [I have] taught you and your [brethren], my sons, concerning them, without omitting any of the things suitable for strengthening you (pl.). But if there is anything written which is (too) obscure in my exposition of the word, I shall explain it to you when you ask. But now, do not be jealous of anyone who is in your number when he is able to help. Many are looking into what I have written to you. These I am instructing about the peace in them and the grace. I greet you together with those who love you in brotherly love' (49.37–50.16).

The teacher also presupposes that truth is not disclosed through human thought, but only through revelation:

> 'There are some, my son Rheginos, who want to learn many things. They have this goal when they are occupied with questions whose answer is lacking. If they succeed with these (answers), they usually think very highly of themselves. But I do not believe that they have stood within the Word of Truth. They seek rather their own rest, which we have received through our Saviour, our Lord the Christ. We received it when we came to know the truth. And in it we came to rest' (43.25–44.2).

The theme of Rheginos is not the resurrection of Jesus Christ, since

131

this is presupposed in the explanations, but the resurrection of believers. Rheginos and his friends were concerned with the question 'in what sense one can and must speak of a resurrection of believers in view of the resurrection of Jesus Christ'.[444] For the fact was that 'there are many who do not believe in it' (44.8f.). Even Rheginos, the spiritual son of the sender, needs to be admonished, 'Do not doubt in the resurrection' (47.1–3), and to be asked: 'Why do you not regard yourself as already risen?' (49.29f.).

The presence of the resurrection is particularly close to the author's heart and he justifies it leaning heavily on Paul. Thus he says in 45.14–46.2:

> 'The Saviour swallowed up death – of this you are not reckoned as being ignorant – for he put aside the world which is perishing. He transformed [it] into an imperishable Aeon and raised it up, having swallowed up the visible by the invisible. And he gave us the way of our immortality. Then, indeed, as the Apostle (= Paul) said, "We suffered with him, and we arose with him, *and we went to heaven with him*." Now if we are manifest in this world wearing him, we are that one's beams, and we are embraced by him until our setting, that is to say, our death in this life. We will be drawn to heaven by him, like beams by the sun, not being restrained by anything. This is the spiritual (pneumatic) resurrection which swallows up the psychic in the same way as the fleshly.'

The basis of the remarks just quoted is the resurrection of Christ, which in connection with I Cor. 15.54 ('When the perishable nature puts on the imperishable, and the mortal puts on immortality, then shall come to pass the saying that is written: "Death is swallowed up in victory ..."') and II Cor. 5.4 ('... we would be ...further clothed, so that what is mortal may be swallowed up by life') is interpreted as the swallowing up of death. Believers have a share in this, i.e. in the way to their own immortality, and this is explicitly based on a saying of the apostle Paul.

The saying is a mixed quotation from various passages (Rom. 8.17; Eph. 2.5f.; Col. 2.12f.), and emphasizes the complete identification of the redeemer and the redeemed. So it is not surprising that the last part of the passage (printed in italics above), which speaks of the ascension of Christ and the Christians together, does not appear in this form in Paul, since the apostle always maintains an eschatological proviso. Nevertheless, it continues to be worth noting that Paul knows of a temporary transportation into heaven (II Cor. 12).[445]

So if this complete correspondence between Christ and Christians is not to be found in Paul, or – to put it more cautiously – if, despite a temporary total identification between Christ and Christians,[446] in Paul an eschatological proviso remains fundamental (see 92 above), Colossians/Ephesians increasingly temper it. They know the complete equality between Christ and Christians as a hidden reality, which has yet to be revealed, not as a temporary state but as a universal condition: according to Col. 2.12, Christians have been buried with Christ and are risen with him; according to Ephesians 2.6, God has made them alive together with Christ and together with him set them on the throne. As was demonstrated above, Ephesians goes furthest in identifying Christ and the Christians. *Here Rheginos takes further some statements which are made in Colossians and above all Ephesians, which already have a basis in Paul.*

This clear evidence is sometimes toned down in two ways. First, it is said that the author of Rheginos attached decisive significance not to Paul himself but to Ephesians, which was already influenced by Gnosis.[447] (Behind this view stands the unexpressed presupposition that Gnosis and Paul are mutually exclusive.[448]) But the author expressly claims the apostle for what he says; indeed, he explicitly associates himself with Paul by using the first person plural. I cannot see that he distinguishes between Ephesians and I Corinthians, both of which he regards as Pauline.

Secondly, the way in which the author leans on Paul and the church's proclamation of the resurrection is regarded as an apologetic ploy. For example, Gaffron writes of the author of Rheginos: 'His intention of reconciling church and Gnostic resurrection faith, and thus defending the orthodoxy of the Gnostics outwardly as well, is unmistakable.'[449] However, this statement is unfair to the author. For at the time when Rheginos was composed, church and Gnostic groups were not yet strictly separated.[450] Rather, the originality of the author's procedure should be assessed correctly, as that of a brilliant interpreter of Paul.[451]

For him, resurrection means a return to the original state of human beings and thus a return to oneself. In it, Christians receive

133

themselves as they were at the beginning (49.35f.). According to 48.33, resurrection is a metaphor for what stands firm (cf. also n.595). It is realized *de facto* by Gnosis, by the recognition of what has always been: 'Why not consider yourself as (already) risen and brought to this?' – in the world of incorruptibility, from which he comes and to which he belongs (49.22–24).[452]

The author stresses the present nature of the resurrection in the same way as the tradition which has been worked over by Ephesians. Cf. Eph. 5.14: 'Awake, O sleeper, and rise from the dead, and Christ shall give you light.' This baptismal cry introduced as a word of scripture ('Therefore it is said', cf. Eph. 4.8) has a poetic form and has numerous parallels in Gnosis. 'Baptism is both "awakening" and "illumination". Christ is the light, but in order to be able to see it one needs to be changed. The form of existence which has not been awakened Is described in Gnosis as sleep, drunkenness or being dead. The one who has not been awakened, the 'old man', thus does not know his lostness. He experiences this in the moment of awakening.'[453]

But the essential difference between what the author of Rheginos says and what Paul says must be emphasized. It lies in two points. First, the author of Rheginos has focussed what he says about resurrection on the individual. Granted, Paul too expresses his personal hope of being with Christ (Phil. 1.23), and the baptismal cry in Eph. 5.14 is addressed to *the individual*, but both for Paul and for the author of Ephesians the resurrection is part of an event which transcends the individual: in Ephesians in the *ekklesia* presented as a cosmic entity,[454] and in Paul as part of God's action to the church made up of Jews and Gentiles. Connected with this, secondly, the resurrection in Rheginos is exclusively an anthropological-christological event, without theo-logy in the real sense. The author of Rheginos separates the resurrection of Christ from the history of God with his people, and formally replaces theology with christology. 'And the world, which is not a purposeless creation but apparently a cosmic mistake, is not a sphere to be redeemed, but a sphere from which to escape.'[455]

At this point a theological criticism is made, the interest of which is abundantly clear. According to Horacio E.Lona, the letter to Rheginos displays 'a way of thinking which is no longer that of the New Testament writings'.[456] This view is misleading, because at that time there was not yet a New Testament, and even if there had been, one could not have spoken of a unitary 'New Testament way of thinking'. Furthermore, this view is uncharitable, because it does not take into account the spiritual affinity between the author of the letter and Paul. Moreover, Malcolm Peel has pointed out that the view of a resurrection body in Rheginos 'is a reasonably faithful interpretation of the Pauline view – more faithful, in fact, than that of many of the heresiologists or early Christendom!'[457]

The Pastoral Epistles as sources for right-wing Paulinism [458]

The designation 'Pastoral Epistles' for I and II Timothy and Titus has become established since the eighteenth century.[459] It arose because these writings contain instructions, prophecies and admonitions for leading the community, i.e. for carrying out the office of pastor. This comprehensive labelling is justified, because the three works within the Pauline writings have a unitary stamp which distinguishes them from all the other letters of Paul: they presuppose the same organization, similar conditions in the community and the same adversaries. Language, style and theological focal points correspond.

In terms of the history of the canon, they are attested only relatively late, but always as a unity. They do not appear in Marcion's collection of letters of Paul,[460] and from this we are to infer that they were not known at least to him.[461] Moreover, since later followers of Marcion accepted the Pastorals, it seems certain that no explicit prohibition of Marcion's against accepting them was known.[462] Irenaeus (180 CE) is the first to know and use them. Indeed the very title of his work against heretics, 'Unmasking and Refutation of the Gnosis Falsely So-Called' (see 15 above) leans explicitly on I Tim. 6.20.[463] In the Muratorian Canon, the earliest extant list of canonical writings (c.200 CE), they follow Philemon; from this we are to conclude that they were added later to an already existing collection of letters of Paul (see 201 below). Behind their number, three, lies the intention to add emphasis to the statements they make.[464] Evidently they were planned *a priori* as a corpus and disseminated with a claim to be valid for the whole of Paul's mission territory. 'But the Pastorals also make a claim to the finality of their interpretation of Paul. What is now said takes the form of an abiding testament of Paul's'.[465]

The Pastorals are therefore 'as indivisibly triplets as Ephesians and Colossians are twins'.[466] However, a theological abyss opens up between the two groups as attempts to interpret Paul, although for both groups of writings Paul was an indispensable ingredient of their faith. 'Common to both groups is the fact that they make an effort to refer the church back to Paul as the apostle who is normative for the church sphere that they are addressing.'[467] At that time it was not only a sign of the radical nature of reality that different groups followed the same tradition and in so doing arrived at completely different, indeed mutually exclusive, interpretations.

The Pastoral Epistles want to encourage the community to remain faithful to the legacy of its Pauline tradition.[468] In II Tim. 2.2 (Paul to Timothy: 'And what you have heard from me before many witnesses entrust to faithful men who will be able to teach others also') a chain of tradition is being established from Paul through his disciple Timothy to the author of the Pastorals, as one of the competent men mentioned there. II Timothy 2.2 and I Tim. 6.20a ('O Timothy, guard what has been entrusted to you![469]) show that the author is guaranteeing the unbroken continuity and reality of the Pauline tradition as he understands it. Formally, we are forced to assume that in the view of the author this was in danger, which is not surprising, given such completely different interpretations of Paul as Colossians, Ephesians and Rheginos.

The author of the Pastorals utilizes the genre of the testament to make Paul speak to his own time. Luke had already done that in the form of Paul's speech in Miletus (Acts 20.17–38), and then the move from a speech attributed to Paul to a letter composed in the name of Paul was not a great one.[470] In other words, here, as in the Miletus speech, Paul is speaking unassailably as one of the elders who are giving instructions for the present. These instructions consist partly of church ordinances (I Tim. 2f.; 5.1–6.2; Titus 1.5–3.11) aimed at organizing the community through the disciples commissioned by the apostle, and partly of detailed remarks about the battle against the heretics (I Tim. 4; 6.3–10; II Tim. 2.14–3.9; Titus 3.8–11).

The church ordinances contain liturgical and hymnic material from worship (I Tim. 1.5f.; 3.16; 6.11f.; 6.15f.; II Tim. 1.9f.; 2.11–13; Titus 3.4–7) and depict the ideal of a middle-class Christianity in which 'discipline, doing right and piety' prevail. In it one spouse is faithful to the other, cares for the children and is hospitable (but not quarrelsome and disputatious). The love of money is the root of all evil (I Tim. 6.10). Christianity is 'responsible to the world and its social norms and must attempt to fulfil these norms in an exemplary way'.[471]

The battle against the heretics whose coming has been prophesied for the end time (I Tim. 4.1; II Tim. 3.1) calls for an uncompromising attitude of defence and exclusion. The detailed treatment of widows (I Tim. 5.3–16) is particularly striking, as in the prohibition against women teaching in I Tim. 2.12f.: 'I permit no woman to teach or to have authority over men; she is to keep silent. For Adam was formed first, then Eve.' This has a parallel in the secondary passage in I Cor. 14.33b–35 (see 86f. above). Another striking observation is the one about women who, 'burdened with sins and swayed by various impulses, will listen to anyone and can never arrive at a knowledge of the truth' (II Tim. 3.6f.).[472] They are said to do this because certain people whom the author condemns as heretics have wormed their way into the houses of these women and captured them (II Tim. 3.6). These are 'men of corrupt mind and counterfeit faith; but they will not get very far, for their folly will be plain to all' (II Tim. 3.8f.). What people is the author attacking?

Because of the expression 'worm their way in', Ulrich B. Müller thinks of opponents (specifically itinerant teachers) who have come into the community of the author of the Pastorals from outside and caused confusion among the women there.[473] But this does not exclude an internal origin of the heresy. Thus I Tim. 1.19 speaks of those who have suffered shipwreck in the faith, and continues in a deliberately stylized way, based on I Cor. 5.5: 'Among them Hymenaeus and Alexander, whom I have delivered to Satan that they may learn not to blaspheme' (1.20). The historical basis is the exclusion from the community of the two persons mentioned. However, that may not have prevented certain circles from gaining influence, as over the women who are referred to. The author seems to be referring to this when at another point he issues the warning, 'Avoid such godless chatter, for it will lead people into more and more ungodliness, and their talk will eat its way like gangrene' (II Tim. 2.16), and in connection with this again mentions two people: 'Among them are Hymenaeus and Philetus, who have swerved from the truth' (II Tim. 2.17f.). But that means that Hymenaeus, Philetus and Alexander are original members of the Pauline group from which the author of Pastorals also comes, but at present are carrying on their own activity outside this association of communities. This similarly happens with a reference to Paul, since they teach that 'the resurrection has already taken place' (II Tim. 2.18).

Now this thesis is not Pauline in itself, but was put forward by disciples of Paul (Eph. 2.6) and also by numerous second-century Gnostics.[474] At this point it can be understood most plausibly as a slogan of the followers of Paul, if it is noted that it was put forward within the Pauline community and was a contributory cause of the break-up of this community.[475]

If we note, further, that the activity of the opponents in the Pastorals is often described as 'teaching' (I Tim. 1.3,7; 4.1; 6.3; II Tim. 4.3; Titus 1.11), it is plausible to assume that they are to be included among the teachers,[476] to whom in the second century not only the Gnostics Valentinus, Ptolemy and Marcus, but e.g. also the Apologists Justin and Tatian belonged. The opponents of the Pastorals were concerned, like e.g. the author of Rheginos (see above, 131–5), to cultivate and develop the legacy of Paul, and have amazing similarities with Ephesians and the opponents of II Thessalonians.

In what follows, we need first to discuss I Tim. 6.20f. and its historical background, because v. 20 is sometimes seen to contain a reference to Marcion's main work, and secondly to answer the question whether Polycarp is the author of the Pastorals.

1. I Tim. 6.20f. and its historical background[477]

The text reads: '20 O Timothy, guard what has been entrusted to you. Avoid the godless chatter and contradictions (*antitheseis*) of what is falsely called Gnosis (= knowledge), 21 for by professing it some have missed the mark as regards the faith.'

Strikingly, many words in the text which are quoted are also used elsewhere in the Pastorals, but not in the other writings of the New Testament: 'what has been entrusted' (= *paratheke*), similarly II Tim. 1.12, 14; 'avoid' (*ektrepesthai*), also I Tim. 1.6; 5.15; II Tim. 4.4 (and in addition Heb.12.13); 'godless chatter' (= *bebeloi kenophoniai*), similarly II Tim. 2.16; 'miss the mark' (= *aposto-chein*), also I Tim. 1.6; II Tim. 2.18.

What particularly sticks out is the formula 'antitheses of what is falsely called Gnosis' as the object of 'avoid' in the accusative; it is not used elsewhere. Elsewhere *epignosis* is used instead of *gnosis*, always combined with 'the truth' (I Tim. 2.4; II Tim. 2.25; 3.7; Titus 1.1). For the formulation 'falsely' cf. I Tim. 4.2, 'false speakers', and similarly the historical Paul: 'false brothers' (Gal. 2.4), 'false apostles' (II Cor. 11.3), 'false witnesses' (I Cor. 15.13). So this 'what is falsely called Gnosis' denotes a Gnosis which is not worthy of the name. The following relative clause ('for by profess-ing it some have missed the mark as regards the faith') makes it clear that 'Gnosis' here picks up the opponents' terminology (as in I Tim. 2.10 'profess' denotes membership of a particular trend). While the author sometimes adds names (as in II Tim. 1.15; 2.17), he is deliberately expressing himself here in general terms. There-fore there may not be too concrete a reference in I Tim. 6.20f. Moreover, we should remember that I Tim. 6.20f. stands at the end of the letter and seeks to issue a general warning against heresies.

If the emphatically general and polemical character of I Tim. 6.20f. is clear, nevertheless the question arises once again whether v. 20 may not also have been coined on the basis of a particular slogan by the opponents. 'Gnosis' could have Gnostic heirs of Paul in view, and 'Antitheses' could refer directly to Marcion's main work. In that case I Tim. 6.20f. would be an evocative formulation by the author of the Pastorals,[478] who is opposing both Marcion and Gnostic disciples of Paul at the same time, by taking up their terminology. However, if there were a reference to Marcion's main work here, one would have to begin from a late dating of Pastorals. Only the next section promises to give some certainty on this question.

2. Is Polycarp the author of the Pastorals?

The following remarks are deliberately made in close association with, and in criticism of, Hans von Campenhausen.[479] Campenhausen seeks to demonstrate the probability of Polycarp being author of the Pastorals both (a) philologically and (b) theologically. Here are his reasons:

(a) 'Four so-called *hapax legomena* which the Pastorals have as compared with the New Testament also occur in Polycarp's short letter to the Philippians' (222).[480] Moreover, the present world-age is regularly described in the Pastorals as *ho nyn aion*. This term 'occurs only in Polycarp (twice) and in the Pastoral Epistles (three times), and is absent from all the other writings of the earliest Christian, apostolic and post-apostolic period' (223).[481] But two other passages which are constantly cited in favour of a dependence of Polycarp on the Pastorals are not convincing: in Phil. 4.1, Polycarp writes: 'The love of money ... is the beginning of all evil. In the awareness that we have brought nothing into the world and also have nothing to take out, we must arm ourselves with the weapons of righteousness.' This has parallels in I Tim. 6.7, 'We brought nothing into the world, and we cannot take anything out of the world', and I Tim. 6.10, 'the love of money is the root of all evil ...'. Polycarp and I Timothy are quoting commonplaces which have the character of wisdom. A dependence of one on the other cannot be proved in this way. Still, the evidence does point to a church tradition common to Polycarp and the Pastorals (224f.).

(b) However, the most remarkable feature which the Pastorals and the letter of Polycarp have in common lies 'not in individual points of contact but in their whole character, i.e. in their content and to a certain degree also in the form of their structure which is conditioned by this' (226). In particular the household tables (Polycarp, Phil. 4–6.2) and their instructions for women, widows, deacons, young men, virgins and presbyters, have parallels in II Tim. 2.2 (young men) and Titus 1.5f. (presbyters). The fight against heretics in Polycarp, Phil. 6.3–7.2, corresponds to that in I Tim. 1.3–20 and 4.1–11 and in Titus 3.8–11. The statement 'The saying is sure' which often appears in the Pastorals (I Tim. 1.15; 3.1; 4.9; II Tim. 2.11; Titus 3.8) recalls Polycarp, Phil. 7.2: 'The word handed down to us from the beginning'. Generally speaking, it can be noted that both Polycarp and the Pastorals have an intrinsic proximity to Paul (211).

The conclusion which follows is that while there is no stringent proof that Polycarp is the author of the Pastorals, there can no longer be any doubt that both authors derive from one and the same milieu. But that also means that the Pastorals were written around 140.

The Pastorals as pseudepigraphical letters

At this point we must return once again to the phenomenon of the Pastorals as pseudepigraphical documents. First of all it must be stated that the author cannot be regarded as a personal disciple of the apostle Paul, unlike the author of Colossians or Ephesians. So if he wants to give the impression that the apostle wrote this letter, his product must be termed a forgery just as bluntly as II Thessalonians was. To the present day, theologians evade this conclusion. Compare, for example, the view of Josef Zmijewski:

'It is by no means the case that the author is merely thinking out what the apostle *would have said had he still been alive*. Rather, what he says and teaches *in fact* corresponds to Pauline paradosis ... And to this extent the Pastoral Epistles – despite their pseudepigraphical character – make just as legitimate a claim to validity as do the authentic letters of Paul, a validity which – independently of the question of "historical" authenticity – arises out of their content and aim and also lays an obligation on us today.'[482]

Here Zmijewski is mixing up the historical plane with the theological plane. In his argument he is using the theological value judgment that the Pastorals in fact embody the Pauline heritage. But this is very questionable (it is enough to compare the difference in the evaluation of women between the historical Paul and the author of the Pastorals). Zmijewski evades the relevant historical questions. However, these are precisely the issue here. And it must be said clearly that even the time in which the author of the Pastorals is writing would not have accepted the kind of disguise that he is using, had it been recognized.

As an example one might refer to the case of the presbyter in Asia Minor about whom Tertullian reports:

'But if they claim the writings which wrongly go under Paul's name [by referring to Thecla's example] as a licence for women's teaching and baptizing, let them know that, in Asia, the presbyter who composed that writing as if he were augmenting it by the title "About Paul" from his own store, after being convicted, and confessing that he had done it from love of Paul, was removed from his office. For how credible would it seem that he who has not permitted a woman even to learn, with overboldness should give a female the power of teaching and of baptizing? Let them be silent, he says, and at home consult their own husbands (I Cor. 14.35)'[483] (Tertullian, *On Baptism*, 17.5).

What were the blameworthy values of this presbyter? He composed a work which wrongly bore the title Acts of Paul. This had nothing to do with Paul, since there baptism was allowed for women. Tertullian sets against this I Cor. 14.35, which for him indicates that the work is inauthentic.[484] Evidently it was expected that the author of the Acts of Paul would have come from the immediate environment of Paul (veneration of Paul was not enough). Now that also means that if at a later time even letters of Paul were to be composed by Christians who had not personally known him, this would cause offence even by the standards of earliest Christianity. Compared with this, the Acts of Paul were a virtually harmless case. They were not attributed to Paul by their author, nor had he claimed to have been present at the events described. Willy Rordorf rightly notes: 'Our presbyter in Asia merely had less luck than his numerous predecessors: his goings-on were relatively quickly unmasked and thus brought into discredit, whereas quite a number of other enterprises which were similar or even harder to justify acquired canonical respect ...'[485]

III Corinthians as an anti-Gnostic and anti-Marcionite writing [486]

In the previous section it became clear how much the author of the Pastorals defended himself against the Gnostic and Marcionite claims on Paul by giving out the letters which he had written as Paul's legacy. In III Cor. the solution to the same problem of how to put up a defence against the Gnostics and Marcion is for Paul in the middle of his missionary work to speak against the false teachers on his own account, taking up the fight to be found in I/II Cor. In this way he puts himself, and at the same time (!) the second-century catholic church, in the right light, since he is defending its confession.

III Corinthians is the answer to a letter containing questions from the Corinthians,[487] in which they refer to the arrival of Simon (Magus) and Cleobius in Corinth. (Previously, in the intro-duction,[488] their coming to Corinth had been mentioned, and Paul's stay in Philippi had been recounted.) The two heretics had said:

'We must not ... appeal to the prophets, and God is not almighty, and there is no resurrection of the flesh, and the creation of man is not God's work, and the Lord is not come in the flesh, nor was he born of Mary, and the world is not of God, but of the angels' (10–15).

The letter from the Corinthians ends with an invitation to Paul: 'Wherefore, brother, make all speed to come hither, that the church of the Corinthians may remain without offence, and the foolishness of these men be made manifest' (16). Here, as in Justin (*I Apol* 26.3) and the Pseudo-Clementines, Simon appears as an arch-heretic. The author of the 'Letter of the Apostles', which probably comes from Egypt, speaks of 'Simon and Cerinthus' as a pair of heretics in the same way as Simon and Cleobius are spoken of here.[489] At any rate, the challenging of the heretics continues in the letter of the Corinthians, which in the second century derives Gnostics and Marcionites from Simon, the first heretic (cf. already Chapter 2 above, 18–21).

In content, pieces of Marcionite and Gnostic doctrine might have been cited in the letter of the Corinthians: the prohibition against referring to the prophets is directed against the custom of proving the coming of Christ by reference to passages from the prophets (cf. below, 148–50), and goes back to Marcion and his disciples. The statement that God is not almighty refers to the God of the Old Testament. He is said to be imperfect and has to be distinguished from the God of love preached by Jesus; in connection with this, human beings are said not to be God's creatures but only creatures of the creator of the world. These doctrines, too, recall Marcion, so that the anti-Marcionite direction of the letter is abundantly clear. (For the details of Marcion's theology see the next chapter [148–69].)

Paul composes a letter in reply to this (= III Cor.).The prescript differs from all the letters of Paul by using the (one-member) Greek form, but there is an imitation of Eph. 3.1 and Philemon in the designation 'prisoner of Jesus Christ' (1). The reference to the many aberrations recalls II Cor. 2.4; the next remark, that Paul is not amazed that the views of the evil one are so rapidly gaining ground (2), takes up Gal. 1.6. After the reference to the imminent coming of the Lord which follows (3), a creed in 5–8 draws on the form of I Cor. 15.3–5. Paul received this from the apostles before him, who were with the Lord all the time (4). This clearly presupposes the criteria of the office of apostle in Acts 1.21.

The creed contains two main statements: (a) the birth of Jesus from Mary (5) and (b) the creation of human beings by God (7). Here the verbs are in the aorist passive (egennethe/eplasthe), and both statements are introduced with hoti (drawing on the fact that the main parts of the creed in I Cor. 15.3–5 are introduced with hoti). To both these main statements are attached explanations or indications of purpose. On (a): Jesus was born of Mary, 'that he might come into this world and redeem all flesh through his own flesh, and that he might raise up from the dead those who are fleshly, even as he has shown himself as our example' (6). On (b): because human beings are the creation of the Father, they have been (sought out by him and) made alive, i.e. redemption follows from creation. The author goes on to derive the following statements from the creed which he has quoted:[490]

9–25: Outline of salvation history

      9–11:   The order of salvation before Christ: the sending

of the Spirit of Christ into the prophets and the
work of the evil one

12–15: The birth of Jesus from Mary by the sending of the
Holy Spirit

16–18: The redemption of the flesh by the body of Christ

19–22: Polemic against those who deny God the Father as
the creator of heaven and earth

23–25: Polemic against those who deny the resurrection

26–32: The resurrection of the flesh

26f.:   The comparison with the grain of wheat (I Cor.
15.37)

28–31: The Old Testament story of Jonah as an argument
for the certainty of the resurrection

32:     The story of Elisha (II Kings 13.21) as an argument for the integrity of the resurrection bodies

34–40: Conclusion

34f.:   Personal matters

36–40: Conditional curse and wish for peace.

In III Corinthians Paul is 'a defender of the confession of the
early Catholic church',[491] though one cannot say that in this letter
there is a 'development of Pauline theology'.[492] Must it not therefore be assumed that the author of III Corinthians wants to put the
apostle to the Gentiles, to whom the heretics have laid claim, in
a proper orthodox light, in order to win him back for the church?
To this conclusion it has been objected that the author of III
Corinthians has 'no more interest than the authors of the
numerous other apocryphal acts of apostles: they all want to report
edifying details from the life of the apostles, deepen the knowledge
of Christians about them and communicate topical "orthodox"
doctrine in the garb of apostolic preaching'.[493]

However, this view is too simple, since the letter is clearly establishing a front or a defence against Gnostic groups. It is no coincidence that the arch-heretic Simon appears at the head of them in
the letter of the Corinthians. The battle is still in full flood, and is
closely connected with the binding character of the creed of the
catholic church that is now coming into being. Moreover, as an
analogy, Lindemann's subsequent reference to the literary genre of
the apocryphal acts of apostles, which merely sought to offer additional information about the canonical acts of apostles,[494] ignores

145

the fact that III Corinthians was originally not an ingredient of the 'apocryphal' Acts of Paul at all.

Summary and results of Chapter 5

We met a variety of documents whose authors claimed to be heirs of Paul. First came Luke. He reserved the second part of Acts for Paul and depicted him as a missionary who, legitimated by the Jerusalem church and ultimately in continuity with Jesus (!), brought the gospel to the Gentiles. For Luke, Paul is not the author of letters, nor is he either an apostle or a teacher of justification by faith (apart from Acts 13.39). When Luke wrote, Paul's legacy was already in dispute. He makes his hero prophesy that after him 'ravening wolves' will come (Acts 20.29). Now we must immediately go on to say that in reality these are only other disciples of Paul. They evidently took up the apostle in a way which was not at all pleasing to Luke. Hence his vilification.

II Thessalonians also reflects turbulence around Paul; its author in an almost ruthless way resorted to extreme polemic and presented Paul's earliest letter as a forgery, when this was interpreted by heretical disciples of Paul in terms of the presence of salvation. His audacious enterprise of a counter-forgery came to a climax in his writing and dissemination of a new 'correct' letter to the Thessalonians utilizing I Thess., which was presented as a forgery.

Colossians opens the circle of *left-wing Paulinism*. It was composed by a close pupil of Paul and sees itself as opposing Gnostics who had appeared in the Pauline missionary territory. These – unlike the Gnostics behind Acts and II Thess. – were not followers of Paul. As the author of Colossians forms Gnosticism and Paulism into an original system, at the latest it becomes clear here that Gnostic and Pauline thought have an affinity.

Ephesians goes a stage further in the direction begun by Colossians and gives the church transcendent roots. On the one hand Paul's ecclesiology is preserved or taken further, and on the other history has become unimportant. Gnosis and catholicism have already entered into a synthesis. The collection of Paul's letters made by the author of Ephesians was a rescue act of unknown extent, and had decisive consequences for all future Christian letters and collections of letters.

Rheginos is just one of many representatives which take up Paul, the recipient of revelation, and understand religious experience in terms of a present resurrection. In some respects one must say that it felt the dynamic that can be noted in the historical Paul and developed it fully – though abandoning the ecclesiology.

In so-called *right-wing Paulinism* (the Pastorals and III Corinthians), church questions come into the foreground: Paul is the church's teacher and embodies its tradition. This is noted without building anything on it. As in II Thess. and II Peter, the future nature of the resurrection and the judgment are literally maintained and thus lost, since the past cannot be maintained literally if it is only extended. Divergent interpreters of Paul like the left-wing Paulinists are ignored and excluded. But the author of the Pastorals did achieve one thing: he consolidated the tradition as armour in the storms of a time in which Paul's brilliant interpretations in part went under. As a 'blind pupil'[495] like the author of III Corinthians, he added Paul to church tradition. The question here, though, is whether the end really justified this means of forgery.

I have omitted from the account so far the other party which was attacked by the Pastorals and III Corinthians, Marcion and his church. Marcion's attempt at reform, which ended with the almost complete annihilation of the 'arch-heretic' and most important disciple of Paul in the second century, will therefore be described in the next chapter.

6

The Arch-Heretic Marcion and His Time

With the shipowner Marcion of Pontus in the second century, a personality emerges to whom a paradoxical verdict going back to Franz Overbeck and taken over by Adolf von Harnack applies: 'Only one Gentile Christian understood Paul – Marcion – and he grossly misunderstood him.'[496] Marcion's action consisted in establishing a canon consisting of letters of Paul and a Gospel, and at the same time banning the Old Testament as Holy Scripture. In order to understand his radical theological remedy, we must first sketch out the use of the Old Testament in the time before Marcion. An account of the life and work of this tragic figure follows after that.

The use of the Old Testament in the period before the emergence of Marcion[497]

General

In the view of the earliest Christians, the passion and resurrection of Jesus took place in accordance with the holy scriptures of the Jewish people (I Cor. 15.3–5). They found prophecies of all the details of his passion and death in this, their Bible, and the evangelist Matthew shows, for example with his repeated formula 'that it might be fulfilled what is said by ...' (Matt. 1.22; 2.5, etc.), how the life and death of Jesus were rooted in the scriptural salvation history. Of course mistakes crept in here. Cf. chiefly Mark 1.2, where there is a quotation from Malachi, although a quotation from the prophet Isaiah is announced, which only follows in v. 3.

The Old Testament was the sacred book right from the beginning, as a Christian and not as a Jewish book.[498] From it could be ascertained the 'revelation of the past, the present and the future' (Barn. 1.7), and from it Paul backed up his doctrine of justification by faith (Gen. 15.6); he regarded the passage of the Israelites through the sea as typology for Christians (I Cor. 10). According to Peter in the *Kergyma Petri*,[499] the books of the prophets 'partly in parables, partly in enigmas, partly with certainty and in clear words name Christ Jesus, and we found his coming, his death, his crucifixion and all the rest of the tortures which the Jews inflicted on him, his resurrection and his assumption to heaven before the destruction of Jerusalem, how all was written that he had to suffer and what would be after him. Recognizing this, we believed God in consequence of what is written of (in reference to) him.'[500]

Even where the Old Testament is not explicitly alleged to be scripture, as for example in the Shepherd of Hermas[501] and in the Letter of Barnabas, which refers to the fact that Christ 'himself prophesies, he himself dwells in your midst' (Barn. 16.9), the holy scriptures are generally treasured, read and learned by heart in the community. Christian teachers like the author of Barnabas are zealous in steeping themselves in scripture, unlocking the mysteries of the divine revelations from it and taking up their treasures, to hand them on to zealous disciples. Underlying this is the unshake-able basic conviction that the Old Testament is always on the side of Christian belief and can never be against it, because it has been fulfilled with the coming of Christ. This certainty is further heightened in the third and fourth generations by comparison with Paul and the New Testament Gospels. Thus the Old Testament becomes a book of Christ and there is no longer any doubt that not only Moses and David but also the prophets awaited the coming of Christ and even foresaw in the Spirit some episodes of his life. And not only this: Christ himself already speaks within the Old Testament as Logos or speaks through his Spirit. However, every-thing depends on perceiving and recognizing this – in contrast to the unbelieving Jews.[502]

Even where Bishop Ignatius of Antioch got into a dispute with opponents in Philadelphia who expounded the Old Testament in a Jewish way, its authority remained intact. Ignatius has heard them say, 'If I do not find it in the archives, I do not believe it to be in the gospel' (Phil. 8.2). He continues: 'And when I said, "It is written", they answered me, "That is just the question"' (ibid.). Evidently Ignatius had appealed to the testimony of scripture, which his opponents had not recognized. (Perhaps he had cited the beloved prophets who had proclaimed Christ [Phil. 9.2].) And when that does not work, he leaves the basis of scripture and immediately appeals to the gospel: 'For me the archives are Jesus Christ, the inviolable archives are his cross and death and his resurrection and faith through him – in which, through your prayer, I want to be justified' (ibid.).

It would not be admissible to see the authority of the Old Testament attacked in such a statement. Three times there are quotations from the Old Testament in Ignatius which are introduced with 'it is written' (Eph. 5.3; Magn. 12; Trall. 8.2), and Abraham, Isaac, Jacob and the prophets have entered salvation through the door (= Jesus) (Philad. 9.1). Therefore no basic dispute over the Old Testament may yet have broken out between Ignatius and his opponents in Philadelphia, although it is clear from the dispute between Ignatius and his opponents that the question of the relationship between the Old Testament and the revelation of Christ would sooner or later need a clear answer.

Individual interpretations of the Old Testament

I shall first quote some examples of interpretations of the Old Testament in the second century which often seem quite remarkable to us. In Justin, *Dial.* 40,[503] the following interpretation can be read (the Old Testament passages to which Justin refers have been added in brackets):

'1 The mystery, then, of the lamb which God enjoined to be sacrificed as the Passover, was a type of Christ; with whose blood, in proportion to their faith in him, they anoint their houses (cf. Ex. 12.7–21), i.e. themselves, who believe on him. For that the creation which God created – namely, Adam – was a house for the spirit which proceeded from God (Gen. 2.7), you all can understand. And this is my proof that this injunction was temporary. 2 God does not permit the lamb of the Passover to be sacrificed in any other place than where his name was named (Deut. 16.5f.); knowing that the days will come, after the suffering of Christ, when even the place in Jerusalem shall be given over to your enemies, and all the offerings, in short, shall cease. 3 And that lamb which was commanded to be wholly roasted (Ex. 12.9) was a symbol of the suffering of the cross which Christ would undergo. For the lamb which is roasted, is roasted and dressed up in the form of the cross. For one spit is transfixed right through from the lower parts up to the head, and one across the back, to which are attached the legs of the lamb. And the two goats which were ordered to be offered during the fast (= the Day of Atonement, Lev. 16.5ff.), of which one was sent away as the scapegoat and the other sacrificed, similarly declared the two appearances of Christ ...'

Justin, *Dial.* 42,1f. makes the following comment on the prediction of the twelve apostles in the Old Testament:

'Moreover, the prescription that twelve bells are to be attached to the robe of the high priest (Ex. 28.33 f.), which hung down to the feet, was a symbol of the twelve apostles, who depend on the power of Christ, the eternal priest; and through their voice all the earth has been filled with the glory and grace of God and of his Christ ...'

At one point the letter of Barnabas combines Gen. 14.14 ('When Abram heard that his kinsman had been taken captive, he armed his servants, born in his house, three hundred and eighteen of them, and went in pursuit as far as Dan'), Gen. 17.23 ('Then Abraham took Ishmael his son and all the slaves born in his house or bought with his money, every male among the men of Abraham's house, and he circumcised the flesh of their foreskins ...'), and Gen. 17.27 ('and all the men of his house, those born in the house and those bought with money from a foreigner, were circumcised with him'), and wants to prove from this that by the circumcision Abraham had already been thinking of the crucifixion of Jesus. He circumcised 318 men. I (= the first letter of the name Jesus) is the figure for ten, H (= the second letter of the name of Jesus) for eight, and T, the sign of the cross, stands for three hundred. The passage can then be read as follows:

'7 Learn fully then, children of love, concerning all things, for Abraham, who first circumcised, did so looking forward in the spirit to Jesus, and had received the doctrines of three letters. 8 For it says, "And Abraham circumcised from his household eighteen men and three hundred." What then was the knowledge that was given to him? Notice that he first mentions the eighteen, and after a pause the three hundred. The eighteen [in Greek figures] is I (= ten) and H (= eight) – you have Jesus – and because the cross was destined to have grace in the T he says "and three hundred" [T is the

Greek figure for 300]. So he indicates Jesus in the two letters and the cross in the other. 9 He knows this who places the gift of his teaching in our hearts. No one has heard a more excellent lesson from me, but I know that you are worthy' (Barnabas 9.7–9).[504]

Justin develops the following 'reasonable proof' for the power of the cross:

'2 For consider all the things in the world, whether without this form they could be administered or have any community. 3 For the sea is not traversed except that trophy which is called a sail abide safe in the ship; and the earth is not ploughed without it; diggers and mechanics do not do their work, except with tools which have this shape. 4 And the human form differs from that of the irrational animals in nothing else than its being erect and having the hands extended, and having on the face extending from the forehead what is called the nose, through which there is respiration for the living creature; and this shows no other form than that of the cross. 5 And so it was said by the prophet, "The breath before our face is the Lord Christ" (Lam.4.20). 6 And the power of this form is shown by your own symbols on what are called banners and trophies, with which all your state possessions are made, using these as the insignia of your power and government, even though you do so unwittingly. 7 And with this form you consecrate the images of your emperors when they die, and you name them gods by inscriptions' (I Apol 55.2–7).

It *must* be said that the examples just cited verge very much on the abstruse and the curious, and at all events are well suited to demonstrate once and for all how strange, peculiar and remote from us early Christianity is. At the same time – despite all their vapidity – they are documents of a spiritual and religious mobility which still had to find a distinctive theological standpoint and therefore showed a certain delight in experimentation.

The sayings of Jesus

At the same time, by way of an appendix, it has to be emphasized that down to the middle of the second century most Christians predominantly quoted and understood the words of Jesus himself[505] in their simple sense. (The allegorization of the parables of Jesus which already begins in the New Testament Gospels [cf. Mark 4.10–20] is hardly representative.)

One might compare the sayings of Jesus in Justin, *I Apol* 15, 1–8,[506] which had perhaps already been collected (the relevant passages in the New Testament Gospels are put in brackets):

'1 Concerning chastity, he uttered such sentiments as these: "Anyone who looks on a woman to lust after her has already committed adultery with her in his heart before God" (Matt. 5.28). 2 And, "If your right eye offends you, cut out, for it is better to enter the kingdom of heaven with one eye than having two eyes to be cast into everlasting fire" (Matt. 18.9). 3 And, "Anyone who marries a woman who is divorced from her husband commits adultery" (Matt. 5.32). 4 And, "There are some who have been made eunuchs of men, and some who were born eunuchs, and some who have made themselves eunuchs for the sake of the kingdom of heaven, but all cannot receive this saying" (Matt. 19.12). 5 So that all who by human law are twice married are sinners in the eyes of the master, and those who look on a woman to lust after her. For not only the one who commits adultery in the act is rejected by him, but also the one who desires to commit adultery; since not only our works but also our thoughts are open before God. 6 And many, both men and women, who have been Christ's disciples from childhood, remain pure at the age of sixty and seventy years; and I boast that I could produce such from every race. 7 For what shall I say, too, of the countless multitude of those who have reformed intemperate habits, and learned these things? For Christ called not the just nor the chaste to repentance, but the ungodly, and the licentious and the unjust; 8 his words being, "I came not to call the righteous, but sinners to repentance" (Luke 5.32). For the heavenly Father desires rather the repentance than the punishment of the sinner.

Reference might also be made to the sayings of Jesus about patience in Justin, *I Apol.* 16, 1f.:

'1 And concerning our being patient of injuries, and ready to serve all, and free from anger, this is what he said: "To him who smites you on one cheek, offer also the other; and do not forbid him who takes away your cloak or coat" (Luke 6.29). 2. "And whoever is angry is in danger of the fire" (Matt. 5.22). "And if any one compels you to go a mile with him, go two with him" (Matt. 5.41). "Let your light so shine before men that they may see it and glorify your Father in heaven" (Matt. 5.16).

Immediately afterwards they are given an illuminating application:

'3 For we ought not to strive, nor has he desired us to be imitators of wicked men, but he has exhorted us to lead all men, by patience and gentleness, from shame and the love of evil. 4 And this indeed is proved in the case of many who were once of your way of thinking but have changed their violent and tyrannical disposition, being overcome either by the constancy which they have witnessed in their neighbours' lives or by the extraordinary forbearance they have observed in their fellow-travellers when defrauded, or by the honesty of those with whom they have transacted business.'[507]

Alongside this, both the words of Jesus and the words of Old Testament prophets are related to his own time. This happens in faithfulness to the conviction that it is 'the work of God, to tell of a thing before it happens, and as it was foretold so to show it happening' (*I Apol.* 12, 10). Thus for example according to Justin, Jesus said the following in anticipation of the heretics of his own time:

Dial 35, 3: '"Many shall come in my name, clothed outwardly in sheep's clothing, but inwardly they are ravening wolves" (Matt. 7.15; 24.5). And, "There shall be schisms and heresies" (I Cor. 11.18f.). And, "Beware of false prophets, who will come to you clothed outwardly in sheep's clothing, but inwardly they are ravening wolves" (Matt. 7.15). "Many false Christs and false apostles shall arise, and shall deceive many of the faithful" (Matt. 24.11, 24).'

Justin goes on to comment:

'There are, therefore, and there were many, my friends, who, coming forward in the name of Jesus, taught both to speak and act impious and blasphemous things; and these are called by us after the name of the men from whom each doctrine and opinion had its origin ... (although they call themselves Christians).'[508]

Considered systematically, in early Christianity six ways of using the Old Testament can be isolated:[509]

1. The Old Testament provided a monotheistic cosmology and approach to nature. For example, at the end of the first century the author of I Clement wants to lead the Corinthian community to the insight that God is free from anger against his whole creation. He then continues:

'1 The heavens moving at his appointment are subject to him in peace; 2 day and night follow the course allotted by him without hindering each other. 3 Sun and moon and the companies of the stars roll on, according to his direction, in harmony, in their appointed courses, and swerve not from them at all. 4 The earth teems according to his will at its proper seasons, and puts forth food in full abundance for men and beasts and all the living things that are on it, with no dissension, and changing none of his decrees. 5 The unsearchable places of the abysses and the unfathomable realms of the world are controlled by the same ordinances. The hollow of the boundless sea is gathered by his working into its allotted places, and does not pass the barriers placed around it, but does even as he enjoined on it; 7 for he said, "Thus far shall you come, and your waves shall be broken within you." 8 The ocean which men cannot pass, and the worlds beyond it, are ruled by the same injunctions of the master. 9 The seasons of spring, summer, autumn and winter give place to one another in peace. 10 The stations of the winds fulfil their service without hindrance at the proper time. The everlasting springs, created for enjoyment and health, supply sustenance for the life of man without fail; and the smallest of animals meet together in concord and peace. 11 All these things did the great Creator and master of the universe ordain to be in peace and concord, and to all things does he do good, and more especially to us who have fled for refuge to his mercies through our Lord Jesus Christ, 12 to whom be the glory and the majesty for ever and ever, Amen' (I Clem. 20.1–12).[510]

2. The Old Testament had long ago announced the appearance, indeed the whole life of Jesus, and the foundation of the church from all nations. Cf. Justin, *I Apol* 49, 1f.:

'And again, how it was said by the same Isaiah that the Gentile nations who were not looking for him should worship him ... And the words are spoken as from the person of Christ; and they are these: "I was manifest to those who did not ask for me" (cf. Isa. 65.1).'

3. Similarly, the Old Testament already points to all that is to come in the future. Cf. Justin, *I Apol.* 52,2:

'For as the things which have already taken place came to pass when foretold, and even though unknown, so shall the things which remain, even though they be unknown and disbelieved, yet come to pass.'

4. The Old Testament in effect contains *all* the principles and institutions of the Christian community like baptism and eucharist (see already I Cor. 10.1–5), and

5. The necessary moral admonitions and – especially in the Psalms – testimonies to a faith which overcomes the world and a spiritual and worship of God which puts all other religions in the shade.

6. The Old Testament attests that the Jewish people are wrong and have either never had a covenant with God or have lost it. Barnabas 4.6–8 is particularly clear here:

'6 And this also I ask you, as being one of yourselves, and especially as loving you all above my own life: take heed to yourselves now, and do not be made like some (people), heaping up your sins and saying that the covenant is both theirs and ours. 7 It is ours: but in this way they finally lost it when Moses had just received it, for the scripture says: "And Moses was on the mountain fasting forty days and forty nights, and he received the covenant from the Lord, tables of stone written with the finger of the hand of the Lord." 8 But they turned to idols and lost it. For thus says the Lord: "Moses, Moses, go down quickly, for the people whom you brought forth out of the land of Egypt have broken the law." And Moses understood and cast the two tables out of his hands and their covenant was broken, in order that the covenant of Jesus the Beloved should be sealed in our hearts in hope and faith.'

In Didache 8.1f. (beginning of the second century) the Jews (following Matt. 6.2, 5, 16) are still generally called hypocrites:

'1 Let not your fasts be with the hypocrites, for they fast on Mondays and Thursdays, but do you fast on Wednesdays and Fridays. 2 And do not pray as the hypocrites, but as the Lord commanded in his gospel, pray thus ...'

This is along the same line as the statements of the author of the Apocalypse (2.9; 3.9), who formally denies the (non-Christian) Jews the name of Jews and dismisses them as a 'synagogue of Satan'.

The last point is particularly important and should be specially emphasized. The self-awareness of the Christian community of being the people of God was shaped above all in its attitude to the Jewish synagogue, whose mere existence was the strongest threat to that self-awareness. Hence the absolutist condemnation in the examples cited. In view of this special dynamic, which already begins with Paul, attempts at mediation by Jewish Christian groups (see Chapter 3 above) to stop this – in vain – or guide it in the right direction did not have a chance and were caught up in the maelstrom of Christian self-assertion.

For example, Justin tells his Jewish discussion partner Trypho that the Old Testament scriptures belong to the Christians, not to the Jews, and he continues: 'For we obey them, while although you read them you do not understand their meaning' (*Dial.* 39.2).

Indeed even the pain of the Jews at the future coming of Jesus was found predicted in the Old Testament.

'10 And what the people of the Jews shall say and do, when they see him coming in glory, has been thus predicted by Zechariah the prophet: "I will command the four winds to gather the scattered children; I will command the north wind to bring them, and the south wind, that it keep not back." 11 And then in Jerusalem, there shall be great lamentation, not the lamentation of mouths or of lips, but the lamentation of the heart, and they shall rend not their garments but their hearts. "Tribe by tribe they shall mourn, and then they shall look on him whom they have pierced; and they shall say, Why, O Lord, have you made us err from your way? The glory which our fathers blessed has for us been turned to shame" (cf. Zech. 12.10–12)' (Justin, *I Apol.* 52, 10–12).

This last piece of evidence to be documented is not only important but also bitter in terms of its effect, since from then on the claim that Christians were the only ones who could interpret the Old Testament dominated Christian theology, and the real Israel in the existence of the Jews was overlooked or Israel was regarded as one of many religions.

Results and criticism

It is evident from what has been said so far that with their typological and allegorical interpretation, Christians, who had been aroused to an enormous self-awareness, had snatched the Old Testament from the (non-Christian) Jews and had made it their own scripture. As the spiritual Israel, the church recognized only a spiritual interpretation of the Old Testament, which discovered in it prophecy of Christ and the church, and rejected all other interpretations. When, for example, Justin's conversation partner Trypho referred to the king in the royal psalms to Solomon – with good historical justification – he was given the following rebuff:

> 'And where it has been said, "O God, give your judgment to the king" (Ps. 72.1), since Solomon was king, you (viz. Jews) say that the Psalm refers to him, although the words of the Psalm expressly proclaim that reference is made to the everlasting king, i.e. to Christ. For Christ is king, and priest, and God, and lord and angel, and man, and captain, and stone, and a Son born, and first made subject to suffering, then returning to heaven, and again coming with glory, and he is preached as having the everlasting kingdom: so I prove from all the Scriptures' (*Dial.* 34, 2).

But somewhere these fantasies had to be submitted to a process of clarification, for as things stood the sacred scripture of the Jews had been handed over defenceless to the most foolish combinations by Christians in 'philological games without precedent'.[511] However, the hope that this process of clarification might perhaps have been initiated by a theologian who was at home in both spheres – the church and the synagogue – was in vain. The external circumstances no longer allowed that, since Gentile Christianity and Judaism were growing increasingly further apart. Rather, the stimulus came from a theologian who further radicalized the opposition between church and Israel. Hans Lietzmann sensitively remarked:

'But if a teacher had come forward, and refused to let himself be blinded by the shimmering gleams of this "spiritual" ingenuity, and had looked the Old Testament plainly and simply in the face, in spite of all cries that he was Judaizing, a catastrophe would have happened. The book would have slipped out of the hands of the Christians again into those of the Jews. If such a teacher had read, and firmly grasped, Paul's doctrine of the abrogation of the Law through Christ, he would have seen how the problem of the Old Testament was to be solved. He would of necessity have come to an understanding that would lead him far from the paths hitherto taken by theologians. This possibility became actuality in Marcion.'[512]

The life and theology of Marcion[513]

Marcion was born in Sinope, in Pontus on the Black Sea, around the end of the first century,[514] the son of a bishop, and lived until around 160 CE. The chronological corner-stones are provided by the report of Clement of Alexandria that he appeared under the Roman emperor Hadrian (117–138 CE) and that he was no longer alive under Marcus Aurelius (161–180 CE).[515] The further piece of information that Marcion was the son of a bishop has occasionally been doubted. But there is no reason to doubt it, because it is not tendentious. Rather, it explains Marcion's preoccupation with Christian belief from his childhood, and also makes it plausible that Marcion may have come in contact with the letter to the Galatians, which was addressed to the communities of north Galatia. This may have been in the archives of the church of Pontus, where his father was bishop.[516]

Marcion left home after a dispute. Church polemical writers report that his father had expelled him from the church because he had seduced a virgin.[517] However, this spiteful tradition has no historical value because later (and probably also earlier) Marcion lived a strictly ascetic life and because 'virgin' here, as in other early Christian sources, also symbolizes the church.[518]

In this tradition Marcion's enemies wanted to say above all that he robbed the church of its innocence. And in a way that is even correct, as will emerge in the course of the account.

Marcion's family must have been very prosperous. According to reliable tradition he was a shipowner (*naukleros*). 'A *naukleros* is a shipowner or captain of his own ship or one that he has leased, in which he trades in his *own* name. The very risky mercantile trade not only presupposes capital but also yields profits.'[519] He may also have received a degree of education as a child. This is suggested by his activity as a textual critic: 'To venture on textual criticism at all presupposes education; the degree of education received at a grammar school was sufficient. If the teacher went through classical texts in the grammar school, first of all the copies which the pupils had in their hands had to be co-ordinated; *enarratio* and *explanatio*, commentary and exegesis, were practised for each one, along with *emendatio*: the text was "improved", purged of errors.'[520]

Because of his later literal interpretation of the Old Testament, it has occasionally been assumed that Marcion was a Jew. However, that is improbable, since at that time the Jews did not always understand the Old Testament literally, but applied various rule of exegesis, as Paul already indicates (see above, 67).[521] Moreover, the tradition that Marcion's father was a bishop suggests that he came to know early Christian writings at home and in the community of which his father was the head.

His journey to the West, undertaken in connection with his break with home and the church in Pontus, suggests a sense of mission. Probably he had already been active on the west coast of Asia Minor, but sought to gain influence there in vain, since according to a tradition Polycarp and Marcion fell out. Thus Irenaeus reports (in Eusebius *HE* IV 14, 7): 'When Marcion once[522] met Polycarp and said to him "Recognize us", Polycarp answered, "I recognize, I recognize the firstborn of Satan!"'[523]

This tradition is particularly vivid, as hate-filled legends are at all times. However, it does seem to reflect the historical knowledge that Polycarp of Smyrna was at a radical distance from Marcion, who seemed to him to be a baneful reformer.[524] This attitude was well in keeping with the customs of the representatives of orthodoxy at that time (the author of the Pastorals, Ignatius, Polycarp) in dealing with 'heretics', as Irenaeus also illustrates immediately after the episode between Marcion and Polycarp. He writes: 'The apostles and disciples had such abhorrence of those who corrupted the truth that they would not even enter into conversation with them' (*Haer* III 3, 4).

In Rome, Marcion got to know the Syrian teacher Cerdo. Cerdo put forward a doctrine of two gods which in the view of many scholars had a great influence on Marcion (see further below, 165). Here he also joined the Roman church[525] and made over to it the proceeds of 200,000 sesterces from the disposal of his ship.[526] He sought and gained influence in this community. He had 'not come to Rome as a notorious heretic who was at all costs to be avoided'.[527] However, in 144 CE[528] a dramatic hearing was held before the presbytery[529] there over his separation (not excommunication), as the reformer could not convince the leaders of the Roman community of the truth of the new insight which he had gained.

In the course of the session Marcion asked the presbyters and teachers of the Roman community what they thought of the following similitude of Jesus: 'No one tears a piece from a new garment and puts it upon an old garment; if he does, he will tear the new, and the piece from the new will not match the old. And no one puts new wine into old wineskins; if he does, the new wine will burst the skins and it will be spilled, and the skins will be destroyed' (Luke 5.36).[530]

When Marcion could not prevail with the call for the 'newness of the gospel'[531] which is implied here, he abruptly parted with the Roman community and founded his own church, which with amazing rapidity spread all over the Roman empire. Indeed, a decade later it was already known among all the peoples of the empire.[532] Marcion's teaching had taken hold with headlong speed, and with it he was evidently meeting the secret desires of many Christians. 'What had dwelt in their inner consciousness in a more or less undefined form until then, acquired through Marcion the definite form that satisfied head and heart. No one can call that a falling away from orthodoxy to heresy.'[533]

The Antitheses

What was the teaching of the orthodox or heretical teacher from Sinope?

It is set down in Marcion's main work, the *Antitheses*, which to some degree represents a commentary on his Bible. The introduction to the *Antitheses* runs: 'O fullness of wealth, folly, might, and ecstasy, that no one can say or think anything beyond it (the gospel) or compare anything with it!'[534]

Here already it is possible to recognize that Marcion's teaching is based on an overwhelming experience. The gospel is exclusively gift, and cannot be compared with anything in this world. Indeed, it cannot really be comprehended in either speech or thought. The reason for this is that in it God enters the world as the stranger. This revelation of the strange God makes Marcion and his community real strangers[535] in this world, which no longer has any power over them. Although the gospel is ineffable and unthinkable, it does endow those to whom it is given with tremendous riches.

At the same time this introduction to the *Antitheses* (like the parables of Jesus about a new patch on an old garment and new wine in old skins) expresses the newness of the gospel and its incompatibility with the old with unparalleled elemental force.[536] The point of Marcion's message is that in the gospel everything is new: 'it does not have links back into history, nor any foundations in creation'.[537]

Marcion's contemporary opponents held his doctrine of two gods against him from the start and wanted to demonstrate that he was a dualist. It is remarkable, and needs explanation, that, as Adolf von Harnack aptly remarked, in 'all these and many other problems ... historiography so far has been essentially content to repeat the short, decided comments of his opponents. Today we are still following their tendency; they wanted to show that he was a dualist but can be refuted from what he allowed to stand in the N(ew) T(estament).'[538]

Andreas Lindemann's influential 1979 book on 'Paul and Earliest Christianity. The Image of the Apostle and the Reception of Pauline Theology in Early Literature to Marcion', which with an extent of more than 400 pages devotes less than 20 to the 'arch-heretic' from Pontus, moves at this well-tried level of interpretation. According to Lindemann, Marcion's starting point was the dualistic distinction between the good God and the just God. Then follows the statement: 'In Paul, talk of God's grace is based ... on the fact that the God who judges (sc. the righteous God) is believed in as the gracious (viz. good) God', and he goes on to remark: 'But Marcion's good God has nothing at all to do with the law – and thus his act of redemption is ultimately not an act of grace at all.'[539] This comment, which is open to misunderstanding, is later made more specific: 'The central statement of the apostle's theology, that by grace God renounces implementing his claim on human beings and pronounces them righteous in Christ by faith, is completely robbed of its meaning by Marcion when he interprets grace as a transition from the sphere of power of the creator into that of the good God.'[540]

At any rate here Lindemann at least concedes to Marcion a doctrine of grace, modifying the sentence first quoted above. But he does him an injustice because he quotes with assent the following question of Tertullian from the sphere of ethics: 'If you (the Marcionites) do not fear God as being good, why do you not boil over into every kind of lust, and so realize that which is, I believe, the main enjoyment of life to all who do not fear God?'(Adv Marc. I 27, 5). He then continues: 'Marcion was the champion of a strictly rigorist ethic, which was based on the notion that no room may be left for the creator God. He could not give a reason for his ethical principles derived from the saving act of the good God.'[541]

To that, the following objections are to be made. First, Tertullian foists on the Marcionites an Epicureanism which Paul's Jewish Christian opponents already wanted to foist on him (Rom. 3.8).[542] In neither case, of course, can that be taken as a serious argument. Secondly, in Paul the ethical foundations do not occupy the first rank, as Lindemann suggests.[543] Thirdly – and connected with this – Paul believes that total sexual asceticism is the best way (I Cor. 7.1: 'It is good for a man not to touch a woman'). Marcion radicalized this side of Pauline ethics and then generalized it by requiring – unlike Paul – all the members of his church to be unmarried. However, at this point an anti-sexual radicalism appears that might almost be called pathological, 'which must be regarded as due to Marcion's social background'.[544] Fourthly, Marcion's experience of grace lies much nearer to Paul than

Lindemann's theological statements will have it. For here, too, as in all areas of living religion, experience precedes theology. In this connection one might ask theological critics in future to take more to heart some statements by Hans Lietzmann which are grounded in historical knowledge: dualistic notions were certainly 'not his starting point, nor in any way the inspiration of his thesis. His main contention is clear enough and does not require the help of such assumptions. Men of that period were accustomed to find a multitude of intermediate beings between God and man, including both the devil and the divine logos. Moreover Marcion's teaching was in reality neither dualistic in its starting point nor in the way in which it was worked out.'[545]

Furthermore, by way of anticipation, reference might be made to Marcion's pupil Apelles, who will be discussed further below: for him the question of the unity of God was the most difficult question of all and as an ingredient of faith is a *notion of faith*. According to Apelles, only belief in the crucified Jesus is important. As the crucified one, this Jesus – putting it in almost a modern way – is the ground of faith. The same is also true for Marcion. We must not get things back to front, as is the wont of the opponents of heresy, old and new.

Marcion's Bible

As well as the *Antitheses* there is the new Marcionite Bible, which contained the Gospel of Luke (purged of Judaistic falsifications) and seven letters of Paul.[546] Marcion did not accept into his canon the Old Testament, which hitherto had been the sacred book of Christianity, since in his view the message that it contained was incompatible with Jesus' gospel of love. He supported this theological decision by rejecting any interpretations of the Old Testament that were not literal, the kind that Christianity before him had abundantly cherished (see 150–2 above). Here he sought clarification completely and fearlessly, and in so doing gave their Bible back to the Jews. Here his procedure is stamped by fanatical matter-of-factness. He looked the Old Testament straight in the eye and – passing over the piety of the psalms and the religion of the prophets – acutely perceived the wretched humanity of the Old Testament God. 'He saw a God who had created a world full of the most deplorable imperfections: a God who had created men, and drove them to fall into sin; who frequently repented of what he had done, and who overlooked the most serious sins in his favourites, although he pursued them cruelly in others.'[547] At the same time he showed an abhorrence of the 'flesh', the 'pollution' of birth and 'the impurity' of the sexual act, which led him into ever deeper antipathy to the creator of this world.[548]

Another dimension of God took shape and developed in Marcion as a result of intensive reading of the accounts of the message of Jesus. In it he found another righteousness than that of the Old Testament, namely the unconditional demand for toleration, forgiveness and love. From this point he was led almost consistently to accept that the God of the Old Testament had to be distinguished from the God of Jesus Christ.

It has been asked whether Marcion derived this distinction between two Gods from Gnosis, specifically from the Gnostic Cerdo, whom Irenaeus calls a forerunner of Marcion. The question is to be answered in the positive, with some reservations (see above, 160). However, a distinction needs to be made. Irenaeus writes:

'Cerdo was one who took his system from the followers of Simon, and came to live at Rome in the time of Hyginus, who held the ninth place in the episcopal succession from the apostles downwards. He taught that the God proclaimed by the law and the prophets was not the Father of our Lord Jesus Christ. For the former was known, but the latter unknown; while the one also was righteous, but the other benevolent. Marcion of Pontus succeeded him, and developed his doctrine. In so doing he advanced the most daring blasphemy against him who is proclaimed as God by the law and the prophets, declaring him to be the author of evils' (*Haer* I 27, 1f.).

However, the redactional character of the link between Cerdo and Marcion made by Irenaeus or his predecessor tells against a direct derivation of Marcion's doctrine of two Gods from Cerdo.[549] Furthermore, as became clear above, the straight-line development of Marcion's thought led to his own distinction between the Creator and Father of Jesus Christ. Cerdo's arguments may have been fruitful here.[550] However, they are in no way the starting point of his thought, which rests on an *overwhelming* experience. So we have to continue to assume that Marcion developed the doctrine of two Gods only at a later date – probably after his separation from the Roman church – and received a stimulus here from Cerdo.

Marcion and the earliest Christian tradition

Now, at the latest, we have to ask: was not Marcion himself clear that at least with the developed form of his doctrine of two Gods he was giving a slap in the face to everything that the earliest Christian witnesses had said about the unity of God, namely that he was not only the Father of Jesus but also the creator of heaven and earth?

Marcion did not feel that in this way he was conflicting with the earliest Christian tradition. Rather, he claimed to be helping to revive what was really the earliest tradition. Repeated reading of the first two chapters of Galatians, which in Paul's own words report how false brethren had slipped in (Gal. 2.4), along with the hypocrisy of Peter and other Jewish Christians (Gal. 2.13), had disclosed to him that the original gospel of Jesus had been falsified by the apostles. He had newly discovered this original gospel and reconstructed it on the basis of the Third Gospel, purified from Jewish additions (e.g. Luke 1–2). But the lying apostles of Jerusalem had not only distorted and altered the gospel and even put several gospels in the place of one gospel; they had even altered and supplemented the letters of the apostle Paul.

To some extent, these falsifications of Jesus and Paul which had taken place robbed Marcion of his naiveté in dealing with church tradition. They shattered his primal trust in the church and led him to regard it as his most personal task to give Christianity the originally pure gospel and the letters of the apostle in their original form. The one gospel – consisting of the Gospel of Luke freed from falsifications – and ten letters of Paul formed the canon of his reformed Christianity, supplemented by the *Antitheses*, which to some degree as a hermeneutical guideline formed an introduction to the New Testament. At the head of his collection of the letters of Paul Marcion quite deliberately put Galatians, by reading which he had arrived at his revolutionary insights; then followed I and II Corinthians, Romans, I and II Thessalonians, Ephesians (called the letter to the Laodiceans by Marcion), Colossians/Philemon, Philippians. The Pastorals were certainly not part of his collection.

As the two letters to the Corinthians and the Thessalonians and Colossians and Philemon (because of the striking similarity of the lists of greetings in both letters) were regarded as a unity, this gave a collection of seven letters of Paul.

Marcion's influence

As we know, Marcion did not find a majority for his reformation in the Roman church, yet he was of unmistakable significance for further developments. Without Marcion there would have been no New Testament, and without this heretic no letters of Paul. (For further justification of this statement see Chapter 9 below.) He was *the* interpreter of Paul in the second century and in any case came closest of all his contemporaries to understanding the apostle to the Gentiles, although he completely misunderstood him.[551] He cut the knot which Paul had tied right through the middle instead of untying it (assuming that that was possible). At all events his opponents[552] were right: according to the testimony of Paul and the early Christian writings, the creator of the world *is* the Father of Jesus Christ. Anyone who tears creation and redemption apart so that they are absolute opposites is no longer on the same side as Paul. However, the same is even more true of Marcion's critics, for whom Paul's understanding of faith[553] and experience of faith, which Marcion and his school had rediscovered, were almost incomprehensible. Hans von Campenhausen sums this up by commenting: 'To the extent that Marcion experiences the gospel once more in its true nature as the redemption of the lost, his theology is primitive Christian in the spirit of Jesus; and in his understanding of faith as freedom from the Mosaic law he is directly akin to Paul.'[554]

A spotlight is thrown on Marcion's reformation by an episode in Rome at the end of the second century. Adolf von Harnack remarked that it was 'the most significant religious dialogue that we have from the earliest church history'.[555] Indeed one can hardly overestimate the significance of the extant source material for this controversy, since here the embattled heretic is himself finally allowed to make some central statements about his position in the faith uncensored.

A Catholic writer named Rhodo disputed with Apelles,[556] the old disciple of Marcion, and composed a report on this dispute of which a fragment has been preserved in Eusebius's *Church History*. Rhodo writes here:

> For the old man Apelles, when he talked with us, was refuted in many wrong statements. Therefore he went on to allege that one ought not to examine doctrine at all, but that everyone should remain in his own belief. For he asserted that they who have placed their hopes in the Crucified will be saved, if only they be found in good works. But he held that the most obscure thing of all was, as I have said, the question of God. For he spoke of a single principle, as also our doctrine does.' (There follows a transitional remark by Eusebius that Rhodo presented the whole teaching of Apelles. Then he continues.) 'But when I said to him, "Whence do you get this proof? or how can you say that there is a single principle, tell us," he replied that the prophecies refute themselves, being absolutely devoid of truth; for they are inconsistent and lying and self-contradictory. But as to how there is a single principle, he said he did not know, but that it was merely his impression. Then on my adjuring him to tell what was true, he swore that he was speaking the truth when he said that he did not understand how there was one uncreated God, but that this was his belief. For my part I laughed, and reproved him, because he said he was a teacher, and yet was unable to establish what he taught' (Eusebius, *HE* V 13, 5–7).

This report makes the following things clear.

First, Apelles is not 'refuted in many wrong statements', as Rhodo puts it at the beginning of the extant report. Rather, contrary to his own interpretation, Rhodo himself is,[557] for his claim to be able to prove his teaching as a theological teacher seems very wooden and arrogant. 'We now know from him that he has listened to the dozen philosophers of the age.'[558]

Secondly, Apelles' survey of the prophetic writings, the contradictions in which he – like his teacher Marcion earlier – has discovered as a 'thorn in the flesh' for any harmonizations of the Bible, is captivating.

Thirdly, the depth of Apelles' message of faith is impressive: he presents the Pauline theology of the cross and an admonition to faith which is made effective through love (cf. Gal. 5.6) with an abruptness which seems unprecedented.[559]

Fourthly, a spirit speaks in Apelles which 'was independent of the outlook of his period, which had grasped a great truth, and which had even epxressed it almost in modern terms, viz. that the religious idea of God does not belong to the sphere of logic, but to that of "emotional" thought'.[560] He is one of the few theologians of the second century who speaks to us directly today.[561] His theology, like that of his teacher Marcion, has doubtless preserved some of the recognition of grace that we find in Jesus and Paul.[562] If it was not possible even in the second century to listen to Marcion and Apelles, this certainly must be remedied today, and the way must finally be paved for their return home to the church.

7

Heresies in the Johannine Writings[563]

The following remarks take up attempts made quite recently to use the brief Johannine letters (II and III John) and the conflict which becomes clearly visible in them as 'windows' on the inner life and history of the Johannine circle. So they are concerned above all with gaining access to the dispute which broke out in the Johannine circle from the perspective of the most personal documents among the Johannine writings, the short letters.

II John and III John as the earliest accessible documents of the Johannine circle

The presuppositions of what follows are, first, the assumption that the Johannine writings originate from Asia Minor, i.e. Ephesus,[564] and secondly, that II and III John are the earliest extant writings of the Johannine circle or the Johannine school.[565] Thirdly, they are relatively close to the origin of this sect-like community association,[566] the fellowship of the friends of Jesus, male and female.[567] The key concepts of this circle are 'truth', 'love', 'knowledge'; and in addition a reference to the 'beginning', the inculcation of the 'commandment', the so-called immanence formulas which describe 'abiding' or 'being' in the new reality; equally characteristic is the Johannine dualism in the contrasting of truth and lie, life and death, love and hatred.

Of course the relationship between the four writings can also be understood differently, as it is e.g. by François Vouga:

'That any information missing or presupposed in II and III John can be found in the corpus of the Gospel of John and I John can be explained most simply by the fact that the Gospel of John and I John are known both to the author of the two short letters and also to those to whom they are addressed (!GL). That this precise over-lapping rests on a common oral heritage is a less plausible approach at an explanation.'[568]

On the other hand, Hartwig Thyen remarks:

'The content, language and style (viz. of II and III John) show that here problems within Johannine Christianity are being dealt with against the background of its specific tradition. Nevertheless we cannot *clearly* see from them that they presupposed the text of the Gospel of John and/or of I John.'[569]

However, first of all relative proximity to the origin of the Johannine community just means a proximity to the beginning that we can perceive. In other words, whatever the real chronological relationship of the four Johannine writings to one another may be, at all events it makes sense to start from the most personal documents of the Johannine circle, the two brief letters, and to attempt a way in from there.

The presbyter mentioned in II and III John is the recognized head of the Johannine school, and *for that reason* he does not need to mention his name.[570] For those receiving the letter 'the presbyter' was enough indication, as they knew the writer of the letter by this unmistakable name.[571] Perhaps it is ultimately thanks to the reputation of this figure in early Christianity that II and III John found a way into the canon.[572] From there it is no great step to regarding these two letters as original documents from the founder of the Johannine school.

To this can be added conjectures which, while they will not underlie the analysis which follows, should at least be kept in view as possibilities. First, 'the elder' (= the presbyter) of II and III John could be identical with the disciple who according to John 21.20–24 died in extreme old age, and to whom the composition of the Fourth Gospel is later attributed.[573] Secondly, we cannot rule out the possibility that 'the elder' of II and III John is to be identified with the presbyter John whose home was in Asia Minor and who is mentioned by Papias (Eusebius, *HE* III 39,4). If these two conjectures were correct, they could add a desirable church-historical depth to the controversies behind the Johannine letters.

But back to II and III John. Their author, the presbyter, is thus a figure who had an authority in the Johannine association of communities. He addresses a private letter to Gaius (= III John) and in it refers to a letter to the community (v. 9). In my view it is simplest to identify this letter with II John.[574] If that is correct, then III John is reacting to the *effect* that II John has had on the community to which it was addressed.[575] That is why III John would be addressed to an individual person, Gaius. He probably lived in the community for which II John was intended, and as a friend of the presbyter served as a go-between who could support brothers sent by the elder (III John 6).[576] In this way the presbyter hopes to regain influence over the half of the community which has fallen away from him, although he has a strong opponent in Diotrephes, who calumniates him and is developing his own authority by force (for details, see 181f. below).

Anyone who is *opposed* to the identification of the letter mentioned in III John 9 with II John must assume that it has been lost or was destroyed by Diotrephes.[577]

The Gospel of John in its final (!) form (chs. 1–21) and I John as a 'homily in the form of a letter' (G. Strecker) later developed out of the association of the presbyter's communities; both bear the stamp of the process of the consolidation of the Johannine circle. In other words, both in part also bear anti-docetic features, but at the same time have combined the earlier Gnostic elements with the 'catholic' elements into a synthesis. The publication of the three letters of John, with the homily addressed in general terms at the beginning (I John), the letter to the church (II John) second and the private letter (III John) at the end, could have followed the lines of the collection of the letters of the apostle Paul (see below 197f.); here the number three has a striking parallel in the triad of the Pastorals.

II John

II John is a real letter, and the way in which more recent publications dispute this is more of a curiosity. Thus no less a scholar than Helmut Koester writes:

'II John is ... not an authentic letter but a not very profound propagation of Johannine statements in the form of a "catholic" letter (the "elect lady" in II John 1 is the church). I and III John are pre-supposed. The title of the author, "the elder", has been borrowed from the latter. From the former derives the confession that Jesus Christ has come in the flesh (II John 7), which is offered as a criterion of right teaching (Didache, II John 9f.). The letter is significant because it shows how after I John an ecclesiasticized Johannine Christianity makes itself the advocate of the fight against the Gnostics.'[578]

The best counter-argument to this is to read the document itself repeatedly. This gives the impression that here a real person is writing to a group of people which really exists.[579]

II John is addressed to a community. The prescript consists of three parts: (*a*) naming of the sender (v. 1: the presbyter'); (*b*) address (v. 1: 'the elect lady and her children'); (*c*) greeting (v. 3). This structure corresponds to that of a Pauline letter to a community. Probably it even comes from there. (The same is to be assumed for Rev. 1.4 [cf. above, 127].)

At the same time, despite the traditional structure of the pre-script, there is no mistaking the Johannine flair: the central Johannine concept 'truth' alone appears four times; the typically Johannine preposition *para* ('from') is used instead of *apo*; and once each we find the specifically Johannine verb 'abide' (v. 9) and the typical phrase 'Jesus Christ, the Son of the Father' (instead of 'the Lord Jesus Christ'). At the end of the prescript stand the Johannine technical terms 'truth' and 'love'.

That the author addresses the community as 'lady' (for the word see below) sometimes gives rise to the conjecture that he did not found it.[580] (In that case a father-child metaphor would have been more likely.) However, this is probably an over-interpretation.

The argument

[1] The sender, the elder (*presbyteros*), is evidently a well-known figure ('the elder' seems virtually to be a title which expresses his dignity). The remark that he loves the children of the community in truth, as do those who know the truth, presupposes more than is said in the few words.

[2] ' ... because of the truth which abides in us and will be with us for ever' confirms this impression. 'Truth' is in any case a central

concept of the sender and the receivers, as is 'abide' (cf. John 8.31).
[3] The greeting of peace is traditional (see 173 above), but is supplemented with two Johannine words, 'truth and love', which also run through the following verses (cf. vv. 4f.: the elder has found the members of the community 'following the *truth*' and now admonishes them to *love* one another).

[4–6] Now follows an admonition to mutual love. The paragraph is a 'summary of Johannine paraenesis' (H.-J. Klauck) which identifies following the truth with following love. Verse 4 says that the elder 'found' some (members of the community) following the truth. This either goes back to a visit by the elder to the community, or a group from the community was with him in order to inform him about what was happening in it. In any case, the elder met members of the community and did not just hear from them.[581]

The relationship between v. 4 and v. 5 is quite remarkable: why does the author make an unconditionally positive statement about the way of life of the community in v. 4 and then in v. 5 admonish it ('lady' as a designation for the community takes up the expression from v. 1) nevertheless to love one another? Evidently in v. 5 the emphasis is on the fact that the community had the commandment 'from the beginning'.

Verse 6 is a variation on v. 5. One might note how 'this is love' is taken up in an effective rhetorical way by 'this is the commandment': commandment (singular) here points back to 'commandment' in v. 5. The community is steadfastly preserving the tradition which as true doctrine (v. 9) becomes the criterion for the distinction between the orthodox community (of the elder) and false teaching.

'The whole complex of the argument is very closely connected with the more extensive polemic against the false teachers in the first letter (2.3–11). These do not keep Jesus' commandments (2.3f.), therefore the truth and God's love is not in them (2.4f.). The "commandments" are concentrated on the one "old" commandment, i.e. the one which was given at that time by Jesus and handed on to the community (2.7f.), which Jesus himself first made possible, which is new each time it is fulfilled, because the one who lives in it demonstrates that the light has overcome the darkness (2.8–10).'[582]

[7–11] These verses give warnings against being led astray by false teaching and detailed instructions as to how this is to be countered. The false teachers are termed 'Antichrist' in keeping with the system of eschatological co-ordinates. And in v. 8 the community is admonished not to set at nought what 'we' (= the presbyter, ceremonial plural) have created. Then it will receive its reward (in the last judgment). According to apocalyptic thought, the false teachers appear in the last time before the end.[583] According to v. 7 they do not confess that Jesus Christ comes in the flesh (*erchomenon en sarki*).

Quite recently, Georg Strecker above all has emphasized the future sense of *erchomenon* and argued that in this passage he can identify the realistic expectation of a future coming of Jesus in the flesh. The presbyter is maintaining the chiliastic notion of an intermediate messianic kingdom as this was perhaps also advocated by Paul (I Cor. 15.23) and – from Asia Minor – the author of Revelation (20.1–20), the presbyter John,[584] Papias,[585] Justin,[586] and also Irenaeus.[587, 588]

This proposal is attractive, because in immediate geographical and chronological proximity to the elder, Bishop Papias of Hierapolis put forward a similar view and his theology was stamped by the presbyter John.[589] Should the 'elder' of II/III John be identical with Papias' presbyter, this would be a plausible historical connection. Furthermore, reference could be made to similar formulations in the early Christian writings to the effect that Jesus will come again in the same flesh as that of the incarnation.[590]

However, the objections to this proposal are considerable:

First, despite the notable proximity of John's and Papias' presbyter to the author of II and III John, it is always questionable to base a general view on one passage (II John 7), which is disputed all the more since *erchomenos* can also be explained in another way (see below).[591] Secondly, the lack of any indication in the context of the letter that the parousia is meant tells against Strecker's proposal.[592] Thirdly, 'confess' in early Christian writings is always used in connection with the death and resurrection of Jesus, and not in connection with the expectation of the parousia.[593] Fourthly, *erchomenos* can be translated both as past (III John 3, the brothers who have come to the elder) and as present. In that case, as in I John (4.2) and the Gospel of John, it refers to the incarnation of

Jesus. Cf. John 1.9: 'The true light that enlightens every man was coming into the world'; John 1.27 (Martha to Jesus): 'Yes, Lord; I believe that you are the Christ, the Son of God, he who is coming into the world.' At the same time the last-mentioned passage shows that coming understood as present can also contain aspects of the past, since the Christ who is coming into the world is the one who has come into the world. Fifthly, the present of the participle may be used to emphasized the personal significance of the incarnation of Jesus.[594]

Thus Ignatius of Antioch 'around the same time finds an even more vivid expression: Jesus is to be "confessed" as the one who is clothed with flesh, as the "bearer of flesh", and anyone who does not accept this has totally denied him.'[595] Cf. further Polycarp 7.1: 'For everyone who does not confess that Jesus Christ has come in the flesh is an anti-Christ.' Here we find a type of confession the main concern of which is to draw lines between orthodoxy and heresy within (!) the Christian community.[596]

The passage from the letter of Polycarp to the Philippians (c. 140 CE) which I have just quoted is sometimes derived in literary terms from I John 4.2 (II John 7).[597] Against that is the observation that Polycarp does not quote at all and that the transition from oral to written tradition is fluid at this period. That means that there is certainly a genetic relationship between the Polycarp passage and I John 4.2 or II John 7. However, this can hardly be regarded as 'scriptural quotation'; rather, Polycarp's confession is 'a well-tried battle cry which comes from a Johannine doctrinal tradition which is not yet very old.'[598] Similarly Polycarp's next sentence, 'And whosoever does not confess the testimony of the cross is of the devil' also sounds Johannine (cf. I John 3.8: 'He who commits sin is of the devil'); indeed even the taunt which Polycarp evidently flings at Marcion (see above, 160) that he is the 'firstborn of Satan' has Johannine colouring (cf. John 8.44: 'the Jews have the devil as their father'). In other words, Polycarp stands with the heirs of the presbyter and the presbyter himself in a battle against Christian heretics who deny the fleshliness of Jesus.

In II John 7, the elder measures the heretics by a confessional formula from whose content they deviate, and puts them in an apocalyptic system of co-ordinates. They are the anti-Christ, who *had to* come. This corresponds to I John 2.18, where the departure of the false teachers similarly has an eschatological basis, and in the next verse the additional information is given: 'They went out from us, but they were not of us; for if they had been of us, they would have continued with us' (I John 2.19).[599]

Accordingly, the clash between heresy and orthodoxy goes back to a split in the Johannine association of communities. The false teachers separated from the community *before* I John was written. The presbyter represents one trend in the Johannine community and the false teachers whom he attacks the other. He thinks it necessary to confess that Jesus Christ comes in the flesh, while the others evidently teach a docetism according to which Jesus Christ does not (completely) come or has come in the flesh.[600] If we glance at the controversies of Ignatius of Antioch with his docetic opponents which were being fought out at the same time, we can see from them that these opponents dispute the corporeality of Jesus (Smyrn.5.2), deny his fleshly resurrection (Smyrn.1.2; 3.1; 7.1, etc.) and emphasize that it was impossible for Jesus to suffer (Trall.10). The details mentioned may also apply to the teaching of the group attacked by the presbyter. But this question was evidently not yet seen as a problem at the beginning of the Johannine community.

Here it is often forgotten that Paul's christology sometimes verged on docetism.[601] Nor are we to expect otherwise for the early period of Christianity in which Paul lived and worked. Here what was later consolidated was still fluid, alive and open. On the one hand, according to Paul, the Son of God is 'born of a woman' (Gal. 4.4), while on the other he assumed only the 'form of a servant' (Phil. 2.7), merely the 'likeness of a human being' (Phil. 2.7) or 'the flesh' (Rom. 8.3).

If we presuppose that the earliest parts of the Gospel of John derive from the beginning of the Johannine community, docetic features in it are unmistakable.[602] The original parts of the Fourth Gospel include all those passages which are stamped by a present eschatology (3.17f.,36; 5.24–27; 11.25f.; 14.18–24). They correspond to Jesus' 'I am' sayings (bread [6.35], vine [15.1–8], light of the world [8.12], resurrection and life [11.25f.]); here the salvation present in Jesus does not need any future supplementation, 'but is totally present in the faith in Jesus' (Philipp Vielhauer). It 'can be described with formulae of reciprocity according to which believers stand in the same unity with the Revealer and Father as these do:

"I am in my Father and you in me and I in you" (14.20; cf. 10.14f.; 17.21, 23).'[603]

Another question is whether the Gospel of John as a whole has an anti-docetic interest.[604] This may already be answered in the affirmative, since the final redactor emphasizes the factuality of baptism (3.5) and eucharist (6.51c–58; 19.34b,35) and the fleshly nature of the risen Jesus.

[9–10] As the fundamental consequence of vv. 7f., v. 9 states that only those who hold fast to the teaching of Christ (as the one who comes in the flesh) have a share in Father and Son. The negative side of this is that anyone who goes further (*proago*), i.e. adopts a *progressive* attitude, has no part in God. At the same time this prepares for v. 10, in which a possible enemy is in view. Here the elder commends rigorous action against the former brothers in faith, who are now putting forward another christological doctrine. He writes: 'If any one comes to you and does not bring this doctrine, do not receive him into the house or give him any greeting.'

This sharp injunction evidently represented a change from the previous practice of welcoming all Christian brothers and sisters.[605] But how concrete was the process of identifying orthodoxy? There are two possibilities. (*a*) The travellers were first welcomed and then tested in worship and/or in the community assembly where they had to say the creed about Jesus' coming in the flesh. (*b*) The travellers were already rejected as heretics on first contact.[606] In that case they must already have been notorious as false teachers. In any case the command by the elder is only more recent.

Walter Bauer calls it an 'anxious instruction', and sees in it a retreat by the orthodox with the aim of preserving 'what could be protected from entanglement with "the world"'.[607] Isn't this thinking too modern? After all, the prime concern is to mark out a position within the association of Johannine communities; here it should be noted that the correct teaching draws a line between heresy and church and that the term 'truth' used so often in II John (and III John) has taken on a close connection with 'doctrine'.[608]

The elder puts the crown on this radical course when he continues: 'For he who greets him shares his wicked work' (v. 11). It is almost as though here we have a clash of two spheres which have become hostile to one another, truth and lie, light and darkness.

A more recent commentator, Georg Strecker, cautiously asks

whether it cannot be 'argued, conversely, that the agape of the Christian community had to be strong enough to support differing doctrinal statements; for not only can doctrine guide agape, but agape can contribute towards defining doctrine'. Then he continues: 'In view of the fact that the existence of his work is evidently at risk, the presbyter can hardly be expected to accept such relativizing of his doctrine at that point in time.'[609]

Strecker puts the contrast on a cognitive level ('can hardly be expected to accept') and strips the text of its feelings and its hatred, which the historian must first identify in order to understand the history of the time.

Here we can refer to similar conduct on the part of Paul. He hands over the man guilty of incest to Satan (I Cor. 5.5),[610] in order to preserve the holiness of the community, and insists on an absolute separation between the sphere of Christ and the realm of demons. The archaic thought that predominates here, which allows no interim solutions and really knows only the opposition between death and life, is strange to the 'enlightened' person, but not to the depths of our unconscious. Indeed, that is how we were, how we are, if it is a question of our 'own power'. Certainly, to use Martin Hengels words, 'the roots of this conduct, strange though it may seem to us, are basically Jewish and dualistic'.[611] Still, they are also human. But does that already make them Christian? At this point Hengel wants to make 'a fundamental distinction between the historical question and the problem of ethical justification or even imitation of the presbyter's attitude today'.[612] We might reflect (as in John 8.44, where the Jews are sons of the devil, or in Phil. 3.2, where Paul's opponents are 'dogs') whether criticism of the content of the statements there is not appropriate on the basis of key Johannine sayings like John 3.16 or I John 4.8, or by the standards of the message of Jesus himself (Matt. 5.43–48; Luke 6.27–36). However, there then follow the sentences: 'But before we condemn the greatest teachers of the primitive church, Paul and John, we should try to understand them as men of their time and in special critical situations against which they had to react. Here in particular the Pauline corpus and the Johannine corpus are closely connected. Both know radical grace, but also the inexorable "no" against any falsification of the message of salvation.'[613]

But one might ask in return: do not the 'heretics' know 'radical grace'? Who provides the criteria for determining whether the message of salvation has been falsified? Here we must go further than Martin Hengel, who – apart from the credal parentheses which he keeps interspersing[614] – never specifically discusses the question of the perspective by which a distinction between true and false teaching has to be made today.

[12–13] These verses form the conclusion to the letter. With Johannine flair ('so that our joy may be complete'), v. 12 expresses a wish to pay a visit. Verse 13 contains a brief greeting at the end of the letter which links up with the 'children of the elect sister' in v. 1. This time, however, the expression denotes the community of the presbyter, from whom the greeting comes, while in v. 1 it relates to the community being addressed. In this way the unity of the two communities is expressly documented.

III John

III John is a private letter to Gaius, of whom a good report has been given in the association of Johannine communities by the travelling brothers. Demetrius, who is evidently bringing the letter, gets an equally good report (v. 12). The letter is stamped with specifically Johannine language: truth (vv. 1, 3 [twice], 4, 8, 12), testimony/testify (vv. 3,6, 12 [three times]), joy (v. 4), beloved/love (vv. 1 [twice], 2,5,6).

The argument

[1] Prescript. Gaius is beloved by the presbyter and is addressed as such three times in the letter (vv. 2, 5, 11). 'Whom I love in the truth' (v. 1b) corresponds to II John 1b ('whom I love in the truth'). Note the key Johannine terms 'love' and 'truth' ('truth' appears six times in the letter).
[2] Instead of the blessing contained in II John, this verse contains a formal prayer for the well-being of the recipient.
[3] Here the sender expresses his joy that the Christian brothers who have come to him have informed him that Gaius is following the truth (cf. the close parallel in II John 4).
[4] A generalization of the individual report. The author feels no greater joy than when he hears that his children are following the truth.

[5] Here the content of following the truth is specified. It relates to an attitude towards unknown brothers who

[6] have born witness to the love of Gaius before the (assembled) community and were received by Gaius and equipped to travel on further (cf. Rom. 15.24; I Cor. 16.6).

[7] An explanation to these missionaries: they are sent out in the name (of Christ) and of course accept nothing from the heathen. 'Like the term *to onoma*, this recalls Jewish behaviour'⁶¹⁵ and corresponds to earliest Christian practice, cf. Matt.10.5: 'Go nowhere among the Gentiles'.

[8] The reason for the need to accept these missionaries: both those who accept and those who are accepted have a share in the same truth, the new reality. There is a word-play here with v. 7.

[9] This gives the reason for the present letter and refers to a letter which the author wrote to the community and which was identified above (172) with II John. An influential member of the community, Diotrephes, does not accept the presbyter, i.e. the brothers sent by him, who similarly had brought II John. The presbyter gives the reason for this non-acceptance: Diotrephes wants to be first.

[10] This contains a reference to a plan of the presbyter (he wants to have a word with Diotrephes) and as a reason for this, developing v. 9 (key word 'accept'), makes additional references to the details of Diotrephes' measures (for the details see below).

[11] This generalizes the concrete situation ('He who does good is of God; but he who does evil has not seen God') and admonishes the recipients to imitate the good.

[12] A double commendation of Demetrius (who is bringing the letter). Like Gaius (v. 3), he has had good testimony from everyone and is also spoken well of by the sender of the letter.

[13f.] These verses have a close parallel in II John 12 (see there).

[15] Greeting: here 'the friends', as those who greet and those who are greeted, is evidently a technical term for the members of the Johannine community.

Historical setting

If there is an allusion in III John 9 to II John,⁶¹⁶ which describes itself as a letter that discerns the spirits, then the following historical setting emerges. The letter with instructions to adopt a radical course towards false teachers evidently did not meet with the good will of Diotrephes. He probably sympathizes with the brothers who are excluded or are to be rejected and retorts in the same vein. Just as the elder calls for a repudiation of the false teachers, now Diotrephes does not accept the emissaries of the presbyter (v. 9) and underlines the violence of his previous behaviour by rejecting those of good will (i.e. those who wanted to offer hospitality to the presbyter's emissaries) from the community (v. 10). At the same time he spreads malicious rumours about the presbyter (ibid.) and in return is accused of being ambitious (v. 9).[617]

Diotrephes is probably the representative of the group being attacked by the presbyter, which has separated from the other Johannine Christians and is advocating a docetic christology (Walter Bauer).[618]

Two objections have been made to this reconstruction:

(a) Time and again it is pointed out that in III John there is no mention of false teachers and *therefore* Diotrephes cannot be the representative of a docetic christology which according to II John 7 the presbyter is condemning.[619] This argument is not convincing, since 'heresy' was an element in a struggle, which was also a power struggle.[620] Moreover we are at a stage when the struggle is developing. That is already expressed by the fact that Diotrephes does not accept the presbyter and his brethren, but the presbyter is nevertheless seeking a dialogue with his adversary.

(b) The other argument similarly disputes the theological background to the controversy and reduces it to questions of hospitality.[621] This is inappropriate, since controversies in early Christianity usually have a theological background as well, and all the more so since in II John right doctrine is explicitly a criterion of the division between Christians; furthermore, III John explicitly refers to II John. (Even if the latter were not the case, the argument advanced earlier would retain its weight.)

The human and theological conflict moves towards a climax which is reached when the presbyter realizes his plan to meet Diotrephes personally in order to restore order. But wasn't that a labour of love? Didn't the elder make a serious error here? Would Diotrephes give in so quickly? At the same time the optimism of the elder shows that the opposing sides do not yet stand over against each other like erratic blocks, but are still relatively fluid. There is a parallel to the close connection between personal conflicts and conflicts of substance and the hostile attitude associated with them in the letters of Paul, especially in II Corinthians, where similarly insults and theological differences are intertwined (see above, 93).

Early church history in Asia Minor at the beginning of the second century issues in a conflict at the end of which there are two trends, one of which converges with other forms of Christianity and goes over into the catholic church, while the other gets swallowed up in the Gnostic maelstrom. When the two short letters of John became an element of the New Testament canon in the wake of the Gospel of John and I John, and thus became holy scripture, a thick veil lay over their original significance, so that they almost ceased to exist. It is a task of historical research which cannot be handed over to any other institution to breathe life into them again, so that we recognize just how human the early Christians were, to some degree like part of ourselves, and finally come to the heart of what is Christian.

8

The Origin of the Apostles' Creed[622]

The so-called Apostles' Creed leads a shadowy existence in scholarly research today.[623] A remark made by Karl Holl three quarters of a century ago still applies: 'The so-called Apostles' Creed is suffering from the disagreeable fate that scholarly research usually becomes seriously concerned with it only in times of church struggle.'[624] The creed which is said in Christian churches on Sundays (though not in the eucharist, where the Niceno-Constantinopolitan Creed is used) comes from the fourth century,[625] but *quite certainly* goes back to a Roman creed from the second century and is to be regarded as a further development of it. At least in its original form it is significant for the present book, since the origin of the Roman creed in any case dates from before the time when the New Testament canon was fixed. In an English translation it reads as follows:[626] here the formulations in the Apostles' Creed used today which have developed beyond the Roman creed or have been changed from it are put in brackets (+ denotes an addition, and a bracket without + represents a change):

I believe in God the Father Almighty (+ Maker of heaven and earth),
and in Christ Jesus his only Son our Lord,
who was born from the Holy Spirit and Mary, the Virgin (who was
 conceived by the Holy Spirit, born of the Virgin Mary),
who under Pontius Pilate was crucified and buried (suffered under
 Pontius Pilate, was crucified, dead and buried)
(+ he descended into hell).
On the third day he rose again from the dead,
ascended into heaven, sits at the right hand of the Father (seated at
 the right hand of God the Father Almighty),
whence he will come to judge the living and the dead,
and in the Holy Spirit,

the holy (+ catholic[627]) church,
(+ the communion of saints),
the remission of sins,
the resurrection of the flesh (+ an eternal life).

A comparison between the old Roman Creed and our Apostles' Creed shows that the latter inserted 'maker of heaven and earth' into the first article. However, that is unimportant, since God's creative activity was an element of faith from the start. In the second article, in the Apostles' Creed above all the differentiation between the Holy Spirit and Mary is striking (the old Roman version could have led to the distortion that Jesus is the Son of the Spirit), as is the addition of Jesus' descent into hell after his death.[628] The third article adds the additional clause 'the communion of saints'.[629]

The deviations are on the whole insignificant and can be disregarded as unimportant for the subsequent argument. But that means that not only the Roman Creed but also our 'Apostles' Creed' is being referred to in what follows.

According to a widespread view, the 'Apostles' Creed' went back to the apostles themselves. Thus Rufinus wrote at the beginning of the fifth century:

'As they were therefore on the point of taking leave of each other, they first settled an agreed norm for their future preaching, so that they might not find themselves, widely separated as they would be, giving out different doctrines to the people they invited to believe in Christ. So they met together in one spot and, being filled with the Holy Spirit, compiled this brief token, as I have said, of their future preaching, each making the contribution he thought fit; and they decreed that it should be handed out as standard teaching to believers.'[630]

Now this narrative of the Twelve gathering together in solemn conclave and composing an apostolic creed is beyond doubt a pious invention. Nevertheless, the fact remains that elements of the Apostles' Creed can already be found in the early Christian period. We must investigate them first, and then go on to outline the further development of the individual elements into the Apostles' Creed.[631]

The first phase of the early Christian credal tradition[632]

Christian 'confessing' begins after 'Easter' (not already during the lifetime of Jesus[633]). Only when bloody Good Friday was not understood as the final end, but through the visions of Christ as the overcoming of death, did the Christian honorific titles for Jesus and statements about the saving power of his death and resurrection come into being. Here is a brief tabular survey:

One-member acclamations that Jesus is the Lord: I Cor. 12.3; Rom. 10.9; Phil. 2.11.

One-member confessions that Jesus is the Christ: Mark 8.29; John 7.26; Acts 9.22, etc.

One-member confessions that Jesus is the Son of God: Mark 3.11; Luke 4.3; Acts 9.30, etc.

Formulae about Jesus' death: Rom. 5.8; 14.15; I Cor. 8.11; Gal. 2.21; I Thess. 5.10.

Formulae about the resurrection: Rom. 4.24; 10.9; I Thess. 1.10.

There is a two-member compilation of various individual formulae (for catechetical purposes) in I Cor. 15.3b–5:

'Christ died for our sins in accordance with the scriptures and was buried (I), he was raised on the third day according to the scriptures and appeared to Cephas, then to the twelve.'

The first phase of the formation of an early Christian creed is thus shaped by 'the designation, as brief as it is unmistakable, of the one divine counterpart the affirmation of which makes individual Christians Christians and distinguishes them from all non-Christians, namely the person of Jesus'.[634]

At the same time the confession of God, the creator, became an element of faith which was taken for granted; here confession of God and confession of Christ were put side by side:

I Cor. 8.6:
'Yet for us there is one God, the Father, from whom are all things and from whom we exist;
and one Lord, Jesus Christ, through whom are all things and through whom we exist.'

I Tim. 2.5f.:
'For there is one God, and there is one mediator between God and men, the man Christ Jesus, who gave himself as a ransom for all ...'

Alongside these binitarian formulations there are also triadic (not trinitarian[635]) phrases:

II Cor. 13.13:
'The grace of the Lord Jesus Christ and the love of God and the fellowship of the Holy Spirit be with you all.'

Matt.28.19:
'Go therefore and make disciples of all nations, baptizing them
in the name of the Father
and of the Son
and of the Holy Spirit.'

Didache 7.1:
'Baptize in the name of the Father
and of the Son
and of the Holy Spirit.'

The second phase of the early Christian credal tradition

The content of the second phase represents a polemical defence against heretics within the community. We already met it in the previous chapter in the discussion of the letters of John (and in Ignatius of Antioch and Polycarp). Here the right doctrine about Christ divides true from false Christians. It consists above all in leaving no doubt about the human nature of Christ: Jesus has really come in the flesh (I John 4.2) or really comes in the flesh (II John 9).[636]

It is no coincidence that in Ignatius we also find a resurrection story independent of Luke 24.36–49. It emphasizes the fleshly character of the resurrection body of Jesus (Smyrn 3.1f.: '1 For I know and believe that he [viz. Jesus] was in the flesh even after the resurrection. 2 And when he came to those about Peter, he said to them, "Take, handle me, and see that I am not a bodiless demon." And immediately they touched him and believed, being intermingled with his flesh and spirit.')

The letters of Ignatius of Antioch contain a large number of confessional statements. They all inculcate into the community what has unconditionally to be maintained in the struggle of Christians against docetism. Cf. the following survey.

Eph. 7.2: 'There is one physician, both fleshly and spiritual, begotten and unbegotten, come in flesh, God, in death, true life, both of Mary and of God, first passible and then impassible, Jesus Christ, our Lord.'

Eph. 18.2: 'For our God, Jesus the Christ, was carried in the womb by Mary according to God's plan – of the seed of David and of the Holy Spirit – who was born and baptized that by his suffering he might purify the water.'

Magn.11: the Magnesians are to believe, 'completely convinced of the birth, and of the suffering, and of the resurrection which took place in the time of the rule of Pontius Pilate – things truly and surely done by Jesus Christ, our hope, from which may none of you be turned.'

Trall. 9.1f.: '1 Be deaf, then, when someone speaks to you apart from Jesus Christ, of the family of David, of Mary, who was truly born, both ate and drank, was truly persecuted and died, as heavenly, earthly, and sub-earthly things looked on, 2 who was also truly raised from the dead, his Father having raised him, in whose likeness his Father will also so raise us up who believe in him through Jesus Christ, apart from whom we do not have true life.'

Smyrn 1.1f.: The Smyrnaeans are 'convinced as to our Lord (that he is) truly of the family of David according to the flesh, Son of God according to the will and power of God, truly born of a virgin, baptized by John that all righteousness might be fulfilled by him, truly nailed for us in the flesh under Pontius Pilate and Herod the tetrarch – from the fruit of which are we, from his divinely blessed passion – that he might raise an ensign to the ages through his resurrection to his saints and believers whether among the Jews or among the Gentiles in the one body of his church.'

In the interests of fighting docetism, Ignatius develops early Christian traditions about Jesus Christ.[637] His theological reflection is an element in that convergence of different early Christian theologies which in the fight against Gnosticism thought it necessary for salvation to maintain the divinity and humanity of Jesus Christ simultaneously.

However, he does not yet know any formally fixed creed. The same is true of his later contemporary, Justin. As I already indicated above (18), the first systematic literary fight against heresies began with Justin. It had not been carried on in this form before, since Bishop Polycarp and those of like mind fought against heretics by forbidding contact with them; by contrast, in his *Syntagma* against the heresies Justin fights against the heretics on the basis of contact with them (otherwise he would not have been able to gain information about them) and derives them from Simon Magus (see ch.2 above). Similarly, in a further work, if it is not identical with the above-mentioned *Syntagma*, he wrote against Marcion. However, Justin still did not have any fixed criterion as to what the Christianity of the church was. So for example he is tolerant towards Jewish Christians, and his comments on the relationship between Jewish and Gentile Christians (Dial 46f.) are carefully thought out.[638] At the same time, a term for 'orthodox' (*orthognomon*) appears in him. However, a lack of *complete* orthodoxy does yet automatically mean that the group concerned belongs among the heretics. Thus in Dial. 80 the resurrection of the flesh and the thousand-year kingdom (in Jerusalem) are elements in the faith of orthodox Christians (*orthognomones*). But alongside this Justin accepts as brothers and sisters those who do not advocate chiliasm and distinguishes the heretics inspired by demons from them.[639]

The great dividing line then lies in the time between Justin and Irenaeus, as Adolf von Harnack was able to demonstrate. He writes:

'What was needed was an apostolic *creed interpreted in a definite way*; for only *through a definite interpretation* could the creed perform the service of defending Christians against Gnostic speculations and the Marcionite understanding of Christianity. In this situation the church of Rome ... put into effect the completed Roman baptismal creed as apostolic in such a way that it proclaimed the anti-Gnostic interpretations necessary in particular cases as its obvious content; it termed the explicit creed ... the rule of truth for faith and made membership of its own church and churches associated with it dependent on the recognition of that rule. What the Roman church put into practice was given a theoretical foundation by Irenaeus and Tertullian.'[640]

With the creed, the Roman church and its leaders had found an eminently practical instrument to use against existing heresies: first, against dividing God into different gods; secondly, against dissolving the humanity of Christ (by an emphasis on the crucifixion and the burial under Pontius Pilate, Jesus' appearance at a particular point of time and his real death were emphasized); and thirdly, against the denial of a future resurrection in the flesh.[641]

On the last point the creed also had an unusually practical and conservative function: it preserved the existing reality by formally guaranteeing its revival. That may have had a social-psychological effect on the broad mass of believers which is not to be under-estimated, since a crude materialism always gains hearts quicker than the concession, which was possible and expressed (!) even then, that it is possible to speak of future things only in images.[642]

The relevance of the Apostles' Creed for today

Karl Holl in his day (1919) wrote the following memorable sentences about the Apostles' Creed:

'Today, we may confidently say that there is no longer a theologian, nor a believer from the community, who can adopt the Apostles' Creed in its real sense. For there is no longer anyone in Christianity, in either the Protestant or the Catholic church, who wants, as this creed does, to make the virgin birth the sole foundation-stone and content of belief in the divine sonship of Jesus.'[643]

However, not only the virgin birth, but also the descent into hell, the resurrection and ascension of Jesus, the future judgment of the living and the dead and the physical resurrection of believers, indeed even the notion of God as the creator of heaven and earth, have become completely incredible or incomprehensible if we examine the meaning of these statements carefully.[644] If they are an enigma, then they can no longer be binding, either, and it is lamentable *that the vast majority of believers are confessing – not* to say droning out – something every Sunday at worship which they no longer understand.

Given that it were possible to communicate to the majority of believers the content of the Apostles' Creed, couldn't the creed then maintain its binding quality? Wolfhart Pannenberg has evidently expressed this view.[645] He writes:

'We can still repeat the creed in church without doing violence to our personal truthfulness as long as we are able to adhere to the intentions behind its statements, critical though we may be of the form these statements take. Today the Apostles' Creed ... is an expression of the identity of Christianity throughout the changing centuries, and over and above the widely varying understandings of the faith. In repeating the creed we are uniting with all Christians; we are not just expressing our personal convictions. That is why it is sufficient if we share the intention behind its statements' (13).

A little later, he continues:

'The more or less obscure discomfort with certain formulations of the Apostles' Creed should not lead to the cheap way out – to the excluding of the creed for use in church and its replacement by other, supposedly more contemporary formulae, which at best could never fulfil the function of the old creeds – that through them the individual Christian can enrol himself in the communion of all Christianity. But even as regards the content of faith, nothing is gained by a change of words. What is needed is an explanation and understanding of the things of the Christian faith, which have found their expression in the ancient credal formulations' (13f.).

Earlier, he had emphasized that 'the reality of the God in whom the Christian faith trusts cannot be had without the so-called "facts" to which the Apostles' Creed points and through which he is identified as this very God' (18).

That is consistent thinking, and it deserves all respect. But it does not seem to me to be the last word. For Pannenberg's view ends up in speaking a dogmatic language, veiled in an outdated metaphysical world-view, which is strange to us modern men and women, in the interest of the identity of Christianity down the centuries. This is abandonment of the self in the interest of an identity of Christian faith, in whatever way that identity is imagined. I do not think that this sacrifice of reason is worth striving for; indeed it is dangerous[646] and outdated.[647]

Moreover we may even doubt whether such a procedure is Christian, if being Christian means constantly going by Jesus of Nazareth.

It is in fact striking that the creed is silent about the period between the virgin birth and the death of Jesus, although the second article is much longer than the first and third. That should not be trivialized by the assumption that the preaching of Jesus is presupposed in the creed, in which Jesus' actions and words take on their real meaning and their authority from the metaphysical foundation of his person and its place in the divine plan of salvation. 'This above all had to be made impregnably firm, and then everything else would follow as a matter of course.'[648] For this supernatural foundation of the activity of Jesus is already the interpretation of people *of that time*, and *today* it possibly leads people away from Jesus himself, by whose presence Christian identity lives in the present and to which it is related. 'His person, he himself, will always appear to us as the decisive thing about Christianity, and not ... doctrine about him.'[649] In other words, filling the gap in the creed between the virgin birth and the death of Jesus seems to be the command of the hour, not only for the theological reason mentioned above, but also as a consequence of historical reconstruction, according to which the appearance of Jesus was the decisive catalyst for the Christian movement.

Finally, such a procedure should not conflict with the fathers of the creed, who emphatically emphasized the true humanity of Jesus in the face of Gnostics. (The divinity of Jesus was not an issue for either party.) Now we must extend our thought further and in a new time work out the essential points of Christian faith.

Before that can happen, in the last chapter, on the basis of what has been worked out so far, and taking into account further factors, in the next chapter I need to sketch out the origin of the New Testament canon.

9

The Origin of the New Testament
Canon[650]

This chapter is concerned with the origin of the New Testament canon. On the one hand it will refer back to previous discussions and take them further (virtually every chapter of this book has dealt with partial aspects of the question of the canon). On the other hand we shall now turn our attention to the whole era of earliest Christianity, starting from individual phenomena in order to draw the main lines by which they are interconnected.

However, one qualification needs to be made immediately: a resolution of this question cannot begin from the term 'canon', since this word is only used as a designation for the Christian Bible after the fourth century.[651] The fact that needs to be explained, rather, is that from a certain point in time there was – suddenly – a normative source of Christian belief. So the question is: '*How* did it happen, or *what* happened, that a certain number of writings was chosen from the abundance of earliest Christian literature, set above the rest in status, and given the same rank as the "scripture" of the Old Testament which had been handed down?'[652]

The real problem is that no direct evidence has survived about *how* the collection of writings which comprise the New Testament was actually made. First, we can only observe that from a certain point in time – in Irenaeus and Tertullian (cf. Chapter 2) – polemic was directed against heretics on the basis of a *particular* collection of writings (which was still open-ended). Secondly, the existence of a New Testament at the end of the second century follows from a remark of Melito of Sardes (c.180), who on a visit to Palestine establishes the number and order of the books of the 'Old Testament' (Eusebius, *HE* IV 26, 13f.) which suggests that we are to assume the existence of a New Testament as well. Thirdly, the so-called Muratorian Canon, which was composed in the West (Rome?) around 200,[653] contains a list of New Testament writings with explanations. In it, the nucleus of the New Testament is clearly established, while the peripheries are still open. According to the Muratorian Canon the New Testament – the recognized scripture of the church – contains the four (New Testament) Gospels, Acts, thirteen letters of Paul, Jude, I and II John, Wisdom and Revelation. The Apocalypse of Peter is rejected by some, and Hermas is allowed only for private use. Different writings which are mentioned at the end of the fragment are to be rejected, as are the letters to the Laodiceans and the Alexandrians. For understandable reasons the author does not mention Hebrews, since this had come into (temporary) discredit in the West, because its harsh words about the impossibility of a second repentance (Heb. 6.4ff.; 10.26f.; 12.16f.) were regarded by the Montanists as justification of their rigorist baptismal practice.[654]

How far back does this collection of the New Testament extend, the outlines of which are fixed at the end of the second century?

Theodore Zahn put the origin of the New Testament at the beginning of the second century. He thought that well before 140 the collection of the four Gospels and the thirteen letters of Paul was being read alongside the writings of the Old Testament throughout the catholic church, and that still other writings like the Apocalypse, Acts, and in some parts of the church also Hebrews, I Peter, James and the letters of John, and perhaps also the Didache, shared in the same honour.[655] But he had an inadequate notion of the New Testament as a sacred foundation document to be set alongside the Old Testament if he concluded the canonical character of the New Testament writings from their use in worship. For reading in worship and canonicity are not the same thing. Adolf von Harnack demonstrated in a way which is still valid today that the formation of the canon, like the origin of the ministry and the rule of faith, is a question which is to be answered both historically and in terms of the history of dogma, and represents a partial aspect of the origin of the early catholic church.[656] But in that case it is clear that there was still no New Testament around 150. Justin in his *Dialogue with Trypho* is a witness to this (cf. above 150–8). He speaks more than extensively about the Old Testament, finds Christ prophesied in it, and uses the reminiscences of the apostles and words of Jesus. However, there is still no trace in Justin of the New Testament as a fixed entity and the basis or starting point for argumentation. Rather, the outline of the New Testament canon first came into being in the course of the second half of the second century, on the one hand by the rejection of writings which did not accord with early catholic teaching, and on the other through the definitive acceptance of certain literary works.[657]

Some results have been extracted from the previous analyses that are relevant to the formation of the New Testament, which developed its present form for practical reasons; these will be further substantiated. They will be prefaced by two paragraphs which are introduced to highlight two basic facts.

The Old Testament as primal canon

The Old Testament read christologically was the primal canon of the young church.[658] People referred to it as holy scripture in scriptural proofs, and later Christian literature had canonical status only if quotations were made from in it in the same way as they were from the Old Testament.

The Lord, the apostles, the prophets and the Spirit

We have already often encountered the phenomenon that words of Jesus had unconditional authority in earliest Christianity. This is the case with Paul (I Cor. 7.10; 9.14; I Thess. 4.15),[659] but also in early collections of Logia (Q, Justin) as forerunners to the Gospel.[660] The apostles and prophets actualize the words of Jesus in the Spirit and therefore demand authority, as his messengers.[661]

The four Gospels

In Chapter 2 it became clear that a collection of four Gospels existed in the time of Irenaeus.[662] Irenaeus justifies it in different ways:

Haer III 11, 8: 'Since there are four zones of the world in which we live, and four principal winds, while the church is scattered throughout all the world, and the "pillar and ground" of the church is the Gospel and the spirit of life, it is fitting that she should have four pillars, breathing out immortality on every side, and vivifying men afresh. From which fact, it is evident that the Word, the artificer of all, the one who sits upon the cherubim and contains all things, he who was manifested to men, has given us the Gospel under four aspects, but bound together by the one Spirit ... Such then as was the course followed by the Son of God, so was also the form of the living creatures, so was also the character of the gospel. For the living creatures are quadriform, and the gospel is quadriform, as is also the course followed by the Lord. For this reason were four principal covenants given to the human race: one, prior to the deluge, under Adam; the second, that after the deluge, under Noah; the third, the giving of the law, under Moses; the fourth ... is the gospel of our Lord Jesus Christ.'

Through these artificial arguments Irenaeus demonstrates that this is a relative novelty. (However, it would be wrong to say that a segregated collection of the Gospels existed only *after* Irenaeus,[663] since 'while Irenaeus certainly justifies the number four, he no longer has to discuss which four they are'.[664]) These four had probably already established themselves previously,[665] even if in the time of Irenaeus there was still a front against the Gospel of John.[666]

The Acts of the Apostles

Acts too can be demonstrated to be holy scripture in Irenaeus and Tertullian. A generation earlier in Justin things were quite different; indeed any knowledge of Acts by Justin can probably be ruled out. Both points can again be defended by reference to Chapter 2 and at the same time be further substantiated.

In his catalogue of heretics in *Haer* I 23–28 Irenaeus had derived all heretics from Simon Magus and also pointed out that Simon had already been mentioned in Acts and had been repudiated there by Peter (*Haer* I 23, 1 [cf. 18f. above]). By contrast, Justin in his repeated mention of Simon Magus[667] does not make any reference to Acts, and the passages from *I Apol* 50, 12 (= Acts 1.8?) and 49.5 (= Acts 13.48?) which are sometimes regarded as allusions to Acts are not compelling.[668] Only with Irenaeus (cf. *Haer* III 12, 1–15) does Acts reappear from its submersion and is immediately recognized everywhere. The reasons for this are self-evident.

Thus the Muratorian Canon says of Acts: 'The acts of all the apostles have been described in a book ...' (lines 34f.). Similarly, the secondary heading is *Praxeis Apostolon*. In other words, Acts serves as a history of all the apostles, although that can hardly be substantiated from its content. Furthermore, Acts is used in the battle against the heretics to confirm the descent of the Spirit upon all the apostles (cf. Tertullian, *Praescr* 22) and to secure the subordination of Paul to the twelve apostles – despite the censuring of Peter by Paul in Gal. 2.11ff. (*Praescr* 23).

Now Tertullian himself says that Acts was rejected by the heretics (*Praescr* 22f.). This was probably a reference to Marcion and his school, who had recognized that the Paul of the letters was incompatible with the Paul of Acts.[669] Acts was used against them and was introduced into the new catholic view, according to which the church rested on the testimony of the gospel and all the apostles; here Acts forms a transition between the two parts of the canon.[670] At the same time Paul is interpreted in an orthodox way.

The letters of Paul (apart from the Pastorals)

Chapters 4–6 produced the following results for the history of the canon in respect of the letters of Paul. The letters of Paul were read aloud at worship in the communities which he founded, as is already evident from the earliest extant letter (I Thess. 5.27: 'I adjure you by the Lord that this letter be read to all the brethren').[671] The communities probably also exchanged the letters among themselves after a certain time (cf. Col. 4.16). It is improbable that Paul himself made a collection of them.[672] However, we should note that Paul had a staff of colleagues with whom he constantly exchanged ideas, and that his disciples must have had some share in the composition of the letters (indeed Paul often mentions co-senders). At all events, the influence of Paul also continued after his death and with it that of his letters, as far as they had been preserved. What happened to them in detail is of course beyond our knowledge. But they lived on in the original theology of Colossians; similarly Ephesians, which builds on Colossians, is eloquent testimony to the liveliness of the circle of disciples, going back to Paul himself.

Whether a collection of letters of Paul was made by the author of Ephesians is – as I said above – disputed. But there is much to suggest that Bishop Onesimus of Ephesus collected a corpus of letters of Paul at the beginning of the second century, in which he arranged them by length, putting Ephesians, which he had written, at the beginning, and Philemon, in which he himself appears as a runaway slave converted by Paul (v. 10), at the end. At any rate this would be a good explanation of how the private letter of Paul to Philemon found its way into the canon, for with it the former slave Onesimus would have created a memorial to himself (thus John Knox). Marcion then made use of this collection, put Galatians at its head and set Ephesians in place of Galatians.

In any case it is certain that more than one letter of Paul could be found in the main places of the Roman empire: thus in Rome at least Romans and I Corinthians were known (I Clem 47.1), and in Antioch (Ignatius) at the beginning of the second century there was a collection of letters of Paul, as there was in Smryna (Polycarp). The author of II Peter also presupposes a completed collection of letters of Paul which in his view is addressed to his own community (II Peter 3.15f.). Now that means that extracts from letters of Paul were also read out in communities which had not been founded by him. But such a use in worship is not to be identified with canonization. It would be a misunderstanding to say that 'the *collections of letters of Paul* stand at the beginning of the process of canonization'.[673]

So the question of the collection and use of letters of Paul is to be distinguished from that of their canonical status.

First of all one might refer to the Jewish Christians hostile to Paul who knew letters of Paul but vehemently rejected both the apostle and his writings.

Then there were irritations within the school of Paul: the foolhardy undertaking of the author of II Thessalonians to bring discredit on I Thessalonians by saying that it is a forgery and replacing it by II Thessalonians puts a spotlight on the struggles. This adventurous attempt was caused by Gnostic Paulinists who, consistently developing I Thessalonians – with reference to Paul – , taught that the end had come. That the Gnostic teachers who are also visible behind the warning of Luke's Paul (Acts 20) attracted large circles among the heirs of Paul becomes clear from Ephesians (and similarly Colossians), which provides an artificial basis for the doctrine of salvation in the present but, in contrast to Gnosis, presents an impressive theology of the church. However, it is not surprising that a Paul understood in such a way became the way into a radical Gnostic individualism (Rheginos).

The commandeering of Paul by the heretics is also reflected in II Peter. This author prizes the wisdom of 'brother' Paul, but at the same time warns against the use of his letters by heretics, who distort them (and other writings).

In other words, Paul was highly controversial at the beginning of the second century. Apart from his implacable opponents there were heirs of Paul in the church (Acts, II Peter), and followers who were semi-Gnostic (Eph/Col) and fully Gnostic (Rheginos).

At the same time it has to be emphasized that at this time the letters of Paul did not have the same status as the writings of the Old Testament and the words of Jesus. It was only when Marcion made the letters of Paul the substance of his Bible, which consisted of the Gospel and the letters of Paul, that a process began at the end of which came the Old Testament and the New Testament (composed of the four Gospels, Acts, the apostolic letters and the apocalypse). Marcion's action in canonizing a certain number of writings is the fact which provided the historical impetus to the development which was completed in church history in the second half of the second century.

Now it is often objected to this thesis that Marcion merely accelerated a movement in the direction of the New Testament canon which would also have taken place without him.[674] Thus Adolf Martin Ritter writes:

'However, it is certain or at least highly probable that after the death of the apostles and their immediate audience, given the "gap in authority" which had come about, sooner or later there was a need to seek the voice of the "Lord" and the apostles in the only place where it could still be heard: in the former oral tradition which had been fixed in writing. But in that case sooner or later the question of the authority of these writings, after and alongside the "Holy Scripture" of the Old Testament, had to arise. In other words, it is extremely probable that a bipartite New Testament canon (of whatever extent) would have developed even without Marcion, purely from beginnings and drives within the church. The appearance of

Marcion then beyond question essentially accelerated this development and provoked a deep shock which had a lasting influence.'[675]

This view raises two questions:

First: Were there not numerous other possibilities of making collections of Christian literature at that time, other than the New Testament? Adolf Harnack alone lists seven approaches.

'1. A collection of late Jewish and Christian prophetic-messianic or prophetic-hortatory books inserted into the Old Testament – thus an expanded and corrected Old Testament.
2. A collection of (late Jewish and) Christian prophetic books standing independently side by side with the Old Testament.
3. A simple collection of Sayings of the Lord, like the common source (Q) of St Matthew and St Luke, standing side by side with the Old Testament.
4. A written Gospel or a collection of several Gospels containing the history of the Crucified and Risen Lord, together with His teaching and commands, standing side by side with the Old Testament.
5. A Gospel (or several), with in addition a more or less comprehensive collection of inspired Christian writings of the most different character and graded prestige, standing side by side with the Old Testament.
6. A systematized "Teaching of the Lord", administered by the "Twelve Apostles", of the character of the "Apostolic Canons, Constitutions, etc.", which also included "Injunctions of the Lord", side by side with the Old Testament and the Gospel.
7. A book of the synthesis or concordance of prophecy and fulfilment in reference to Jesus Christ, the Apostles, and the Church, standing side by side with the Old Testament.'[676]

Harnack continues: 'It can still be shown today that in the second century each of these "New Testaments", or additions to the Old Testament, not only were possible, but were actually present in embryo; and further it can be shown why they did not come to full life or perished.'[677] Ritter leaves this fully out of account.

Secondly, would Paul, i.e. the existing collection of Pauline letters, have been canonized without Marcion? It seems that it was the Pastorals, directed against Marcion, which first made the apostle to the Gentiles respectable (see below). Now Ritter does not explicitly mention the apostle Paul, but speaks in general terms of a bipartite New Testament canon in the process of formation, consisting of the Lord and the apostles. But as the second part of what was later the New Testament consisted primarily and essentially of letters of Paul, the assertion made by Ritter has to be decided on the question of the authority of the letters of Paul. Here, however, considerable reservations have to be expressed about his thesis, since 'without Marcion in literary history the letters of Paul would have shared the fate of the letters of Ignatius, if not that of the apocryphal Gospels'.[678]

The Pastoral Epistles

One way towards an orthodox interpretation of Paul – for the purpose of warding off Marcion – was for a bishop like Polycarp or a churchman from his environment to write the Pastoral Epistles around the middle of the second century in order to give the church a guideline for understanding Paul. (Later, as I showed above, the author of III Corinthians undertook this attempt.) Irenaeus and Tertullian were fond of employing the Pastorals in their battle against Gnosis and Marcion.[679] The very title of Irenaeus' five books against the heretics ('Unmasking and Refutation of Gnosis Falsely So-Called') is orientated on a phrase in I Timothy (6.20), and the work begins with a quotation from I Tim. 1.4. These two important quotations already indicate that the Pastorals played a decisive role in the reception of Paul[680] – and thus completely fulfilled the purpose which their author had intended – even if Irenaeus fights his battle with Gnosis (and Marcion) as a battle over the correct exegesis of the letters of Paul.[681]

The Pastorals were written all together and were added to the already existing collection of letters of Paul. In the Muratorian Canon they come *after* Philemon, which formerly concluded the collection of letters of Paul that had been arranged by length. The corpus of the Pastorals was patched on to it; in the Muratorian Canon Titus comes first, and then the two letters to Timothy. This order derives from the author of the Muratorian Canon, who makes the single letter to Philemon parallel to that to Titus and only then makes the two letters to Timothy follow.

The Letter to the Hebrews[682]

The earliest trace that Hebrews has left behind in early Christianity is I Clement 36.2–5. Here Heb.1.3–5,7, 13 is written out without any special reference. It follows from this that it was already held in esteem in the Roman community at the end of the first century. Its further way into the New Testament canon was very bumpy and not achieved without changes to its form. This is the literary puzzle that it poses, since it has the ending of a letter (13.18–25) but not the beginning. As the end of Hebrews is stylized as a letter of Paul[683] but its content is un-Pauline, it seems likely that the conclusion of Hebrews should be seen as the addition of a Paulinist who in this way is claiming the letter for the Pauline tradition. The church rewarded him. In the East, Hebrews was counted among the canonical Pauline letters (including the Deutero-Paulines) after the third century. In the West, Hebrews had a more difficult time; the Muratorian Canon does not even mention it (for the reason see 194 above). Gaius (for whom see 204 below) disputes its validity for similarly dogmatic reasons,[684] probably because the author of Hebrews taught that repentance could only be made once (Heb. 6.4–6). Irenaeus in his five-volume work against the heretics uses all the letters of Paul (except Philemon) and repeatedly cites them under the name of the apostle. But he does not quote Hebrews once. He does not regard it as an apostolic writing, but doubtless knows it.[685] The same goes for Tertullian. Although he cites it in his Montanist period, he does not speak of it as an apostolic testimony.[686]

The Catholic Epistles[687]

Since Eusebius,[688] James, I and II Peter, I, II and III John and Jude have been known as 'Catholic Epistles'. Of these, I Peter and I John gained respect earliest, while the other five letters had a more difficult time, for various reasons. But there is evidence to suggest that II Peter gained canonical status in the wake of I Peter, and II and III John – as indicated above – because of the esteem in which the Gospel and I John were held. James and Jude came last, probably because of the information about their senders.[689]

Their number, seven, is important.[690] It corresponds to the existing collection of the letters of Paul consisting of twice seven letters (including Hebrews), and according to the dogma of the person who collected them the corpus differs from the letters of Paul addressed to individual churches by being meant to be addressed to all. (Beyond question that does not apply to II and III John.)

That they were part of the New Testament canon was still not so certain at the end of the second century as it was in the case of the four Gospels, Acts and the thirteen letters of Paul which have already been mentioned. Moreover we must take into account that the canonization of the individual writings took place in different ways. For example, it became clear in Chapter 7 that the three letters of John were published together (on the basis of the first Pauline corpus, with a general letter at the beginning and a personal letter at the end), and probably only became an ingredient of the New Testament canon as a corpus.

On the whole, we shall not go wrong in assuming that it was the collection of Paul's letters – at whatever stage – which stimulated and made possible the collection of the Catholic Epistles. Without the collection of Paul's letters there would have been no second part of the New Testament, i.e. probably no New Testament at all.

The Apocalypse of John

The canonical status of this writing was long disputed in the catholic church. Justin names John the son of Zebedee as its author (Dial 81,4) and refers to it as evidence of the chiliasm which he advocated. Of course the chiliast Papias also regards it as trustworthy,[691] and in the Muratorian Canon it belongs among the writings accepted by the church. The canon states:

'Also of the revelations we accept only those of John and Peter, which (latter) some of our people do not want to have read in the church. But Hermas wrote the Shepherd quite lately in our time in the city of Rome, when on the throne of the church of the city of Rome the bishop Pius, his brother, was seated. And therefore it ought indeed to be read, but it cannot be read publicly in the church to the other people either among the prophets, whose number is settled, or among the apostles to the end of time' (lines 71–80).

However, the perceptible reserve here towards the Apocalypse of Peter[692] and Hermas[693] already indicates that there was general resistance to apocalyptic in some Christian groups.[694] This becomes even clearer, and is also sparked off by the Apocalypse of John, when in the middle of the second century in Asia Minor, with reference to the saying about the Paraclete in the Gospel of John, so-called Montanism saw the coming of the Holy Spirit which is announced there fulfilled, and estimated the Apocalypse highly. Resistance formed against the Montanists. The Roman presbyter Gaius, who was active in Rome at the time of Bishop Zephyrinus there (c.198–217), wrote a dialogue with the Montanist Proclus[695] in which he abruptly attributed the Gospel of and Apocalypse of John to Cerinthus, known through tradition as a heretic, and thus presented them as forgeries.[696]

Dionysius of Alexandria attributes the charge that the Apocalypse was a forgery by Cerinthus to his own forebears. (As he is writing in the middle of the third century, the tradition which he is handing down goes back at least to the end of the second century.) On the Apocalypse of John, Dionysius writes:

'1 Some indeed of those before our time rejected and altogether impugned the book, examining it chapter by chapter and declaring it to be unintelligible and illogical, and its title false. 2 For they say that it is not John's, nor yet an apocalypse, since it is veiled by its great thick curtain of unintelligibility; and that the author of this book was not only not one of the apostles, nor even one of the saints or those belonging to the church, but Cerinthus, the same who created the sect called Cerinthian after him, since he desired to affix to his own forgery a name worthy of credit. 3 For this was the doctrine which he taught, that the kingdom of Christ would be on earth; and he dreamed that it would consist in those things which formed the object of his own desires (for he was a lover of the body and altogether carnal), in the full satisfaction of the belly and lower lusts, that is, in feasts and carousals and marriages and (as a means, he thought, of procuring these under a better name) in festivals and sacrifices and slayings of victims' (Eusebius, *HE* VII 25, 1–3).

However, Dionysius does not dare to reject the Apocalypse. He continues: 'I should not dare to reject the book ... but, reckoning that my perception is inadequate to form a perception concerning it, I hold that the interpretation of each passage is in some way hidden and more wonderful' (Eusebius, *HE* VII 25, 5). But he nevertheless doubts that John the disciple of the Lord is the author of the writing, and regards another John as its author (Eusebius, *HE* VII 25, 16).

Only in the fourth century did the debate over the authenticity and canonicity of the Apocalypse settle down. Basically, at this time the unresolved problem of the chiliasm highly valued by Papias, Justin and Irenaeus was removed.

To conclude the question of the origin of the New Testament canon, we can say with Hans von Campenhausen: 'It is undisputed that both the Old and the New Testaments had in essence already reached their final form and significance around the year 200. The minor variations which still persist, and are occasionally the subject of further discussion, co-exist perfectly happily with the over-riding conviction that Christians everywhere possess one and the same Bible. For the fundamental understanding of the canon they are of no importance.'[697]

Result

The processes which have been sketched out indicate a slow but inexorable growth of the Christian Bible. At the beginning stood the Old Testament as primal canon. At the end of the first century Christians would have 'proudly and without hesitation said yes to the question whether their community possessed a holy and binding book of divine revelation: the church possessed such books, the "law and the prophets", what is now called the Old Testament'.[698]

Closely connected with this was the authority of the now present Lord Jesus, who in his words and in his Spirit spoke to the communities.

To that was directly attached the authority of those in office, i.e. the Twelve, the apostles, the prophets. That is also true of Paul and his community. When the first generation had formally died off, a gap in authority was opened up. For who was to continue to lead the communities, the church?

Now we must not under-estimate the specific dynamic of individual communities. Much followed automatically from tradition and from customary practices. Liturgical forms had long since been established and were a social-psychological necessity. The rule of faith and 'everything that was regarded as the apostolic legacy'[699] formed a fixed nucleus. But the Spirit, too, continued to speak through the prophets and other vehicles.[700] Things could not go on like this indefinitely.

A heretic, Marcion, provided the decisive stimulus towards the New Testament. When he canonized (the) letters of Paul alongside the Gospel of Luke, he formally compelled the church to give them a canonical status – or wholly to reject them. That is all the more amazing, since the theology of the church which canonized the letters of Paul was utterly un-Pauline. *So it is extremely ironical that Paul in particular occupied the greatest place in the new canon and that all the others letters came into the New Testament in the wake of this heretic.* However, that was only possible because his disciples cherished his legacy and preserved his letters from destruction. Finally, by a mission and theology in the grand style Paul first created the preconditions of his canonization and the canon, whereas other heads of the first community evidently had not trained competent disciples. But let us not fool ourselves. Those who canonized him were not aware of the theological dynamite in what from then on they regarded as the Word of God.

Retrospect

Despite all the uncertainties in historical reconstruction, we may say that the assertion that the New Testament is infallible, without contradiction, or united in what it says, is untenable. Historical consideration of the origin of the New Testament makes the walls of church and theology, in so far as they are grounded in the New Testament as a Word of God, collapse like a house of cards. That applies even more to the use of the Old Testament as holy scripture.

Granted, Hans von Campenhausen, to whom the present work owes so much, takes a different view. He believes:

'The essential significance of the canon and its theological meaning need not change ... despite this scientific revolution. Even an Old Testament read critically remains the book of a history which leads up to Christ and probably also predicts him, without which Christ himself cannot be understood. Even a New Testament read critically remains the only source from which we can learn who and what Christ really was – and historical research in particular first helps us to a full knowledge of his character and uniqueness. Certainly faith never arises – any more than it did in the early church – merely through reading Holy Scripture, and Christ, not the canon, is its real subject; but scripture read in faith with reason simply remains "the guideline". If it is not bound to the canon which – in the widest sense – attests the history of Christ, belief in Christ in any church would become an illusion.'[701]

Against that, however, it must be stated without illusion and historically (!): First, the Old Testament does not necessarily lead to Christ. Secondly, only historical research helps us to know who Jesus of Nazareth really was, and it is he, and not the Christ of faith, who is the norm of what is Christian today. Campenhausen is an example of the theologian who in the end returns to the safe haven of dogma instead of remaining true to history.[702]

The concluding remarks of the author of the most recent 'history of the theology of earliest Christianity' are quite shattering:

'With the formation of the New Testament no new truth arose, but the churches came together in defence against untruth by collecting the foundation documents of the truth which were familiar to them and elevating them to the status of a common possession. We should look at the New Testament in the same way today. For whatever distinguishes or even divides the Christians in the different confessions from one another, the New Testament binds them together, and if they allow themselves to be bound together by this New Testament they are bound together in the truth.'[703]

This relativizes all historical questions and their possible relevance to faith today and ultimately saves them for the church – whatever one may understand by that.

Rather, the positive aspect of the reconstruction of the history of the canon offered above is that a very human side of early Christianity becomes visible in it. Here individuals and groups are struggling over the right understanding of the tradition which has been handed down, over Jesus and Paul; they are asking about what is true and false, good and evil, but above all they have a

10

The Christianity of the First Two Centuries, Jesus and Ourselves

Alfred Loisy posed the problem of the relationship between Jesus and the church which appealed to him after his death with the often-quoted formula: 'Jesus proclaimed the kingdom of God, and it was the church that came.'[704] This statement was subsequently often understood to mean that the development into the church represents a falsification of the gospel of Jesus.[705] The misunderstanding here could not be greater, since Loisy specifically wanted to challenge this view (that of Adolf Harnack[706]), as emerges from the continuation of the sentence I have just quoted.

> 'It (viz. the church) came, enlarging the form of the gospel, which it was impossible to preserve as it was, as soon as the passion closed the ministry of Jesus. There is no institution on the earth or in history whose status and value may not be questioned if the principle is established that nothing may exist except in its original form. Such a principle is contrary to the law of life, which is movement and a continual effort of adaptation to conditions always new and perpetually changing. Christianity has not escaped this law, and cannot be reproached for submission to it. It could not do otherwise than it has done.'[707]

If we presuppose that Jesus is the foundation of Christian faith, then in fact the further development of its preaching is not apostasy, but even necessary in view of a changed situation. In other words, a living memory of this origin, which is to be called for here, is more than a mere repetition of the words of Jesus. The decision whether the church has remained faithful to Jesus must therefore be made by other criteria.

The following section has been written with constant heed to E. P. Sanders' warning that many New Testament scholars write books about Jesus in which they discover that he corresponds with their own version of Christianity.[708] The question to be discussed here is what Jesus wanted and did. It was already touched on in ch.2 and will now be taken further.

Jesus formally lived out for his disciples the message of the boundless grace of God – in word and action. Human beings have nothing to boast about to God (cf. Luke 18.10–14). The word of salvation is for the poor (Matt. 11.5) and the outcast (Matt. 21.28–31; Luke 15.4–10; 15.11–32). To state it pointedly, according to Jesus' preaching, God seeks out the lost, and they do not have to repent first.[709] At the centre of his message stands the kingdom of God, which begins to come about with him – completely of its own accord. The kingdom of God literally breaks into the present, so that from now on all life is lived in the presence of God. Jesus speaks to God as a loving Father, and what he says about faith, which presupposes the Old Testament concept of God's faithfulness, includes the unconditional certainty that faith is no longer just a roving desire, but rests on God (cf. Isa. 7.9: 'If you do not believe, you will not be established') and includes the total renunciation of calculation or previous achievements (Luke 18.10–14). In Jesus God's gate is as wide as the heavens, at a particular time, in a particular place, in a specific person. His announcement of the kingly rule of God was accompanied by a praxis which opened up participation in the kingdom of God to sinners – or better, the godless – unconditionally. And there was more. Jesus interpreted the law of Moses in the light of love, the holy tradition from the perspective of whether it serves men and women. He focussed this provocatively in the rule-of-thumb formula: the sabbath is made for the sake of human beings, and not vice versa (cf. Mark 2.27).

In all this a reduction of theology is to be noted in Jesus, which is orientated on the unconditional nature of the promise of salvation for individuals as well.

Jesus' actions and words are based on a picture of God which was quite unknown to many of his contemporaries. For Jesus, this unknown God is also the creator, as emerges from the way in which a parallel is drawn between the dawning kingdom of God and the morning of creation (Mark 10.6–8/Gen. 2.24).

With all this Jesus was not founding Christianity, since it was to his own people that he turned to call them to repentance. He did not develop a programme of world mission. The election of Israel is not disputed, but is always presupposed.

The question whether Jesus applied any of the countless christological titles to himself is probably to be decided in the negative.[710] The way in which he understood himself cannot be grasped in a christological title. Nevertheless, behind his words and actions there seems to be a self which claims unconditional authority for itself, is bound up with God – as Jesus understands him – in the most intimate way, and appears in the name of God.

In this connection we may regard as credible the statement that Jesus also forgave sins in the name of God,[711] passing over the institutions in Judaism which were prescribed for that (temple, sacrifice, Day of Atonement). (The Gospel of John appropriately expresses the substance of Jesus' activity, heightened in symbolic terms, when it makes Jesus say of himself that he is the Way, the Truth and the Life [John 14.6].) But that made Jesus a heretic, who would have to pay for it sooner or later with his life.

The term 'co-humanity' is not a full expression of the person and activity of Jesus. He was bound up in a particular understanding of God, on behalf of whom he claimed to act. But that does not immediately make him the sinless Son of God that New Testament writings portray him as.[712] Thus in Paul the notion of sinlessness is conditioned by the view that only such a Christ laden with our sins and as a representative sacrifice could be punished with death in our place (cf. Rom. 5.8; II Cor. 5.14f.; Gal. 3.13). We can see how this conclusion was arrived at within the framework of the thought of that time, but it is in no way a binding thought pattern today,[713] even less so as Jesus was not sinless even by his own understanding.[714] In fact he had himself baptized by John 'for the forgiveness of sins' (Mark 1.9),[715] and called only God good (Mark 10.17f.).[716] In this way 'Jesus took the side of sinful humankind'.[717] The cross-check that Jesus understood himself as a sinner is provided by the First Evangelist, who reinterpreted the baptism of Jesus (Matt. 3.14: John to Jesus, 'I need to be baptized by you, and do you come to me?'); the Fourth Evangelist, who did not think that this had taken place (cf. John 1.29–34: Jesus' baptism by John can be recognized only by those who know of it; 3.22f.; 4.1: John and Jesus baptize at the same time); and the Gospel of the Nazareans, according to which Jesus explicitly repudiated his own baptism by John with the words, 'Wherein have I sinned that I should go and be baptized by him?'[718] In other words, from a very early point in time Jesus' estimation of himself as a sinner, which can be seen behind the earliest tradition, is corrected in the direction of the dogma of Jesus' sinlessness.[719]

Jesus' humanity also shows itself in the fact that his expectation of the imminent coming of the kingdom of God and that of the new temple was shattered by harsh reality. So he was not only not sinless but not even 'inerrant'. This fact has of course been disputed or reinterpreted by dogmatic theologians. Thus Wolfhart Pannenberg thinks that Jesus' expectation of an imminent end was fulfilled, not by the world as a whole, but in his person through his resurrection.[720] So Jesus was not deceived. However, this desperate apologetic expedient comes to grief on the simple fact that the resurrection of Jesus is not a historical event.

What remains of Jesus today is not an eschatological mistake but a picture of human beings and of God, a wisdom and an ethic. For me he is not the Son of God to whom I pray, but the Messiah who moves me to do the same sort of thing as he did and who in this way can become the basis for my life.

The subsequent Christian generations which appealed to Jesus are to be measured by such a picture. However, once again it should be emphasized that Jesus neither foresaw nor deliberately wanted them: he expected the kingdom of God. Nevertheless, it makes sense to ask whether the appeal to Jesus at that point was correct. At any rate this possibility must not be dismissed *a priori*.

But isn't an answer to the question whether the reference to Jesus was right made problematical from the start by the fact that the subsequent Christian generations always and above all meant the Risen Christ when they referred to Jesus? Doesn't this reduce the whole Christ to the historical Jesus in an underhand way? At first sight my proposal may seem doubtful. But there is no other choice, since on the basis of the vision hypothesis the 'Risen Christ' is always the interpreted Jesus. These interpretations[721] can be in line with Jesus, or not. At all events each is to be measured by the reconstructed picture of the historical Jesus. I shall go on to undertake this task.

The Jerusalem community and Jesus (on Chapter 3)

As a result of his vision, the first witness, *Peter*, understood Jesus better than he had during his lifetime. Only now did it become clear to him that Jesus' activity and message were stamped by three elements: the forgiveness of sins, the experience of life and the experience of eternity. In other words, in this vision of Peter and in the vision of subsequent witnesses to the resurrection, Jesus himself and his work came into their own, within the framework of eschatological notions.

During Jesus' lifetime, *James* was reserved towards his brother. Then after a vision of the Risen Christ he rapidly became the leading force in the Jerusalem community. His strict observance of the law was akin to Jesus, in that Jesus too wanted to realize the original purpose of the Torah. But the two men differed over the question of observing individual regulations and in the freedom which Jesus adopted to law and tradition. However, these differences should not be exaggerated either. James worked for decades in Jerusalem, Jesus for the most part in Galilee; James lived a settled life, Jesus was an itinerant preacher. Nevertheless, one cannot avoid the ultimate verdict that James increasingly shed the spirit of Jesus.

James' followers were condemned as heretics. There were several reasons for that. In the meantime Christianity had become increasingly Gentile Christian; it had completely changed its first form, and all at once James' followers were caught between the stools of the developing catholic church on the one hand and the new rabbinic orthodoxy which was in process of formation on the other. Instead of being seen as a permanent indication that the catholic church had a Jewish root, in what must be called a historical scandal they were identified with Gnostics and Marcionites. That is how unfair fate can be. But the fact that even a mission to the Gentiles was later undertaken from their ranks and that the circumcision of Gentile Christians was no longer advocated subsequently justified their arch-enemy, Paul.

Paul (on Chapter 4)

The apostle to the Gentiles is sometimes understood as the second founder of Christianity[722] – surely wrongly so. Although Paul had no personal dealings with Jesus and got to know Jesus' preaching only through the Hellenists whom he persecuted, Jesus' message corresponded not only to his earlier unconscious strivings but also to his later developed theology. For Jesus, unconditional love was the answer to the kingdom of God; for Paul, it was the answer to God's righteousness. Here for both Jesus and Paul there was a 'now already' and a 'not yet'. With the preaching of Jesus the kingdom of God broke into the present and embraced all who followed him; the righteousness of God preached by Paul had been made manifest in the gospel – for all believers. But its final realization was as much still to come as was Jesus' kingdom of God. *In substance, both teach the justification of the godless.* In the case of Jesus that is expressed in the way in which he turns to the rejected; in the case of Paul, in his teaching that boasting should be abandoned, putting men and women in the position of beggars before God.[723]

For both, Jerusalem is the centre of the world, and both come to grief there. They are ardent visionaries of a new Jerusalem, which Paul sees realized in the church consisting of Gentiles and Jews, and Jesus sees realized in the new temple to which Gentiles also have access.

Viewed from a historical distance, both the apostle and his Lord are original Jews whose fate was to be taken over by Gentiles – with devastating consequences for the Jewish people.

The heirs of Paul (on Chapter 5)

The heirs of Paul kept his memory alive, but soon split into several branches. The real heart of Pauline theology, the doctrine of justification, combined with the dynamic of the 'now already' and 'not yet', was usually either dropped, or lived on only in slogans. The foolhardy attempt of the author of II Thessalonians to put Paul's first letter out of action shows how all-too-humanly even the heirs of Paul tended to behave.

On the left wing of Paulinism the Gnostic speculation which is already around with Paul breaks through, but it is exploited by the author of Ephesians in a constructive way for church thought. Here beyond question there is influence from the historical Paul, who used the idea of the church against his own disciples (enthusiasts) in Corinth and also saw his own position in the framework of the new people of God made up of Gentiles and Jews – i.e. in terms which transcend the individual.

The author of Ephesians, who may have known the historical Paul and is perhaps identical with the former slave Onesimus, arranged the first collection of Paul's letters, to make the voice of his master heard. At the same time there was a concern to safeguard the identity of the church within the framework of the Roman empire. It was threatened where Gnostic individualists had discovered Paul for themselves and had unconstrainedly bent his theology in a personal direction, taking left-wing Paulinism further. But here, at least in part, did they not have Paul and Jesus on their side? These say 'I' more than all the other figures in the New Testament, and did not sink into the collective.

The right-wing Paulinists preserved Paul without any great theological depth and handed down faithfully his statements about the end which had not yet come, while at the same time vilifying the left-wing Paulinists. They were also already in part reacting to the second-century interpreter of Paul, Marcion, who founded a church. To some degree they were blind disciples. Yet without them there would not have been canonical letters of Paul in the framework of the Catholic church (cf. n.681).

Marcion (on Chapter 6)

Marcion and his church are the great motive power in second-century church history. The son of the Bishop of Pontus brought clarity into the theological confusion of the second century and found a rule of interpretation, what today would be called a hermeneutical principle. He showed as a model for all theology *that Christian faith (and any faith) must be able to state its concern precisely if it is not to sink into the sphere of groundless speculation and theological games.* His religion is close to Jesus and Paul, in that he recognized and stated that human beings are dependent on grace and that God *gives* this to them. However, from this he draws the basically false conclusion that the God who gives is not the creator. In this way he loses himself in the world and literally by-passes the reality which surrounds him. *Marcion did not understand that Jesus proclaimed the unknown God as creator of the world.* However, because of his religious ardour, based on the principle of grace, his rediscovery of Paul and his crucial effect on theological development in the second century, he was a great man.

The concept of heresy is inevitably present wherever the church is. Heresy is the attempt at a living view of religion, even if in extreme cases the fossilized form of the church is destroyed.[724] After Marcion has done his duty, he cannot simply be allowed to disappear from the scene. Rather, even the greatest heretic of the second century must be brought home into the present form of Christianity. He is the torchbearer of the fire which went out from Jesus and Paul.

The Johannine circle (on Chapter 7)

In this other offshoot of Jesus, who valued more than other Jesus' commandment to love, we find the clearest definition of what Jesus is, a definition which can still be repeated today: the way, the truth and the life. However, this clarity was soon disturbed by disputes over the humanity of Jesus to the point of a *de facto* departure from Jesus' commandment to love, which becomes clear in the bitter fight of the presbyter against Diotrephes. All this is not said in a condescending way. The departure from Jesus' commandment to love is governed by the demarcation of heretics. It became necessary when people had become convinced that the right christological doctrine was necessary for salvation.

Would it not have been better to leave the question of the humanity of Jesus vague, as had been the case in an early stage of the Johannine circle and e.g. in Paul, and to have kept to a naive docetism? In the second century, the time for such openness was probably not favourable, and the need or the wish for the organization of a church was similarly opposed to a tolerant attitude in this question. On the other hand, it was also absolutely right to strengthen the assertion that Jesus had really become man, even if the full consequences of this could not yet be recognized. However, it is then depressing to see what became of Jesus' commandment to love at a certain stage of Johannine Christianity.[725]

The Apostles' Creed (on Chapter 8)

Because of dogmatic pressure, the Apostles' Creed has totally stripped Jesus of Nazareth of his life, although at the same time traditions of Jesus' words and actions were known and were being read out. But they did not have, or did not yet have, the same status as the dogmatic statements. On the other hand the fact of the humanity of Jesus is preserved in the Apostles' Creed, and it is also striking that there is no anti-Jewish polemic in the depiction of his passion. That is to be seen in a positive light in view of the anti-Judaism which was also widespread in the second century (cf. also above, 157).

The New Testament and the Old Testament as Holy Scripture (on Chapter 9)

At the end of the second century, the New Testament along with the Old Testament was given authority in the church, and it has retained this status in all the churches to the present day. However venerable this authority may be, it has to be said unsparingly that the canonical New Testament as such is the basis not only of all confessions, but also of more or less all sects in the present.[726] For who can continue to dispute the contradictions in the christologies of the New Testament, not to mention the difficulty, if not impossibility, of an honest christological interpretation of the Old Testament? The only truthful way to use the New Testament is to measure its individual writings and individual statements by the words and actions of Jesus and to read the Old Testament as a document of Jewish faith which Jesus, Paul and the first Christians shared.[727] But it would be nonsensical to assert that the writings of the Old Testament point to the coming of Jesus. Marcion effectively put an end to these games, though they have continued down to the present, and we should not go back behind his insights.[728]

However, the human view and reading of the Bible also offers rich gain. Julius Wellhausen rightly commented: 'People have become unaccustomed to putting the demands of ordinary, human speech to the text of the Bible.'[729] Now if the texts of the Bible are understood as human speech, at a first moment they may lose their heavenly splendour because they have been stripped of their authority and inspiration. But if they are really close to God, they cannot but lead us to God. So I do not believe in the Bible as the word of God to us, but in Jesus who, pressed down by the rubble of church tradition, stands *behind* the New Testament texts and has to be regarded as the criterion of all so-called Holy Scripture.

I regard the question whether the Bible is still to be preserved at all as Holy Scripture in the church as an artificial problem, which does not fall within the competence of scholarship and is to be answered in terms of the pragmatics of the church. (For example it is also a vexed question whether or not our history belongs to us.) The only important thing here is the insight that the Holy Scripture of the New Testament is a sum of human answers to the appearance of Jesus. (Those who regard it differently must see how they can reconcile this with their consciences, in view of the clear historical evidence.) So in no circumstances can I follow the decision of the church in the second century and regard both New and Old Testament as the word of God;[730] I regard it as an early Christian collection which has grown up historically. Thus the New Testament canon is also an indication of the humanity of faith, and how Christian it is must be measured by the first Christian, Jesus. The 'word of God of scripture' may in no circumstances drown out the voice of Jesus of Nazareth (Ernst Käsemann).

I regard it as a positive sign in the present that interest in Jesus has risen enormously. Indeed somehow there is an intimation that Jesus is still the great unknown, whose message aims at seeking hearts inside and outside the church. *Jesus is still always the one who is to come*, and does not allow us so quickly to return to the order of the day through what is apparently well known.

With Jesus[731] we have the unmerited stroke of luck that we can once again turn away from dogmatic phraseology to the reality of the life which is given us, in resolution, courage and clear-sightedness. Jesus still confronts us today with the decision whether his word is truth when he says, 'Blessed are those who do not take offence at me.'

Epilogue: Ten Golden Words

1. The view of the Bible as the Word of God or as Holy Scripture belongs to a past time. Today it hinders understanding. The Bible is the word of human beings.

2. The idea of the sinlessness of Jesus belongs to a past age. It hinders understanding of the human being Jesus. Jesus is either fully a human being or not a human being at all.

3. Jesus proclaims the unknown God and his rule. He understands, measures and lives out the tradition by love, which first allows us to live in a human way, open to the world and indeed reasonably, in the freedom of the children of God, and to remain true to God's creation.

4. As the first Christian, Jesus remains the criterion for what is Christian in the Bible, in history and in the present.

5. The church is the community of people who have been touched by Jesus, who celebrate his coming and seek the truth.

6. The heretics of the second century, men and women, are at least as close to Jesus as the orthodox, and must be welcomed back into the church.

7. In the conflict between the church and truthfulness, truthfulness has the priority.

8. In theology and the church there is a need to turn from phraseology to reality in order to survive.

9. Theologians must keep learning to say 'I', and if need be to contradict the tradition.

10. A fragment of religion which has been experienced and recognized is worth more than an orthodoxy which is fully known. A tiny ray of the light of Jesus in my life is more important than any orthodoxy.

Appendices

1. *Justin, Dialogue with the Jew Trypho* 46,1–2; 47,1–5

46,1 Trypho asked me, 'But if some, even now, wish to observe the institutions given by Moses, and yet believe in this Jesus who was crucified, recognizing him to be the Christ of God, and that it is given to him to be absolute judge of all, and that his is the everlasting kingdom, can they also be saved?'

2 I replied, 'Let us consider this question also together, whether one may now observe all the institutions of Moses.'

He answered, 'No. For we know that, as you said, it is possible to sacrifice the Passover lamb or the goats ordained for the fast only in Jerusalem; and that all the other offerings, too, are possible only there.'

And I said, 'Tell me then yourself, please, some things which can be observed; for you will be persuaded that, though a man does not keep or has not performed the eternal decrees, he may assuredly be saved.'

Trypho: 'To keep the sabbath, to be circumcised, to observe months, and to be washed if you touch anything prohibited by Moses or after sexual intercourse...'

47,1 Trypho asked: 'But if some one, knowing that this is so, after he recognizes that Jesus is the Christ, and has believed in him and follows him, wishes also to observe these institutions, will he be saved?'

I replied: 'In my opinion, Trypho, he will be saved if he does not strive in every way to persuade other men – I mean those Gentiles who have been circumcised by Christ and freed from error – to observe the same things as himself, telling them that they will not be saved unless they do so. This you did yourself at the beginning of our discussion, when you declared that I would not saved unless I observe these institutions.'

2 Trypho declared: 'You could say "In my opinion such a man will be saved" only if there are people who claim that such will not be saved.'

'Trypho,' I replied, 'there are such people and people who do not venture to have any dealings with or to extend hospitality to those who have been mentioned. I do not agree with them. But if some, through narrow-mindedness, wish to observe such institutions as were given by Moses, expecting some virtue from them, though we believe that they were appointed by reason of the harshness of the people's hearts, as well as hoping in this Christ, and if they wish to perform the eternal and natural acts of righteousness and piety, yet choose to live with the Christians and the faithful as I said before, not inducing them either to be circumcised like themselves, or to keep the Sabbath, or to observe any other such ceremonies, then I think that we ought to accept them and associate with them in all things as kinsmen and brethren. 3 But if, Trypho,' I continued, 'some of your race, who claim to believe in this Christ, compel those Gentiles who believe in this Christ to love in all respects according to the law given by Moses, or choose not to associate so intimately with them, in the same way in this case I do not acknowledge them. 4 But I believe that even those who have been led astray by them to observe the legal dispensation along with their confession of God in Christ will certainly be saved if they continue to confess the Christ of God. However, I firmly dispute that those who have confessed and known this man to be Christ, yet have gone back for some reason to the legal dispensation, and have denied that this man is Christ, and have not repented before death, shall be saved. 5 Furthermore, I dispute that those of the seed of Abraham who live according to the law and do not believe in this Christ before death, shall be saved, and especially those who have cursed and still curse this very Christ in the synagogue, and everything by which they might obtain salvation and escape the vengeance of fire.'

(Translation based on Ante-Nicene Fathers, Vol. I, ed. A. Cleveland Coxe, 1885; Greek text in Edgar J. Goodspeed, *Die ältesten Apologeten. Texte mit kurzen Einleitungen*, 1914, 143–6)

2. III Corinthians

1 Paul, the prisoner of Jesus Christ, in (the midst of) many tribulations, to the brethren in Corinth – greeting! 2 I do not wonder that the opinions of the evil one are so quickly gaining ground. 3 For my Lord Jesus Christ will quickly come, since he is rejected by those who falsify his words. 4 I delivered to you in the beginning what I also received from the apostles who were before me, who at all times were together with Jesus Christ, 5 that our Lord Jesus Christ was born of Mary of the seed of David, when the Holy Spirit was sent down from heaven by the Father into her, 6 that he might come into this world and redeem all flesh through his own flesh, and that he might raise up from the dead us who are fleshly, even as he has shown himself as our example. 7 And since the man was created by his Father, 8 for this reason he was also sought when he went to his corruption, that he might be made alive by sonship. 9 For the God who is almighty over all things, who made heaven and earth, first sent the prophets to the Jews, that they might be snatched away from their sins; 10 for he had determined to save the house of Israel. Now he sent a portion of the spirit of Christ into the prophets, who at many times proclaimed the inerrant worship of God. 11 But since (the prince who was unrighteous) wished himself to be (God), he influenced them and so fettered all human flesh to desire. 12 God, the almighty, who is righteous and did not want to repudiate his own creation, 13 sent the Holy Spirit through fire into Mary the Galilean, (14 who believed with all her heart, and she received the Holy Spirit in her body that Jesus might enter into the world,) 15 in order that through the same flesh by the corruption of which he held sway, the evil one might be conquered, and convinced that he was not God. 16 For by his own body Jesus Christ has saved all flesh 17 by representing a temple of righteousness in his body, 18 through whom we are freed. 19 They are thus not children of righteousness but children of wrath, who reject the providence of God, saying that heaven and earth and all that is in them are not

223

works of the Father, 20 for they have the accursed faith of the serpent. 21 From them turn away, and flee from their teaching! (22 For you are not sons of disobedience but of the most dearly beloved church. 23 Therefore the time of the resurrection is proclaimed.) 24 As for those who tell you that there is no resurrection of the flesh, for them there will be no resurrection, 25 who do not believe in him who is thus risen. 26 For indeed, you Corinthians, they do not know about the sowing of wheat or the other seeds, that they are cast naked into the ground and when they have perished below are raised again by the will of God as a body and clothed, 27 so that the body which was cast off (into the earth) is not only raised up, but also abundantly blessed. 28 If it is necessary that we derive the similitude not just from the seeds, but from nobler bodies, 29 know that Jonah the son of Amathios, when he would not preach in Nineveh, but fled, was swallowed by a whale, 30 and after three days and three nights God heard Jonah's prayer out of the deepest abyss, and no part of him was damaged, not even a hair or an eyelid. 31 How much more, O you of little faith, will he raise you up who have believed in Christ Jesus as he himself was raised up? 32 And if, when a corpse was thrown by the children of Israel upon the bones of the prophet Elisha, the man's body rose up, so you also who have been cast upon the body and bones and Spirit of the Lord shall rise up on that day with your flesh whole. 34 Now if you receive anything else, do not cause me trouble; 35 for I have these fetters on my hand that I may gain Christ, and his marks in my body that I may attain to the resurrection from the dead. 36 And if anyone abides by the rule which he received through the blessed prophets and the holy gospel, he shall receive a reward. 37 But if anyone turns aside from this, there is fire for him and for those who go before him in the way, 38 since they are godless men, a generation of vipers; 39 from these turn away in the power of the Lord, 40 and peace will be with you. Amen.

Translated from Papyrus Bodmer X, ed. Michel Testuz, *Papyrus Bodmer X–XII*, 1959, 33–45, on the basis of Schneemelcher-Wilson (n.243), 255–6, with some emendations.

3. *The Letter to Rheginos from Nag Hammadi*

(43,25) There are some, my son Rheginos, who want to learn many things. They have this goal when they are occupied with questions whose answer is lacking. 30 If they succeed with these (answers), they usually think very highly of themselves. But I do not think that they have stood within the Word of Truth. They seek 35 rather their own rest, which we have received through our Saviour, our Lord the Christ. 44,1 We received it when we came to know the truth. And in it we came to rest.

But since you ask us 5 as is fitting and in friendliness about the resurrection, I am writing you (to say) that it is necessary. To be sure, there are many who do not believe in it, but there are some (few) 10 who find it. So then, let us discuss the matter.

How did the Lord proclaim things while he existed 15 in the flesh and when he revealed himself as Son of God? He went around in this place (= the world) in which you live, speaking 20 against the law of nature – but I call it (= the law) 'death'. Now the Son of God, Rheginos, was son of man; and he embraced both (natures), 25 as he possessed the humanity and the divinity, so that on the one hand he might vanquish death through his being Son of God, 30 and that on the other hand through the Son of Man the restoration to the Pleroma might occur. For he was originally from above, 35 a seed of the Truth, before the structure had come into being in which many dominions and divinities came into existence.

I know that I am presenting 45,1 the solution in difficult terms, but there is nothing difficult in the Word of Truth – because 5 the solution comes into the middle so as not to leave anything hidden, but to disclose all things openly concerning coming to be. The destruction 10 of evil on the one hand, and the revelation of the elect on the other, *that* is the bringing forth of truth and the Spirit; Grace is of the Truth. The Saviour swallowed up 15 death – you are not reckoned among the ignorant – for he put aside the world which is perishing. He

225

transformed [it] into an imperishable Aeon and raised it up, having 20 swallowed up the visible by the invisible. And he gave us the way of our immortality. Then, indeed, as the Apostle (= Paul) 25 said, 'We suffered with him, and we arose with him. and we went to heaven with him.' Now if we are manifest in 30 this world wearing him, we are that one's beams, and we are embraced by him until our setting: that is 35 to say our death in this life. We will be drawn to heaven by him, like beams by the sun, not being restrained by anything. This is 40 the spiritual (pneumatic) resurrection 46,1 which swallows up the psychic in the same way as the fleshly.

But if there is anyone who does not believe, it is not 5 (possible) to persuade him. For it is the principle of faith, my son, and not that which belongs to persuasion: the dead shall arise!

And there is one who believes among the philosophers who are in this place (= the world). 10 At least he will arise. And let not the philosopher who is in these places have cause to believe that he is one who returns by himself. And through our faith we have known the Son of 15 Man, and we have come to believe that he arose from among the dead. This is he of whom we say, 'He has become the destruction of death.' For he is a great one 20 in whom one believes and those who believe (in him) are (also) great. The thought of those who are saved shall not perish; the mind of those who have known him shall not perish. 25 Therefore, we are elected to salvation and redemption, since we are predestined from the beginning not to fall into the foolishness of those who are without knowledge, 30 but we shall enter into the wisdom of those who have known the Truth. Indeed, the Truth which is kept cannot be abandoned, nor did it (ever) come into being.

35 Strong is the system of the Pleroma; small is that which broke loose (and) became (the) world. But the All is what is encompassed. It has not 47,1 come into being; it was existing. So, do not doubt concerning the resurrection, my son Rheginos. For if you were not existing 5 in the flesh, you received flesh when you entered this world. Why should you not receive flesh when you ascend into the Aeon, which is better than the flesh, though 10 it is (at the same time the) cause of life for it (= the flesh). That which came into being on your account, is it not yours? But does not what is yours exist with you? Yet, while you are in these places, what is it that you 15 lack? This is what you have been making every effort to learn. The afterbirth of the body is old age, and you are perishable. You have 20 loss as a gain, for you will not give up something exquisite if you depart. The bad has the

property of diminution, but there is grace for it. Nothing, 25 then, redeems us from these places, but the All – which we are – we are saved. We have received salvation utterly. Let us think in this way! 30 Let us comprehend in this way!

But there are some (who) wish to understand in the enquiry about those things they are looking into, whether he who is saved, if he leaves 35 his body behind, will be saved immediately. Let no one doubt concern this: (in the old fetters) the visible members which are dead 48 shall not be saved: for (only) the living [members] which exist within them will rise.

What, then, is the resurrection? 5 It is the continuing manifestation of those who have risen. For if you remember reading in the Gospel, 'Elijah appeared and Moses 10 with him' (Mark 9.4 parr), do not think the resurrection is an illusion. It is no illusion, but it is truth. Indeed, it is more fitting to say that the 15 world is an illusion – rather than the resurrection which has come into being through our Lord the Saviour, Jesus, the Christ.

20 But what am I teaching you now? Those who are living shall die. How illusory is their life! The rich have become poor, 25 and the kings have been overthrown. Everything is prone to change, the world is an illusion – not to disparage things 30 even more. But the resurrection does not have this aforesaid character, for it is the truth which stands firm, and it is the revelation of 35 what is, and the transformation of things, and a transition into a new being. For imperishability 49,1 [comes] down upon the perishable, and the light streams over the darkness, swallowing it up. And the Pleroma 5 fills up the deficiency. These are the symbols and the images of the resurrection; that is what produces the good. Therefore, do not 10 think (only) in part, O Rheginos, nor live in conformity with this flesh for the sake of unity, but depart from the divisions and the 15 fetters, and already you have the resurrection.

For if he who will die knows about himself that he will die – even if he spends many 20 years in this life, he is brought to this – why not consider yourself as risen and (already) brought to this? 25 If you have the resurrection but continue as if you are to die, and yet one knows that he has died, why, then, do I let your 30 lack of practice go?

It is fitting for each one to practise in a number of ways, in order to be (thus) released from this element, that he may not fall into error but shall receive himself 35 as he first was.

These things I have received from the generosity of my 50,1 Lord,

Jesus, the Christ. [I have] taught you and your [brethren], my sons, concerning them, without omitting any of the things suitable for strengthening you. 5 But if there is anything written which is (too) obscure in my exposition of the word, I shall explain it to you when you (pl.) ask. But now, do not be jealous of anyone who is in your number 10 when he is able to help. Many are looking into what I have written to you. These I am instructing about the peace in them and the grace. 15 I greet you together with those who love you in brotherly love.

The Treatise on the Resurrection.

The basis for the present translation is the edition of the text from NHS XXXII (Harold W. Attridge, *Nag Hammadi Codex* I [The Jung Codex], 1985)

Notes

1. Gerd Lüdemann, *Untersuchungen zur simonianischen Gnosis*, GTA 1, 1975; cf. my summary and development of this in 'The Acts of the Apostles and the Beginning of Simonian Gnosis', *NTS* 33, 1987, 420–6 (with bibliography). The most recent article on Simon Magus is by Klaus Berger, 'Propaganda und Gegenpropaganda im frühen Christentum: Simon Magus als Gestalt des samaritanischen Christentums', in *Religious Propaganda and Missionary Competition in the New Testament World. Essays Honoring Dieter Georgi*, NT.S 74, 1994, 313–17 (= id., *Theologiegeschichte des Urchristentums. Theologie des Neuen Testaments*, 1994, 159–62). His conclusion is: 'What has hitherto been regarded as an exotic heresy (the "Gnosis" of Simon Magus) is in origin a schism among Samaritan Christians. Luke merely states that there are non-apostolic Christians there' (316). Later, he claims, 'the further course of the schismatic Samaritan Christians led into Gnosis' (ibid.). Berger's article is written without asking any redaction-critical questions and in sovereign disregard of the history of the tradition of Simonian Gnosis which – according to the consensus of scholars – assimilated Christian features only at a secondary stage. Furthermore, there can hardly be serious dispute that the statement about Simon's baptism (Acts 8.13) derives from his opponents, who in this way wanted to emphasize his subordination to Christian missionaries like Philip. Here Berger's unexplained confidence in the historical reliability of Acts takes its revenge. According to Berger, however, plausibility is 'the only criterion for a historical reconstruction' (Berger, *Theologiegeschichte*, 133). But that would also allow the stories of Karl May to be proved historical (Conzelmann). And precisely what does it mean when Berger says, 'We trust Luke's accounts... but by no means in a naive way' (ibid., 141)? In order to avoid misunderstanding, let me make it clear that in contrast to a large number of redaction critics I regard the historical value of Acts as high, though this verdict applies mainly to the historical value of the traditions used by its author (cf. Gerd Lüdemann, *Early Christianity according to the Traditions in Acts. A Commentary*, 1987). It is a long way from here to the way in which Berger deals with Acts!

2. The most important are: *Opposition to Paul in Jewish Christianity*, 1989; 'Zur Geschichte des ältesten Christentums in Rom. I. Valentin und

Marcion, II. Ptolemäus und Justin', *ZNW* 70, 1979, 86–114; 'Zum Antipaulinismus im frühen Christentum', *EvTh* 40, 1980, 437–55.

3. Gerd Lüdemann, *The Resurrection of Jesus: History, Experience, Theology*, 1994. Cf. Hansjürgen Verweyen (ed.), *Osterglaube ohne Auferstehung? Diskussion mit Gerd Lüdemann*, QD 155, 1995; Alexander Bommarius (ed.), *Fand die Auferstehung wirklich statt? Eine Diskussion mit Gerd Lüdemann*, 1995.

4. Cf. Adolf Harnack, *Lehrbuch der Dogmengeschichte* III, 1890, viii. Here Harnack expresses the wish to 'help to break the real great power in the theological struggles of the present – ignorance'.

5. It appears in a blatant form in an article by Jan Ross in the *Frankfurter Allgemeine Zeitung* of 15 April 1995, 29, in which under the headline 'The Enlightenment of Jesus' the historicity of Matt. 27.62–66 (the guard on the tomb at the instigation of the Jews, to prevent the theft of Jesus' body by disciples) is presupposed right from the start. That is not just deception but – when repeated today – sheer anti-Judaism.

6. Gotthold Ephraim Lessing, *Werke, Achter Band, Theologiekritische Schriften III, Philosophische Schriften*, 1979, 309–13, 335–41.

7. Gustav Krüger, *Die Entstehung des Neuen Testaments*, 1896, 26.

8. Cf. Hartmut Stegemann, *Die Essener, Qumran, Johannes der Täufer und Jesus. Ein Sachbuch*, ¹1994.

9. *The Nag Hammadi Library in English. Translated by Members of the Coptic Library Project of the Institute for Antiquity and Christianity*, 1977. This translation has meanwhile been published in a third, revised edition (1988). It was a truly historic moment when at the annual meeting of the Society of Biblical Literature in San Francisco in December 1977 this pioneering work of North American biblical scholarship was presented to the public. It made symbolically clear that the former predominance of German exegesis had come to an end for ever. However, it is also clear that German biblical scholarship in the time of Harnack would not have missed the opportunity to make a swift translation of this pioneering discovery.

10. On this see e.g. James M. Robinson, 'Die Bedeutung der gnostischen Nag Hammadi Texte für die neutestamentliche Wissenschaft', in *Religious Propaganda* (n.1), 23–41. James D. G. Dunn, *The Parting of the Ways Between Christianity and Judaism and their Significance for the Character of Christianity*, 1991, remarks sweepingly – without having worked on even one Nag-Hammadi writing himself – that the texts have no significance for a pre-Christian idea of a redeemer. He continues: 'The Nag Hammadi fever which afflicted some NT scholars is like the Mandean fever of an earlier generation. It is a persistent virus, but we may entertain a good hope that the healthy body of historical criticism will shake it off in due course' (11). Now the question of a pre-Christian redeemer figure is

certainly not the only point on which the Nag Hammadi texts may be a help in interpreting the New Testament. Furthermore, the absolutist tone in which Dunn expresses his opinion is alienating. That at least in Germany rather more Nag Hammadi fever would be appropriate is evident from the most recent Introduction to the New Testament by Udo Schnelle, *Einleitung in das Neue Testament*, UTB 1830, 1994. He only occasionally touches on the Nag Hammadi texts and at no point goes into the Gospel of Thomas, the earlier parts of which in all probability go back to the pre-synoptic tradition and in part to Jesus himself. Cf. the impressive analyses in Robert W.Funk, Roy W. Hoover, The Jesus Seminar, *The Five Gospels. The Search for the Authentic Words*, 1993, 471–532, and previously in the German-language area Philipp Vielhauer, *Geschichte der urchristlichen Literatur*, 1975, 618–35.

11. Friedrich Nietzsche, *Human, All Too Human*, trans. Helen Zimmern, 1909, I, 257.

12. Cf. Ulrich Luz, in Pinchas Lapide and id., *Der Jude Jesus. Thesen eines Juden. Antworten eines Christen*, 1979, 160f.

13. Stefan Alkier (*Urchristentum. Zur Geschichte und Theologie einer exegetischen Disziplin*, BHTh 83, 1993) offers a history of the concept of 'primitive Christianity' and suggests dispensing with it in the future because it is understood in too positive a sense. (The 'predominant impression of unity, originality, normativity [is given] if one continues to use the term *primitive Christianity*' [264]) He suggests that it should be replaced with 'early Christianity', a term which is already used frequently. I think that this proposal for a linguistic rule is artificial, and will return to it elsewhere (*ThR* 61, 1996).

14. On this cf. most recently Jürgen Becker, *Das Urchristentum als gegliederte Epoche*, SBS 155, 1993. In my view he concludes the period of primitive Christianity too early, seeing the years 120 and 130 CE as 'the transitional area ... which marks the limit of earliest Christianity as a *terminus ad quem*' (12). By contrast, Henning Paulsen, 'Zur Wissenschaft vom Urchristentum und der alten Kirche – ein methodischer Versuch', ZNW 68, 1977, 200–30: 210, remarks: 'The transition from primitive Christianity to the early church, which can be recognized in exemplary fashion in the completion of canonization, takes place in the years between 150 and180.' For further reasons see below.

15. However, other divisions at present predominate in the literature and in theological and church consciousness generally, e.g. into an apostolic and a post-apostolic age (cf. only Leonhard Goppelt, *Die apostolische und nachapostolische Zeit*, KIG A, ²1966); these will be ignored in the present account, even if they are understood not as a value judgment but merely as chronological terms. The reason for this is that the

concept of an 'apostolic age' 'is an idea, the product of a picture of history, even if this picture was first drawn at an early stage. Of course, there were followers of Jesus who formed the nucleus of the primitive community after his death or after Easter. The founding of the primitive community is identical with the constituting of the circle of the twelve (I Cor. 15.3ff.). But the twelve are not the "twelve apostles". This idea is only developed in the "post-apostolic age", and this gives rise to the "apostolic age". The twelve have no concrete influence on the theology and the form of the church generally. They are influential only as an idea' (Hans Conzelmann, *An Outline of the Theology of the New Testament*, 1969, 290f.; cf. id., 'Die Frage der Einheit der neutestamentlichen Schriften', in J.M. Hollenbach and Hugo Staudinger [eds.], *Moderne Exegese und historische Wissenschaft*, 1972, 67–76: 69f., and the discussion of the 'idea' of an apostolic age which is documented in the same collection [143–5]). However, academic theology can only be concerned with concepts which develop from the subject-matter *itself* and not, as in the case of the 'apostolic age', with fictions of the third (!) generation of early Christianity. Similarly, terms like 'New Testament period' or 'post-New Testament period', which are common in the literature should strictly be avoided in so far as they are meant to denote historical eras, since at that time there was no such thing as the New Testament. For further reasons see below.

16. But cf. now Falk Wagner, *Zur gegenwärtigen Lage des Protestantismus*, 1995, 83: 'The assertion that the historical beginnings of Christianity at the same time guarantee its normative origin and its validity down the ages cannot be substantiated in argument ... As a rule the beginnings of a new movement... are still poor and undeveloped.' Even proximity to Jesus in space and time is inadequate, and 'may not play a constitutive role in the intellectual explanation of the content of "Jesus the Christ", which is not available to the senses' (84). Now if the later proclamation of Jesus was already contained in his words and story (see below, 214f.), then nearness to Jesus in space and time, as a living memory, is to be striven for (see further below, 209).

17. 'If Christianity depends directly on the differentiated history of the earthly Jesus and the original recollection of it, those writings which contain the authentic and original knowledge of the earthly appearances of Jesus have a particular and irreplaceable significance in the framework of Christian theology and the church' (Gunther Wenz, 'Sola Scriptura? Erwägungen zum reformatorischen Schriftprinzip', in Jan Rohls and id. [eds.], *Vernunft des Glaubens. Wissenschaftliche Theologie und kirchliche Lehre [FS Wolfhart Pannenberg]*, 1988, 540–67, here 564).

18. Where he does quote a saying of Jesus (Smyrn.3.2), it is not

canonical and comes from apocryphal writings about the 'risen' Jesus. For the text of this saying cf. below 187f.

19. 'The history of early Christianity can be made historically plausible only if we start from Jesus himself and make this history begin there' (Berger, *Theologiegeschichte* [n.1], 103).

20. Cf. Johann Salomo Semler, *Abhandlung von freier Untersuchung des Canons*, 4 vols., 1771–75; also Gottfried Hornig, *Die Anfänge der historisch-kritischen Theologie. Johann Salomo Semlers Schriftverständnis und Luther*, FSThR 8, 1961; Werner Georg Kümmel, *The New Testament. The History of the Investigation of its Problems*, 1972 (select readings and illuminating explanations).

21. Cf. Adolf Harnack, *Bible Reading in the Early Church*, 1912, 12 (on the historical criticism of the Bible which begins with Semler): 'From this time dates the gradual dissolution of orthodox Protestantism; henceforth it could free itself from the burden of the letter, the burden of the Bible, to receive in exchange the Bible as the fundamental historical document of religion and a book of comfort that knows no terror.'

22. Cf. the volume which arose out of the Dresden Congress of Theologians in 1990, Hans Heinrich Schmid and Joachim Mehlhausen (eds.), *Sola Scriptura. Das reformatorische Schriftprinzip in der säkularen Welt*, 1991; Richard Ziegert (ed.), *Die Zukunft des Schriftprinzips, Bibel im Gespräch* 2, 1994. Ziegert speaks of the 'disaster in the content of the Dresden Congress of Theologians' (8) and in the book which he has edited does not want to 'get stuck in its aporias'. As an outstanding example of a new beginning in the volume edited by Ziegert, mention should be made of Falk Wagner, 'Auch der Teufel zitiert die Bibel. Das Christentum zwischen Autoritätsanspruch und Krise des Schriftprinzips' (236–58), an article which is reprinted in Wagner, *Lage* (n.17), 68–88.

23. Wolfhart Pannenberg, 'The Crisis of the Scriptural Principle' (1962), in *Basic Questions in Theology* 1, 1970, 1–14. Cf. also the article by Pannenberg's pupil Wenz, 'Sola' (n.16). Wenz gives an instructive account of the understanding of scripture by the magisterium of the Roman Catholic church, works out the Reformation theology of scripture and attempts a reformulation of the Reformation principle of scripture under modern conditions. Wenz emphasizes *a priori* that without (Pannenberg's) perspective of the theology of the resurrection 'the problem of scripture, too, cannot be taken to an appropriate solution' (541). Semler's unreservedly positive view proves welcome: Semler unmasks 'as an anachronistic fiction the tacit assumption at least of those early Protestant theologians who hold a strict theory of verbal inspiration that from the beginning there was a limited, unchangeable canon' and 'arrives at the "assertion that only in the second century was a beginning made on the

collection of the New Testament writings, that those lists of the canon which gradually came into being in the individual church provinces were of very different extents, and that the delimitation of the canon in its now familiar form was the result of a process lasting over centuries, of rival traditions and ecclesiastical compromises"' (555; here Wenz is citing Hornig, *Anfänge* [n.20 above], 60). Certainly Wenz states that 'the first word of theology towards historical investigation must not be negative and immunizing but positive and open' (561). Nevertheless, 'if it is to be theologically appropriate and soteriologically helpful, any view of the earthly life of the crucified Jesus of Nazareth has to have the Easter event as a presupposition behind which it is impossible to go' (562). In return, however, one may ask: what is concrete about Easter? Wenz's teacher Pannenberg at least made an attempt to answer this question.

24. Cf. Friedrich Beisser, *Claritas scripturae bei Martin Luther*, 1966; Rudolf Hermann, *Von der Klarheit der Heiligen Schrift. Untersuchungen und Erläuterungen über Luthers Lehre von der Schrift in De Servo Arbitrio*, 1957; Reinar Bring, *Luthers Anschauung von der Bibel*, 1951.

25. Cf. also the account by Ulrich Luz, 'Einheit und Vielfalt neutestamentlicher Theologien', in id. and Hans Weder, *Die Mitte des Neuen Testaments. Einheit und Vielfalt neutestamentlicher Theologie (FS Eduard Schweizer)*, 1983, 142–61.

26. Similarly again today Reinhard Slenczka, *Kirchliche Entscheidungen in theologischer Verantwortung. Grundlagen – Kriterien – Grenzen*, 1991; he argues that it is a mistake to say that 'holy scripture *contains* God's word in human discourse' (59), but it is not the word of God, since 'this view separates the spirit and the letter in Holy Scripture' (ibid.). Rather, '*the Holy Scripture of the Old and New Testaments is the word of the triune God in which he makes himself known and through which he speaks and acts in the present*' (38). On this cf. my remarks 'Zwischen Karfreitag und Ostern', in Hansjürgen Verweyen (ed.), *Osterglaube ohne Auferstehung? Diskussion mit Gerd Lüdemann*, QD 155, ²1995, 13–46: 14–16.

27. Emanuel Hirsch, 'Verkündigung und Zwiesprache', in Joachim Ringleben (ed.), *Christentumgeschichte und Wahrheitsbewusstsein. Studien zur Theologie Emanuel Hirschs*, TBT 50, 1992, 247–54: 247.

38. It is to some degree the exegetical variant of the Word of God theology, and is closely related to it.

29. It is no coincidence that Hans Conzelmann's 1974 collection of articles (BEvTh 65) bears the title *Theologie als Schriftauslegung*. For the question whether theology must necessarily be exegesis cf. the acute comments of Hans-Joachim Dörger, *Kirche in der Öffentlichkeit*, 1979, 86–8.

30. Cf. the popular phrase 'get behind something', 'get to the bottom of',

i.e. discover the real situation, the true history. In the phrases quoted, English (and German) contains what has already been conceptualized as 'hermeneutical suspicion'. Cf. also the protest by Jörg Baur, 'Sola Scriptura – historisches Erbe und bleibende Bedeutung', in Schmid/Mehlhausen, *Sola* (n.22), 19–43: 43: 'This word of scripture which concerns us is not robbed of its power by containing in itself the difference between event and word which is brought out by criticism, since it does not claim to provide information about facts or to surpass the achievements of reason in competition with the scientific knowledge of the world. Therefore there is no need, either, to assure oneself of the truth of the word in history "behind the texts".'

31. Günter Klein, *Rekonstruction und Interpretation*, BEvTh 50, 1969, preface. Cf. similarly Udo Schnelle, 'Sachgemässe Schriftauslegung', *NT* 30, 1988, 115–31:131: the historical-critical method 'understands ... itself as having a function which serves the word of God'. (In this article there is no mention of the problem of the canon.)

32. For criticism cf. my article 'Die Religionsgeschichtliche Schule und ihre Konsequenzen für die Neutestamentliche Wissenschaft', in Hans Martin Müller (ed.), *Kulturprotestantismus. Beiträge zu einer Gestalt des modernen Christentums*, 1992, 311–38.

33. It is not doing Hans Conzelmann an injustice to say that his *History of Primitive Christianity*, 1973, is not an exception. He tells the reader right at the beginning that he is presenting 'more of a presentation of historical *problems* that call for study than a flowing historical narrative which he can assimilate with pleasure (sic!). The reason for this lies in the very nature of the case' (13). 'A "pleasing" (sic!) presentation would above all have to follow the course of external events and bring out the dramatic high points ... The new teaching does not spread, so to speak, by contagion. It is borne through the world by witnesses of the faith because the Lord of the church wills to be recognized as Lord of the *world*. Therein the church knows that the success is not the result of human cleverness; it is the Lord himself who "adds" believers (Acts 2.47)' (14). What is the purpose of the polemic against the 'agreeable' account? Of course a historical account will also have to take account of all those factors which Conzelmann seeks to bracket off. Furthermore, what is the function and expressive power of the statement that the Lord himself adds believers? Presumably the kind of twofold concept of history which Heinrich Ott has diagnosed in the case of Rudolf Bultmann (*Geschichte und Heilsgeschichte in der Theologie Rudolf Bultmanns*, 1954) also underlies Conzelmann's account: history is understood (a) as external history and (b) as historicity (*tua res agitur*), as though the two could be separated. The theological judgments then often no longer have anything to do with empirical

history (e.g. Paul's negative judgments on Judaism as a religion of righteousness by works [cf. Lüdemann, 'Schule' [n.32], 329f.). Moreover Conzelmann's book has a critically corrected Lukan outline and therefore (!) does not touch historically and theologically on many questions like e.g. that of the historical context of the Gospels. The highly learned work of his old age, *Gentiles – Jews – Christians. Polemics and Apologetics in the Greco-Roman Era* (1981), 1991 in particular also shows the difficulty he has with the trend of scholarship which stands close to historicism (cf. his polemical introduction).

34. Leonhard Goppelt, *Christentum und Judentum im ersten und zweiten Jahrhundert. Ein Aufriss der Urgeschichte der Kirche*, BFCTh 2/55, 1954 (references to the book are put in brackets in the text); cf. also id., *Die apostolische und nachapostolische Zeit*, KIG A, ²1966.

35. For criticism of Goppelt, *Christentum*, cf. Georg Strecker, ZKG 67, 1955/56, 157–63.

36. Cf. on this Ernst Käsemann (ed.), *Das Neue Testament als Kanon. Dokumentation und kritische Analyse zur gegenwärtigen Diskussion*, 1970.

37. Gustav Krüger, *Das Dogma vom neuen Testament*, 1896, 4 (his italics).

38. A survey of the dedications and prefaces to theological and academic books would be rewarding here. To give just two examples, which could easily be multiplied: in the preface to his commentary on Romans, Ulrich Wilckens writes that one only understands Paul if one prays with him. 'Anyone who on going through Romans becomes aware how all the lines of Paul's thought move towards the *ingens miraculum* of this event in the death and resurrection of Jesus and thus the conceptual structure of the whole movement of his thought calls for and makes possible a rethinking in this direction which will constantly fall into prayer, into worship, in such reflection' (Ulrich Wilckens, *Der Brief an die Römer* (Röm 1–5], EKK VI/1, 1978, vi). Gerhard Sellin (*Der Streit um die Auferstehung der Toten. Eine religionsgeschichtliche und exegetische Untersuchung zu 1 Korinther 15*, FRLANT 138, 1986) already remarks in his foreword: 'The Corinthian idealism is unmasked as a style of self-glorification which awards itself eternity' (5). In that case who could dare possibly to contradict Paul and take sides with his opponents, though they were also Christians? Furthermore, it is significant that right up to its twenty-fifth edition, the *Novum Testamentum Graece*, i.e. the scholarly (!) edition of the Greek New Testament, could contain as quasi-missionary-pastoral advice a saying of the Pietist Johann Albrecht Bengel from 1734: '*Te totum applica ad textum; rem totam applica ad te*' ('Apply yourself totally to the text, apply the content totally to yourself').

39. Cf. only Karl Barth, *Church Dogmatics*, 1936ff.; Hermann Diem, *Theologie als kirchliche Wissenschaft. Handreichung zur Einübung ihrer Probleme*, 1951; id., *Dogmatik. Ihr Weg zwischen Historismus und Existentialismus*, 1955; id., *Theologie als kirchliche Wissenschaft. Handreichung zur Einübung ihrer Probleme III, Die Kirche und ihre Praxis*, 1963. See also Hans Martin Müller, 'Kirchliche Praxis als Zielpunkt der Universitätstheologie', *Pastoraltheologie* 79, 1990, 317–26. Underlying his remarks is the conviction that the academic quality of theology in particular depends on its evangelical character and *therefore* the confessional links of the Protestant faculties of theology are to be affirmed.

40. Cf. my article 'Das Wissenschaftsverständnis der Religionsgeschichtlichen Schule im Rahmen des Kulturprotestantismus', in Hans Martin Müller (ed.), *Kulturprotestantismus. Beiträge zu einer Gestalt des modernen Christentums*, 1992, 78–107: 102f. (with bibliography). Cf. in addition Johannes Gottschick, *Die Kirchlichkeit der s.(ogenannten) k.(irchlichen) Theologie geprüft*, 1890. (In this work Gottschick examines the 'right of the claim to the prerogative of representing the church which is raised by a particular trend in theology' [v] and arrives at a negative result.)

41. Oskar Pfister, *Die Aufgabe der Wissenschaft vom christlichen Glauben in der Gegenwart*, 1923, 13.

42. Cf. Carl Albrecht Bernoulli, *Die wissenschaftliche und die kirchliche Methode in der Theologie*, 1897; Gustav Krüger, 'Die unkirchliche Theologie', *ChW* 14, 1900, 804–7; id., *Der Historismus und die Bibel*, 1925, 20 n.23: 'I still do not want to retract anything from my article on "unchurchly theology"... The development has demonstrated fully that what I more hinted than said there is correct.' The development to which he was referring is on p.16: 'I see a danger to this life itself in the exclusiveness with which people (today) retreat to the Bible as the sole foundation document of our religious life.'

43. Wilhelm Herrmann, *ThLZ* 23, 1898, 65 (= review of Bernouilli, *Methode* [n.42]).

44. Klaus Berger, *Hermeneutik des Neuen Testaments*, 1988, 112.

45. Cf. e.g. Joachim Jeremias, *The Eucharistic Words of Jesus*, 1966, 8. This opinion has often been accepted in the subsequent period.

46. Wolfgang Schenk, 'Textverarbeitung in Frühjudentum, Frühkirche und Gnosis', in Karl-Wolfgang Tröger (ed.), *Altes Testament – Frühjudentum – Gnosis*, 1980, 299–313: 313. Cf. also the remark on 309: 'Any exegetical work and academic discussion among scholars on the meaning of a text would be impossible or nonsensical if the hermeneutical theory were correct that there was no possibility of decoding the objective content of a text as a theoretical construction of the meaning of a

work, i.e. if there were no interpretation that was immanent within the work.'

47. Wayne A.Meeks, *The First Urban Christians. The Social World of the Apostle Paul*, 1983, 1f.

48. Cf. E.P.Sanders, *Jesus and Judaism*, 1985, 63.

49. Gerhard Ebeling, 'The Significance of the Critical Historical Method for Church and Theology in Protestantism', in *Word and Faith*, 1963, 17–61: 60. Cf. also Gerhard Ebeling, *Theologie und Verkündigung. Ein Gespräch mit Rudolf Bultmann*, HUTh 1, 1962, 1–9 (on 'the tension between academic theology and the preaching of the church').

50. *Institutiones historiae ecclesiasticae novi testamenti*, 1726 and 1737, enlarged to modern times 1741, revised 1755. The basic work on Mosheim continues to be Emanuel Hirsch, *Geschichte der neuern evange- lischen Theologie* II, ⁴1968, 354–9 (a book which ought to be translated into English); cf. his brief characterization: 'A cool clear head and an unprejudiced scholar, in whose cradle the fairy put the gift of scientific method, keeping himself far from the conflicts and fights of men, untouched by Pietism, but committed to the interests of a state church administration aiming without prejudice at popular education, praising everywhere the golden mean, his influence stems...from the insight and achievement that is his...' (354).

51. Cf. Walter Nigg, *Die Epochen der Kirchengeschichtsschreibung*, 1934, 110.

52. For attempts in the present to turn the wheel back in connection with the 'resurrection' of Jesus see n.281 below.

53. Bernd Moeller, 'Johann Lorenz von Mosheim und die Gründung der Göttinger Universität', in id. (ed.), *Theologie in Göttingen. Eine Vorlesungsreihe*, 1987, 9–40:19f. Moeller does not agree with Hirsch, *Geschichte* II (n.50), 355, that Mosheim deliberately detached church history from his theology, 'at any rate not if the concept of theology is sufficiently wide' (22). But this criticism does not apply, since Hirsch explicitly says of Mosheim that according to him 'theology is ... only dogmatics and ethics' (355). On this see further Ekkehard Mühlenberg, 'Dogmatik und Kirchengeschichte', in Rohls and Wenz (eds.), *Vernunft des Glaubens* (n.17), 436–53: 440–4.

54. For the present discussion on the task of church history cf. Peter Meinhold, *Geschichte der kirchlichen Historiographie* II, OA III/5, 1967, 481–544 (with extracts from texts); Raymund Kottje (ed.), *Kirchen- geschichte heute. Geschichtswissenschaft oder Theologie?*, with contribu- tions by Norbert Brox, Erwin Iserloh, Hubert Jedin, Heinrich Lutz and Peter Stockmeier, 1970; Christoph Markschies, *Arbeitsbuch Kirchen- geschichte*, UTB 1857, 1995, 150–3; Friedrich de Boor, 'Kirchengeschichte

oder Auslegungsgeschichte?', *TLZ* 97, 1972, cols.401–14; the author is critical of Gerhard Ebeling, *Kirchengeschichte als Geschichte der Auslegung der Heiligen Schrift*, SgV 189, 1947 (= id., *Wort Gottes und Tradition. Studien zu einer Hermeneutik der Konfessionen*, KiKonf 7, 1964, 9–27), and emphasizes that church history only becomes understandable 'if account is taken of the political, social and cultural forces which have influenced the course of church history from outside, but very much also from within' (412). Ebeling's approach is not relevant to my own work since at the beginning of Christianity stands not the New Testament – or the Old Testament either – but Jesus himself, whose special character is not parallel to that of the New Testament canon, as Ebeling curiously thinks (*Kirchengeschichte*, 23).

55. Cf. E. Troeltsch, 'Voraussetzungslose Wissenschaft' (1897), in id., *Gesammelte Schriften II. Zur religiösen Lage, Religionsphilosophie und Ethik*, 1913, 183–92.

56. Cf. Eduard Spranger, *Der Sinn der Voraussetzungslosigkeit in den Geisteswissenschaften*, SAB, phil.-hist.Klasse, 1929, 2–30.

57. The last sentences are quoted literally from Walter Nigg, *Franz Overbeck. Versuch einer Würdigung*, 1931, 112ff., who bases himself on the unpublished papers of Franz Overbeck.

58. Franz Overbeck, 'Nachlass Historica', in Nigg, *Overbeck* (n.57), 114.

59. Cf. Lüdemann, *Christianity* (n.1), 21; cf. also Leander E. Keck, 'Is the New Testament a Field of Study? or, From Outler to Overbeck and Back', *The Second Century* 1, 1981, 19–35.

60. Cf. Franz Overbeck, *Zur Geschichte des Kanons*, 1880 (= 1965), 72; cf. Nigg, *Overbeck* (n.57), 115.

61. For the historical orientation of New Testament study cf. the programmatic article by Martin Hengel, 'Aufgaben der neutestamentlichen Wissenschaft', *NTS* 40, 1994, 321–57, which is great in its way. But I have the following criticism to make. Despite all the admirable breadth of his view of the setting of early Christianity and what led up to it and followed from it historically, Hengel remains imprisoned in dialectical theology and all the weaknesses in the investigation of earliest Christianity which stem from it. What else is one to say of the following statements? The New Testament, Hengel argues, 'is... about "God's free address", his "claim" on us, his wilful creatures: Heb.1.1–2; John 1.1–18. As a Christian theologian I cannot go back on that' (328 n.26). The view that there was only a contradictory multiplicity of messages in the early Christian period is 'also contradicted by the amazing cohesion of the Christian communities at the end of the first century and in the second, indeed by the fact that despite all the special movements and divisions the one church, what we

call the "early church", could take shape' (349). Hengel here presupposes without considering the matter that the so-called early church in the second century could *rightly* appeal to the beginnings, going back to Jesus, and the heretics could not. But that is precisely the question! At this point the dogmatic standpoint of the old master of Tübingen, in whom radical historical criticism and dogmatics (of what kind?) manifestly stand side by side in abrupt juxtaposition, takes its revenge. Elsewhere I have written on Joachim Jeremias and Otto Michel and the generation of their pupils which includes Hengel, as a pupil of Michel (the article is dedicated to his memory), that in contrast to Bultmann and his pupils they had an unclarified relationship to supernaturalism (Lüdemann, 'Schule' [n.32], 333). Hengel dismisses this article in a note (328 n.6) with the misleading remark that it *refers* to the larger study by Heikki Räisänen (*Beyond New Testament Theology. A Story and a Programme*, 1990). But what I wrote was that my article had *points of contact* with Räisänen's work (311 n.1). So at this point I would like emphatically to repeat that Hengel has an unclarified relationship to supernaturalism, since for him there are certain absolute fixed points in New Testament theology ('the church', 'God's free address', and so on – all terms from the arsenal of a dogmatic theology).

62. For him, in addition to Nigg, *Overbeck* (n.57), in general see the admirable account by Niklaus Peter, *Im Schatten der Modernität. Franz Overbecks Weg zur 'Christlichkeit unserer heutigen Theologie'*, 1992.

63. Nigg, *Overbeck* (n.57), 126.

64. Ibid., 127.

65. Here it makes the claim credible for others: cf. Dietz Lange, *Erfahrung und die Glaubwürdigkeit des Glaubens*, HUTh 18, 1984.

66. Erich Seeberg, *Krisis der Kirche und des Christentums heute*, SGV 185, 1939, 22. The sentence continues: 'However, be this as it may, all authentic theology has its source in experienced religion, and the broad aim of all theological work is – we may confidently say – to engender religion' (22f.).

67. Wilhelm Bousset, *Kyrios Christos. A History of the Belief in Christ from the Beginnings of Christianity to Irenaeus* (²1921), 1970.

68. Cf. Walter Schmithals, *Theologiegeschichte des Urchristentums. Eine problemgeschichtliche Darstellung*, 1994; Berger, *Theologiegeschichte* (n.1).

69. Cf. E.P.Meijering, *Die Hellenisierung des Christentums im Urteil Adolf von Harnacks*, 1985.

70. Cf. Peter Lampe, *Die stadtrömischen Christen in den ersten beiden Jahrhunderten*, WUNT II/18, ²1989.

71. Cf. Winfried Elliger, *Paulus in Griechenland. Philippi, Thessalonich, Athen, Korinth*, SBS 92/93, 1978.

72. Cf. Matthias Günther, *Die Frühgeschichte des Christentums in Ephesus*, Arbeiten zur Religion und Geschichte des Urchristentums 1, 1995 (with bibliography).

73. Cf. Lukas Bormann, *Philippi. Stadt und Christengemeinde zur Zeit des Schreibens des Paulus*, NT.S 78, 1995.

74. Cf. Frederick W.Norris, 'Antiochien I', *TRE* 3, 1978, 99–103 (with bibliography).

75. Cf. Kurt Rudolph, 'Das frühe Christentum in Ägypten. Zwischen Häresie und Orthodoxie', *Riggisberger Berichte* I, 1993, 21–31 (with bibliography).

76. See Walter Nigg, *Das Buch der Ketzer*, ⁴1962; Roland H. Bainton (ed.), *Concerning Heretics. Whether They Are to be Persecuted and How They Are to be Treated. A Collection of the Opinions of Learned Men both Ancient and Modern. An Anyonymous Work attributed to Sebastian Castellio*, 1965; Hans-Jürgen Schulz (ed.), *Die Wahrheit der Ketzer*, 1968; Hans-Georg Beck, *Vom Umgang mit Ketzern. Der Glaube der kleinen Leute und die Macht der Theologen*, 1993.

77. Alfred Schindler, 'Häresie II. Kirchengeschichtlich', *TRE* 14, 1985, 318–41: 320.

78. Cf. also Alain Le Boulluec, *La notion d'hérésie dans la littérature grecque des IIe–IIIe siècles, tome I: De Justin à Irénée, tome II: Clément d'Alexandrie et Origène*, 1985; Norbert Brox, 'Häresie', *RAC* 13, 1986, 248–97; Kurt Rudolph, 'Heresy', *The Encyclopedia of Religion* 6, 1987, 269–77.

79. The German word *Ketzer* derives from terms for the 'Cathars' (Greek *katharoi* = the pure; Italian *gazzari*). 'The Cathari or "neo-Manichaeans" were connected with dualistic heretics in the East. Their main characteristic was therefore their strict asceticism' (Karl Heussi, *Kompendium der Kirchengeschichte*, ¹²1960, 217).

80. Adolf Hilgenfeld, *Die Ketzergeschichte des Urchristenthums urkundlich dargestellt*, 1884 (= 1966). For Hilgenfeld see Lüdemann, *Opposition* (n.2), 18–20 and 229f. (with bibliography). Hilgenfeld was *not* a personal pupil of F.C.Baur; he did not even know him personally (on Christoph Markschies, 'Alte und neue Texte und Forschungen zu Valentin und den Anfängen der "Valentinianischen" Gnosis – Von J. E. Grabe und F. C. Baur bis B. Aland', in Alexander Böhlig and id. [ed.], *Gnosis und Manichäismus. Forschungen und Studien zu Texten von Valentin und Mani sowie zu den Bibliotheken von Nag Hammadi und Medinet Madi*, BZNW 72, 1994, 39–111: 49).

81. Gottfried Arnold, *Unpartheyische Kirchen- und Ketzer-Historie vom Anfänge des Neuen Testaments biss auf das Jahr Christi 1688*, Teil I/II, 1699; Teil III/IV, 1700; Johann Lorenz von Mosheim, *Versuch einer*

unpartheiischen und gründlichen Ketzergeschichte, 1746; id., *Ander-weitiger Versuch einer vollständigen und unpartheyischen Ketzer-geschichte*, 1748; C. W. Franz Walch, *Ketzergeschichte* (11 vols.), 1762–85.

82. For the anti-heretical works of the first century cf. Chapter 2 below.

83. Walter Bauer, *Orthodoxy and Heresy in Earliest Christianity* (1934, ²1964); a revised American edition appeared in Philadelphia and London in 1971 under the aegis of the Philadelphia Seminar on Christian Origins. Cf. the review of the German second edition by Hans Dieter Betz, 'Orthodoxy and Heresy in Primitive Christianity', *Int* 19 ,1965, 299–311. For Walter Bauer, cf. Georg Strecker, 'Walter Bauer – Exeget, Philologe und Historiker', in id., *Eschaton und Historie*, 1979, 360–6. Strecker also edited *Walter Bauer, Aufsatz und Kleine Schriften*, 1967. Adolf Martin Ritter, '"Orthodoxie", "Häresie" und die Einheit der Kirche in vorkon-stantinischer Zeit', in id., *Charisma und Caritas*, 1993, 249–64: 249f. with bibliography, rightly emphasizes that the discussion of Bauer's work is not yet finished. On p.250 he speaks of the 'towering significance of Bauer's book'. Cf. also Helmut Koester, *Ancient Christian Gospels. Their History and Development*, 1990, xxx: 'The appearance of a second edition of this epochal work thirty years after its original publication and four years after the death of its author as well as the publication of an English translation signified a fundamental change in the climate of scholarship.' For the further reception of Bauer's work cf. Daniel J. Harrington, 'The Reception of Walter Bauer's *Orthodoxy and Heresy in Earliest Christianity during the Last Decade*', HTR 73, 1980, 287–98 (a splendid survey which accuses Bauer methodologically of a failure to take sociological theories into account [e.g. Max Weber] and theologically of a lack of interest in theology in the narrower sense); cf. also Robert L. Wilken, 'Diversity and Unity in Early Christianity', *The Second Century* 1, 1981, 101–10; Gary T. Burke, 'Walter Bauer and Celsus: The Shape of Late Second-Century Christianity', *The Second Century* 4, 1984, 1–8; Margaret Y. Macdonald, *The Pauline Churches. A Socio-historical Study of Institutionalization in the Pauline and Deutero-Pauline Writings*, SNTS.MS 60, 1988, 225–34 (who argues that Bauer is dealing in the history of ideas); Birger A. Pearson, *Gnosticism, Judaism, and Egyptian Christianity*, 1990, 194–213 ('Gnosticism in Early Egyptian Christianity'); Michel Desjardins, 'Bauer and Beyond: On Recent Scholarly Discussion of Hairesis in the Early Christian Era', *The Second Century* 8, 1991, 65–82. For the historical problem of heresy and orthodoxy cf. also Martin Elze, 'Häresie und Einheit der Kirche im 2.Jahrhundert', ZThK 71, 1974, 389–409; Josef Blank, 'Zum Problem "Häresie und Orthodoxie"', in Gerhard Dautzenberg, Helmut Merklein and Karlheinz Müller (eds.), *Zur Geschichte des Urchristentums*, QD 87, 1979, 142–60. Finally, the theo-

logical problem of the topic 'heretics in early Christianity' should be noted; for this see Helmut Köster, 'Häretiker im Urchristentum als theologisches Problem', in *Zeit und Geschichte. Dankesgabe an Rudolf Bultmann zum 80.Geburtstag* (ed. Erich Dinkler), 1964, 61–76; here there are passionate statements and a programme (cf. e.g. 71) which as far as I know Köster did not take up later: he declares heresy to be virtually a failure of demythologizing in earliest Christianity (73–6). Cf. similarly James D. G. Dunn, *Unity and Diversity in the New Testament. An Inquiry into the Character of Earliest Christianity*, ²1990, 266 (on the successors to the earliest Jewish Christians): 'One of the earliest heresies was conservatism' (he puts this in italics). On pp.1–7 of his book Dunn explicitly argues with Bauer, *Orthodoxy*; however, he does not follow him, but in fact works in a markedly systematic way on the basis of the New Testament. At the end of his learned book there are reflections on the function of the New Testament canon (374–88). The formal concluding sentence runs: 'Only when we recognize the unity in diversity of the NT and the diversity in unity of the NT and the ways they interact, only then can the NT continue to function as canon' (388). Arland J. Hultgren, *The Rise of Normative Christianity*, 1994, offers a caricature of Bauer (9–13), and unlike Baur fails to take seriously the second century, when orthodox Christianity emerged.

84. This passion, which is directed against the view of history taken in Eusebius' *History of the Church* (cf. Bauer, *Orthodoxy*, 165 n.33, 191f.), often cannot be seen because of the gigantic historical knowledge that Bauer presupposes in his account and among his readers (!). Is it fortuitous that Bauer's work appeared in the Nazi period, when, as in the time of Eusebius, a political theology was called for?

85. Bauer, *Orthodoxy*, xxi–v. Cf. also Bauer's note on his work which was reprinted in Bauer, *Aufsätze* (n.83), 229–33. Cf. also already Friedrich Nitzsch, *Grundriss der Christlichen Dogmengeschichte* I, 1870, 35: '... only from the standpoint of orthodoxy as it was later fixed can the doctrinal disputes of the first post-apostolic century be set in the perspective of a defensive war of the "church" against heretics. From a historical perspective it appears, rather, as a battle between different main Christian parties (formally still with equal rights), of which one, that of the apostolic positives, won a decisive victory towards the end of the second century.'

86. Cf. Lüdemann, 'Wissenschaftsverständnis' (n.40), 107.

87. Cf. the critical comments by Hans-Dietrich Altendorf (review of the German edition in *ThLZ* 91, 1966, 192–5); 'The book refrains from any theological reflection; it is written in an explicitly "profane" way, and in some parts there are tones which recall Gibbon and Renan' (193). Altendorf asks: 'How do orthodoxy and heresy relate to one another in

sustance?' (ibid). He continues: 'No can one suppress the question whether the deliberately distanced nature of the treatment of disputes within the church, touching on the casual, is really adequate... Not only church politics is at stake, but also the human spirit – and perhaps even more?' (194). Altendorf also thinks 'that this somewhat lax hypothetical view of things, developed with some coldness, is sometimes all too readily accepted and put to theological use by the theological side' (ibid.). Ernst Käsemann, *The Testament of Jesus. A Study of the Gospel of John in the Light of Chapter 17*, 1968, 75 n.1, replied to this: 'It is easy to declare that "a truly historical understanding cannot be gained in this manner". If only it were clear what is meant by a "truly historical understanding"... Furthermore, the historian with the bird's eye view is also confronted not only by the spirit in history, but also by everyday existence, which is usually more or less confusing and contradictory. Finally, for us who have learned from Bauer and Bultmann to be told by someone within the academic community that earlier exegetes of the New Testament had a closer relationship to the Church than we seem to have is a bit much! We spent half a lifetime in the pastorate and were formed by it. Again, we may be permitted to ask, which church is actually meant? We ourselves have experienced to our sorrow "the wild mish-mash" in the church and we are therefore aware of ecclesiastical mythology and the legends which continue to grow exuberantly even since 1945. On the basis of our experiences within the church, we as exegetes tend towards criticism of the tradition. Can we not postulate at least as a possible working hypothesis that the everyday life of primitive Christianity was determined by similar realities which also produced a "wild mish-mash"? We do not operate completely without practical experience, even if some no longer remember and others do not want to know.' Hans-Dietrich Altendorf replied to this criticism ('Zum Stichwort Rechtgläubigkeit und Ketzerei im ältesten Christentum', *ZKG* 80, 1969, 61–74): 'Käsemann's chastizing of my review of Bauer's book... overlooks the fact that it was not concerned with the denial of everyday church life with its contradictoriness and its humanity, but with a question of historiography. I did not have the naivety to paint church history on a gold background, but I think that one can also describe complicated, contradictiory and distressed conditions within the framework of the possible' (73 n.50).

88. Cf. Wilhelm Schneemelcher, 'Walter Bauer als Kirchenhistoriker', *NTS* 9, 1962/63, 11–22, though he does not see Bauer's work as being profane historiography. He writes: 'Rather, it must be seen as an attempt to do justice to the fact that church history is never the history of the kingdom of God, but rather the history of the gospel in this world. But in this way Bauer is a pioneer in showing a legitimate understanding of church

history as a theological discipline' (2). Reflections of this kind cannot be found (happily?) in Bauer. Nor have they been registered elsewhere in the later influence of his work. Similarly, the remarks by Rowan Williams ('Does it Make Sense to Speak of Pre-Nicene Orthodoxy?', in id. (ed.), *The Making of Orthodoxy. Essays in Honour of Henry Chadwick*, 1989, 1–23), which in other respects are worth noting, miss the point of Bauer's view of the 'essence of the Christian faith as a principle beyond history and speech' (4) and at best relate to undigested bits of his theological education.

89. Cf. also my criticism in Lüdemann, 'Schule' (n.32), 326f., which examines Bauer's tacit presupposition that the Roman community was never shaped by Gnostics and *therefore* was able to lead the fight against Gnosticism. (Additionally see the evidence that the Valentinian Florinus, who was a presbyter of the Roman [!] community around 190 CE, put forward doctrines in the church which were first complained about by Irenaeus [Eusebius, *HE* V, 20,4].) But this false estimation does not alter the fruitfulness of Bauer's questions in any way. For the work by Thomas A.Robinson (*The Bauer Thesis Examined. The Geography of Heresy in the Early Christian Church*, 1988), which I cite in my article mentioned above, 328 n.79, cf. my review in *ThR* 61, 1996. For Bauer's treatment of the Roman community cf. also Klaus Koschorke, 'Eine gnostische Pfingstpredigt. Zur Auseinandersetzung zwischen gnostichem und kirchlichem Christentum am Beispiel der ⟨Epistula Petri ad Philippum⟩ (NHC VIII,2)', *ZThK* 74, 1977, 323–43: 337f.

90. Cf. the informative survey by Alexander Böhlig, 'Die Bedeutung der Funde von Medinet Madi und Nag Hammadi für die Erforschung des Gnostizismus', in id. and Christoph Markschies (eds.), *Gnosis und Manichäismus* (n.80), 113–242. See also Hans-Martin Schenke, 'Nag Hammadi', *TRE* 23, 1994, 731–6.

91. Cf. the new journal *Apocrypha. Le champ des apocryphes*, 1, 1990f.

92. See the journal *The Second Century*, founded in 1981 (since 1993 the *Journal of Early Christian Studies*).

93. For more detail see below, Chapter 9.

94. Bauer, *Orthodoxy* (n.83), 234.

95. The polemic in Rom. 16.17–20 cannot change any of the evidence indicated above. For the problem see still Bauer, *Orthodoxy* (n.83), 236 n.11 and Helmut Köster, 'Häretiker im Urchristentum', *RGG³* , 1959, 17–21.

96. For I Cor. 5.1ff. cf further Meeks, *First Urban Christians* (n.47), 127ff.

97. For a bibliography see: Hans Lietzmann, *A History of the Early Church*, Vol.2, *The Founding of the Church Universal*, 1938, 204–15;

Ellen Flesseman-van Leer, *Tradition and Scripture in the Early Church*, 1954, 100–44; Georg Günter Blum, *Tradition und Sukzession. Studien zum Normbegriff des Apostolischen von Paulus bis Irenäus*, AGTL 9, 1963 (and on this Karlmann Beyschlag, *ThLZ* 92, 1967, 112–15); Hans von Campenhausen, *Ecclesiastical Authority and Spiritual Power in the Church of the First Three Centuries*, 1969; id., 'Irenäus und das Neue Testament', *ThLZ* 90, 1965, 1–8; id., *The Fathers of the Greek Church*, 1963; Norbert Brox, *Offenbarung, Gnosis und gnostischer Mythos bei Irenäus von Lyon*, 1966; Elaine Pagels, *The Gnostic Gospels*, 1980; Carl Andresen, 'Die Anfänge christlicher Lehrentwicklung', in id. (ed.), *Handbuch der Dogmen- und Theologiegeschichte* I, 1982, 1–98: 79–98 ('Die biblische Theologie des Irenäus von Lyon'); Hans-Jochen Jaschke, 'Irenäus von Lyon', TRE 16, 1987, 258–68. Cf. Gérard Vallée, *A Study in Anti-Gnostic Polemics. Irenaeus, Hippolytus and Epiphanius*, 1981, 9–40; Rolf Noormann, *Irenäus als Paulusinterpret. Zur Rezeption und Wirkung der paulinischen und deuteropaulinischen Briefe im Werk des Irenäus von Lyon*, WUNT II/66, 1994.

98. The translation of Irenaeus' 'Against the Heresies' is based on that by A. Cleveland Coxe in The Ante-Nicene Fathers, Vol.1, 1887; the translation of 'The Demonstration of the Apostolic Preaching' is based on that by J. Armitage Robinson, 1920.

99. Greek title in Eusebius *HE* V 7,1; the Latin title runs *Adversus omnes haereses*. Ten-volume edition in Sources Chrétiennes (1969ff.).

100. Here the concordance of Bruno Rynders, *Lexique comparé du texte grec et des versions latine, arménienne et syriaque de l'"Adversus Haereses" de Saint Irénée*, 2 vols, 1954, offers indispensable help.

101. Hippolytus lived at the beginning of the third century in Rome and was one of the most fertile early Christian writers in Greek. His work against the Gnostics is the learned *Refutatio omnium haeresium* (= *Ref*), which derives the heresies from Greek philosophy. Of the ten books, the second and third and the beginning of the fourth are lost (edition in GCS 26, 1916 [Paul Wendland] and in PTS 25, 1986 [Miroslav Markovich]), cf. Vallée, *Study* (n.97), 41–62.

102. Epiphanius of Salamis (c.315–403) composed a Panarion ('Doctor's Chest' [= *Haer*]) against eighty heresies which are described at length (edition GCS 25–27; English translation by Frank Williams, *The Panarion of Epiphanius of Salamis*, Book I [sects 1–46], NHS XXXV, 1987; Books II and III [Sects 47–80, *De fide*], NHS XXXVI, 1994. Cf. Vallée, *Study* [n.97], 63–91).

103. Theodoret of Cyrrhus (c.395–c.460) composed a history of heretics in five volumes (edition, PG 83).

104. Eusebius (260/65–339/40) was bishop of Caesarea in Palestine. A

fertile writer, he had a pioneering influence on earlier church historiography. His *historia ekklesiastike* contains numerous quotations from lost writings and goes down to 324: English translation, introduction and notes by Hugh Jackson Lawlor and John Ernest Leonard Oulton, 2 vols., 1927.

105. The biblical passages in brackets indicate the passages to which Irenaeus is evidently referring.

106. For the translation see n.98.

107. Women are already the object of 'heretical' instruction in II Tim. 3.6. Cf. further the letter of Ptolemy to Flora, preserved in Epiphanius, *Haer* 33,3,1–33,7,10. Flora is a well-educated woman whom the Christian teacher Ptolemaeus wants to win over to Christianity by showing her the significance of the various laws of the Old Testament and their relation to the words of Jesus. Probably Ptolemaeus was denounced by Flora's husband out of jealousy and subsequently executed (cf. Justin, *II Apol.* 2.9–13). That would make the Gnostic the first known Roman martyr.

108. The description of this reaction by a church father is historically unique, though it is not suprising, given the unbridled polemic of Irenaeus.

109. Possibly the descriptions of the doctrine of the 'heretics' in Hippolytus' work which deviate from those in Irenaeus arise out of more precise study by this very learned opponent of heretics; in other words, he will have done all he could to gather as much material as possible. The reports of Irenaeus on the one hand and Hippolytus on the other, which differ in content over *the same* Gnostic groups (Simonians, Basilidians and others), present great problems to scholars. Cf. Lüdemann, *Untersuchungen* (n.1), 104.

110. Campenhausen, *Fathers of the Greek Church* (n.97), 20.

111. Brox, *Offenbarung* (n.97) thinks that Irenaeus has 'seen through his manifold, muddled contrast in so far as he can reduce all the variations to a few basic errors and mistaken attitudes without sparing the reader wearisome and difficult individual refutations, predominantly of scriptural exegesis' (12). But the question is whether he does justice to these groups. At any rate he also includes the Ebionites (I 26) among the united front of Gnostics and in fact equally identifies Marcionites with Valentinians on the one hand and Ebionites on the other. In no way is that historically correct, although – as I have remarked – Irenaeus' unification had a great effect on church history.

112. Among modern scholars, Karlmann Beyschlag, *Simon Magus und die christliche Gnosis*, WUNT 16, 1974, 16f. n.19 and 141f. n.24, in particular has drawn attention to the character of the section *Haer* I 23–28 (see my review in *ZKG* 87, 1976, 346–51).

113. The list given below is orientated on Beyschlag, *Simon Magus* (n.112), 141f. no.24.

114. Günter Klein, 'Der Synkretismus als theologisches Problem in der ältesten christlichen Apologetik', *ZThK* 64, 1967, 40–82 (= id., *Rekonstruktion und Interpretation*, BEvTh 50, 1969, 262–301: 299).

115. Brox, *Offenbarung* (n.97), 128f.

116. Immediately after this quotation, Irenaeus writes: 'To this course many nations of those barbarians who believe in Christ assent, having salvation written in their hearts by the Spirit, without paper or ink, and, carefully preserving the ancient tradition, believing in one God, the Creator of heaven and earth, and all things therein, by means of Christ Jesus, the Son of God; who, because of his surpassing love towards his creation, condescended to be born of the virgin, he himself uniting man through himself to God, and having suffered under Pontius Pilate, and rising again, and having been received up in splendour, shall come in glory, the Saviour of those who are saved, and the Judge of those who are judged' (*Haer* III 4, 2). Here we already see how the rule of truth is bound up with creeds.

117. For what follows cf. Karl Holl, 'Tertullian als Schriftsteller' (1897) = id., *Gesammelte Aufsätze zur Kirchengeschichte* III, 1928, 1–12; Lietzmann, *Founding* (n.97), 218–25; Flesseman-van Leer, *Tradition* (n.97), 145–85; Hans von Campenhausen, *The Fathers of the Latin Church*, 1964, 4–35; Timothy D. Barnes, *Tertullian, A Historical and Literary Study*, 1984. Cf. also John F. Jansen, 'Tertullian and the New Testament', *The Second Century* 2, 1982, 191–207; L. W. Countryman, 'Tertullian and the Regula Fidei', ibid., 208–27; Robert D. Sider, 'Approaches to Tertullian: A Study of Recent Scholarship', ibid., 228–60. The translations of Tertullian which follow are based on Vol. 3 of the Ante-Nicene Fathers, by A.Cleveland Coxe, 1885.

118. Montanism – named after Montanus, who appeared in the Phrygian village of Ardabau in the middle of the second century as an eschatological Paraclete (John 14.16), is the earliest clearly visible example of apocalyptic enthusiasm in the early church. The sayings of the Paraclete about revelation called for rigorous church discipline, e.g. the excommunication of those who had committed mortal sins, a prohibition against remarriage and a rule of heightened fasting. Cf. n.700 below.

119. *Apol.* 18.4: 'Once these things were with us, too, the theme of ridicule. We are of your (i.e. the pagans') stock and nature: men are made, not born Christians.'

120. Holl, *Tertullian* (n.117), 6.

121. Klaus Koschorke ('"Suchen und Finden" in der Auseinandersetzung zwischen gnostischem und kirchlichem Christentum', *WuD* NF 14, 1977, 51–65) has evaluated the tractate 'Authoritative Teaching' (NHC VI,3) from the Nag Hammadi writings for this question. 33.16–26

is particularly interesting: 'Furthermore, if they (viz. orthodox Christians) find someone else who asks about his salvation, their hardness of heart sets to work upon that man. And if he (the quester) does not stop asking, they kill him by their cruelty, thinking that they have done a good thing for themselves. Indeed they are sons of the devil!' (cf. Koschorke, 'Suchen', 56f.).

122. Cf. *Adversus Praxean* (against the Monarchians); *Adversus Marcionem* (against Marcion and the Marcionites); *Adversus Hermogenen, De Carne Christi, Scorpiace, De resurrectione mortuorum, De anima* (all writings against Gnostics of different species).

123. Holl, 'Tertullian' (n.117), 8.

124. *De Ieiunio*, 17.

125. *De Pudicitia* 1,5–9: '5 It is our own good things whose position is now sinking; it is the system of Christian chastity which is being shaken to its foundations – which derives its all from heaven; its nature, through the bath of regeneration; its discipline, through the power of preaching; its penal rigour through the judgments which each Testament exhibits; and is subject to a more constant external compulsion, arising from the apprehension or the desire of the eternal fire or kingdom. 6 In opposition to this, chastity – and I could not have concealed the fact – has issued a decree, and a peremptory one at that. The Pontifex Maximus, that is, the bishop of bishops, issues an edict: "I forgive the sins of adultery and fornication to those who have shown repentance." 7 What a decree, but not one which one could entitle "A good deed"! And where shall this generosity be made known? On the very spot, I suppose, at the very gates of the sensual desires under the red lights of the brothels, where sin itself is at home. There is the place where the pardon will have to be given, where one can enter only with the hope of grace. 8 But it is in the church that this edict will be read out, and the church is Christ's virgin. That virgin who is true, who is chaste, who is holy, should not hear such a shameful thing. 9 She has no one to whom she could announce this forgiveness, and if she did, she would not promise forgiveness, since the earthly temple of God could be called a den of thieves rather than a brothel.'

126. Cf. Berthold Altaner, *Patrology*, 1960, 166.

127. Brox, 'Offenbarung' (n.97), 101. Cf. Harnack, *Bible Reading* (n.21),48–54.

128. For what follows see Pagels, *Gnostic Gospels* (n.97), 102–18.

129. Cf. now from a Gnostic perspective the 'Apocalypse of Peter' from Nag Hammadi (NHC VII,3) (with the comments by Klaus Koschorke, 'Die Polemik der Gnostiker gegen das kirchliche Christentum', *NHS* XIII, 1978, 11–90). Cf. the polemic in 79.22–31: 'And there shall be others of those who are outside our number who name themselves bishops and also

deacons, as if they have received their authority from God... These people are dry canals.'

130. Cf. Christopher R.Smith, 'Chiliasm and Recapitulation in the Theology of Irenaeus', *VigChr* 48, 1994, 113–331; Horacio E. Lona, *Über die Auferstehung des Fleisches, Studien zur frühchristlichen Eschatologie*, BZNW 66, 1993, 211–13.

131. Cf. Tertullian, *De Resurrectione mortuorum* 48–63, esp. 48–51. Cf. Irenaeus, *Haer.* V 9–14 and on this Noormann, *Irenäus* (n.97), 501–16, though he understands 'Irenaeus' defence of the resurrection of the flesh as a continuation of the battle waged by Paul in I Cor. 15' (516). But in Paul there is no idea of the continuity of the flesh (on 515). From Nag Hammadi, the tractate The Testimony of Truth (NHC IX, 3) is an eloquent testimony to the rejection of the church's belief in the resurrection (cf. 36,26–37,1f.): 'In contrast to the Gnostic, who by virtue of his self-knowledge – namely the knowledge of his true origin... is already redeemed in the world from the world and has "perfect life", the church's faith awaits even for the future none other than the continuation (or restoration) of the present sarkic existence; he hopes in the flesh, though this is doomed to decay' (Koschorke, 'Polemik' [n.129], 119f.).

132. Tertullian, *De Resurrectione mortuorum* 60: 'For the judgment of God requires that man be kept entire. However, he cannot be entire without his limbs, of the substance of which... he consists.'

133. *The state of research*: the sources for the following account are the authentic letters of Paul and Acts. For the period afterwards there are only documents on individual pieces of information (the martyrdom of James in 62 [Josephus, *Antt.* XX, 199f.; Hegesippus in Eusebius, *HE* II 23]; the 'flight' of the earliest community to Pella [Eusebius, *HE* III 5, 3]; reports about the kinsfolk of Jesus [Hegesippus in Eusebius, *HE* III 20, 1–6]; lists of bishops of Jerusalem in Eusebius *HE* IV 5,3; V 12; Justin, *Dial.* 46f. [see below, 221f.]; Irenaeus, *Haer* I, 26; PsCl [see below, 57–60]).

The following is based on my monograph *Opposition to Paul in Jewish Christianity*, 1989. This book, which attempts to demonstrate hostility to Paul as a constant of Jerusalem Christianity and its successors (including the relatives of Jesus), has gone almost unnoticed in research into Jewish Christianity – probably also because the German title (*Paulus der Heidenapostel II, Antipaulinismus im frühen Christentum*, FRLANT 130, ²1990) does not contain the key phrase 'Jewish Christianity'. Cf. only Ray A. Pritz, *Nazarene Jewish Christianity from the End of the New Testament Period until its Disappearance in the Fourth Century*, SPB 37, 1988; Simon C.Mimouni, 'Pour une définition nouvelle du judéo-christianisme ancien', *NTS* 38, 1992, 161–86; Richard Bauckham, *Jude and the Relatives of Jesus in the Early Church*, 1990. Despite Jude 17f., the author argues that this work is authentic and comes from Jude, the brother of James, though this is to be ruled out since there it looks back to the apostles as bearers of tradition (v.17) and attributes a message about the last time to them (v.18). This is a stylistic characteristic typical of a later generation (cf. I Tim. 4.1; II Tim. 3.1; II Thess. 2.3). Berger, *Theologiegeschichte* (n.1), also argues for the considerable antiquity of Jude, though without commenting on the question of authorship; he writes: 'The archaic character of the opponents of Jude and the fact that the mercy of Christ is still absent (cf. e.g. I Thess. 1.10b) preclude a late dating of the letter' (249). Cf. also the latest substantial contribution on the topic of Jewish Christianity, Joan E.Taylor, *Christians and Holy Places. The Myth of Jewish-Christian Origins*, 1993 (with bibliography). See also Martin Hengel, 'Jacobus der Herrenbruder – der erste "Papst"?', in *Glaube und Eschatologie. Festschrift für Werner Georg Kümmel zum 80. Geburtstag* (ed. Erich Grässer and Otto Merk), 1985, 71–104; Gösta Lindeskog, *Das jüdisch-christliche Problem. Randglosssen zu einer Forschungsepoche*, AUUHR 9, 1986, 56–84; Wilhelm Pratscher, *Der Herrenbruder Jakobus und die Jakobustradition*, FRLANT 139, 1987 (with rather too strong a tendency to harmonize the tensions between James and Paul); Jack T. Sanders, *Schismatics, Sectarians, Dissidents, Deviants. The First One Hundred Years of Jewish-Christian Relations*, 1993.

Research into Jerusalem Christianity is still hindered by the fact that the current histories of earliest Christianity as a rule only extend the period of time to be discussed to the beginning of the second century or merely give a few references. Cf. only Conzelmann, *History* (n.33), 134–8; Wilhelm Schneemelcher, *Das Urchristentum*, 1981; Ludger Schenke, *Die Urgemeinde*, 1986. Cf. also Gerhard Dautzenberg and Karlheinz Müller (eds.), *Zur Geschichte des Urchristentums*, QD 87, 1979. Moreover the history of *Jerusalem* Christianity is seldom in the forefront of interest (not even in the welcome advance by Helmut Koester and James M. Robinson, *Trajectories through Early Christianity*, 1971; cf. also Helmut Koester, *Einführung in das Neue Testament*, 1980, 637–47 [there is an English version, published in Berlin, *Introduction to the New Testament*, 1983, but this was not accessible for the translator]; but cf. now Bernd Wander, *Trennungsprozesse zwischen Frühem Christentum und Judentum im 1.Jahrhundert n.Chr. Datierbare Abfolgen zwischen der Hinrichtung Jesu und der Zerstörung des Jerusalemer Tempels*, TANZ 16, 1994, a work which despite all the intuition of its author has an unjustified trust in the historical value of Acts *in toto* and only because of that can criticize the distinction between primary source (= authentic letters of Paul) and secondary source (= Acts)(47). The only more recent contribution to scholarship which goes into the question of the nature of Jerusalem Christianity before and after the Jewish War is Carsten Colpe, *Das Siegel der Propheten. Historische Beziehungen zwischen Judentum, Judenchristentum, Heidentum und frühem Islam*, ANTZ 3, 1990, 38–89. Dunn, *Unity* (n.83), promises more than he offers since he does not analyse the sources from the second century at all, though he often speaks of 'Ebionites'. Moreover it is factually inappropriate to accuse the second-century Jewish Christians of not showing any development in their theology (thus 265f.). By what criteria is this judgment made?

Of the earlier literature, Johannes Weiss, *Earliest Christianity* (1917), 1937 reissued 1959 (2 vols.), is still worth noting, especially I, 14–82, 258–76; II, 707–39, and then Hans Joachim Schoeps, *Theologie und Geschichte des Judenchristentums*, 1949, which Wilhelm Schneemelcher ('Das Problem des Judenchristentums', *VuF* 5, 1949/50, 229–38) criticized over-sharply. Hans Joachim Schoeps responded to this (and other criticisms) in *Urgemeinde, Judenchristentum, Gnosis*, 1956. It is the merit of Georg Strecker to have rehabilitated the Pseudo-Clementines for the question of the history of Jewish Christianity – in the face of the hyper-criticism of his former teacher Schneemelcher, whose judgments betray some emotional hostility (thus Schoeps, *Urgemeinde*, 3); cf. Georg Strecker, *Das Judenchristentum in den Pseudoklementinen*, TU 70, 1958, ²1981; id., postscript to Walter Bauer, *Orthodoxy and Heresy* (n.83), 241–85; id., 'Judenchristentum', *TRE* 17, 1988, 310–25. In *Das Judenchristentum. Untersuchungen über Gruppenbildungen und Parteikämpfe in der frühen Christenheit*, Dalp-Taschenbücher 376, 1964, Hans Joachim Schoeps presented a popular account of his researches; cf. id., *Aus frühchristlicher Zeit*, 1950; *Paul. The Theology of the Apostle in the Light of Jewish Religious History*, 1961; *Studien zur unbekannten Geistesgeschichte*, 1963. It is worth noting that Hans Dieter Betz points out in his influential commentary on *Galatians* that the work of Hans Joachim Schoeps has become important to him for his new view of Paul and Jewish Christianity (Hans Dieter Betz, Galatians, Hermeneia, 1988, 5f.).

134. Eusebius is referring back to *HE* II 23, where he twice reports the martyrdom of James, once in connection with Hegesippus (23.16–18) and then in connection with Josephus, *Antt.* XX, 199–203 (23,21–24).

135. Cf. how Eusebius interprets the Jewish War in another passage. In *HE* III 7, 5–9, he writes: '6 When one compares the words of our Saviour with the other accounts of the historian (viz. Josephus) concerning the whole war, how can one fail to be amazed, and to admit how truly divine and surpassingly marvellous our Saviour's prescience and foretelling were? 7 There is no need, therefore, to add anything to these accounts of the events which happened to the whole nation after the Saviour's passion,

and after those voices had been uttered in which the whole multitude of the Jews asked that the robber and murderer should be saved from death (Mark 15.6–15), but begged that the Prince of Life should be taken away from them. 8 But it may be right to mention as well those events which go to establish the loving-kindness of that all-gracious Providence, which for forty whole years after their crime against the Christ postponed their destruction. During all these years the greater number of the apostles and disciples, and James himself, the first bishop there, who was called the Lord's brother, were still alive and made their abode in the city of Jerualem itself, thus remaining, as it were, that place's most sure bulwark. 9 For the divine visitation was still long-suffering, if after all they might repent of what they had done, and so obtain pardon and salvation; and besides this great long-suffering, marvellous signs were vouchsafed them by God of what was to happen to them should they not repent. These matters also have been deemed worthy of mention by the aforesaid historian (viz. Josephus), and we cannot do better than lay them before the readers of this work' (there follows a quotation from Josephus, *BJ* VI, 288–304).

136. If it were a construction of Eusebius himself, he would have reported a return of the community to Jerusalem, since according to him there was an unbroken continuity in the Jerusalem church (see 29 below). Cf. Jürgen Wehnert, 'Die Auswanderung der Jerusalemer Christen nach Pella – historisches Faktum oder theologische Konstruktion?', *ZKG* 102, 1991, 231–55: 236f.

137. Lüdemann, *Opposition* (n.133), 200–13.

138. Wehnert, 'Auswanderung' (n.136), says that the exodus of the Jerusalem community after the death of James took place in 62 (248ff.). His main evidence for this is *Pseudo-Clementine Recognitions* I 71: the Jerusalem Christians went to Jericho after the murderous attack on James by the hostile Paul: 'Jericho, on the borders of Judaea, was an ancient crossroads from which it was also possible to reach Pella, on the edge of the Jordan valley, without a detour' (250). Wander, *Trennungsprozesse* (n.133), refers on the one hand to Wehnert, who says that this was an emigration (not a flight) (269), but then later again speaks of a flight followed by a return to Jerusalem (288). That will not do.

139. Hegesippus in Eusebius, *HE* III, 32,3.

140. Cf. the cycle of legends about Narcissus in Eusebius, *HE* VI 9,1–11,4.

141. Cf. Carl Andresen, *Die Kirchen der alten Christenheit*, 1971, 214. For the problem of the lists of bishops cf. Roelof van den Broek, 'Der *Brief des Jakobus an Quadratus* und das Problem der judenchristlichen Bischöfe von Jerusalem (Eusebius, *HE* IV, 5, 1–3)', in *Text and Testimony. Essays*

on New Testament and Apocryphal Literature in Honour of A. F. J. Klijn, edited by T. Baarda, A. Hillhorst, G. P. Luttikhuizen and A. S. van der Woude, 1988, 56–65.

142. Cf. Lüdemann, *Opposition* (n.133), 165f.

143. For the details cf. Lüdemann, *Opposition* (n.133,) 123–5.

144. For Cochaba as the abode of Ebionites cf. Epiphanius, *Haer* 30, 2, 7f.; Eusebius, *Onomasticon* 172, 1ff.(cf. further Lüdemann, *Opposition* [n.133], 124–5.

145. In his *Homily on the Passion*, only discovered this century, Melito looks back on this stay and accuses the Jews of having crucified Jesus in the midst of Jerusalem (72; 93f.). Cf. Melito of Sardis, *Homily on the Passion*, ed. Campbell Bonner, 1940.

146. 'And for apostates let there be no hope, and mayest thou speedily blot out the wicked rulers in our day and may the Nazarenes (= Christians) and Minim (= heretics) perish in a moment. Blessed art thou, O Lord, who bows down the wicked.' Cf. also the cursing of Jewish Christians in synagogue worship attested by Justin, *Dial* 16.4; 47.5. See also Klaus Wengst, *Bedrängte Gemeinde und verherrlichter Christus. Ein Versuch über das Johannesevangelium*, 1990, 89–104 ('Der Ausschluss aus der Synagogue als Erfahrung von "Ketzern"').

147. The following is based on Lüdemann, *Resurrection* (n.3), 173ff. Cf. also Colpe, *Siegel* (n.3), 60–7. Colpe presupposes a generally ecstatic disposition among those left behind in Jerusalem (60). The death of Jesus was a shock which only made 'sense with the interpretations, not already with the mere trances' (ibid.). 'The spontaneous reaction to the execution was the exodus of evidently all the men and perhaps some of the women to Galilee' (ibid.); Mark 16.7 'provides subsequent legitimation for a process which had evidently already taken place' (63). 'The new orientations first began in Galilee. They consisted in visions which were immediately combined with instructions that amount to the earliest interpretations. These represented in turn the basis of the later interpretations for which there was already a rich store of possible points of contact in the tradition of Israel: exaltations of Enoch (from Gen.5.24 to the books of Enoch) and Elijah (from II Kings 2.11 to the Elijah apocalypses) from life, temporary transportations of Ezra (IV Ezra 14.9, 49f.) and Baruch (SyrBar 13.3 etc.) to obtain heavenly information, ascension after death (in some works reported of Moses, Isaiah and some rabbis), resurrections of martyrs (from II Macc. to Rev.11) and outpourings of the Spirit of God (from Joel 3 to the rituals of the great pilgrimage festivals). The first instructions required the men to return to Jerusalem…; the interpretation included in them indicated that the kingdom of God would come about there – and not in Galilee' (60f.). Cf. also Colpe, *Siegel*, 61f., on the ascension from the cross

as the earliest tradition. Cf. also Georg Bertram in *TDNT* VIII, 604–12 (with bibliography); *EWNT* III, 981f.

148. The following is based on E. P. Sanders, *Jesus and Judaism*, 1985, 61–76; id., *The Historical Figure of Jesus*, 1993, 249–64. Cf. also Helmut Mödritzer, *Stigma und Charisma im Neuen Testament und seiner Umwelt. Zur Soziologie des Urchristentums*, NTOA 28, 1994, 147–56. Jacob Neusner, 'Geldwechsler im Tempel – von der Mischnah her erklärt', *ThZ* 45, 1989, 81–4, criticizes Sanders: 'Anyone who understood the theological conception of the whole offering will have found an action in which the tables of the moneychangers were overthrown incomprehensible' (83). He argues that Jesus himself replaced the whole offering (Ex. 30.16) in the temple, by which atonement for sins was achieved, with the eucharist, which communicated the forgiveness of sins (84). The fact that Jesus himself did *not* institute the eucharist tells against this.

149. I Kings 11.29–39 (Ahijah of Shiloh tears his new cloak into twelve pieces); Isa.8.1–4 (Isaiah displays a tablet with names written on it); Hos.1,2–9 (Hosea marries the prostitute Gomer and has children of prostitution), etc.

150. Mödritzer, *Stigma* (n.148), 150, following Sanders, *Jesus* (n.148), 71.

151. Translation based on the classic version by William Whiston, revised by D. S. Margoliouth (1906), 1960.

152. For Jesus son of Ananus see the remarks by Rebecca Gray, *Prophetic Figures in Late Second Temple Jewish Palestine. The Evidence from Josephus*, 1993, 158f. It should be emphasized that this Jesus had no recognizable connection with the Jerusalem community and was not a 'Christian'.

153. Jürgen Roloff, *Die Kirche im Neuen Testament*, ENT 10, 1993, 61, again differs completely: 'It is clear that these appearances were not individual visionary ecstatic experiences which served to provide religious assurance that Jesus continued to live before God. Rather, in them Jesus showed himself to be the one who had been appointed eschatological messianic ruler of Israel by the action of God. That explains why the motive of sending and commissioning is inherent not only in I Cor. 15.5 but also in the old accounts of appearances in the Gospels (Matt. 28.16–20; Luke 24.36–49; John 20.19–23) which deal with appearances of the risen Christ to the group of Twelve.' What precisely does Roloff mean by Jesus' showing of himself? A supernatural event? Cf. similarly Pannenberg, 'Auferstehung' (n.281).

154. On this cf. Berger, *Theologiegeschichte* (n.1),131–9.

155. Dieter Georgi (*Der Armen zu gedenken. Die Geschichte der Kollekte des Paulus für Jerusalem*, second revised and expanded edition

1994), has stated that the women known from the story of the visit to the tomb in Mark 16.1–8 'were the first leaders of the Jerusalem community' (109). But as long as it is only *asserted* that experiences of Easter appearances underlie Mark 16.1–7 (108) and that in Mark 16.8 'there is an echo of real fear of the male disciples who fled to Galilee' (109), this thesis is improbable. I have demonstrated that John 20.11–17 is *late* in the history of the tradition (Lüdemann, *Resurrection* [n.3], 152–60).

156. The expression comes from Anton Vögtle, *Die Dynamik des Anfangs. Leben und Fragen der jungen Kirche*, 1988.

157. Ernst Haenchen, *The Acts of the Apostles*, 1974, 258: '"A group of men and women had come together in faith in Jesus Christ and in the expectation of his return, and they led in Jerusalem a quiet and even in the Jewish sense 'devout' life"' (here Haenchen is quoting Martin Dibelius, *Studies in the Acts of the Apostles*, 1956, 124). Haenchen goes on to speak of 'a modest existence... in which the winning of souls for the Lord went on in the quiet personal encounter of man with man'.

158. I use this name to denote the author of the Gospel of Luke and Acts, though the real author is still unknown.

159. Cf. Martin Hengel, 'Between Jesus and Paul. The "Hellenists", the "Seven" and Stephen (Acts 6,1–15; 7.54–83)' (1975), in id., *Between Jesus and Paul*, 1983, 1–29, and my analysis of the relevant Acts texts in Lüdemann, *Christianity* (n.1), 73–92 (Acts 6.1–8.3). Cf. recently e.g. Dieter Sänger, *Die Verkündigung des Gekreuzigten und Israel*, WUNT 75, 1994, 226–41 (with bibliography). The consensus which is becoming established is that these Hellenists were critical of the law – in whatever way – and thus paved the way for Pauline thought. Cf. now Berger, *Theologiegeschichte* (n.1), 140–9.

160. Cf. Karl Holl, 'Der Kirchenbegriff des Paulus in seinem Verhältnis zu dem der Urgemeinde' (1921), in id., *Gesammelte Aufsätze zur Kirchengeschichte* II, 1928, 44–67: 50. Following Schlatter, Holl points out that the earliest community distinguishes between appearance and vision. He continues: 'How far the distinction can in fact be taken is another question which is not relevant at this point. The decisive thing is that it was believed to be possible to draw a line here. Therefore the visions of the martyrs were never thought to have the same weight as the appearances to the apostles' (50 n.1).

161. Cf. Berger, *Theologiegeschichte* (n.1), 144f.

162. In its tradition, this text certainly goes back to a historical nucleus. We can assume that the quotation in Stephen's speech (= v.56) is tradition which the author of Acts has worked into the introduction to the speech (= v.55, cf. the word for word correspondences between the introduction and the speech). Along with Rev.1.13–16, the text or the tradition under-

lying it is really part of a report of a resurrection appearance. Cf. James M. Robinson, 'Jesus – From Easter to Valentinus (or to the Apostles' Creed)', *JBL* 101, 1982, 5–37: 10.

163. For the following section cf. especially Colpe, *Siegel* (n.133), 67–72.

164. Colpe, *Siegel*, 67.

165. It should be explicitly emphasized that the people involved in this were not aware of the factors which will be worked out in what follows. Similarly, those who later reinterpreted the message of Paul, which was wholly rooted in the expectation of an imminent end, were not aware that they were making a change. Even Paul in the later letters was not aware that all at once he had given up the expectation of a return of Jesus in his lifetime. But it is legitimate for scholars to demonstrate the real changes in order to get behind things and understand (not just explain) a strange history.

166. On this cf. Wilhelm Heitmüller, *'Im Namen Jesu'. Eine sprach- und religionsgeschichtliche Untersuchung zum Neuen Testament, speziell zur altchristlichen Taufe*, FRLANT 2, 1903.

167. Mark 1.4. On this cf. below 211f.

168. Thus Colpe, *Siegel* (n.133), 70f.

169. Cf. Lüdemann, *Christianity* (n.1), 73–9.

170. Cf. Eduard Schwartz in Lüdemann, *Christianity*, 79.

171. Cf. already 35 and n.159 above.

172. Colpe, *Siegel* (n.133), 79.

173. For me the old theory that Mark 9.2–8 is an Easter story (Mark 9.9 seems to indicate this) is becoming increasingly probable and – this is relatively new – is connected with the appointment of the 'Three' to their office.

174. Cf. Colpe, *Siegel* (n.133), 81 and before that Ethelbert Stauffer, 'Zum Kalifat des Jacobus', ZRGG 4, 1952, 193–214. This thesis is also supported by the remarkable fact that soon afterwards James was sole leader of the Jerusalem community and that the physical successors to Jesus were highly respected in Palestine after 70 (see 30 below).

175. Cf. Colpe, *Siegel* (n.133), 81.

176. See Holl, 'Kirchenbegriff' (n.160).

177. Cf. Hengel, 'Jakobus' (n.133), 95.

178. Cf. Lüdemann, *Opposition* (n.133), 73f.

179. In this connection one might recall the view of Julius Wellhausen, (*Kritische Analyse der Apostelgeschichte*, AGG.PH, NF 15.2, 1914): Acts 15 'smoothes the waves with holy oil; Paul indicates that the proceedings were all too human. To him the earliest period does not appear in the mist of sacred history; he allows himself to speak quite ironically of men like

James and Peter. It should also be noted that the dispute was not settled and brought to an end with the apostolic decision, as it appears in Acts, but continued for a long time afterwards' (29f.).

180. Greek *kataskopesai*; Holl, 'Kirchenbegriff' (n.160), rightly asks whether 'the expression *kataskopesai* does not have a similar explanation to *katatome* in Phil.3.2, i.e. whether what Paul called *kataskopein* was not meant by the earliest community more as an *episkopein*' (57).

181. This should not be understood to mean that though he was not *forced*, nevertheless he allowed himself to be circumcised *voluntarily*.

182. The expression 'free from the law' which is used in the secondary literature, and which I myself have also used, is inappropriate in that Paul was never an antinomian, and handed on positive ethical demands to his communities which correspond to parts of the Old Testament. On the other hand, the expression is to some degree justified, since in his doctrine of justification Paul in principle prescribes justification by grace alone without the works of the law. In what follows I am keeping the phrase 'free from the law' because I know of no better one.

183. Cf. I Macc. 12.11 and for the philological question of the meaning of the word, Klaus Berger, 'Almosen für Israel', *NTS* 23, 1977, 180–204: 196 and n.69.

184. Rudolf Bultmann, 'Ethische und mystische Religion im Urchristentum', *ChW* 34, 1920, 725–31: 730.

185. Ethelbert Stauffer, 'Petrus und Jakobus in Jerusalem', in Maximilian Roesle and Oscar Cullmann (eds.), *Begegnung der Christen (FS Otto Karrer)*, 1959, 361–72: here 370 ('church tax').

186. Dieter Georgi, *Die Geschichte der Kollekte des Paulus für Jerusalem*, ThF 38, 1965, 72f.

187. Berger, 'Almosen' (n.183), 200.

188. Cf. Bengt Holmberg, *Paul and Power*, CB.NT II, 1978, 39: 'The leaders of Jerusalem can harldy have shared, or even known of, the Pauline view.'

189. Cf. Holl, 'Kirchenbegriff' (as n.160), 61.

190. Cf. Georg Strecker, 'Ebioniten', *RAC* 4, 1959, 487–500. Strecker later withdrew this thesis (to my mind wrongly) in his postscript to Bauer, *Orthodoxy* (n.83), 272f.

191. For these last two terms cf. Conzelmann, *Outline* (n.15), 34.

192. For what follows cf. the basic article by E.P. Sanders, 'Jewish Association with Gentiles in Galatians 2:11–14', in *The Conversation Continues. Essays on Paul and John. In Honor of J. Louis Martyn*, ed. Robert T. Fortna and Beverly R. Gaventa, 1990, 170–88. Cf. also id., *Jewish Law from Jesus to the Mishnah*, 1990, 283–308. In both works Sanders is replying to James D.G. Dunn ('The Incident in Antioch [Gal.

2.11–18]', *JSNT* 18, 1993, 3–57), according to whom the Jewish (Christian) people in Antioch were under pressure from Jerusalem Pharisees who wanted to enforce the two following points: 1. Jews should not have dealings with Gentiles, since these were unclean; 2. food should be tithed in the Diaspora.

193. Cf. the laws on clean and unclean animals in Lev.11; Deut.14.3–20.

194. Cf. Lev.27.30–33; Num.18.21–32.

195. Cf. the Apostolic Decree (Acts 15.29; 21.25). On this see now Jürgen Wehnert, *Die Reinheit des Gottesvolkes aus Juden und Heiden. Studien zum historischen und theologischen Hintergrund des sog. Aposteldekrets*, theological habilitation, Göttingen 1995.

196. Johannes Munck, *Paul and the Salvation of Mankind*, 1959, 290: 'Paul collects voluntarily for Jerusalem, although the church there, in spite of its poverty, uses its modest means to pay the travelling expenses of people who are to oppose the apostle in the Gentile Christian churches. Paul is therefore supposed to have collected money voluntarily for the benefit of the Jerusalem Judaizing mission in his own churches. Let anyone believe that who can. These untenable assertions must, of course, be rejected.' For Munck's general tendency cf. Lüdemann, *Opposition* (n.133), 23–5.

197. For what follows cf. Lüdemann, *Christianity* (n.1), 230–6; also Jürgen Becker, *Paulus. Der Apostel der Völker*, 1989, 48–60; Walter Rebell, *Gehorsam und Unabhängigkeit. Eine sozialpsychologische Studie zu Paulus*, 1986, 49–52. Hengel, 'Jakobus' (n.133), in an article marked by great historical knowledge, specifically takes no account of the question of the outcome of the collection (cf. esp. 92–8 ['Jakobus und Paulus'] and 95f.), although this question, which is decisive for Paul's self-understanding, cries out for an answer. Hengel, who regards Acts 21 as an eyewitness account, merely remarks laconically that perhaps with the fulfilment of the vow of the four Nazirites 'the question of the collection, about the acceptance of which Paul himself had doubts in Rom. 15.31, was clarified' (96). A book by E.P. Sanders (*Paul*, 1991) which is otherwise marked by a critical treatment of Acts, presupposes: 'The collection was accepted by James, and so Paul's worry about a rupture caused by the "false brethren" came to nothing (Acts 21.17–26)' (15). However, this assumption is probably not justified, for the reasons given in the text.

198. Josephus, *Antt.* XX 199–203 (see 49f. below); Hegesippus in Eusebius, *HE* II 23, 4–6.

199. Cf. Gerd Lüdemann, *Paul, Apostle to the Gentiles. Studies in Chronology*, 1984, 66f. (with further formulae).

200. In addition to the commentaries cf. Berger, 'Almosen' (n.183), 111 n.51, who sees here a reference to the real significance of the collection, namely that as alms from Pauline communities to Israel it was a demonstration of social solidarity, so that they would have the status of godfearers. However, the 'alms' are a Lukan motif. Of the 13 instances in the New Testament, 10 are from Luke/Acts, and 8 of these are from the Acts of the Apostles.

201. Cf. the basic work by Georg Strecker, 'Die sogenannte Zweite Jerusalemreise des Paulus (Act. 11.27–30)' (1962), in id., *Eschaton und Historie*, 1979, 132–41.

202. Cf. Holmberg, *Paul* (n.188), 43 (with bibliography).

203. Georgi, *Geschichte* (n.186), 89.

204. Cf. the scholars mentioned in Lüdemann, *Opposition* (n.133), 251 n.117, who have similarly supported the theory of the rejection of the collection.

205. Becker, *Paulus* (n.197), 483.

206. Ibid., 484.

207. Cf. Martin Hengel, *The Zealots, The Investigation into the Jewish Freedom Movement in the Period from Herod I Until 70 AD*, 1989, 200–6. In addition the halakhoth contained among other things twelve prohibitions of pagan foods and the prohibition of the Greek language and statements by pagan witnesses before the court. It is impossible to arrive at a precise dating, but the decree belongs in the period before the Jewish War. The refusal 'to accept consecrated gifts or sacrifices from non-Jews ... was the external cause of the outbreak of the Jewish War' (Hengel, *Zealots*, 205, referring to Josephus, *BJ* II 409f.; cf. also Wander, *Trennungprozesse* [n.133], 240).

208. Jacob Taubes, *Die Politische Theologie des Paulus*, 1993, 28. Taubes emphasizes well how concerned Paul was for legitimation in handing over the collection (30f.).

209. Translation by Louis H.Feldman, *Josephus* IX, LCL,1965.

210. Hengel, 'Jakobus' (n.133), 73f.

211. For what follows see Hengel, 'Jakobus', 73ff.

212. Cf. the cautious discussion by August Strobel, *Die Stunde der Wahrheit*, WUNT 21, 1980, 31–6.

213. Hengel, 'Jakobus' (n.133), 80. By contrast, Berger, *Theologiegeschichte* (n.1), makes less of a differentiation: 'The notices that James lived all his life as a Nazirite at the temple and devoted himself to prayer are credible (cf. e.g. Eusebius, *HE* II 23, 4–6). This explains the connection between Paul and the Nazirate of Jerusalem Christians (Acts 21.26)' (159). By way of criticism it should be said that the passage from Eusebius' *Church History* cited by Berger, which goes back to Hegesippus, is histori-

cally already a further development. Moreover the combination of the note in Hegesippus with Acts 21.26 rests on an arbitrary association.

214. Hengel, 'Jakobus', 97. In fact Hengel, too, depicts James as specifically not being a law breaker.

215. Cf. Lüdemann, *Opposition* (n.133), 62.

216. Translation from Ante-Nicene Fathers (n.98).

217. Cf. Georg Strecker, 'Ebioniten', *RAC* 4, 1959, 487–500: 487. Cf. also above, 30.

218. Adolf von Harnack, *Judentum und Judenchristentum in Justins Dialog mit Trypho*, TU 39.1, 1913, 47–92, is still basic. Cf. also Oscar Skarsaune, 'Justin, der Märtyrer', *TRE* 17, 1988, 471–8. What I go on to say in part leans heavily on Lüdemann, *Opposition* (n.133), 150–3, without substantiating points in detail.

219. Unfortunately this text has not been reprinted or analysed in the useful and wide-ranging book by A. F. J. Klijn and G. Reinink, *Patristic Evidence for Jewish-Christian Sects*, NT.S, 1973.

220. For Justin cf. above, 18.

221. Cf. Hermann Lichtenberger, 'Synkretistische Züge in jüdischen und judenchristlichen Taufbewegungen', in *Jews and Christians*, WUNT 66, 1992, 85–97 (bibliography). However, objection should be made to Lichtenberger's uncritical use of the monograph by G. P. Luttikhuizen, *The Revelation of Elchasai*, TSAJ 8, 1985 (on this see F. S. Jones in *JbAC* 30, 1987, 200–9). As long as Georg Strecker, 'Elkesai' (1959), in id., *Eschaton und Historie*, 1979, 320–33, whom Lichtenberger does not mention once, has not been refuted, Elkesai will have to be reckoned a Jewish Christian; cf. also Lüdemann, *Opposition* (n.133), 129–39.

222. Peter von der Osten-Sacken, 'Römer 9–11 als Schibbolet christlicher Theologie', in id., *Evangelium und Tora. Aufsätze zu Paulus*, ThB 77, 1987, 294–314: 297f.

223. Ernst Dassmann, *Der Stachel im Fleisch. Paulus in der frühchristlichen Literatur bis Irenäus*, 1979, 245.

224. Andreas Lindemann, *Paulus im ältesten Christentum. Das Bild des Apostels und die Rezeption der paulinischen Theologie in der frühchristlichen Literatur bis Marcion*, BHTh 58, 1979, 366.

225. For details cf Lüdemann, 'Geschichte' (n.2), 109f.; Theodore Stylianopoulos, *Justin Martyr and the Mosaic Law*, SBLDS 20, 1975.

226. Dassmann, *Paulus* (n.223), 247f. But Bauer, *Orthodoxy* (n.83), to whom Dassmann refers in his argument, differs from Dassmann in thinking it doubtful that Justin used the letters of Paul. Of possible allusions to the letters of Paul in Justin he writes: 'Such allusions are of no help to me, since at best they spring up occasionally from the subconscious, but evidence no kind of living relationship with Paul' (215).

227. For a bibliography cf. Lüdemann, *Opposition* (n.133), 298–304. A commentary (with German translation) on the Pseudo-Clementine Homilies by Gerd Lüdemann and Jürgen Wehnert is virtually complete. The translations below are based on it. The standard edition of the texts comes from Bernhard Rehm (GCS 422); the third edition revised by Georg Strecker appeared in 1992.

228. On this cf Klijn/Reinink, *Evidence* (n.219), 22–39, 44–6.

229. Hans Joachim Schoeps, *Paul* (n.133), 79. It should be emphasized that at the narrative level of the latest stratum there is polemic against Simon Magus, but in part Paul is meant. Here I presuppose this generally accepted verdict of scholarship and only use those texts in which there is manifestly a reference to Paul.

230. Schoeps, *Paul* (n.133), 82.

231. Bauer, *Orthodoxy* (n.83), 236.

232. *On the state of research*: the literature on Paul is overwhelming. Year by year so many works are written that no individual can read them all any more. The conclusion drawn by some scholars, that from now on they should concentrate on only one of Paul's letters, is not a good thing. So the following references are very subjective. Albert Schweitzer, *Geschichte der paulinischen Forschung*, 1910, gives information about research into Paul in the nineteenth century. Ferdinand Christian Baur, *Paulus, der Apostel Jesu Christi*, 1845 (1866/67² in two volumes) is still worth reading; also Hermann Lüdemann, *Die paulinische Anthropologie*, 1872. Reports on research into Paul were given by Rudolf Bultmann, *ThR* 1, 1929, 26–39; id., *ThR* 6, 1934, 229–46; id., 8, 1936, 1–22; Otto Merk, *ThR* 53, 1988, 1–81; Hans Hübner, *ANRW* II, 25, 4, 1987, 2649–80 (since 1945); Béda Rigaux, *Paulus und seine Briefe. Der Stand der Forschung*, 1964; Werner Georg Kümmel, *The New Testament. A History of the Investigation of its Problems*, 1972; id., *Das Neue Testament im 20.Jahrhundert. Ein Forschungsbericht*, SBS 50, 1970, 93–105. Cf. also Karl Heinrich Rengstorf (ed.), *Das Paulusbild in der neueren deutschen Forschung*, WdF 24, ³1982. Bultmann's statement that the significance of Paul (for world history) was that he was the first Christian theologian (*ThR* 1929, 59) has had an influence on many contributions to the German literature on Paul. Accordingly, the letters of Paul have been interpreted strongly in terms of their theological purpose or from a unitary starting point. Correct though it is, this approach has often led to historically very forced constructions of the positions of opponents (aiming at a hermeneutical contribution). One need only recall the débacle of the attempt by Walter Schmithals to find Gnostic opponents in every letter of Paul (for a summary cf. id., *Neues Testament und Gnosis*, EdF 208, 1984); for criticism see Lüdemann, *Paul* (n.199), 206–9; *Opposition to Paul* (n.133), passim.

A revival in research was brought about by the rediscovery of Paul's Jewish matrix (W. D. Davies, *Paul and Rabbinic Judaism* [4]1980; cf. now the admirable work by Peter J. Tomson, *Paul and the Jewish Law. Halakha in the Letters of the Apostle to the Gentiles*, CRINT III.1, 1990) and large-scale comparisons beween Paul and Judaism (E. P. Sanders, *Paul and Palestinian Judaism*, 1977). This has had lasting influence on English-language research, but so far has unjustly been insufficiently noted in Germany. At present no one knows the Hellenistic side of Paul, which is equally important, better than Hans Dieter Betz, *Paulinische Studien, Gesammelte Aufsätze* III, 1994 (with bibliography). There are some highly interesting Jewish interpretations of the apostle to the Gentiles: Joseph Klausner, *From Jesus to Paul*, 1944; Schoeps, *Paul* (n.133); Richard L. Rubenstein, *My Brother Paul*, 1972; Schalom Ben-Chorin, *Der Völkerapostel in jüdischer Sicht*, [3]1983; Alan F. Segal, *Paul the Convert. The Apostolate and Apostasy of Saul the Pharisee*, 1990; and Jacob Taubes, *Die Politische Theologie des Paulus*, 1993; cf. further Lindeskog, *Problem* (n.133), 85–103.

Jürgen Becker, *Paulus. Der Apostel der Völker*, 1989, is a full, non-technical account of Paul with adequate attention to historical and theological questions. The thesis of Hermann Detering (*Der gefälschte Paulus. Das Urchristentum im Zwielicht*, 1995), that the letters of Paul come from the second century, is mistaken and is refuted by the existing sources. Further important literature on Paul is referred to at individual points in the text.

233. For the question how we are to regard the phenomenon it denotes (as a forgery?), cf. 105–8 below.

234. For criticism cf. 120–30 below.

235. Cf. Lüdemann, *Christianity* (n.1). This book has certainly been only partially successful. Whereas some scholars defend the reliability of Acts in almost every detail (most recently Rainer Riesner, *Die Frühzeit des Paulus. Studien zur Chronologie, Missionsstrategie und Theologie*, WUNT 71, 1994 [with bibliography]), others – above all under the influence of the great commentary by Ernst Haenchen (1974) – continue to be sceptical about the second part of Acts. But Becker, *Paulus* (n.232), 16, rightly comments: 'Only the laborious course of carefully weighing up arguments in each individual instance can help us further. Neither sweeping condemnation nor the postulate that Acts has high value help us further in the quest for historical truth.' The monograph by Claus-Jürgen Thornton, *Der Zeuge des Zeugen. Lukas als Historiker der Paulusreisen*, WUNT 56, 1991, has left me somewhat perplexed. It is beyond question enviably learned and presents the best possible defence of the view that Luke the companion of Paul is the author of Acts. But Thornton's remarks on the

historical value of the individual details given by Luke are too mysterious for me. Thus he writes at the end: 'We treat Luke as if he looked at what happened through a certain pair of spectacles... In no way are we doing justice to Luke the man and Christian historian. His theological understanding is not a scheme of interpretation which he could so to speak paint subsequently on "objective" facts. *His view of history presents itself to him at the same time as he experiences it.* He does not wear any spectacles through which he looks at history but which he could also take off. He perceives through his eyes. He wants to be an eye-witness to what he can see with his eyes' (367). Is that to be the result of Thornton's stupendous learning? What else is left to us than to ask in return what really happened? Furthermore, why does Thornton treat professional colleagues so roughly? Surely that betrays uncertainty and hinders the dialogue on which even Thornton is dependent? Cf. also the review of Thornton's book by Gottfried Schille, *ThLZ* 118, 1993, 139–41, which says all that needs to be said about Thornton's style in dealing with authors who hold other views.

236. Cf. Lüdemann, *Paul* (n.199), passim.

237. Cf. already Ernst von Dobschütz, *Probleme des Apostolischen Zeitalters*, 1904, 5: 'In particular I believe that the individual reports can often be trusted more than is usually the case at present. It is simply that the credibility of individual pieces of tradition has been put in doubt as a result of a false chronological ordering on the part of the author.'

238. For the conflicts in Acts cf. Jürgen Roloff, 'Konflikte und Konfliktlösungen in der Apostelgeschichte', in Claus Bussmann and Walter Radl (eds.), *Der Treue Gottes trauen. Beiträge zum Werk des Lukas (FS Gerhard Schneider)*, 1991, 111–26.

239. Acts 14.4, 14, where Paul and Barnabas are called apostles, only seems to be an exception. Here Luke is following a source which uses 'apostle' to denote emissaries of the community – and not witnesses to the resurrection. Cf. above, 40.

240. Christoph Burchard, *Der dreizehnte Zeuge*, FRLANT 103, 1970; id., 'Paulus in der Apostelgeschichte', EvTh 10, 1950, 1–15 (= *Aufsätze zum Neuen Testament* I, ThB 31, 1965, 9–27).

242. Epiphanius, *Haer* 30, 16, 6–9 in the so-called 'ascensions of James' Cf. the comments in Lüdemann, *Opposition to Paul* (n.133), 80f. (which also contains the whole fragment of text).

243. Acts of Paul 7, in Wilhelm Schneemelcher and R. McL. Wilson (eds.), *New Testament Apocrypha* II, 1992, 252. Cf. the introduction by Schneemelcher, 213–36.

244. Acts of Paul and Thecla, in ibid., 239. Cf. also R. M. Grant, 'The Description of Paul in the Acts of Paul and Thecla', *VigChr* 36, 1982, 1–4:

he argues that here Paul is given the attributes of an leader in antiquity. Cf. also Ernst Dassmann, *Paulus in frühchristlicher Frömmigkeit und Kunst*, Rheinisch-Westfälische Akademie der Wissenschaften, Vorträge G 256, 1982.

245. For the author of the Acts of Paul see below, 141f.

246. In the following section I am referring, sometimes word for word, to Lüdemann, *Resurrection* (n.3), 74–84; Lüdemann, 'Karfreitag' (n.26), 33–40, without noting the fact.

247. Cf. for what follows Heinrich Weinel, *Paulus: Der Mensch und sein Werk: Die Anfänge des Christentums, der Kirche und des Dogmas*, Lebensfragen, 1904, 13f.; Meeks, *First Urban Christians* (n.47), 9ff.

248. Becker, *Paulus* (n.197), 35.

249. Others conjecture Damascus as Paul's home town. Cf. Koester, *Einführung* (n.133), 531: 'Some features of his theology, like his marked apocalyptic expectation – certainly a Jewish legacy that he did not first take over from Christians – fit better into a milieu and church which was not so markedly Hellenistic as one must assume for Tarsus.' *By way of criticism*: we have a tradition for Tarsus which can be connected with the biography of Paul on the basis of the letters, but not for Damascus. Moreover Paul was probably trained neither in Tarsus nor in Damascus, but in Jerusalem (see 66 below). Cf. also Sanders, *Paul* (n.232), 543, on the question of the derivation of the apocalyptic elements in Paul.

250. Cf. Martin Hengel (*The Pre-Christian Paul*, 1991, 38): 'Greek was Paul's mother tongue, but he also had a command of Hebrew, the "holy language" of scripture and liturgy, and Aramaic, the vernacular of Jewish Palestine. A Pharisee who was faithful to the law and a "Hebrew of the Hebrews" who spoke only Greek would be a strange mixture.' Cf. also Becker, *Paulus* (n.197), 54f.

251. Cf. now Martin Hengel and Anna Maria Schwemer (eds.), *Die Septuaginta zwischen Judentum und Christentum*, WUNT 72, 1994.

252. For the following brief account of the Pharisees cf. Berndt Schaller ('Pharisäer', *EKL* ³1992, 1177f.), to whom I am also grateful for personal instruction on this matter. Present research into the Pharisees produces a chaotic picture; cf. only Peter Schäfer, 'Der vorrabbinische Pharisäismus', in Martin Hengel and Ulrich Heckel (eds.), *Paulus und das antike Judentum*, WUNT 58, 1992, 125–72 (with bibliography). The problem relates to whether or not we have sources for the reconstruction of Pharisaism in the first century. The only (ex-)Pharisee from the period before 70 CE about whom sources survive is the apostle Paul. The other source is Josephus, who at the beginning of the second century claims to have been a Pharisee (*Vita* 10–12) and whose work is the basic source for the history of Judaism in the first centuries BCE and CE. There is argument

over the attribution of individual sources (e.g. the Psalms of Solomon or the *Assumptio Mosis*) to the Pharisees which is sometimes customary. However, the importance of the New Testament Gospels from the period after 70 is not to be underestimated, although they contain a polemical picture of the Pharisees. For more recent literature see Hengel, *Paul* (n.250); Günter Stemberger, *Pharisäer, Sadduzäer, Essener*, SBS 144, 1991; Steve Mason, *Flavius Josephus on the Pharisees*, StPB 39, 1991. From an earlier period Julius Wellhausen, *Die Pharisäer und die Sadducäer. Eine Untersuchung zur inneren jüdischen Geschichte*, 1874 (= ³1967) is stilll important; it was the first work to regard the Psalms of Solomon as Pharisaic and is probably still right in conjecturing that the influence of the Pharisees on the people was considerable, even if Wellhausen's remarks are highly polemical. Cf. e.g. the statement: 'They (viz. the Pharisees) never took the human side in matters of God but always opposed it' (101); 'the remarkably indirect approach in relation to God, the lack of freedom with which Paul expresses himself, is a main characteristic of the dominant (viz. Pharisaic) piety of those days' (19).

253. Cf. Dan. 12.2f.: 'And many of those who sleep in the dust of the earth shall awaken, some to everlasting life, and some to shame and everlasting contempt'; and Ezek.37 (esp. v.12): 'Thus says the Lord God: Behold, I will open your graves, and raise you from your graves, O my people; and I will bring you home into the land of Israel.'

254. For the question whether Josephus was really a Pharisee, see n.252 above.

255. Sanders, *Law* (n.192), 236, differs; he puts the fulfilment of the commandments for purity only in third place: 'Study of the law and of their extra-biblical traditions, along with belief in life after death, were the two main marks of the Pharisees – not tithes and purity' (236).

256. Klaus Berger ('Jesus als Pharisäer und frühe Christen als Pharisäer', *NT* 30, 1988, 231–62) uses far too wide a concept of Pharisee and begins from the doubtful presupposition of an extended Diaspora Pharisaism.

257. So it might be only half true that I Cor. 15.8f. formulates the correlation of inferiority and posteriority and thus serves to express the self-disparagement which often occurs in rhetoric (Michael Wolter, *Die Pastoralbriefe als Paulustradition*, FRLANT 146, 1988, 55). Thus this is not a *captatio benevolentiae*; Paul means it seriously. The introduction of rhetorical categories only makes interpretation more difficult. Unfortunately many historically important details of information are being formally explained away today with reference to rhetoric. When Paul writes in I Cor. 14.18 that he speaks more in tongues than all the Corinthians, Friedrich Wilhelm Horn (*Das Angeld des Geistes. Studien zur paulinischen Pneumatologie*, FRLANT 154, 1992) regards this as rhetori-

cally motivated and unhistorical (255f.). But even if Paul is exaggerating here, for understandable reasons – he is in fact arguing – the aspect of glossolalia in Paul cannot be completely disputed or limited to the degree that it disappears from his personal piety.

258. William Wrede, 'Paulus', *RGV* I 5–6, 1904, in Rengstorf, *Paulusbild* (n.232), 23.

259. Cf. Ernest Renan, *Saint Paul*, 1888, 13.

260. He was probably not a widower, as Joachim Jeremias argues, 'War Paulus Witwer?', *ZNW* 25, 1926, 310–12.

261. Tos. Jebamoth 8.4; cf. Albrecht Oepke, 'Probleme der vorchristlicher Zeit des Paulus' (1933), in Rengstorf, *Paulusbild* (n.232), 410–46: 431.

262. Cf. Hengel, *Paul* (n.250), 292 (discussion of his article).

263. Cf. Werner Georg Kümmel, *Römer 7 und das Bild des Menschen im Neuen Testament. Zwei Studien*, ThB 53, 157.

264. Carl Gustav Jung, 'The Psychological Foundations of Belief in Spirits' (1928), in id., *Collected Works* 8, 1960, 301–18.

265. Gerd Theissen, *Psychological Aspects of Pauline Theology*, 1987, 244. It should be emphatically stressed that Theissen distinguishes the thesis of an unconscious conflict over the law behind Rom. 7 from the view that an unconscious attraction to the Christian faith was associated with this. He writes: 'We admit that we can say nothing about an unconscious Christianity of the pre-Christian Paul' (237). But in my view the two belong together (see below).

266. Kümmel, *Römer 7* (n.263), 1–60.

267. See n.250. Subsequent references to this work are in brackets in the text.

268. Rudolf Bultmann, 'Römer 7 und die Anthropologie des Paulus' (1932) = id., *Exegetica*, 1967, 198–209: 199.

269. Cf. also Theissen, *Aspects* (n.265), 209 n.25.

270. For the exegetical literature see the relevant commentaries.

271. Ulrich Wilckens, *Der Brief an die Römer* (Röm 6–11), EKK VI/2, 1980, 79.

272. Cf. the examples from antiquity in Theissen, *Aspects* (n.265), 224f.

273. But cf. Ezek. 20.25: 'Moreover I (= Yahweh) gave them statutes that were not good and ordinances by which they could not have life.'

274. For the tradition analysis of the sentence Rom. 7.15b cf. Theissen (n.265), 211–21.

275. Cf. 'For I do not do what I want, but I do the very thing I hate' (v.15b) with 'For I do not do the good I want, but the evil I do not want is what I do' (v.19).

276. Cf. e.g. Conzelmann, *Outline* (n.15), 228–35.

277. On the above cf. Theissen (n.265), 231.

278. The following reflections make the controversy between Bultmann 'Römer 7' (n.268, 198–209) and Paul Althaus (*Paulus und Luther über den Menschen*, 1938) valuable for the question of a conscious or an unconscious conflict in the biography of Paul underlying Rom. 7. Althaus saw the split as a conflict between willing and acting; Bultmann dissociates himself from this subjectivistic anthropology and sees the conflict as trans-subjective. I replace 'trans-subjective' with 'unconscious' and see in Rom. 7 both kinds of split, a moral-ethical and thus a conscious one, and an unconscious one. Cf. Rudolf Bultmann, *Theology of the New Testament* I, 1952, 248f. (with a correction to his original position).

279. Oskar Pfister, 'Die Entwicklung des Apostels Paulus', *Imago* 6, 1920, 243–90: 269. References to this work are given below in the text.

280. For the reasons see Lüdemann, 'Karfreitag' (n.26), 27–9.

281. It need hardly also be said that the assumption 'that the Risen Christ made himself known' must be excluded from a historical account because it is indebted to supernaturalist thought. It is remarkable that Wolfhart Pannenberg again introduces it as an argument against my book *The Resurrection of Jesus*. Cf. Wolfhart Pannenberg, 'Die Auferstehung Jesu – Historie und Theologie', *ZThK* 91, 1994, 318–28: 323 (= lecture in Göttingen, 23 June 1994). For a response cf. Lüdemann, 'Karfreitag' (n.26), 32 n.65.

282. Cf. Lüdemann, *Resurrection* (n.3), 81–4.

283. As a witness beyond suspicion for the view that the Easter appearances were visions cf. Gerhard Ebeling, *Dogmatik des christlichen Glaubens* II.2, *Der Glaube an Gott als Versöhner der Welt*, 1979, 299: 'But despite all the problems which arise from such a view, there is no compelling reason against subsuming all the appearances historically under the same category and describing them as visions.'

284. Such a misunderstanding underlies e.g. Jürgen Roloff's review of my *Resurrection* (n.3) in *BZ* NF 39, 1995, 133–7.

285. Cf. Hans Weder, *Das Kreuz Jesu bei Paulus. Ein Versuch, über den Geschichtsbezug des christlichen Glaubens nachzudenken*, FRLANT 125, 1981, 121–224; Christian Dietzfelbinger, *Die Berufung des Paulus als Ursprung seiner Theologie*, WMANT 58, 1985, passim.

286. Cf. in an analogous way the fact that the statements about the resurrection of Jesus in I Cor. 15.4 are in the perfect, whereas the death of Jesus, his burial and his appearance to Cephas are in the aorist tense.

287. Cf. the discussion of the reception of the book in Lüdemann, *Paul, Apostle to the Gentiles* (n.199), 289–94. The reference constantly made to the fact that Orosius (VII 6, 15) dates the expulsion of the Jews from Rome to 49 and that this fits Acts 18.2 is pointless when it is recognized that this

date was calculated by an informant of Orosius on the basis of Acts (!) (cf. Gerd Lüdemann, 'Das Judenedikt des Claudius [Apg 18,2]', in Claus Bussmann and Walter Radl [eds.], *Der Treue Gottes trauen. Beiträge zum Werk des Lukas* [FS Gerhard Schneider], 1991, 289–98). At the same time it should be emphasized that before calculating an absolute date the most important issue here is whether I Thess. comes from the period before the Apostolic Council. Numerous recent works on the chronology of Paul agree on this point – which risks being forgotten; cf. only Robert Jewett, *Dating Paul's Life*, 1979, 89–94; Jerome Murphy-O'Connor, 'Pauline Mission before the Jerusalem Conference', *RB* 89, 1982, 71–91.

288. The term 'millenarian movement' has been coined for this phenomenon, cf. John Gager, 'Das Ende der Zeit und die Entstehung von Gemeinschaften', in Wayne A. Meeks (ed.), *Zur Soziologie des Urchristentums*, ThB 62, 1979, 88–130.

289. Cf. his biography in Gerd Lüdemann and Martin Schröder, *Die Religionsgeschichtliche Schule in Göttingen. Eine Dokumentation*, 1987, 89; also Berthold Lannert, *Die Wiederentdeckung der neutestamentlichen Eschatologie durch Johannes Weiss*, TANZ 2, 1989.

290. Johannes Weiss, *Jesus' Proclamation of the Kingdom of God* (1892), ed. Richard H.Hiers and David L.Holland, 1971. The second fully revised German edition of this work, *Die Predigt Jesu vom Reich Gottes*, appeared in 1900, now extended to 210pp. Here I keep to the first edition, from which the English translation was made, and only resort to the second where there are differences or expansions.

291. Cf. the masterly article by Friedrich Wilhelm Graf, 'Kulturprotestantismus. Zur Begriffsgeschichte einer theologiepolitischen Chiffre', *Archiv für Begriffsgeschichte* 28, 1984 (1987), 214–68 (= in Hans Martin Müller [ed.], *Kulturprotestantismus. Beiträge zu einer Gestalt des modernen Christentums*, 1992, 21–77). The identification of the kingdom of God with the consummation of culture described above in the text relates to all three of the definitions of cultural Protestantism mentioned by Graf.

292. Weiss, *Preaching* (n.290), 73.

293. Weiss, *Preaching* (n.290), 74, with reference to Rev.12.7–17. Weiss also makes a general reference in the second edition to Job 1–2 (the fate of the patient is predetermined in heaven), and to Dan 10.13/11.1 (the battle of the nations on earth runs parallel to the battle of the archangel Michael against the 'princes' of Persia and Greece) and II Macc.5.2f. (the angels join in the fight in the clouds when Antiochus goes against Egypt).

294. Weiss, *Preaching* (n.290), 92 (reference to Luke 17; Mark 13).

295. Weiss, *Preaching* (n.290), 130.

296. For the text see Lüdemann, *Paul* (n.199), 205–42. I am glad that

this exegesis has been a fruitful contribution to research into I Thess. and has largely found acceptance, even if some contradiction was of course unavoidable. Cf. only Helmut Merklein, 'Der Theologe als Prophet. Zur Funktion prophetischen Redens im theologischen Diskurs des Paulus', NTS 38, 1992, 402–24: 405 n.10: 'If I take issue above all with Gerd Lüdemann in what follows, that is because when I began my reflections I was still convinced by his thesis.' According to Merklein, the reason for the sorrow of the Thessalonians was not their ignorance about a resurrection of the dead but their inability to combine parousia and resurrection of the dead into an integral event' (407). For criticism of this see already Lüdemann, Paul, 211f. Merklein defines I Thess. 4.15b as Paul himself speaking as a prophet here (418), whereas I termed the verse a Pauline summary of the word of the Lord in vv.16f. (Paul, 231). In my view the difference is not a serious one.

297. This undertakes for all the biblical writings the so-called 'canonical criticism' which conjures up the names of James A. Sanders and Brevard S. Childs. For the New Testament see Robert W. Wall and Eugene E. Lemcio, The New Testament as Canon. A Reader in Canonical Criticism, JSNTSSS 76, 1992. Cf. further Eckard Schnabel, 'Die Entwürfe von B.S. Childs and H. Gese bezüglich des Kanons', in Gerhard Maier (ed.), Der Kanon der Bibel, 1990, 102–52. It should be sufficiently clear from what has been said in the text that I can only regard 'canonical criticism' without previous historical reconstruction as an error, since its representatives do not respect the authors of the original biblical documents sufficiently. James Barr (Holy Scripture, Canon, Authority, Criticism, 1983) has emphasized that the main question of theology is not relevance but truth (118). That also applies to history. Cf. also Richard R. Topping, 'The Canon and the Truth: Brevard Childs and James Barr on the Canon and the Historical Critical Method', TJT 8, 1992, 239–60.

298. Cf. a remark by Overbeck, Geschichte (n.60), 1, which is worth noting: 'It is in the nature of all canonization to make its objects unknowable, and one can also say of all the writings of our New Testament that at the moment of their canonization they ceased to be understood. They have been transposed into the higher sphere of an eternal norm for the church, not without a dense veil having been spread over their origin, their original relationships and their original meaning' (see further below, under ch.9).

299. Andreas Lindemann ('Paulus und die korinthische Eschatologie. Zur These von einer "Entwicklung" im paulinischen Denken', NTS 37, 1991, 373–99) remarks: 'In that case, after another death in Thessalonica a new Pauline argument would have been needed' (378 n.21). No! The model of I Thess. 4.13–17 continues to maintain its validity unchanged. It

does not need to be changed as long as the deaths are the exception. Later Lindemann focusses his criticism on my exegesis of I Thess. 4.13–17, by writing that Paul does not say how many people the 'we' in I Thess 4.17 would refer to (389). *Answer*: Paul does not say it in so many words, but he does clearly presuppose that he is reckoning with a survival of the Thessalonians and his own person to the parousia. In my view, anyone who in exegesis only goes by the explicit statements of Paul, and does not take into account their presuppositions and what is taken for granted in them, is not fully involved in exegesis and is in danger of losing sight of the living person of Paul.

300. Between I Thess. and I Cor. Paul wrote at least a further letter, the so-called 'previous' letter (I Cor. 5.19), but this has not survived.

301. Merklein, 'Theologe' (n.296), vigorously disputes this because it is not 'all' that is negated but 'fallen asleep'. He continues: 'That means that he (viz.Paul) limits the presupposition on which he has made the previous remarks (I Cor. 15.35–49). He concedes that these remarks do not apply to all (because *not all* have fallen asleep)' (422, his italics). Isn't Merklein here in fact saying the same thing as I am?

302. Berger, *Theologiegeschichte* (n.1), puts I Thess. 4 and I Cor. 15 side by side and recognizes clear differences. He writes: 'However, this is not a purposeful development but relates to events which were conditioned by questions arising out of the situation' (442). Like Merklein, 'Theologe' (n.296), Berger does not take sufficiently into account the fact that I Thess. was written in Corinth and therefore I Cor. 15.51f. can be regarded as a continuation of I Thess. 4.13ff., the teaching of which was communicated to the Corinthians on the visit on which Paul founded the community. We are to presuppose that the readers of what later became I Corinthians were acquainted with the stage of Paul's teaching which is expressed in I Thess. 4. I Cor. 15 cannot be seen independently of I Thess. 4 and simply put alongside this text.

303. Berger, *Theologiegeschichte* (n.1), brings rhetorical reasons into play here and writes: 'The expectation of an imminent end has more of a rhetorical function in I Cor. 15; by including himself among those who are still alive (v.52b; literally I Thess. 4.17), he increases his credibility in describing the matter' (43). But was there also a rhetorical reason for what Paul says in I Thess. 4.17?

304. There is an illuminating account of the interpretation of II Cor. 5.1–10 in Friedrich Gustav Lang, *2 Korinther 5, 1–10 in der neueren Forschung*, BGBE 16, 1973, 1989, 44.

305. Cf. here Udo Schnelle, *Wandlungen in paulinischen Denken*, SBS 137, 1989, 44.

306. Cf. Anton Vögtle, 'Röm 13,11–14 und die "Nah"-Erwartung'

(1976), in id., *Offenbarunsgeschehen und Wirkungsgeschichte. Neutestamentliche Beiträge*, 1985, 191–204.

307. Cf. by way of example the analysis by Georg Strecker, *Eschaton und Historie*, 1979, 154–6.

308. Thus most recently Peter Wick, *Der Philipperbrief. Der formale Aufbau des Briefes als Schüssel zum Verständnis seines Inhalts*, BWANT 135, 1993; Schnelle, *Einleitung* (n.10), 164–7.

309. Cf. already I Thess. 5.10: (Christ has died for us) 'that whether we wake or sleep (= die), we live with him' (cf. Lüdemann, *Paul* [n.199] , 213).

310. Fritz Buri, *Die Bedeutung der neutestamentlichen Eschatologie für die neuere protestantische Theologie. Ein Versuch zur Klärung des Problems der Eschatologie und zu einem neuen Verständnis ihres eigentlichen Anliegens*, 1935, 113–34. (Unfortunately Erich Grässer, *Die Naherwartung Jesu*, SBS 61, 1973, 43, does not go further into this important work of Buri's.) Buri (1–112) gives a still penetrating critique of the attempts (which have not diminished since his time) to rescue at least elements of the New Testament notion of the future. A. Emanuel Biedermann (*Die freie Theologie oder Philosophie und Christentum in Streit und Frieden*, 1844) had already remarked on this: the 'earliest Christian world view no longer exists' (70); 'there is *no longer any* theologian who still adopts completely the earliest Christian view of the world and has made the notions which we find in the New Testament writings his own – when we read what they actually say and do not start from anything *a priori*, to find in them nothing other than what we have otherwise already made our own' (71). 'One has already long felt that, basically, if one identified Christianity directly with the earliest Christian view of the world ... one would be doing away with it completely' (73).

311. Cf. John G.Gager, *Kingdom and Community. The Social World of Early Christianity*, 1975, 20ff. (taking note of the important book by Leon Festinger, Henry W.Riecken and Stanley Schachter, *Wehn Prophecy Fails*, 1956). As in certain groups of earliest Christianity and in Qumran, so too in the group studied by the American team, the failure of the future to turn out as prophesied did not cause a serious crisis. On the contrary, when the essence of the faith of this group (the destruction of the world on 21 December) had been unequivocally refuted, the members did not react by giving up their faith but by intensifying their previous preaching to the pagans (Gager, *Kingdom*, 39).

312. Cf. Lüdemann, *Paul* (n.199), 116 n.41. The commentary on Gal. 5.11 is contained in Gal. 6.12. So Gal. 5.11 is to be paraphrased as follows: 'If I preach circumcision like my opponents, what am I being persecuted for? After all it is they who, by causing you to be circumcised, want to escape persecution so that the scandal of the cross is removed.'

313. Berger, *Theologiegeschichte* (n.10), now differs: 'That Paul preaches in Damascus in the synagogues indicates that he is engaged in mission to the Jews (Acts 9.22). Therefore he is probably also silent about this time in Gal. 1' (235). As Acts 9.2 is based on the Lukan (!) scheme (cf. Acts 15.5, 28), Berger's reflections can be left aside. They are another example of his arbitrary use of Acts.

314. I do *not* want to dispute here that Paul occasionally preached the Gospel to Jews. But he did not regard this preaching as a special task. For the question where in particular Paul met Gentiles to preach the gospel to them cf. Marius Reiser, 'Hat Paulus Heiden bekehrt?', *BZ* NF 39, 1995, 76–91 (with bibliography). However, Reiser's view that Paul gained Gentiles (almost) exclusively in the synagogue is overdrawn. Paul often enough had to get out of the way because of the resistance of local Jews. Cf. also the important article by Christoph Burchhard, 'Formen der Vermittlungen christlichen Glaubens im Neuen Testament', *EvTh* 38, 1978, 313–40: 315–20 (on Paul) and the splendid book by Martin Goodman, *Mission and Conversion. Proselytizing in the Religious History of the Roman Empire*, 1994.

315. Of course in reality it is not always possible to make a clean distinction between the mission to the Gentiles and the mission to the Jews. For example, in Timothy Paul had gained a Jewish-Christian fellow-worker, circumcised him because of his Jewish mother (Acts 16.1–3) and also accepted Jews into his communities. Nevertheless, none of this alters the general correctness of what is said above.

316. This is emphasized by way of dissociation from the widespread suggestion that as an effervescent genius Paul did everything alone. The simple observation that in the majority of the extant letters Paul mentions others who join with him in sending them already tells against this. Cf. the study by Wolf-Henning Ollrog, *Paulus und seine Mitarbeiter. Untersuchungen zu Theorie und Praxis der paulinischen Mission*, WMANT 50, 1979; for Paul's women colleagues see also below, 88.

317. Nevertheless 'it still remains difficult to explain how Paul could connect the mission to the Gentiles so closely with the Damascus vision' (G. P. Wetter, 'Die Damaskusvision und das paulinische Evangelium', in *Festgabe für Adolf Jülicher zum 70. Geburtstag am 26. Januar 1927*, 1927, 80–92: 83). Wetter continues: 'one must assume that the facts were heavily adjusted by the apostle's later experiences'. In his view, 'who has called' (Gal. 1.15) points to the Damascus vision, 'reveal' (1.16) denotes 'the way in which Paul has received his distinctive gospel all the time' (82). The 'vision at Paul's conversion is not a unique experience, but only the first in a long series' (ibid.). The correct insight here is that in Gal. 1.15f. the interpretation of the Damascus vision as a prophetic call has accrued

at a secondary stage (cf. Isa. 49.1; Jer. 1.5). For the problem cf. Traugott Holtz, 'Zum Selbstverständnis des Apostels Paulus' (1966), in id., *Geschichte und Theologie des Urchristentums*, WUNT 57, 1991, 129–39; Karl-Wilhelm Niebuhr, *Heidenapostel aus Israel. Die jüdische Identität des Paulus nach ihrer Darstellung in seinen Briefen*, WUNT 63, 1992.

318. Cf. Karl-Wilhelm Niebuhr, *Gesetz und Paränese*, WUNT II/28, 1987; Eckart Reinmuth, *Geist und Gesetz. Studien zu Voraussetzungen und Inhalt der paulinischen Paränese*, ThA 44, 1985, 22–41 (on the warning against unchastity and greed in early Christian literature). Roman Heiligental (*Zwischen Henoch und Paulus. Studien zum theologie-geschichtlichen Ort des Judasbriefes*, TANZ 6, 1992), finds Pharisaic categories of thought in I Thess. 4.1–8 (52f.). without clarifying his own picture of Pharisees. To the degree that it corresponds to that of Berger, *Jesus* (n.256), the plausibility of this thesis must be doubted. The same goes for Wander, *Trennungsprozesse* (n.133), 161.

319. Peter Brown, *Body and Society: Men, Women and Sexual Renunciation in Early Christianity*, 1990, 51. Cf. as an illustration Rom. 1.24–27: '24 Therefore God gave them (the pagans) up in the lusts of their hearts to impurity, to the dishonouring of their bodies among themselves, 25 because they exchanged the truth about God for a lie and worshipped and served the creature rather than the creator... 26 Therefore God gave them up to dishonourable passions. Their women exchanged natural relations for unnatural, 27 and the men likewise gave up natural relations with women and were consumed with passion for one another, men committing shameless acts with men...'

320. Cf. Hans Conzelmann, *First Corinthians*, Hermeneia, 1975, 190f.

321. Wolfgang Schrage, *Ethics of the New Testament*, 1988, 225.

322. Cf. Luise Schottroff, *Lydia's Impatient Sisters. A Feminist Social History of Early Christianity*, 1995, 128f.

323. Cf. on this Beverly R. Gaventa, 'The Maternity of Paul: An Exegetical Study of Galatians 4: 19', in *Conversation* (n.192), 189–201.

324. Elisabeth Schüssler-Fiorenza, *In Memory of Her. A Feminist Reconstruction of Christian Origins*, 1983, 235.

325. Cf. Judith M. Lieu, 'Circumcision, Women and Salvation', *NTS* 40, 1994, 358–70.

326. Cf. Schüssler-Fiorenza, *In Memory* (n.323), 236.

327. For the heading cf. Schrage, *Ethics* (n.321), 211–16, to whom the next section is indebted. Quotations from this work are given in brackets in the following text.

328. Cf. Conzelmann, *First Corinthians* (n.320), 219–20 (parallels from the history of religions). As there is no christology at all in I Cor. 13, he argues that this section reflects 'Paul's Hellenistic Jewish schooling' (220).

329. Cf. Richard Reitzenstein, *Die hellenistischen Mysterienreligionen nach ihren Grundgedanken und Wirkungen*, [3]1927 (= 1966), 333–93.

330. On Sellin, *Streit* (n.38). For criticism cf. e.g. Becker, *Paulus* (n.232), 120.

331. I am presupposing that the statements on suffering made about the apostle also apply to the Christian; cf. Helmut Köster, 'Apostel und Gemeinde in den Briefen an die Thessalonischer', in Dieter Lührmann and Georg Strecker (eds.), *Kirche* (FS Günther Bornkamm), 1980, 287–98. Erhard Güttgemanns, *Der leidende Apostel und sein Herr. Studien zur paulinischen Christologie*, FRLANT 90, 1966, had differed.

332. For the parallels between Paul and Jesus cf. Eberhard Jüngel, *Paulus und Jesus. Eine Untersuchung zur Präzisierung der Frage nach dem Ursprung der Christologie*, HUTh 1 [3]1967. According to Jüngel, Paul's doctrine of justification corresponds to Jesus' preaching of the kingdom of God. Cf. also the important remarks by James M.Robinson, *The New Quest of the Historical Jesus*, 1959, 111–24 on the similar (!) understandings of existence in the historical Jesus and the early kergyma; these need new reflection on them.

333. Cf. II Cor. 10.1f., 10, 18; 12.16.

334. Cf. the remarks by William Wrede, 'Paulus', *RGV* I 5/6, 1904, in Rengstorf, *Paulusbild* (n.232), 21.

335. Cf. Lüdemann, *Opposition to Paul* (n.133), 110f. It should be noted that in Rom. 3.8 Paul is quoting a slogan directed against him and is not formulating it himself, as e.g. in Rom. 6.1. In other words, the slogan was formulated specifically against Paul and circulated.

336. Cf. Melito of Sardis, *Homily on the Passion* (n.145), 72–99, esp.94–99: '94 Hear, all you families of mankind, and see: an unprecedented murder has been committed in the midst of Jerusalem, in the city of the law, in the city of the Hebrews, in the city of the prophets, in the city that was acclaimed as righteous! And who was murdered? And who is the murderer? I am ashamed to tell, and yet I must tell. Had the murder taken place at night, or had (the Lord) been killed in the wilderness, it would have been well to hold our peace. But the unjust murder of the righteous took place in the midst of a public place, in the midst of the city, where all saw it. 95 And so he was raised upon a high cross, and a title was set upon it, making known the one who was slain. Who was he? It is hard to say, but it is even more terrible not to say. Hear and tremble before the one who made heaven and earth tremble! 96 The one who hung the earth in its place was hanged, the one who fixed the heavens was fixed (on the cross); the one who made all things fast was made fast upon the wood. The master has been insulted, God has been murdered, the king of Israel has been slain by an Israelite hand. 97 What an unprecedented murder,

what an unprecedented crime! The Lord was deformed, with his body naked, and was not even though worthy of a covering so that he was not seen (naked). For this reason the stars turned away and the day darkened, to hide the one who had been stripped naked on the cross, shrouding not the body of the Lord, but the eyes of these men. 98 And though the people did not tremble, the earth trembled; though the people did not fear, the heavens were afraid; though the people did not rend their garments, the heaven rent (its); though the people did not lament, the Lord thundered from heaven and the Most High lifted up his voice. 99 Why, O Israel, did you not quake before the Lord? Why were you not terrified before the Lord? Why did you not lament over the firstborn? Why did you not rend you garments for the Lord hanging there? The Lord has abandoned you; you found no mercy for him. You have destroyed the Lord, and so you have been utterly destroyed. And now you are lying there dead.'

337. On this see the different examples from Christian writing of the second century below, 155f. For Irenaeus cf. Noormann, *Irenäus* (n.97), 420–6.

338. For what follows cf. Gerd Lüdemann, 'Paulus und das Judentum', *TEH* 212, 1983 (with bibliography), in the as yet unpublished revision of which Jens-Uwe Krüger has helped me; of course the secondary literature on this topic is legion. Cf. most recently e.g. Sänger, *Verkündigung* (n.159); Becker, *Paulus* (n.197), 486–502; Richard H. Bell, *Provoked to Jealousy. The Origin and Purpose of the Jealousy Motif in Romans 9–11*, WUNT II/63, 1994 (with bibliography). Also important are Gerd Theissen, *Judentum und Christentum bei Paulus. Sozialgeschichtliche Überlegungen zu einem beginnenden Schisma*, WUNT 58, 1991, 331–56, and Peter von der Osten-Sacken, 'Römer 9–11 als Schibbolet christlicher Theologie', in id. (ed.), *Evangelium und Tora. Aufsätze zu Paulus*, ThB 77, 1987, 294–314, and other articles by the same author reprinted in the same volume; Niebuhr, *Heidenapostel* (n.317), and Karl P. Donfried (ed.), *The Romans Debate*, Revised and Expanded Edition ²1991. Of the more recent commentaries on Romans see especially James D. G. Dunn, *Romans 9–16*, WBC 38d, 1988.

339. At present the most recent monograph on this passage is by Carol J. Schlueter, *Filling up the Measure. Polemical Hyperbole in I Thessalonians 2.14–16*, JSNTSS 98, 1994; cf. also the important study by Rainer Kampling, 'Eine auslegungsgeschichtliche Skizze zu 1 Thess 2, 14–16', in Dietrich-Alex Koch and Hermann Lichtenberger (eds.), *Begegnungen zwischen Christentum und Judentum in Antike und Mittelalter (FS Heinz Schreckenberg)*, 1993, 183–213. The thesis which is occasionally put forward, that I Thess 2.14–16 is an interpolation, is untenable (cf. Lüdemann, 'Judentum' [n.338], 25–7 [with bibliography]).

340. Cf. Odil Hannes Steck, *Israel und das gewaltsame Geschick der Propheten. Untersuchungen zur Überlieferung des deuteronomistischen Geschichtsbildes im Alten Testament, Spätjudentum und Urchristentum*, WMANT 23, 1967; Hans-Joachim Schoeps. 'Die jüdischen Propheten-morde', in id., *Aus frühchristlicher Zeit. Religionsgeschichtliche Untersuchungen*, 1950, 126–43.

341. Mark 14.64: 'And they all (viz, the members of the supreme council) condemned him as deserving death'; John 19.7: 'The Jews answered him (viz. Pilate), "We have a law, and by that law he ought to die..."' Cf. Wolfgang Reinbold, *Der älteste Bericht über den Tod Jesu. Literarische Analyse und historische Kritik der Passionsdarstellungen der Evangelisten*, BZNW 69, 1994.

342. Cf. only Phil. 2.6–11, expanded by 'to death on the cross' (v.8b); Rom. 3.25f., expanded by 'through faith' (v.25); Gal.3.26–28, expanded by 'through faith' (v.26). As a summary see Vielhauer, *Geschichte* (n.10), 9–57.

343. Cf. the apt commentary by Günter Kegel, *Glaube ja. Kirche nein? Anstiftung zu einer neuen Reformation*, 1994, 126f.

344. Anyone who reads the New Testament as the word of God to us will not be able to avoid going out immediately to carry on a mission to all unbelieving Jews and Gentiles (cf. Lüdemann, *Resurrection* [n.3], 10 and n.49).

345. Sanders, *Paul* (n.232), 549.

346. The impression that Paul could only found churches but not lead them is certainly not completely false.

347. Cf Christoph Burchard, *Der Dreizehnte Zeuge. Traditions- und kompositionsgeschichtliche Untersuchungen zu Lukas' Darstellung der Frühzeit des Paulus*, FRLANT 103, 1970.

348. Cf. Jürgen Wehnert, *Die Wir-Passagen der Apostelgeschichte. Ein lukanisches Stilmittel aus jüdischen Tradition*, GTA 40, 1989.

349. *The state of research*: the investigation of pseudepigraphy in early Christianity basically began only twenty-five years ago. The milestones in it are Kurt von Fritz (ed.), *Pseudepigrapha I. Pseudopythagorica – Lettres de Platon – Littérature pseudépigraphique juïve*, 1972, and Wolfgang Speyer, *Die literarische Fälschung im heidnischen und christlichen Altertum. Ein Versuch ihrer Deutung*, HKAW I, 2, 1971, a book which translated into action Wrede's wish 'that one day soon a new treatment of the problem of literary pseudonymity in earliest Christianity may be given us which is undertaken with comprehensive means' (William Wrede, 'Miscellen', ZNW I, 1900, 66–85: 78 n.1). Norbert Brox, *Falsche Verfasserangaben. Zur Erklärung der frühchristlichen Pseudepigraphie*, SBS 79, 1975; id. (ed.), *Pseudepigraphie in der heidnischen und jüdisch-*

christlichen Antike, WdF CDLXXXIV, 1977, has made the greatest contribution towards applying the results to early Christianity aimed at by Speyer.

Kurt Aland ('Falsche Verfasserangaben? Zur Pseudonymität im früh-christlichen Schrifttum', *ThRv* 75, 1979, 1–10 [cf. the response by Norbert Brox, 'Methodenfragen der Pseudepigraphie-Forschung', ibid., 275–8) has sharply protested in this and other publications (cf. most recently *Supplementa zu den Neutestamentlichen und Kirchengeschichtlichen Entwürfen*, 1990, 158–76 ['Noch einmal; Das Problem der Anonymität und Pseudonymität in der christlichen Literatur der ersten beiden Jahrhunderte']) against the approach which puts the pseudepigraphy of early Christianity up to 150 CE in the history of ancient pseudepigraphy. That is grounded in the unhistorical notion that it does not do justice to the *Sitz im Leben* of the earliest Christian literature in question and the historical development (cf. e.g. *ThRv*, 1979, col.3). He argues that the pseudepigraphical writings came into being in a climate in which there were still no concrete author personalities, but only anonymity and pseudonymity. If Aland were right, the problem – which for him, at any rate, is only a Roman Catholic one (!) – is again immediately resolved. 'No Christian before 150 CE was interested in authorship; each individual writing commended itself as charismatic or prophetic on the basis of content alone, and for earliest Christianity a pseudo-problem has been introduced into scholarship. Pseudepigraphy after this period is something quite different from that in the earliest Christian writings' (Brox, *ThRv* 1979, col. 277).

Cf. further Horst R.Balz, 'Anonymität und Pseudepigraphie im Ur-christentum. Überlegungen zum literarischen und theologischen Problem der urchristlichen und gemeinantiken Pseudepigraphie', *ZThK* 66, 1970, 403–36; Michael Wolter, 'Die anonymen Schriften des Neuen Testaments. Annäherungsversuch an ein literarisches Phänomen', *ZNW* 79, 1988, 1–16 ('If, as Aland rightly states, in authentic letters the mention of the name is conditioned by the literary genre, the pseudonymous letters of the New Testament claimed as "inauthentic letters" also fulfil this external condition. Only they give a false author's name, and it is this phenomenon that has to be explained' [3]).

David E. Meade, *Pseudonymity and Canon. An Investigation into the Relationship of Authorships and Authorities in Jewish and Earliest Christian Tradition*, WUNT 39, 1986, mixes up historical and theological perspectives; i.e., he requires from scholars a concept of the canon for today (cf. 3). Bruce M. Metzger, 'Literary Forgeries and Canonical Pseudepigrapha', *JBL* 91, 1972, 3–24, had previously adopted a similarly apologetic approach.

350. Friedrich Delitzsch, *Die grosse Täuschung. Kritische Betrachtungen zu den alttestamentlichen Berichten über Israels Eindringen in Kanaan, die Gottesoffenbarungen vom Sinai und die Wirksamkeit der Propheten*, 1920, 5f. The Old Testament scholar mentioned in the quotation is probably August Dillmann (1823–1894); cf. Reinhard G. Lehmann, *Friedrich Delitzsch und der Babel-Bibel-Streit*, OBO 133, 1994, 60–6. I need hardly emphasize that at this point I am concerned only with Delitzsch's autobiographical note and the abiding insight expressed in it, and not with the fatal influence of his book *Die grosse Täuschung* and the antisemitic accents contained in it (cf. Lehmann, *Delitzsch*, passim).

351. Cf. e.g. Frederik Torm, *Die Psychologie der Pseudonymität im Hinblick auf die Literatur des Christentums*, 1932.

352. The same is true of James, I and II Peter and Jude. A distinction has to be made between the false attributions which are elements in the texts in question and the later headings which attribute the literary documents to particular persons (I, II, III John to John and the four Gospels to Matthew, Mark, Luke and John). The latter originally appeared anonymously, whereas the two short letters of John name the presbyter as the sender (I John does not mention any sender, but a collective of authors).

353. Schnelle, *Einleitung* (n.10). Quotations from this book will be indicated in brackets in the text.

354. This is at least in contradiction to Schnelle's dating of II Peter to around 110 CE (486). Particular care should be taken here with a global dating. For is not III Corinthians, which appeared in the middle of the second century, also a pseudepigraphical letter (see 143–6 below)?

355. Norbert Brox, 'Zum Problemstand in der Erforschung der altchristlichen Pseudepigraphie' (1973) = id., *Pseudepigraphie* (n.349), 311–34. Passages from this article are indicated in brackets in the text.

356. Brox, ibid. refers to Iamblichus, *De vita Pythagorica* 198: 'Now if it is granted that the writings currently in circulation in part come from Pythagoras and otherwise are designated on the basis of what he said (so that the Pythagoreans have not given out that these writings are their own property, but attribute them to Pythagoras as his work), it is clear from all this that Pythagoras was sufficiently experienced in all wisdom.'

357. Martin Hengel, 'Anonymität, Pseudepigraphie und "Literarische Fälschung" in der jüdisch-hellenistischen Literatur', in Fritz, *Pseudepigrapha* I (n.349), 229–308: 283.

358. Brox, *Problemstand* (n.355), 322f.

359. Jacob Speigl, review of Brox, *Pseudepigraphie* (n.349), *JbAC* 20, 1977, 194f.: 195.

360. Bauer, *Orthodoxy* (n.83), 74f.

361. Cf. the classic study by Ernst Käsemann, 'An Apologia for

Primitive Christian Eschatology' (1952), in id., *Essays on New Testament Themes*, 1964, 169–195, and the contribution by Kurt Aland, 'Das Ende der Zeiten. Über die Naherwartung im Neuen Testament und in der frühen Kirche', in id., *Neutestamentliche Entwürfe*, ThB 63, 1979, 124–82 (on II Peter: 148–50), which provides the necessary church-historical depth.

362. The reason given for this ('For ever since the fathers fell asleep, all things have continued as they were from the beginning of creation' [v.4]) is rejected in II Peter 3.5–7. The supposition that since the creation everything has remained unchanged is incorrect, since as a result of the flood the world has already once been annihilated (v.6). For the sake of simplicity, I have passed over this line of argument in the text.

363. Here there should be no dispute that 'the scepticism echoing in the thesis of the opponents... has parallels not only in the matter of the delay of the parousia, but also in the formulation of parallels in the history of early Christian theology. This is true above all in respect of I Clem.23.2 and II Clem.11.3' (Henning Paulsen, *Der Zweite Petrusbrief und der Judasbrief*, KEK XII/2, 1992, 132). Cf also below in the text.

364. Cf. Ignatius, Eph.12.1: Paul 'mentions you in every letter'. Similarly, this evidently presupposes a collection of the letters of Paul.

365. William Wrede, *Die Echtheit des zweiten Thessalonicherbriefs untersucht*, TU 24.2, 1903, 72; Anton Vögtle, *Der Judasbrief/ Der zweite Petrusbrief*, EKK XXII, 1994, 264 (alongside this Vögtle is thinking 'above all of the Pauline doctrine of grace and freedom, which the dissidents falsely interpret in terms of the justification of this libertinism...' [ibid.]). Paulsen, *Petrusbrief* (n.363), differs. But cf. also Lindemann, *Paulus* (n.224), 262 n.202.

366. Heinrich Julius Holtzmann, 'Zum zweiten Thessalonicherbrief', ZNW 2, 1901, 97–108: 107f., thought that II Thess., II Peter and John 21 basically had their origin in one and the same interest, namely to 'remedy a severe hurt to the earliest Christian belief in the future'.

367. Cf. the synoptic survey in Wrede, *Echtheit* (n.365), 3–12, 24–7; Wolfgang Trilling ('Literarische Paulusimitation im 2. Thessalonicherbrief', in Karl Kertelge [ed.], *Paulus in den neutestamentlichen Spätschriften*, QD 89, 1981, 146–56) remarks on Wrede's work: 'Wrede's demonstrations represent the most important basis for subsequent scholarship and are still regarded as valid today. Here one must simply make the qualification that Wrede often wants to understand the literary dependence of I Thess. too narrowly as a literal "writing out", and thus leaves the author too little scope' (147f.). Cf. also the synoptic contrast in Willi Marxsen, *Der Zweite Thessalonicherbrief*, ZBK 11,2, 1982, 19–28.

368. Werner Georg Kümmel, *Introduction to the New Testament*, 1975, 268: 'II Thess is most comprehensible, therefore, if Paul himself wrote II

Thess a few weeks after he had written I Thess, when the first letter was still fresh in his mind.'

369. Cf. the survey in Schnelle, *Einleitung* (n.10), 371f.

370. Thus already Hugo Grotius (1640); cf. Vielhauer, *Geschichte* (n.10), 97 n.13.

371. Adolf Harnack, 'Das Problem des zweiten Thessalonicherbriefs', *SB* 1910, 560–78 (= id., *Kleine Schriften zur alten Kirche* II, 1980, 560–78). Harnack comments on Wrede's study that it has 'shown that the authenticity of the second letter cannot be maintained if it is said to have been written to the same community some months after the first', but objects 'that even Wrede's acuteness could not succeed in making comprehensible the purpose and aim of the forgery' (574f.).

372. E.g. the statement in the kerygma that Christ died for us and was raised 'according to the scriptures' (I Cor. 15.3–5) immediately required to be given content.

373. Cf. Wrede's view at another point: 'I maintain that things themselves are sometimes most radical, and that one therefore can hardly be reproached for presenting them as they are', William Wrede, *The Messianic Secret in the Gospels* (1901), 1971, 2.

374. Cf. Adolf Hilgenfeld, 'Die beiden Briefe an die Thessalonicher nach Inhalt und Ursprung', *ZWTh* 5, 1862, 225–64: 249f., 262; id., *Historisch-kritische Einleitung in das Neue Testament*, 1875, 636. At the present time Andreas Lindemann, 'Zum Abfassungszweck des Zweiten Thessalonicherbriefs', *ZNW* 68, 1977, 35–47: 47, has latched on to this thesis: '... the author of II Thess. evidently felt compelled to conceive of his work as a substitute for I Thess.' (cf. 39), and Marxsen, *Zweiter Thessalonicherbrief* (n.367), presupposes it in his substantial commentary: 'I think it certain that II Thess. was meant to suppress I Thess.' (35 n.9). Cf. previously already Martin Rist, 'Pseudepigraphy and the Early Christians', in *Studies in New Testament and Early Christian Literature. Essays in Honor of Allen P. Wikgren* (ed. David Edward Aune), NT.S 33, 1972, 75–91: 82f.

375. For a bibliography cf. the titles mentioned in n.349: Speyer, *Fälschung*; Brox, *Verfasserangaben*; Brox, *Pseudepigraphie*.

376. Cf. Brox, 'Problemstand' (n.355).

377. For the reference of *hos di'hemon* to *epistole* cf. Lindemann, 'Abfassungszweck' (n.374), 37. Because of the position of *hos di'hemon* immediately behind *epistole* this reference is in any case improbable. If the *hos di hemon* similarly referred to the other two members (expression of the spirit, word), it would not alter the reference to the *epistole*. Harald Hegermann, 'Der geschichtliche Ort der Pastoralbriefe', in *Theologische Versuche* II, ed. Joachim Rogge and Gottfried Schille, 1970, 47–64: 49f., differs, Hegermann translates: 'Nor through a letter, *as through* us', and

concludes: 'So (?) there is no reference to the possibility of letters which have been slipped in' (50).

378. Greek *hos di'hemon*. Here, as in Rom. 9.32; II Cor. 10.2; 11.17; 13.7, the Greek particle *hos* introduces a fabricated or objectively false property (cf. Gerhard Schneider, *EWNT* III, 1983, 1216) and is meant to indicate that the letter does not come from Paul. Trilling, *Zweiter Brief* (n.380), incorrectly translates: 'Neither through an expression of the spirit nor through a word nor through a letter as coming from us, who allegedly say that...' (68).

379. Greek: *enesteken he hemera tou kyriou*. Willi Marxsen, *Einleitung in das Neue Testament. Eine Einführung in ihre Probleme*, ⁴1978, 52, argues that the correct translation is 'The day of the Lord is here', not 'is imminent' (against Vielhauer, *Geschichte* [n.10], 93f.). This assertion, which is often made, is hardly appropriate. Rather, it should be interpreted in terms of the context (cf. Conzelmann, *First Corinthians* [n.320], on I Cor. 7.26 [132 n.14]). For the problem see 118 below.

380. Wolfgang Trilling, *Der zweite Brief an die Thessalonicher*, EKK XIV, 1980, 128f., 155.

381. Wrede, *Echtheit* (n.365), 60.

382. Lindemann, 'Abfassungszweck' (n.374), 37. Cf. similarly Franz Laub, 'Paulinische Autorität in nachpaulinischer Zeit (II Thess.)', in Raymond F.Collins (ed.), *The Thessalonian Correspondence*, BETL LXXXVII, 1990, 403–317, here 408f. Unfortunately Trilling, *Zweiter Brief* (n.380), does not investigate the question whether v.15 relates to I Thess. or II Thess. In my view it is only because of this that he can reject Lindemann's replacement hypothesis. Glenn S. Holland, *The Tradition that You Received from Us: 2 Thessalonians in the Pauline Tradition*, HuTh 24, 1988, 151f., is equally unsatisfcactory. His proposal that the author of II Thessalonians is the first editor of I Thessalonians is improbable, as no new letter would have had to be composed to send out, and the misused earlier letter (= I Thess) would hardly have been preserved. The thinking here is too modern.

383. Anyone who recognizes an allusion to I Thess. in II Thess. 2.2 has to accept the displacement hypothesis. In a contradictory way Schnelle, *Einleitung* (n.10), 373, says on II Thess. 2.2: 'Moreover II Thess. 2.2 suggests that the authors also claimed the authority of Paul through pseudepigraphy.'

384. 'Word of mouth' is governed by the situation of the letter.

385. Marxsen, *Zweiter Thessalonicherbrief* (n.367), 11f.

386. Cf. ibid., 80.

387. Cf. I Thess. 4.17.

388. Translation based on G.Nathanael Bonwetsch (ed.), *Hippolyt's*

Kommentar zum Buche Daniel und die Fragmente des Kommentars zum Hohenliede, GCS, 1897, 232.

389. Cf. II Thess. 2.2.

390. Cf. also Wrede, *Echtheit* (n.365), 49.

391. Cf. Marxsen, *Zweiter Thessalonicherbrief* (n.367), 103.

392. Friedrich Nietzsche, *Beyond Good and Evil*, trans.Helen Zimmern, 1909, no.68.

393. Schnelle, *Einleitung* (n.10), 377. He continues: 'Would it have been possible to call I Thess. a forgery around forty years after its composition? The marked leaning on I Thess. suggests that the author of II Thess. was convinced of the authenticity of the letter he had before him. In that case he would have indicated that I Thess. was a forgery against his better judgment. This is not a procedure that could be imputed to a New Testament author.' Evidently the fact that II Thess. is in the New Testament canon makes Schnelle immune to particular historical possibilities.

394. Peter Müller, *Anfänge der Paulusschule. Dargestellt am 2 Thessalonicherbrief und Kolosserbrief*, AThANT 74, 1988, 319, speaks of a second improved edition represented by II Thess. This comes very close to the displacement hypothesis.

395. Henning Graf Reventlow, *Epochen der Bibelauslegung, I, Vom Alten Testament bis Origenes*, 1990, 102.

396. According to Lindemann, *Paulus* (n.224), 44 n.5, the opponents of II Thessalonians were not Gnostics or champions of enthusiasm but rather apocalyptists (cf. 2.2, 'day of the Lord'), or (?), 133, 'enthusiastic circles'. Cf. also Marxsen, *Einleitung* (n.379), 55: 'So it may be most probable that in the time after Paul an author unknown to us is combating Gnostic enthusiasm. Here it is striking that both the enthusiasts and the author refer to Paul' (similarly II Peter 3.15f.).

397. Here and below, Gnosis is understood as the knowledge of divine mysteries which is reserved for an elite and which among the disciples of Paul is combined with a presentist eschatology (for the definition of 'Gnosis' and how it differs from 'Gnosticism', in which an identity of being between the redeemer and the redeemed is expressed, cf. Lüdemann, *Untersuchungen* [n.1], 102f.).

398. The personal sections of I Thess. (2.1–3.10 [excluding 2.9]) were in fact omitted from II Thess.

399. Holtzmann, *Thessalonicherbrief* (n.366), 107.

400. Lindemann, 'Abfassungszweck' (n.374), 133f.

401. Lindemann, *Paulus* (n.224), 133.

402 Thus Vielhauer, *Geschichte* (n.100), 101. Cf. Lindemann, *Paulus* (n.224), 133f.

403. Lindemann, *Paulus*, 134.

404. Cf. Koester, *Einführung* (n.133), 682, and Herbert Braun, 'Zur nachpaulinischen Herkunft des zweiten Thessalonicherbriefes' (1952/53), in id., *Gesammelte Studien zum Neuen Testament und seiner Umwelt*, 1962, 205–9, which is still worth reading.

405. But cf. the verdict of Hans Conzelmann ('Die Schule des Paulus', in *Theologia Crucis – Signum Crucis. FS für Erich Dinkler zum 70. Geburtstag* [ed. Carl Andresen and Günter Klein], 1979, 85–96): 'Formally the opponents are right. They are evidently orthodox Paulinists and have I Thess. on their side. Nevertheless, the theological vote has to be for II Thess. The opponents are certainly repeating Paul's statements. But they evidently have not grasped their significance. They cannot transfer Paul's eschatological statements to a new situation. They have not grasped the historical significance of the eschatology as an interpretation of the present time. They are only formally orthodox, and have moved from orthodoxy to enthusiasm. That, too, is part of the effect of Paul' (95f.). But one might ask whether the author of II Thess. understood Paul theologically.

406. For the canonization of I and II Thess. cf. the relationship of I and II Kings to I and II Chronicles and the remarks on this by Morton Smith, *Palestinian Parties and Politics that Shaped the Old Testament*, 1971, 11: both were canonized, although there are contradictions between them, and II Chronicles was perhaps intended to replace I and II Kings.

407. For the literature, in addition to the commentaries cf. Lindemann, *Paulus* (n.224), 38–42, 114–30; id., *Die Aufhebung der Zeit,. Geschichtsverständnis und Eschatologie im Epheserbrief*, StNT 12, 1975; Karl Martin Fischer, *Tendenz und Absicht des Epheserbriefes*, FRLANT 111, 1973; Victor Paul Furnish, 'On Putting Paul in His Place', *JBL* 113, 1994, 3–17 (with bibliography); Horacio E. Lona, *Die Eschatologie im Kolosser- und Epheserbrief*, fzb 48, 1984, 171–80; Müller, *Anfänge* (n.394).

408. Cf. Lindemann, *Aufhebung* (n.406), 46f.

409. Unless Timothy, the co-sender of the letter, was the author of Colossians. Cf. e.g. Eduard Schweizer (*Der Brief an die Kolosser*, EKK XII, 1976), who because of the personal notes and greetings in Col.4.7–18, shrinks from the thesis of a complete inauthenticity of Colossians, i.e. what he calls 'such a refined forgery' (24) and considers whether the co-sender Titus could have 'composed the letter in both names when Paul's prison conditions prevented it' (26).

410. On II Peter, see above 109f.

411. Conzelmann, *Outline* (n.15), 314.

412. For this and the next section see Vielhauer, *Geschichte* (n.10), 197–200.

413. For the next section see Vielhauer, *Geschichte* (n.10), 192–5.

414. Has this humility something to do with the self-humiliation of Christ in the Philippians hymn (Phil. 2.8)?

415. The relationship between asceticism over food (Col.2.16a) and the observance of particular times (Col.2.16b) may have a basis here.

416. Cf. Vielhauer, *Geschichte* (n.10), 194.

417. Ibid., 202f.

418. Cf. Lindemann, *Paulus* (n.224), 121f.

419. Ibid., 121 n.44.

420. For a bibliography cf. Helmut Merkel, 'Der Epheserbrief in der neueren exegetischen Diskussion', *ANRW* II, 25.4, 1987, 3156–246; Eberhard Faust, *Pax Christi et Pax Caesaris. Religionsgeschichtliche, traditionsgeschichtliche und sozialgeschichtliche Studien zum Epheserbrief*, NTOA 24, 1993.

421. Hans Conzelmann, *Der Brief an die Epheser*, NTD 8, [15]1981, 84–124: 88.

422. Papyrus 46, Vaticanus, original version of Sinaiticus. Cf. the discussion in Rudolf Schnackenburg, *Der Brief an die Epheser*, EKK X, 1982, 37–9.

423. Vielhauer, *Geschichte* (n.10), 215.

424. Cf. Koester, *Einführung* (n.133), 705. Lindemann, *Paulus* (n.10), 129, is reserved about this assumption because in his view 'a literary dependence can be claimed with some probability' only for I Corinthians (ibid). Cf. the tabular summary of the results of the careful work of Albert E. Barnett, *Paul Becomes a Literary Influence*, 1941, 40 (individual analyses on 2–39). Here I presuppose that Barnett's investigations are correct.

425. Adolf Jülicher, *Einleitung in das Neue Testament*, [5/6]1906, 127; cf. also Weiss, *Earliest Christianity* (n.133) II, 684: 'And it has not yet been settled, whether the author of the Epistle to the Ephesians is not the same person as the collector of the Pauline corpus.'

426. Edgar J. Goodspeed, *The Meaning of Ephesians*, 1933; id., *The Key to Ephesians*, 1956; cf. similarly C.L. Mitton, *The Epistle to the Ephesians*, 1951.

427. Cf. only Mitton, *Epistle* (n.426), 263–7.

428. Cf. Albert E. Barnett, *The New Testament. Its Making and Meaning*, 1946, 181, and before that Edgar J. Goodspeed, *The Formation of the New Testament*, 1926, 22f.; id., *New Solutions of New Testament Problems*, 1927, 21–8. Martin Karrer (*Die Johannesoffenbarung als Brief. Studien zu ihrem literarischen, historischen und theologischen Ort*, FRLANT 140, 1986), makes criticism of Goodspeed's thesis too simple. He writes: 'In America to the present day his hypothesis exercises a certain

fascination, but it is untenable simply because of its view of 1.4–20 as a covering letter to the document which can be maintained only by ignoring Rev. 22.21. For with this the analogy to the postulated Pauline collection, for which moreover there is no ancient evidence, collapses' (33). By way of criticism: Rev. 22.21 merely suggests that the work was read out in worship and says nothing about the model on which the author orientated himself. So the striking parallels between the Pauline corpus and Revelation remain.

429. The proposal by John Knox (*Philemon Among the Letters of Paul. A New View of Its Place and Development*, ²1959), that Onesimus is to be identified with the bishop of Ephesus of the same name at the beginning of the second century (cf. Ignatius, *Eph* 1.3), and that he made the first collection of Paul's letters without the Pastorals, deserves special mention. Only this explains the remarkable fact that the letter to Philemon was part of the collection, something about which Tertullian was amazed (91). David Trobisch, *Die Entstehung der Pastoralbriefsammlung. Studien zu den Anfängen christlicher Publizistik*, NTOA 10, 1989, 115–17 (cf. 131), rightly emphasizes the attractiveness of this hypothesis, but falsely attributes to Knox the view that the Pastorals belonged to this collection (116). I shall return to this suggestion later (130 below).

430. Vielhauer, *Geschichte* (n.10), 215. For criticism cf. further Andreas Lindemann, 'Bemerkungen zu den Adressaten und zum Anlass des Epheserbriefes', ZNW 67, 1976, 235–51: 240f.

431. Cf. Schnackenburg, *Epheser* (n.422), 28.

432. Cf. the analysis of the cosmological terms in Ephesians by Lindemann, *Aufhebung* (n.407), 49–63.

433. Cf. Helmut Merklein, 'Paulinische Theologie in der Rezeption des Kolosser- und Epheserbriefes', in Karl Kertelge (ed.), *Paulus in den neutestamentliche Spätschriften*, QD 89, 1981, 25–69: 44; cf. Schnelle, *Einleitung* (n.10), 363 (with bibliography).

434. Cf. Lindemann, *Aufhebung* (n.407), 196–9.

435. Ibid., 64f.

436. Cf. further Schnackenburg, *Epheser* (n.422), 28.

437. Franz Mussner, *Der Brief an die Epheser*, ÖTK 10, 1982, 30, differs.

438. To support this view, Goodspeed, *Meaning* (n.426), 42, referred to Eph. 3.3f.: '3 How the mystery was made known to me by revelation, as I have written *briefly*. 4 When you read this you can perceive my insight into the mystery of Christ.' He argues that the mode of expression refers to a later reader of an earlier work; in other words, the author is referring his readership to the other letters of the apostle, written earlier, which are now in a collection – with Ephesians at their head. However, it is questionable

whether 'briefly' (*en oligo*) can denote the whole collection of Paul's letters. Cf. rightly Schnackenburg, *Epheser* (n.422), 133.

439. Henry Chadwick, 'Die Absicht des Epheserbriefes', ZNW 51, 1960, 145–53: 149.

440. Cf. Adolf von Harnack, *Marcion. Das Evangelium vom fremden Gott. Neue Studien zu Marcion*, TU 45.1, ²1924 (= 1960), 168f.*, though he thinks that Marcion was the first to arrange the remaining letters of Paul by length.

441. For a new translation of the Letter to Rheginos see below, 225–8. For a bibliography see Malcolm Lee Peel, *The Epistle to Rheginos. A Valentinian Letter on the Resurrection*, 1969; Lona, *Eschatologie* (n.407), 396–404; Hans-Georg Gaffron, 'Eine gnostische Apologie des Auferstehungsglaubens. Bemerkungen zur "Epistula ad Rheginum"', in Günther Bornkamm and Karl Rahner (eds.), *Die Zeit Jesu (FS Heinrich Schlier)*, 1970, 218–27; Robert Haardt, 'Die "Abhandlung über die Auferstehung" des Codex Jung aus der Bibliothek gnostischer koptischer Schriften aus Nag Hammadi. Bemerkungen zu ausgewählten Motiven', *Kairos* 12, 1970, 241–69; Klaus Koschorke, 'Paulus in den Nag-Hammadi-Texten', ZThK 78, 1981, 177–205; here esp.196–200. Cf. also *Nag Hammadi Texts and the Bible. A Synopsis and Index* (edited by Craig A. Evans, Robert L. Webb and Richard A. Wiebe), NTTS 18, 1993, 42–7 (biblical allusions or quotations in the Letter to Rheginos), 434f. (secondary literature).

442. Cf. above, xvi.

443. Cf. the remarks by Peel, *Rheginos* (n.441), 156–80.

444. Gaffron, 'Apologie' (n.441), 220.

445. For the acceptance of II Cor. 12 in Gnosis cf. the Apocalypse of Peter (NHC V/2) and Hans-Josef Klauck, *Die Himmelfahrt des Paulus (2 Kor 12,2–4) in der koptischen Paulusapokalypse aus Nag Hammadi (NHC V/2)*, SNTU, A.10, 1985, 151–90.

446. Cf.: God has revealed his Son in Paul (Gal. 1.15); Christ lives in Paul (Gal. 2.20); he is in believers (Rom. 8.10); Paul has been crucified with Christ (Gal. 2.19); the Christians are in Christ (Gal. 3.26, 28, etc.).

447. Cf. Andreas Lindemann, 'Der Apostel Paulus im 2.Jahrhundert', in Jean-Marie Sevrin (ed.), *The New Testament in Early Christianity*, BETL LXXXVI, 1989, 39–67: 57.

448. At another point Lindemann states this pointedly: 'The Gnostics evidently did not see any specific affinity between their own thought and the theology of Paul' (Lindemann, *Paulus* [n.224], 400), Thus not only is there an *objective* diastasis between Gnosis and Paulinism, but *subjectively*, too, the Gnostics did not see any similarities between themselves and the apostle. However, the latter assertion is now clearly contradicted by the

numerous examples from the Nag Hammadi writings which make clear the extent to which 'Gnostic theologians understood themselves as authorized interpreters of "the apostle"' (Koschorke, 'Paulus' [n.444], 180).

449. Gaffron, 'Apologie' (n.441), 227. It is similarly unsatisfactory to speak of a re-Christianizing of Gnostic thought with reference to Rheginos (thus e.g.Ernst Dassmann, 'Paulus in der Gnosis', *JbAC* 22, 1979, 123–38: 130).

450. Christoph Markschies, *Valentinus Gnosticus? Untersuchungen zur valentinianischen Gnosis mit einem Kommentar zu den Fragmenten Valentins*, WUNT 65, 1992, rightly emphasizes how close Valentinus is to the mainstream church, although his identification of Valentinus as a Gnostic goes too far.

451. Ekkehard Mühlenberg, 'Wirklichkeitserfahrung und Theologie bei dem Gnostiker Basilides', *KuD* 18, 1972, 161–75:174, rightly points out that e.g. the cosmology of the Basilidians took more seriously than Irenaeus and the theologians after him the (Pauline) statement that human beings are universally sinful. We need to take more note than before of how Christian the Gnostics of the second century were!

452. Cf. Peel, *Rheginos* (n. 441), 141f.

453. Conzelmann, *Epheserbrief* (n.421), 117. For the text see Fischer, *Tendenz* (n.407), 140–6, and Gospel of Truth (NHC I,3): 'Through him (i.e. Jesus) he (God?) enlightens those who through forgetfulness are in darkness. He illuminated them; he gave them a way' (18.17–19).

454. But cf. Vielhauer, *Geschichte* (n.10), who remarks on Ephesians: 'The important step from a mysticism which is individual or practised in exclusive circles to an ecclesiology with a mystical colouring has been taken' (215). In this case Rheginos is adopting positions which Ephesians works over or corrects.

455. Cf. Peel, *Rheginos* (n. 441), 146.

456. Lona, *Eschatologie* (n.407), 403f. (there then follow the differences between Ephesians and Paul worked out above).

457. Cf. Peel, *Rheginos* (n. 441), 148.

458. *The state of research*: the consensus among scholars today is that the historical Paul cannot be the author of the Pastorals, either directly or indirectly (say with the help of a secretary). This common view was pioneered, after preparatory work, by Ferdinand Christian Baur (*Die sogenannten Pastoralbriefe des Apostels Paulus aufs neue kritisch untersucht*, 1835), and finds representatively broad confirmation in the commentaries by Jürgen Roloff (*Der Erste Timotheusbrief*, EKK XV, 1988) and Lorenz Oberlinner (*Die Pastoralbriefe*, HThK XI/2, 1994, 1995). Even on a first unprejudiced reading of all three letters, one comes up against a world of language and thought which differs from that of the historical Paul.

So it was not surprising that in the past large areas of scholarship measured the Pastorals against Paul himself and passed a correspondingly negative judgment on them. There can no longer be any question of that. Probably the greatest expert on the Pastorals, Jürgen Roloff (in addition to his commentary on I Timothy cf. his *Die Kirche im Neuen Testament*, 1993, 250–67 [a section on 'God's orderly household: the Pastorals']) has energetically called for a new evaluation and in so doing represents a broad stream of international New Testament scholarship (cf. also Schnelle, *Einleitung* [n.10], 399–401). In so far as the negative value judgments on the Pastorals were of a dogmatic nature, one can agree with Roloff. But with the application of strictly historical criteria and a rooting of the Pastorals in their original situation, a verdict on them must look different (see below 135–42), even if Roloff's following comments on the Pastorals point in another direction. 'Thus by their presence in the biblical canon the Pastoral Epistles ensure that at its centre ecumenical dialogue must always be a dialogue about scripture' (Roloff, *Kirche*, 267). *Question*: in that case is the canon or history the foundation for critical judgment?

459. On this see the learned survey by P. N. Harrison, *The Problem of the Pastoral Epistles*, 1921, 13–16.

460. Cf. Harnack, *Marcion* (n.440), 170*-2*.

461. Lindemann, *Paulus* (n.224), in all seriousness thinks it possible that they were 'overlooked' by Marcion (148). That is a counsel of desperation, which is not improved by the reference he makes to the narrower manuscript tradition of the Pastorals as compared with the other letters of Paul. For while the earliest manuscript of the letters of Paul, Papyrus 46, from the time around 200, does not contain the Pastorals, it does not contain II Thessalonians and Philemon either. Codex B (fourth century) does not contain the Pastorals either (nor does it contain Philemon and Revelation).

462. Cf. Harnack, *Marcion* (n.440), 170f.*

463. For the use of the Pastorals by Irenaeus cf. below, 202.

464. Cf. the letters of John, which were similarly published as a threesome (see below 203).

465. Peter Trummer, *Die Paulustradition der Pastoralbriefe*, BET 8, 1978, 74; cf. id., 'Corpus Paulinum – Corpus Pastorale. Zur Ortung der Paulustradition in den Pastoralbriefen', in Karl Kertelge (ed.), *Paulus in den neutestamentlichen Spätschriften*, QD 89, 1981, 122–45. Trummer rightly emphasizes that the Pastorals are to be interpreted as a pseudepigraphical corpus.

466. Heinrich Julius Holtzmann, *Lehrbuch der historisch-kritischen Einleitung in das Neue Testament*, ³1892, 274.

467. Roloff, *Kirche* (n.458), 223.

468. Cf. Michael Wolter, *Die Pastoralbriefe als Paulustradition*, FRLANT 146, 1988, 269.

469. Greek: *ten paratheken phylaxon*. The term *paratheke* occurs only in Hermas, *Mand.* 3.2 in early Christianity outside II Tim. 1.12, 14 and in the Pastorals is always used in connection with 'preserving'. Cf. Wolter, *Pastoralbriefe* (n.468), 114–30. The term *paratheke* comes from ancient deposit law. Paul is the depositor of the *paratheke*. With its introduction 'is combined... the intention of explicitly bringing out and maintaining the integrity of the tradition and thus the unbroken continuity between the apostle and the community in the present... The positions advocated by him (viz. the author of the Pastorals) as one of the *pistoi anthropoi* mentioned in II Tim. 2.2 stand in unbroken continuity with Paul as the archegete of the tradition who is the basis of the identity of his community' (Wolter, *Pastoralbriefe*, 120).

470. Cf. Harrison, *Problem* (n.459), 12f.

471. Koester, *Einführung* (n.133), 741.

472. Behind this may stand emancipatory tendencies in women's circles which have a positive parallel in the Acts of Paul. Cf. Dennis Ronald MacDonald, *The Legend and the Apostle: The Battle for Paul in Story and Canon*, 1983; Willy Rordorf, 'Nochmals: Paulusakten und Pastoralbriefe', in Gerald F. Hawthone (ed.), *Tradition and Interpretation in the New Testament (FS E.Earle Ellis)*, 1987, 319–27.

473. Ulrich B.Müller, *Zur frühchristlichen Theologiegeschichte*, 1976, 62.

474. Cf. the Letter to Rheginos (see above, 131–5) and Gospel of Philip (NHC II,3), 73,1–8: 'Those who say they will die first and (only then) rise are in error. If they do not first receive the resurrection while they live, when they die they will receive nothing. So also when speaking about baptism they say, "Baptism is a great thing, because if people receive it they will live."'

475. Michael Wolter has protested against the thesis that the conflict discussed here was a controversy within Pauline Christianity. According to Wolter, what tells against this is 'above all the relationship of the priority theme, which goes beyond tradition, to Paul as the guarantor of tradition. It is used wherever the legitimation of personalized lines of tradition *including* their archegete is intended, so that its involvement would not make sense if the opponents were appealing to Paul!' (Wolter, *Pastoralbriefe* [n.468], 265). *Answer*: these reflections are far too subtle for the author of the Pastorals. In his view his opponent's appeal to Paul was illegitimate, and of course his own appeal was correct. Their Paul was a phantom, his Paul was real. As the opponents in any case had a wrong understanding of Paul, the use of the theme of priority which

Wolter brings into play was legitimate in the eyes of the author of the Pastorals.

476. Cf. Egbert Schlarb, *Die gesunde Lehre. Haresie und Wahrheit im Spiegel der Pastoralbriefe*, MThSt 29, 1990, 133–41 (on the 'sociological' context of the teachers).

477. I am grateful to my colleague C. Joachim Classen (letter of 23 June 1994) for his instruction on I Tim. 6.20f.

478. Cf. Egbert Schlarb, 'Miszelle zu 1 Tim. 6, 20', ZNW 77, 1986, 276–81: 281: 'Thus it is possible to regard I Tim. 6.20 as a deliberate formulation by the author of the Pastorals which draws up fronts: striking in its linguistic and stylistic clarity, typical in its exclusive abruptness.' Schlarb's repudiation at the same point of the thesis that there is an allusion to Marcion's main work is not compelling. Redaction does not exclude tradition.

479. Hans von Campenhausen, 'Polykarp von Smyrna und die Pastoralbriefe' (1951), in id., *Aus der Frühzeit des Christentums. Studien zur Kirchengeschichte des ersten und zweiten Jahrhunderts*, 1963, 197–252. References to this work are indicated in the following text in brackets.

480. *mataiologia* (2.1); *egkrates, diabolos, dilogos* (all in 5.2).

481. Phil. 5.2; 9.2; I Tim. 6.17; II Tim. 4.10; Titus 2.13.

482. Josef Zmijewski, 'Die Pastoralbriefe als pseudepigraphische Schriften – Beschreibung, Erklärung, Bewertung', in *SNTU*.A 4, 1979, 91–118:118.

483. Cf. also the somewhat divergent translation in Schneemelcher-Wilson II (n.243), 214. Schneemelcher rightly persists in regarding 'by referring to Thecla's example' as an interpolation. Here is the Latin text by way of comparison: '*Quodsi quae Acta Pauli quae perperam scripta sunt [exemplum Theclae] ad licentiam mulierum docendi tinguendique defendunt, sciant in Asia presbyterum qui eam scripturam construxit quasi titulo Pauli de suo cumulans conuictum atque confessum id se amore Pauli fecisse loco decessisse. Quam enim fidei proximum uidetur ut is docendi et tinguendi daret feminae potestatem qui nec discere quidem constanter mulieri permisit? Taceant, inquit, et domi uiros suos consulant*' (ed. Borleffs, CChrSL 1, 1954, 219f.).

484. Schottroff, *Sisters* (n.322), 130: 'This man (viz., the presbyter) was dismissed, ostensibly not because he had composed a work in the name or to the honour of Paul (many admirers of Paul had done so at that time) but because women relied on his writing to support their case and legitimate their action in Paul's name.' Doubtless this writing was used by women, but that was hardly the reason for the removal of the presbyter.

485. Willy Rordorf, 'In welchem Verhältnis stehen die apokryphen

Paulusakten zur kanonischen Apostelgeschichte und zu den Pastoral-briefen?', in *Text and Testimony (FS A. F. J. Klijn)*, 1988, 225–42: 226.

486. *The state of research*: For a long time III Corinthians was regarded as an original ingredient of the Acts of Paul, which have been handed down in fragments, even by Walter Bauer, who had already recognized the importance of this letter for the problem of orthodoxy and heresy in early Christianity (Bauer, *Orthodoxy* [n.83], 39f.; 39–43 on the historical significance of the Acts of Paul or III Cor.). This was for the most part done with reference to the Coptic Heidelberg Papyrus discovered in 1894 and published in 1904 (Carl Schmidt, *Acta Pauli aus der Heidelberger koptischen Papyrushandschrift*, Nr 1, 1904 [the papyrus comes from the sixth century]). The publication of the Greek Bodmer Papyrus from the beginning of the third century (M.Testuz, *Papyrus Bodmer X–XII*, 1959, 30–45) has not only finally clarified the Greek origin of III Cor. (Adolf Harnack even offered a Greek retro-translation, id., 'Untersuchungen über den apokryphen Briefwechsel der Korinther mit dem Apostel Paulus' [1905], in *Kleine Schriften zur Alten Kirche, Berliner Akademieschriften 1890–1907*, 1980, 737–69: 752–62), but has also shown that III Cor. originally circulated separately and was connected with the Acts of Paul only at a secondary stage (cf. now the consensus in Schneemelcher-Wilson II [n.243], 217f.).

We will have to imagine the development as follows: first came III Corinthians (written in the middle of the second century); then the letter of questions from the Corinthians was composed and added, and later a piece was added which linked the letter of questions with III Corinthians and introduced the correspondence. The correspondence was then fitted into the Acts of Paul. Cf. further Martin Rist, 'III Corinthians as a Pseudepigraphic Refutation of Marcionism', *The Iliff Review* 26, 1969, 498–58, who distinguished between introduction (= A), a letter of Corinthian questions (= B), transition (= C) and letter of Paul to the Corinthians (= D). Three of these elements (letter of questions, transition, III Corinthians) are to be found in the canon of the Syrian church and the Acts of Paul, whereas the Bodmer Papyrus mentioned above contains only the Greek text of the two letters without interim report and introduction.

The essential literature on III Corinthians (in addition to what has already been mentioned) is: A.F.J. Klijn, 'The Apocryphal Correspondence between Paul and the Corinthians', *VigChr* 17, 1963, 2–23; Lona, *Auferstehung* (n.130), 155–71. Appendix 2 below contains a translation of III Corinthians. In the time of Aphrahat (died after 345) and Ephraem (306–373), the correspondence was in the Syrian Bible (though the Bardesanites did not recognize it), in the Armenian Bible and in some Latin copies of the Bible.

487. Translation in Schneemelcher-Wilson II (n.243), 254.

488. Ibid.

489. The opening sentences run: 'What Jesus Christ revealed to his disciples as a letter, and how Jesus Christ revealed the letter of the council of the apostles, the disciples of Jesus Christ, to the Catholics; which was written because of the false apostles Simon and Cerinthus, that no one should follow them – for in them is deceit with which they kill men' (translation in Wilhelm Schneemelcher and R. McL. Wilson, *New Testament Apocrypha* I, ²1991, 252).

490. For the division cf. also Lona, *Auferstehung* (n.130), 159, whom I follow in part.

491. Koester, *Einführung* (n.133), 738.

492. Lindemann, *Paulus* (n.224), 374.

493. Ibid., 375.

494. Ibid.

495. 'The disciple... who has no eyes for the weaknesses of the doctrine, the religion, and so forth, dazzled by the aspect of the master and by his reverence for him, has on that account usually more power than the master himself. Without blind disciples the influence of a man and his work has never yet become great. To help a doctrine to victory often means only so to mix it with stupidity that the weight of the latter carries off also the victory of the former' (Friedrich Nietzsche, *Human, All-Too-Human*, trans. Helen Zimmern, 1909, I, 122, p.127). Cf. also I, 126, p. 129: 'For the greatest achievements of the people who are called geniuses and saints it is necessary that they should secure interpreters by force, who *misunderstand* them for the good of mankind.'

496. Adolf Harnack, *Lehrbuch der Dogmengeschichte* I, ⁴1909, 100.

497. The literature is overwhelming. Hans von Campenhausen, 'Das Alte Testament als Bibel der Kirche vom Ausgang des Urchristentums bis zur Entstehung des Neuen Testaments', in id., *Aus der Frühzeit des Christentums. Studien zur Kirchengeschichte des ersten und zweiten Jahrhunderts*, 1963, 152–96, and id., *The Formation of the Christian Bible*, 1972, are important. From the earlier literature, Ludwig Diestel, *Geschichte des Alten Testamentes in der christlichen Kirche*, 1869, 15–67, is useful.

498. 'It would be historically quite an inadequate description of the state of affairs to want to say that the Old Testament – wholly or in part – was *still* valid for Christians, as though some reflection had preceded the recognition, and as if the possession of the miraculous and infallible book had not been in the eyes of Christians one of the most illuminating and commendable advantages of the new religion. One cannot struggle powerfully enough with the notion that at that time there was no intimation that one

day a second holy scripture would be formed alongside and indeed above the first' (William Wrede, *Untersuchungen zum ersten Clemensbrief*, 1891, 75f.).

499. This writing, which has survived in fragments, comes from the beginning of the second century: on it cf. Schneemelcher-Wilson (n.243), 34–41.

500. Clement of Alexandria, *Stromateis*, VI 15, 128, in Schneemelcher II, 40: for 'foundation' I read 'destruction',

501. 'The layman Hermas, although he shows himself to be a prophet and a prolific writer, evidently has very little or no knowledge of the Holy Scriptures, and such laymen were naturally always in the majority' (Harnack, *Bible Reading* [n.21], 38). For the problem cf. Norbert Brox, *Der Hirt des Hermas*, KAV 7, 1991, 49–55.

502. For the last paragraph cf. Campenhausen, 'Testament' (n.497), 157.

503. The translation of Justin comes from the Ante-Nicene Library of Christian Fathers.

504. The translations of the Apostolic Fathers are from *The Apostolic Fathers* (2 vols.), trans. Kirsopp Lake, LCL, 1925, except for the translations of Ignatius, which are from William R. Schoedel, *Ignatius of Antioch*, Hermeneia, 1985.

505. For the question of the origin of individual sayings of the Lord in general see Chapter 9 below. In most cases, as for example in Justin (cf. below), the Gospel of Matthew was the origin of the individual sayings of the Lord. But alongside this there was a fluid oral tradition and there were also regular collections of sayings which were written down in the pre-synoptic tradition and which in the second century found an offshoot in the Gospel of Thomas (NHC II,2).

506. Sayings of Jesus about love of neighbour follow in 15.9–17.

507. Sayings of Jesus about truthfulness follow in 16.5–7, on living according to the teaching of Jesus in 16.8–14.

508. Cf. Justin, *I Apology* 26.6: 'All those who belong to their tendency (Justin had previously mentioned Simon, Menander, Marcion and their followers) are called … Christians.'

509. For what follows see Harnack, *Lehrbuch* I (n.496), 195f.

510. The translation is based on *The Apostolic Fathers* (n.504).

511. Friedrich Nietzsche, *The Dawn of Day*, trans J. M. Kennedy, 1911, I 84, pp.85f. The whole passage is worth quoting: 'When all is said and done, however, what can be expected from the effects of a religion which, during the centuries when it was being firmly established, enacted that huge philological farce concerning the Old Testament? I refer to that attempt to tear the Old Testament from the hands of the Jews on the

pretext that it contained only Christian doctrines and *belonged* to the Christians as the true people of Israel, while the Jews had merely arrogated it to themselves without authority. This was followed by a mania of would-be interpretation and falsification, which could not in any circumstances have been allied with a good conscience. However strongly Jewish savants protested, it was everywhere sedulously asserted that the Old Testament alluded everywhere to Christ, and nothing but Christ, more especially his cross, and thus, wherever reference was made to wood, a rod, a ladder, a twig, a tree, a willow, or a staff, such a reference could not but be a prophecy relating to the wood of the Cross: even the setting-up of the Unicorn and the Brazen Serpent, even Moses stretching forth his hands in prayer – yea, the very spits on which the Easter lambs were roasted: all these were allusions to the Cross, and, as it were preludes to it! Did any one who kept on asserting these things ever *believe* in them?'

512. Cf. Hans Lietzmann, *A History of the Early Church*, Vol.1, *The Beginnings of the Christian Church* (1932), ³1953, 249.

513. *The state of research.* Bibliography: cf. Gustav Krüger, 'Marcion', *RE*³ 12, 1903, 266–77; Harnack, *Marcion* (n.440); Johannes von Walther, *Christentum und Frömmigkeit. Gesammelte Vorträge und Aufsätze*, 1941, 41–62 ('Marcion' [1928]); Lüdemann, *Geschichte* (n.2); Barbara Aland, 'Marcion/Marcioniten', *TRE* 22, 1992, 89–101 (with bibliography); Gerhard May, 'Marcion in Contemporary Views: Results and Open Questions', *The Second Century* 6.3, 1987/88, 129–51; R. Joseph Hoffmann, *Marcion: On the Restitution of Christianity. An Essay on the Development of Radical Paulinist Theology in the Second Century*, AAR.AS 46, 1984. Hoffmann has rightly raised the question of a pre-Roman activity of Marcion, but has put it against the background of a questionable reconstruction of the anti-Marcionite activity of Polycarp and Ignatius; cf. Gerhard May, 'Ein neues Markionbild?', *ThR* 51, 1986, 404–13, with the view also put forward by Aland, 'Marcion', and already Krüger, 'Marcion', that Marcion only became a Christian in Rome; thus also Jürgen Regull, *Die antimarkionitischen Evangelienprologe*, 1969, 177–95 (on 'Marcion's heretical activity before Rome). May, 'Markionbild', 407, has recently claimed with reference to Tertullian, *Praescr* 30, that Marcion first became a Christian in Rome (similarly already Krüger, 'Marcion', 267f.). But in that case the whole of Epiphanius' report (see n.529 below) must be rejected as unhistorical and not just the polemic that Marcion seduced a virgin. However, that would be difficult: first, because the note that Marcion was the son of a bishop has no bias. Secondly, it explains Marcion's scriptural learning; and thirdly, Tertullian, to whom May appeals, allows the possibility that Marcion had already been a Christian before his stay in Rome. Tertullian,

Praescr 30, writes: 'Marcion joined the church in Rome.' Tertullian, *Adv Marc* 4.4, says that Marcion gave a gift of money to the community *in primo calore fidei*. Krüger, 'Marcion', 267, comments on this: 'The mode of expression allows ... no other conclusion than that in T(ertullian)'s view M(arcion) first became a Christian in Rome.' The opposite can even be supported by the quotations from Tertullian. That is clear from the context in the two relevant passages. In *Adv Marc* 4.4.3 Tertullian says that Marcion formerly believed the Gospel of Luke of the orthodox church, and still at a point in time when he made his gift of money; a little later he had then been expelled from the community along with his money. Of course the *primus calor fidei* first seems to denote a conversion experience, but what tells against that is the fact that there is no mention of a conversion, and Tertullian would certainly have evaluated a conversion in quite a different way. Rather, *primus calor fidei* means that Marcion was in the first phase of his belief when he made his gift of money, and that this phase was one of deep faith – how could it have been otherwise in an orthodox Christian? This reflection is supported by the remark *prima apud nos fides* a sentence later. For here *prima* certainly denotes a state of Marcion's faith which lasted longer, the first phase of orthodoxy in which Marcion had lived in the Roman community.

An investigation of *Praescr* 30 yields the same result. Here Tertullian writes: 'For it is a well known fact that those men (viz. Marcion, Valentinus) lived not so long ago, in the reign of Antoninus for the most part, and that they at first (*primo*) were believers in the doctrine of the Catholic Church, in the church of Rome under the episcopate of the blessed Eleutherus, until on account of their ever restless curiosity, with which they even infected the brethren, they were more than once expelled. Marcion, indeed, went despite the 200,000 sesterces which he had brought into the church, and, when banished at last to a permanent excommunication, they scattered abroad the poison of their doctrines.'

It cannot be read out of this passage, either, that Marcion and Valentinus with him had first become orthodox Christians in Rome. Tertullian writes only that Valentinus and Marcion had been orthodox Christians in a first period and later were removed from the church after a lengthy period of dispute. *Primo*, the tradition of which is not certain, here means 'initially, in the first stage', and thus denotes a state which lasted for some time.

Harnack's *Marcion* has now – after seventy years – been translated into English, but without its appendixes of 455 pages in all and without the *Neue Studien zu Marcion*. Cf. *Marcion, The Gospel of the Alien God*, trans. John E. Steely and Lyle O. Bierma, Durham, NC 1990. However, because of the abridgement and the relative inaccessibility of the book, the translations here have been made from the original, to which page references are given. May, 'Markionbild', 404, writes on Harnack's work: 'At any rate it has become increasingly clear over the growing passage of time to what a considerable degree Harnack's interpretation is the result of a time-conditioned modernization.'

514. Hoffmann, *Marcion* (n.513), dates this essentially earlier (70 CE).

515. *Strom* VII 16, 106f.: the information that Marcion (together with other heretics like Basilides) appeared as early as the time of Hadrian is credible, because in general the church fathers are concerned to distance the heretics chronologicaly as far as possible from the apostles.

516. Cf. Carl Andresen, 'Die Anfänge christlicher Lehrentwicklung', in id. (ed), *Handbuch der Dogmen- und Theologiegeschichte* I, 1982, 1–98: 63.

517. Thus according to Epiphanius, *Haer* 42, 1, 4; Pseudo-Tertullian, *Haer* 6, 2. Filastrius, *Haer* 45, writes that in Ephesus Marcion 'was condemned by John the evangelist and the presbyter'.

518. Cf. Hegesippus in Eusebius *HE* IV 22, 4: 'As the church (viz., in the time when James was bishop of Jerusalem) was not yet stained by vain teaching, it was called a virgin.' Cf. Shaye J.D. Cohen, 'A Virgin Defiled: Some Rabbinic and Christian views on the Origins of Heresy', *USQR* 35, 1980, 1–11.

519. Peter Lampe, *Die stadtrömischen Christen in den ersten beiden Jahrhunderten. Untersuchungen zur Sozialgeschichte*, WUNT II/18, ²1989, 204f.

520. Ibid., 215.

521. E.g. in Judaism the Song of Songs could become holy scripture only by transferred exegesis. The bride was usually Israel and God the beloved.

522. The tradition handed down by Irenaeus does not give a location for the encounter. It is connected with Polycarp's stay in Rome. For an analysis cf. Lüdemann, *Geschichte* (n.2), 89f.

523. Cf. Harnack, *Marcion* (n.440), 5*: Harnack conjectures Papias' work as Irenaeus' source at this point.

524. However, this episode could in theory also have taken place after Marcion's stay in Rome, especially if we see Marcion's church reflected behind the 'us'. Cf. Harnack, *Marcion*, 4f.*, though he prefers an earlier date. We can rule out the possibility of its having taken place actually during Polycarp's stay in Rome (cf. already n.513 above). 'That this did not take place first in Rome but already in Asia Minor is not stated explicitly, but is certainly to be assumed: in Rome it would have been too late for such an attempt at a rapprochement' (Campenhausen, 'Polykarp' [n.479], 216 n.79).

525. It is sometimes assumed that this was no longer possible after the

clash with Polycarp in Asia Minor (cf. Regull, *Evangelienprologe* [n.513], 177–95). However, this rests on a division between orthodoxy and heresy which is inadmissible for this early period.

526. Tertullian, *Praesc* 30; *Adv Marc* IV 3, 2, in Harnack, *Marcion* (n.440), 17*.

527. Cf. Harnack, *Marcion* (n.440), 17*.

528. According to Tertullian (*Adv Marc* I 19,2), the followers of Marcion estimate 115 years and six and a half months between Jesus' appearance in the fifteenth year of the Emperor Tiberius (= 29 CE, cf. Luke 3.1) and Marcion's foundation of the church (= 144 CE); cf. Adolf Harnack, *Geschichte der altchristlichen Literatur bis Eusebius, II: Die Chronologie, 1: Die Chronologie der Literatur bis Irenäus nebst einleitenden Untersuchungen*, ²1958, 297–311; id., *Marcion* (n.440), 20*.

529. Source: Epiphanius, *Haer* 42, 1, 7–2, 8 (cf. my analysis, Lüdemann, *Geschichte* [n.2], 96 n.28).

530. According to another tradition Marcion presented to the leadership of the Roman church the saying of Jesus: 'For no good tree bears bad fruit, nor again does a bad tree bear good fruit (Luke 6.43)' (Pseudo-Tertullian, in Harnack, *Marcion* [n.440], 25* and n.1).

531. Cf. Adolf von Harnack, 'Die Neuheit des Evangeliums nach Marcion' (1929), in id., *Aus der Werkstatt des Vollendeten*, 1930, 128–43.

532. Justin, *I Apol* 25, 5: *dia pan genos anthropon*. If Justin cannot interest the Roman emperor, to whom the *Apology* is addressed, in Marcion's heresy, nevertheless he does not neglect denouncing Marcion and his followers politically – perhaps aroused by his attention. He ends the section on Marcion, along with Simon and Menander in *I Apol*. 26.7: 'And whether they perpetrate those fabulous and shameful deeds – the upsetting of the lamp, and promiscuous intercourse, and eating human flesh – we know not; but we do know that they are neither persecuted nor put to death by you, at least on account of their opinions.'

533. Bauer, *Orthodoxy* (n.83), 194.

534. Cf. Lietzmann, *Beginnings* (n.512), 274 and n.1. One might recall the famous hymn 'Amazing Grace' by John Newton. It is worth recalling that Newton, the son of a ship-master who was arrested and spent two years as the slave of a slave trader, became a Christian after experincing the unlimited grace of God that relates not only to white people but also to black people. Here his experience resembled that of Marcion.

535. 'All Christians at that time believed that they were strangers on earth. M.(arcion) corrected this belief: *God is the stranger* who is leading them from their homeland of oppression and misery into a quite new home of which hitherto they have not even had an inkling' (Harnack, *Marcion* [n.440], 4f.). Why doesn't the highly-learned Habilitation thesis by

Reinhard Feldmeier (*Die Christen als Fremde. Der Metapher der Fremde in der antiken Welt, im Urchristentum und im 1.Petrusbrief*, WUNT 64, 1992) devote a single line to this?

536. However, according to Karlmann Beyschlag (*Grundriss der Dogmengeschichte I: Gott und Welt*, ²1988), Marcion's cry of jubilation is 'nothing but a negation' (161 n.215). I want to correct this average view in the account above.

537. Harnack, 'Neuheit' (n.531), 129: 'The two experiences which meant everything to him were the experience of redemption through faith in the God revealed in Christ and the experience of the evil and damnation of the world in all its "righteousness". Evidently these two experiences were intimately connected in him, so that we cannot ask which comes first; however, from the tone that they have in him and the firm fact that he was formerly a Catholic Christian, a significant aspect can be contributed to his characterization' (139f.).

538. Cf. Harnack, *Marcion* (n.440), 20f.

539. Lindemann, *Paulus* (n.224), 386.

540. Ibid., 390.

541. Ibid., 386.

542. Cf. Lüdemann, *Opposition* (n.133), 109–11.

543. Paul knows e.g. commandments which are a matter of course (cf. I Cor. 5 and all the decisions relating to unchastity). Cf. further above 85f.

544. Cf. Lietzmann, *Beginnings* (n.512), 251; cf. Harnack, 'Neuheit' (n.531), 140f.

545. Cf. Lietzmann, *Beginnings* (n.512), 253. Even Paul knows a host of divine beings (I Cor. 8.5) and in II Cor. 4.4 speaks of 'the god of this age who has blinded the minds of unbelievers'.

546. Cf. below, 167.

547. Cf. Lietzmann, *Beginnings* (n.512), 251.

548. Cf. above, 163f. with n.545.

549. Cf. Lüdemann, *Untersuchungen* (n.1), 36f.

550. For a discussion of Marcion's relation to Gnosis cf. Lindemann, *Paulus* (n.224), 388f. (with bibliography).

551. 'Although Marcion undoubtedly misunderstood Paul at certain vital points, there can be no question that he came nearer to understanding him than did, say, the author of I Timothy' (John Knox, *Marcion and the New Testament* [1942], 1980, 13).

552. E.P.Meijering (*Tertullian contra Marcion. Gotteslehre in der Polemik Adversus Marcionem I–II*, 1977) writes on Tertullian, the scourge of heretics, in his relationship to Marcion: 'This book describes and analyses the fight between two unequal opponents: the acute but not very original Tertullian and Marcion, who is far superior to him in profundity

and originality. The only reason why the outcome is in favour of Tertullian is that Marcion (or the Marcionites) does not get a chance to fight back. Marcion shares this fate with most of the heretics in early Christianity: his writings have been lost and we have only the fragments of them which his opponents quote against him more or less accurately in their writings' (IX).

553. Cf. Harnack, *Studien* (n.440), 9: 'I do not know how it can be indicated any more clearly that M(arcion) stakes everything *on faith*, sees an *inner transformation* brought about by faith (from sinner to good), makes Christ's death on the cross the content of this faith, *and thus in this decisive piece of doctrine is an authentic disciple of Paul*. That he has the ransom paid to the creator of the world is not the basis here for any essential difference from the religious altitude, since at the time he most clearly indicates that this is a matter of the justification of the impious and that for him the transformation of the sinner brought about by faith is the decisive thing.'

554. Campenhausen, *Formation* (n.497), 149. The continuation of the quotation runs: 'But the tension between law and faith, which dominates Paul's theology, has in Marcion become simple contradiction; and the redemption of those lost in the world becomes hatred toward the creation, toward all the gods at work "in Nature", and toward the cruelly unjust Creator of this world himself.'

555. Harnack, *Marcion* [n.440], 180 (printed in italics in Harnack).

556. For him cf. Harnack, *Marcion* (n.440), 177–96, 404*–20*; Lampe, *Christen* (n.519), 350f. Harnack's view that the content of the conversation with Rhodo reflects some resignation on the part of Apelles (Apelles says 'that what he had formerly judged to be a matter of knowledge is now a subjective determination lying outside knowledge'[187]) can be left aside here.

557. 'Presumably, Apelles considered himself to be the victor' (Bauer, *Orthodoxy* [n.83], 132).

558. Harnack, *Marcion* (n.440), 187 n.2 (on 188).

559. The absolute 'the Crucified' is unique in the whole of literature after Paul (cf. Harnack, *Marcion* [n.440], 182).

560. Cf. Lietzmann, *Beginnings* (n.512), 263.

561. Cf. Harnack, *Marcion* (n.440), 187.

562. Cf. Lietzmann, *Beginnings* (n.512), 263.

563. *The state of research*: The Gospel of John and the three letters of John, and for some scholars also Revelation, are regarded as belonging to the Johannine writings. Since Revelation is included only by a minority, it will not be taken into account here. (For the problem cf. Jörg Frey, 'Erwägungen zum Verhältnis der Johannesapokalypse zu den übrigen Schriften des Corpus Johanneum', in Martin Hengel, *Die johanneische*

Frage. Ein Lösungsversuch, WUNT 67, 1993, 326–49 [with biblio-graphy]. This article is not in the English edition, *The Johannine Question*, 1989, which appeared earlier and represents a less fully documented version of the work.) At any rate no one today can any longer overlook research into the Gospel of John and the three letters. It is welcome that some scholars have written commentaries on all four documents (Rudolf Bultmann, Rudolf Schnackenburg and Raymond E. Brown) and thus have presented a relatively unitary account of these four writings, which belong together.

Several stages of research into John can be distinguished (for what follows cf. Vielhauer, *Geschichte* [n.10], 411–15; in each case the most recent literature on individual texts is mentioned and used):

First, the question of whether the Gospel was written by John the dis-ciple of Jesus, whose calling is narrated in Mark 1.19f., was discussed particularly intensively in the nineteenth century, and in general the critical consensus was reached that the author was someone other than this John.

Secondly, in the subsequent period the main interest of Johannine research was in source criticism. An attempt was made to separate authentic from inauthentic texts within the Gospel by means of source criticism or – starting from offensive features and contradictions in the structure of the Gospel – to free a basic document from redactional revisions of it. To this was added an attempt to reconstruct the original Gospel by transpositions of the text. Finally, by means of word-statistical investigations, some scholars investigated the typical stylistic peculiarities of John as compared to the other New Testament writings and how these are distributed over the Gospel. Sometimes this led to the conclusion that the source-critical method was fruitless when applied to the Gospel of John and that the Gospel was therefore a unity.

Thirdly, the question what context in the history of religion is to be given to the Gospel of John or its sources is a further ongoing theme of research into John; this of course is closely connected with the new dis-coveries in particular times. (In the 1920s, the Mandaeans played an important role; in the 1950s the Qumran texts; and at present the Nag-Hammadi discoveries, at last accessible, invite comparison.) The problem here also arose out of the observation that in term of its mode of speech, conceptuality and world of ideas the Gospel of John is clearly different from the Synoptics. Here, however, generally speaking, the champions of a Gnostic origin of the Gospel and those of a Jewish syncretistic origin oppose each other.

Fourthly, the theme which attracted increasing interest in the period after the Second World War was the question of the theological message

301

of the Gospel of John. But here, too, a considerable variety of opinions can be noted. At the same time, in this respect it can be noted that occasionally the theological and hermeneutical problem is treated without any consideration of the historical question and that in more recent literary investigations these historical questions no longer have a role.

Fifthly, attempts at defining the concrete location of the Johannine writings have increasingly interested scholars in recent years. Here reference should be made in particular to the investigations by J. Louis Martyn, *History and Theology in the Fourth Gospel*, 1948; Raymond E. Brown, *The Community of the Beloved Disciple*, 1979; and Klaus Wengst, *Bedrängte Gemeinde und verherrlichter Christus. Ein Versuch über das Johannesevangelium*, ³1990. These works arose out of renewed reflection on the significance of giving the Johannine circle a social and historical location, but at the same time also as a reaction to one-sided theological hermeneutical analysis. Those who defend the right to seek a historical location are not concerned with dissolving what the text actually says but are trying to understand the text in the conditions in which the people by whom and for whom it was composed and who received it actually lived (cf. Wengst, *Gemeinde*, 48). Ernst Käsemann already commented critically on the one-sided theological and hermeneutical analysis of the Gospel of John by Rudolf Bultmann:

'It is no coincidence that the most recent great commentary on John by R. Bultmann is highly sceptical, and judges that the argument over the problem of authorship is valueless for real exegesis. Such an assertion seems to me to go too far. Any detail which allows us to comprehend the historical location more sharply at the same time prevents us from getting lost in the sphere of speculation' (Ernst Käsemann, 'Ketzer und Zeuge. Zum johanneischen Verfasserproblem' [1951], in id., *Exegetische Versuche und Besinnungen* I, 1960, 168–87: 169).

Sixthly, here, taking into account the perspective of this last-mentioned branch of scholarship, the (short) letters and the conflict which has broken out in them are used as a starting point for reconstructing the origin of the Johannine circle. The remarks of mine which follow take this up. Here the commentary by Georg Strecker, *Die Johannesbriefe*, KEK 14, 1989, and the great monograph by Martin Hengel mentioned above, *The Johannine Question*, have become particularly important for me. In addition Bauer's *Orthodoxy* (n.83), constantly mentioned above, and the article by Käsemann, 'Ketzer und Zeuge', already mentioned, are relevant works for these problems.

564. Thus the whole patristic tradition in conjunction with the narratives about the apostle John or the presbyter of the same name (cf. only Eusebius, *HE* III 23, 6–19; 39.5f., etc.).

565. We need not take the designations 'circle' and 'school' too specifically. For example Justin's school in Rome (cf. Lüdemann, 'Geschichte' [n.2], 103f.) differs considerably from the Johannine school, which is part of an association.

566. This is meant sociologically, and refers to the evidence that runs through all the Johannine writings, that the community sees itself faced with a hostile world. 'Thus the Johannine literature gives rise to a completely dualistic image: a small group of believers stands in isolation over against "the world", which by nature belongs to the "things below", i.e. to darkness and the devil' (Wayne A. Meeks, 'Die Funktion des vom Himmel herabgestiegenen Offenbarers für das Selbstverständnis der johanneischen Gemeinde', in id., [ed.], *Zur Soziologie des Urchristentums*, ThB 62, 1979, 245–83: 277. Cf. also Walter Rebell, *Gemeinde als Gegenwelt. Zur soziologischen und didaktischen Funktion des Johannesevangeliums*, BET 20, 1987).

567. Cf. also Roloff, *Kirche* (n.458), 290–309 (XI. Die Gemeinschaft der Freunde Jesu: Die johanneischen Schriften).

568. François Vouga, *Die Johannesbriefe*, HNT 15/III 1990, 15. Cf. in this connection also the precise investigations into the relationship between the individual Johannine letters by Hans-Josef Klauck, *Die Johannesbriefe*, EdF 276, 1991, 109–24.

569. Hartwig Thyen, 'Johannesbriefe', *TRE* 17, 1988, 186–200: 186f.

570. The reasons produced against this by Walter Schmithals (*Johannesevangelium und Johannesbriefe*, BZNW 64, 1992) are pure postulates; thus for example Schmithals doubts whether II John is an authentic letter and whether there was a Johannine school at all (287). U.H.J.Körtner (*Papias von Hierapolis. Ein Beitrag zur Geschichte des frühen Christentums*, FRLANT 133, 1983) regards II/III John 'as pseudonymous writings which fictitiously derive from the presbyter John, who was known to the readers' (199). But in this case the question arises whether he was not himself the author. For the presbyter cf. Klauck, *Johannesbriefe* (n.568), 116–21.

571. Klauck, *Johannesbriefe*, 117.

572. Cf. Strecker, *Johannesbriefe* (n.563), 22.

573. Cf. Hengel, *Question* (n.563), 133f.

574. Thus already Ferdinand Christian Baur, 'Die johanneischen Briefe. Ein Beitrag zur Geschichte des Kanons', *ThJB* 7, 1848, 293–337:329; cf. also Strecker, *Johannesbriefe*, 357f., 368; cf. Vouga, *Johannesbriefe* (n.568), 91 (either II John or a lost letter of commendation the content of which corresponded to vv.3–8); Hengel, *Question* (n.563), 138. By contrast, Jens W. Taeger ('Der konservative Rebell. Zum Widerstand des Diotrephes gegen den Presbyter', *ZNW* 78, 1987, 267–87) thinks that the

identification of the letter to the community (III John 9) with II John cannot be substantiated (27 n.28), but neglects to ask whether this identification is not the most obvious hypothesis. His further reference to Adolf Harnack, *Über den dritten Johannesbrief*, TU 15/3b, 1897, 10 n.1, is not convincing (ibid., cf. n.575). For the identification of II John with the letter mentioned in III John 9 cf. below n.616.

575. It is therefore too simple when Harnack, *Johannesbrief* (n.574) objects to the identification of II John with the letter mentioned in III John 9 that 'there is simply no mention of false teachings in III John – even with Diotrephes – whereas II John does not mention Diotrephes, nor are there discussions of the violations of the community by an ambitious president' (10 n.1). Harnack's further objection (ibid.), that the earliest tradition does not know a connection between the two short letters of John, is untenable (see 203 below). In particular the similarity of the language and structure is an argument for the immediate chronological proximity of the two letters and therefore makes the identification advocated above even more probable.

576. Cf. Georg Strecker, 'Chiliasmus und Doketismus in der johanneischen Schule', *KuD* 38, 1992, 30–46: 34.

577. Cf. Hans-Josef Klauck, *Der zweite und dritte Johannesbrief*, EKK XXIII/2, 1992, 100; id., *Johannesbriefe* (n.568), 35–7, 'Verlorene Johannesbriefe?'). Klauck observes: 'The textual variants (on v.9) already signalize the difficulty that people had with this letter of the presbyter' (*Johannesbriefe*, 35). Although Klauck thinks that the letter mentioned in III John 9 has been lost, he can write that Diotrephes 'applied ... the principle from II John 9 – no acceptance of messengers from the dissidents in the house – to all itinerant missionaries on the move' (*Johannesbriefe*, 162).

578. Koester, *Einführung* (n.133), 635. Schmithals, *Johannesevangelium* (n.570), 286, argues that II John corresponds to I John and is a catholic letter, addressed to all communities which have to ward off the Gnostic heresy. As its content corresponds so completely with I John, it cannot be thought an authentic letter. Körtner, *Papias* (n.570), similarly regards II John as a later compendium of I John (199).

579. For II John (and III John) as a conventional Hellenistic letter cf. especially Robert W.Funk, 'The Form and Structure of II and III John', *JBL* 86, 1987, 424–30 (= 'The Apostolic Presence: John the Elder', in id., *Parables and Presence. Forms of the New Testament Tradition*, 1982, 103–10). Although in the original article Funk leaves open the question whether II/III John are letters which were really sent, he now (because of the new title of the article) seems to answer it in the affirmative.

580. Cf. Strecker, *Johannesbriefe* (n.563), 139.

581. Cf. Hengel, *Question* (n.563), 39

582. Ibid., 40 and 171 n.64.

583. Cf. Mark 13.22ff.; Acts 20.29f.; II Thess. 2.3ff.; I Tim. 4.1ff.; II Tim. 3.1ff.; 4.3ff.; II Peter 2.1.

584. There is no explicit account that the presbyter John was a chiliast. But this follows compellingly from the fact that he was the chief informant of the chiliast Papias (n.585)(cf. Eusebius, *HE* III 39,4).

585. Eusebius, *HE* III, 39, 11f.: 'And Papias has quoted other things also, as coming to him from unwritten tradition: for instance, certain strange parables of the Saviour and teachings of his, and some other things of a rather mythical character. And among these is his statement that there will be a certain period of a thousand years after the resurrection from the dead, when the kingdom of Christ will be set up in a material order upon this earth. I imagine that he got these ideas through a misinterpretation of the apostolic accounts, for he did not understand what they said mystically and in figurative language.' In immediate connection with this, Eusebius attests Papias 'spiritual limitation' (III 39.13).

586. *Dial.* 80.5: 'But I and others, who are right-minded Christians on all points, are assured that there will be a resurretion of the dead, and a thousand years in Jerusalem, which will be built, adorned and enlarged, as the prophets Ezekiel and Isaiah and others declare.'

587. Irenaeus, *Haer* V 33, 3. The blessing of Isaac from Gen.27.27 'belongs... to the times of the kingdom, when the righteous shall bear rule upon their rising from the dead; when also the creation, having been renewed and set free, shall fructify with an abundance of all kinds of food, from the dew of heaven, and from the fertility of the earth.'

588. Cf. Strecker, *Johannesbriefe* (n.563), 335f.

589. Cf. Eusebius, *HE* III 39,7: 'Papias acknowledges that he received the discourses of the apostles from those who had been their followers, but says that he was himself an actual hearer of Aristion and of John the elder. Certainly he mentions them by name frequently in his treatises and sets forth their traditions.'

590. Cf. Irenaeus, *Haer* III 16, 8: 'It is one and the same Christ to whom the gates of heaven were opened, because of his taking upon him flesh; who shall also come in the same flesh in which he suffered, revealing the glory of the Father'; Tertullian, *On the Flesh of Christ* 24.4: 'It is only good that the one who suffered will come again from heaven, and the one who rose again from the dead shall be seen by all. Those who crucified him will see him and acknowledge him; that is to say the same flesh against which they raged, and without which it would be impossible for him either to exist or to be seen.'

591. Cf. Klauck, *Johannesbriefe* (n.568), 114.

592. Cf. Judith M. Lieu, *The Second and Third Epistle of John: History and Background*, 1986, 85.

593. It would be 'unparalleled for the expectation of the parousia to be the content of the *homologein*' (Conzelmann, *Outline* [n.15], 361). Nor is a reference to the pre-Pauline formula I Thess. 1.9f. much more help, since this does not mention a *homologein*. On the other hand, it does not follow from the two arguments advanced above against Strecker's early dating of the two short letters of John that the sequence of these letters cannot be reversed. See above in the text.

594. Cf. Hans von Campenhausen, 'Das Bekenntnis im Urchristentum' (1972), in *Urchristliches und Altkirchliches. Vorträge und Aufsätze*, 1979, 217–72: 254.

595. Campenhausen, 'Bekenntnis', 255, referring to Smyrn.5.2. At the same time it should be emphasized that Christian Gnostics could interpret the becoming *flesh* in a docetic sense. Cf. the Gospel of Truth (NHC I,3): 'He gave them the means of knowing the knowledge of the Father and the revelation of his Son. For when they had seen him and had heard him, he granted them to taste him (cf. John 6.52–58) and smell him and to touch the beloved Son (cf. John 20.20, 27). When he had appeared instructing them about the Father, the incomprehensible one, when he had breathed into them (cf. John 20.22) what is in the mind, doing his will (cf. John 4.34), when many had received the light, they turned to him... They did not see his likeness and had not known him. For he came by means of fleshly appearance (cf. I John 4.2; II John 7) while nothing blocked his course because it was incorruptibility and irresistibility' (30.24–31.9). By contrast, the Gospel of Philip (NHC II,3) explicitly emphasizes the resurrection in this flesh (57.18). However, this is no crass materialism, but resurrection as a metaphor for what is firm. In this connection cf. 56.26–57.19: 'Some are afraid lest they rise naked. Because of this they wish to rise in the flesh, and [they] do not know that it is those who wear the [flesh] who are not naked. "Flesh [and blood shall] not [be able] to inherit the kingdom of God." What is this which will not inherit? This which is on us. But what is this very thing which will inherit? It is that which belongs to Jesus and his blood. Because of this he said, "He who shall not eat my flesh and drink my blood has not life in him." What is it? His flesh is the word and his blood is the Holy Spirit. He who has received flesh is the word and his blood is the Holy Spirit. He who has received these has food and he has drink and clothing. I find fault with the others who say that it (the flesh) will not rise. Then both of them are at fault. You say that the flesh will not rise. But tell me what will rise, that we may honour you (as a teacher). You say the spirit in the flesh, and it is also this (spark of) light in the flesh. But this too (that you have mentioned) is a

matter which is in the flesh, for whatever you shall say, you say nothing outside the flesh. It is necessary to rise in this flesh, since everything exists in it.' According to the linguistic theory of the Gospel of Philip, reality first discloses itself through images. Cf. 53.23–54.1: 'Names given to worldly (things) are very deceptive, for they divert our thoughts from what is correct to what is incorrect. Thus one who hears the word "God" does not perceive what is correct, but perceives what is incorrect. So also with "the Father" and "the Son" and "the Holy Spirit" and "life" and "light" and "resurrection" and "the church" and all the rest – people do not perceive what is correct, unless they have come to know what is correct. The names which are heard are in the world...' Cf. further Lona, *Auferstehung* (n.150), 235–56.

596. Cf. Adolf Martin Ritter, *Charisma und Caritas. Aufsätze zur Geschichte der Alten Kirche*, 1993, 121.

597. Cf. Klauck, *Johannesbriefe* (n.568), 17.

598. Hengel, *Question* (n.563), 16 (the fuller German text, *Johanneische Frage*, 73, which is translated here, differs slightly).

599. For the construction cf. Strecker, *Johannesbriefe* (n.563), 124 n.19.

600. For docetism, cf. Udo Schnelle, *Antidocetic Christology in the Gospel of John*, 1992, 76–82. Strecker, *Johannesbriefe*, on the basis of his own reconstruction of the Johannine circle, imagines the origin of the opposing position as follows: 'A challenge to the realistic position of the presbyter could have been the cause of the origin of a rival docetic christology of the kind that is characteristic of the heretics ... At the time of the composition of I John and of the Gospel its nucleus (viz. that of the school) had swung over to a moderate "church" position; the rival docetic wing, dissociation from which was being attempted, was presumably older' (124). By way of criticism: docetism is not necessarily a position opposed to chiliasm.

601. Cf. Bauer, Orthodoxy (n.83), 234, and Harnack, *Lehrbuch der Dogmengeschichte* I (n.496), 215 and passim.

602. In them to a large degree 'the earthly life of Jesus is ... a backdrop for the Son of God proceeding through the world of man ... and as the scene of the inbreaking of the heavenly glory' 'The message of the God who walks on the face of the earth finds its correspondence in the community which, being conscious of its mission, is without a feeling of solidarity for the world... The notion of the liberated community takes the place of the concept of the new world' (Ernst Käsemann, *The Testament of Jesus. A Study of the Gospel of John in the Light of Chapter 17*, 1968, 13, 65).

603. For this and the next section see Vielhauer, *Geschichte* (n.10), 197–200.

604. Thus especially Schnelle, *Christology* (n.600). Cf. already the protest against this by Käsemann, *Testament* (n.602), 26 n.41: 'The assertion, quite generally accepted today, that the Fourth Gospel is anti-docetic, is completely unproven.'

605. Cf. Didache 12.1: 'Let everyone who comes in the name of the Lord be received!'

606. For Polycarp's repudiation of Marcion cf. above 160.

607. Bauer, *Orthodoxy* (n.83), 92f.

608. Roland Bergmeier, 'Zum Verfasserproblem des II. und III. Johannesbriefes', ZNW 57, 1966, 93–100, exaggerates: he argues that truth is used as an embodiment of Christian teaching (II John 9), which is simply handed down in the community. But the simple identification of truth and doctrine can hardly be maintained. Cf. also Rudolf Schnackenburg, 'Zum Begriff der "Wahrheit" in den beiden kleinen Johannesbriefen', BZ 11, 1967, 253–8.

609. Strecker, *Johannesbriefe* (n.563), 347f.

610. See above 13. Cf. further I Tim. 1.20; Acts 2.22f.

611. Hengel, *Question* (n.563), 44f.

612. Ibid., 45.

613. Ibid.

614. Cf. ibid.,72, as a quotation from Karl Barth, or the author's remark on the Gospel of John that he was the first person in early Christianity to grasp the *vere homo et vere deus* as the starting point for authentic christology in all its depth (*Johanneische Frage*, 257, cf. 266; cf. *Johannine Question*, 103). By way of criticism: I am firmly convinced that the doctrine of two natures from the early church cannot help us today to say who Jesus is, quite apart from the fact that Hengel merely cites this tradition and does not interpret it at all.

615. Hengel, *Johanneische Frage* (n.563), 127f.

616. Cf. n.574. Klauck, *Johannesbriefe* (n.568), 99, discusses this possibility and rejects it: 'We do not ultimately know what stood in the letter of v.9a'. Similarly Abraham Malherbe, 'The Inhospitality of Diotrephes', in *God's Christ and His People. Studies in Honour of Nils Alstrup Dahl*, 1977, 222–32: 231 n.40. 'This is not a reference to II John … The circumstances envisaged in the two are different.'

617. Cf. Klauck, *Johannesbriefe* (n.568), 158–63 ('Der "herrschsüchtige Diotrephes"'), esp. 161 and n.46.

618. Cf. Strecker, *Johannesbriefe* (n.563), 365–8 ('Excursus: Diotrephes und der Presbyter').

619. Cf. most recently Taeger, 'Rebell' (n.574), 269, 279, and already above n.575.

620. As a parallel note the controversy between Paul and his opponents

in II Cor, where the personal matters at least in part come ahead of the theological ones.

621. Thus Malherbe, 'Hospitality' (n.616), 228: 'We must be content with the fact that we do not know what Diotrephes' reasons were for his conduct. We are limited to the Elder's view of the matter, and he sees in it a purely personal issue.'

622. *The state of research.* The standard book today on the Apostles' Creed is J.N.D. Kelly, *Early Christian Creeds*, 1950; cf. also the article on the Apostles' Creed in *TRE* 3, 1978, 528–54 (Frederick Ercolo Vokes); *RGG*¹ 1, 1909, 99–601 (Gustav Krüger); *RGG*² 1, 1927, 443–6 (Hans Lietzmann); *RGG*³ 1, 1957, 51–13 (Alfred Adam). Paul Feine, *Die Gestalt des apostolischen Glaubensbekenntnisses in der Zeit des Neuen Testaments*, 1925, is a curious book, as the title already indicates (cf. the review by Adolf von Harnack, *ThLZ* 50, 1925, 393–5). Cf. also Hans von Campenhausen, 'Das Bekenntnis im Urchristentum', *ZNW* 63, 1972 = id., *Urchristliches und Altkirchliches*, 1979, 217–72; Vielhauer, *Geschichte* (n.10), 9–68 ('pre-literary forms').

At this point we should recall the dispute over the Apostles' Creed which caused a great furore a century ago (cf. Karl H. Neufeld, 'Adolf Harnacks Konflikt mit der Kirche. Weg-Stationen zum "Wesen des Christentums"', *IThS* 4, 1979, 114–32). It was sparked off by the dismissal of the Württemberg pastor Christoph Schrempf, who with an appeal to his conscience refused to say the Apostles' Creed at baptisms and in worship. Adolf Harnack, when asked for his opinion on the Schrempf affair by students in Berlin, gave an answer at the end of the summer semester of 1892; it was finally published the same year and raised a storm of protests and declarations of solidarity. Cf. Adolf Harnack, 'Das apostolische Glaubensbekenntnis, ein geschichtlicher Bericht nebst einer Einleitung und einem Nachwort' (1892), in id., *Reden und Aufsätze* I, 1904, 219–64. From the host of literature cf. only Karl Sell, 'Zur Kirchenfrage und ueber evangelischen Gebrauch von kirchlichen Formeln, insbesondere von Glaubensbekenntnissen', *ZThK* 3, 1893, 140–80; Wilhelm Herrmann, 'Ergebnisse des Streites um das Apostolikum', *ZThK* 4, 1894, 291–303 (cf. the introductory sentence on 291): 'In my time I have joined many people in complaining that by publishing his answer to the students, Harnack gave our opponents the welcome opportunity of arousing the piety of the orthodox community against us with a semblance of justice ... Nevertheless, I now rejoice at the blessing that this storm has brought to the evangelical church'. Cf. the assessment of the dispute by Walter Nigg, *Geschichte des religiösen Liberalismus*, 1937, 284f.: 'The dispute over the Apostles' Creed grew out of the Schrempf "affair" as a matter of conscience. It was as it were a rebellion of the truth against a creed which was no longer felt to be true. Thus the issue in this question was the honesty of the intellectual existence of the theologian. This existential question, which urgently called for an answer that could be applied in practice, was deflected into dangerous academic waters by the intervention of the professors. That made the whole affair harmless, for one can discuss *ad infinitum* the scholarly significance of the Apostles' Creed without changing the oppressed situation of the pastor in office to the slightest degree. The dispute over the Apostles' Creed, which after Schrempf "could have been a page of honour in the history of the Protestant church" could in this way be condemned to complete ineffectiveness.'

623. For this see most recently Willy Rordorf, 'Bedeutung und Grenze der altkirchlichen Glaubensbekenntnisse (Apostolikum und Nicaeno-Constantinopolitanum)', *ThZ* 51, 1995, 50–64 (with bibliography).

624. Karl Holl, 'Zur Auslegung des 2.Artikels des sog.apostolischen Glaubensbekenntnisses' (1919), in id., *Gesammelte Aufsätze zur Kirchengeschichte II. Der Osten*, 1928, 115–22: 122. Wolfhart Pannenberg, *The Apostles' Creed In the Light of Today's Questions*, 1973, is an exception here.

625. Cf. Kelly, *Creeds*, (n.622), 398–434.

626. Ibid., 102.

627. As is well known, Luther inserted 'Christian'.

628. Cf. Kelly, *Creeds*, (n.622), 378–83.

629. Cf. ibid., 388–97.

630. Ibid., 1f.

631. 'But the second-century conviction that the "rule" of faith believed and taught in the Catholic church had been inherited from the Apostles contains more than a germ of truth. Not only was the content of that rule, in all essentials, foreshadowed by the "pattern of teaching" accepted in the apostolic church, but its characteristic lineaments and outline found their prototype in the confessions and credal summaries contained in the New Testament documents' (Kelly, *Creeds* [n.622], 29).

632. Cf. 'Glaubensbekenntnis(se) IV. Neues Testament', *TRE* 13, 1984, 392–9 (Klaus Wengst); 'V.Alte Kirche', ibid,. 399–412 (Adolf Martin Ritter), which lists the most important literature.

633. Thus, however, Campenhausen, 'Bekenntnis' (n.622), 220. He sees the starting point in the 'authentic' saying of Jesus in Matt. 10.32: 'Every one who acknowledges me before men, I also will acknowledge before my Father who is in heaven.' But the logion in Matt. 10.32 certainly does not come from Jesus (cf. Funk/Hoover, *Gospels* [n.10]), 173).

634. Campenhausen, 'Bekenntnis' (n.622), 219.

635. Were these trinitarian formulations it would be implied that the doctrine of the Trinity already underlay these texts. However, there

can be no question of that – hence the neutral expression 'triadic' formulations.

636. The emphatically anti-docetic features of some of the resurrection narratives are also to be understood in this connection. Cf. Luke 24.36–49 and the report in John 20.19–23 which is dependent on it (for the reasons cf. Lüdemann, *Resurrection* [n.3], 161f.).

637. Campenhausen, 'Bekenntnis' (n.622), 271.

638. Cf. above 53f.

639. E.g. *I Apol* 26.1 says: 'After Christ's ascension from heaven the devils put forward certain men who said they themselves were gods.' Following this Justin cites the following examples for Simon, Menander and Marcion (*I Apol* 26, 2–5, see above 19).

640. Harnack, *Lehrbuch* I (n.496), 360f.

641. Cf. the passages from Irenaeus and Tertullian quoted in Ch.6 (n.590) on the correspondence betwen Jesus' fleshly appearance and his return in the flesh.

642. *All* early Christians who use allegorical exegesis exclusively presuppose this, e.g. the Valentinian Heracleon, but also Clement of Alexandria and Origen. Cf. also the examples from the newly discovered Nag Hammadi texts given in n.595 above.

643. Karl Holl, 'Zur Auslegung des 2.Artikels des sog. apostolischen Glaubensbekenntnisses' (1919), in id., *Gesammelte Aufsätze zur Kirchengeschichte II, Der Osten*, 1928, 115–22: 121.

644. Cf. the offence caused at the time by John A. T. Robinson, *Honest to God*, 1963; and on it David L. Edwards (ed.), *The Honest to God Debate*, 1963; John Bowden (ed.), *Thirty Years of Honesty. Honest to God Then and Now*, 1993.

645. Pannenberg, *Creed* (n.624). References to this book are given in brackets in the text.

646. One might think of the dictum of Adolf von Harnack: 'That is the side-effect of dogma. It does harm when one has it and it does harm when one has had it. These after-effects are even the worst.'

647. Cf. also Holl, 'Auslegung' (n.624), 122: 'The so-called Apostles' Creed is a monument which an unusual formative power and an unusually definitive conviction have joined together in creating. But it is not granted to any human being to bring forth something timeless, something eternally valid. He can always only confess what he and his time believes. And unless they want to live in another way, the churches cannot avoid reinterpreting their own creeds in the course of the centuries. If they hold rigidly to the content or completely to the wording which was once fixed, they condemn themselves to death.'

648. Lietzmann, *Founding* (n.97), 117.

649. Gustav Krüger, *Das Dogma von der Dreieinigkeit und Gottmenschheit in seiner geschichtlichen Entwicklung*, Lebensfragen, 1905, 298.

650. *The state of research.* Carsten Colpe, 'Heilige Schriften', *RAC* 14, 1988, 184–223, gives an instructive survey from a history-of-religions perspective. There is a history of the New Testament canon in any major scholarly Introduction to the New Testament; as representatives see Adolf Hilgenfeld, *Historisch-kritische Einleitung in das Neue Testament*, 1875, 27–163; Heinrich Julius Holtzmann, *Lehrbuch der historisch-kritischen Einleitung in das Neue Testament*, [3]1892, 75–154; Friedrich Bleek, *Einleitung in das Neue Testament*, [4]1886, 821–84; Adolf Jülicher, *Einleitung in das Neue Testament*, [5/6]1906, 418–517; Kümmel, *Introduction* (n.368), 475–93; Vielhauer, *Geschichte* (n.10), 774–865. Cf. also the outstandingly learned work by Theodor Zahn, *Geschichte des neutestamentlichen Kanons. I: Das Neue Testament vor Origenes. Erste Hälfte*, 1888; *Zweite Hälfte*, 1889; *II. Urkunden und Belege zum ersten und dritten Band*, 1890; id., *Grundriss der Geschichte des neutestamentlichen Kanons. Eine Ergänzung zu der Einleitung in das Neue Testament*, [2]1904; Johannes Leipoldt, *Geschichte des neutestamentlichen Kanons. Erster Teil: Die Entstehung*, 1907; Hans Lietzmann, 'Wie wurden die Bücher des Neuen Testaments Heilige Schrift?' (1907), in id., *Kleine Schriften* II, TU 68, 1958, 15–98; Adolf von Harnack, *The Origin of the New Testament and the Most Important Consequences of the New Creation* (1914), 1925; also Karl-Heinz Ohlig, *Woher nimmt die Kirche ihre Autorität? Zum Verhältnis von Schriftkanon, Kirche und Jesus*, 1970; id., *Die theologische Begründung des neutestamentlichen Kanons in der alten Kirche*, KBANT, 1972; Alexander Sand, *Kanon. Von den Anfängen bis zum Fragmentum Muratorianum*, Handbuch der Dogmengeschichte I 3 a (1), 1974. Cf. further Wilhelm Schneemelcher, 'Bibel III', *TRE* 6, 1980, 22–48; Robert W. Funk, 'The New Testament as Tradition and Canon', in id., *Parables and Presence. Forms of the New Testament Tradition*, 1982, 151–86; Wilhelm Schneemelcher and R. McL. Wilson, *New Testament Apocrypha* I, [2]1991, 9–50 (with translations of the most important sources); A. F. J. Klijn, 'Die Entstehungsgeschichte des Neuen Testaments', ANRW II 26.1, 1992, 64–97.

Hans von Campenhausen, *The Formation of the Christian Bible*, 1972, is basic to the following discussion. It is a standard work on the forces and motives which led to the formation of the canon, putting special emphasis on the role of Marcion's canon for the New Testament canon. On his project Campenhausen writes:

'In my view... it is possible...given the requisite caution, to reconstruct the main lines of the formation of the canon. The man who wants to know too much loses the thread, and in the end learns nothing; the man who turns his attention to what is actually there perceives to his astonishment that the links are by no means as obscure as had first appeared. The right course is not to concentrate simply on isolated individual texts but – more in the manner of the historian than of the literary critic – to observe those lines which link up and finally form a discernible pattern.

More recent, usually popular works, do not come up to the level of those mentioned (cf. the survey in Harry Y. Gamble, 'The Canon of the New Testament', in *The New Testament and its Modern Interpreters*, ed. Eldon Jay Epp and George W. MacRae, 1989, 201–43 [with bibliography]) and no further account will be taken of them here. A few further individual contributions will be mentioned at appropriate points in the text.

In some respects Bruce M. Metzger, *The Canon of the New Testament*, 1987, represents an international neo-conservative consensus which is also evident in the positive acceptance of his thesis by Ernst Dassmann (id., 'Wer schuf den Kanon des Neuen Testaments?', *JBCh* 3, 1988, 275–83). According to Metzger the origin of the canon and the selection or rejection of individual writings was normal and logical. The selection was made on the basis of what was self-evident and 'the survival of the fittest' (286). But what does 'fittest' mean here? Certainly Metzger's book is fascinating for its learning and comprehensive knowledge. But his theological attitude corresponds to that of the church fathers; it is far removed from being historical. Cf. only his verdict on 287: 'No books or collection of books from the ancient Church can be compared with the New Testament in importance for Christian history or doctrine.' Who has ever disputed this commonplace? The problem is that so much that is mutually exclusive has been brought together in collecting the New Testament. At another point Metzger makes critical comments on Helmut Koester's requirement that apocryphal and New Testament Gospels should be treated side by side and remarks: 'To give the impression that, from the point of view of material content, they stand on a par is to betray a lamentable lack of sensitivity.' (166 n.3). In view of this strong dogmatic tendency, one always needs to be careful in using Metzger's book.

Much can still be learned today from the controversy between Adolf Harnack (*Das Neue Testament um das Jahr 200. Theodor Zahn's Geschichte des neutestamentlichen Kanons [Erster Band. Erste Hälfte] geprüft*, 1889) and Theodor Zahn (*Einige Bemerkungen zu Adolf Harnack's Prüfung der Geschichte des neutestamentlichen Kanons [Erster Band. Erste Hälfte*, 1889]). (Cf. Neufeld, *Konflikt* [n.622], 182, and the assiduous work by Uwe Swarat, *Alte Kirche und Neues Testament. Theodor Zahn als Patristiker*, 1991, 331–49.) With historical corrrectness Harnack emphasizes the fact that the New Testament is a new creation, though of course the individual ingredients already existed previously. Zahn's 'account is not a history but a flight from history, because the criticism is tendential criticism' (Harnack, *Das Neue Testament*, 110).

651. Cf. Vielhauer, *Geschichte* (n.10), 775.

652. Ibid., 780f.

653. English translation in Schneemelcher-Wilson I (n.489), 34–6. In addition to the literature mentioned there cf. also Overbeck, *Geschichte* (n.60), 71–142; Adolf von Harnack, 'Über den Verfasser und den literarischen Charakter des Muratorischen Fragments', ZNW 24, 1925, 1–16; Arnold Ehrhardt, 'The Gospels in the Muratorian Fragment' (1953), in id., *The Framework of the New Testament Stories*, 1964, 11–36; Everett Ferguson, 'Canon Muratori: Date and Provenance', in *Studia Patristica* XVII, Part 2, 677–83. The renewed displacement of the Muratorian Canon to the fourth century by Geoffrey M.Hahneman (*The Muratorian Fragment and the Development of the Canon*, 1992) is improbable, since in this case the 'Shepherd of Hermas could not have been composed in the middle of the second century, and this is certain for other reasons'. Cf. CanMur 73–77: 'But Hermas wrote the Shepherd quite lately in our time in the city of Rome, when on the throne of the church of the city of Rome the bishop Pius, his brother, was seated.'

654. Cf. Campenhausen, *Formation* (n.497), 232f. Cf. further above, n.118.

655. Cf. Zahn, *Grundriss* (n.650), 35.

656. Cf. also Harnack, *Origin* (n.650), 218–29 (Appendix 6, which is an examination of Zahn's conclusions on the origin of the New Testament).

657. Uwe Swarat ('Das Werden des neuttestamentlichen Kanons', in Gerhard Maier [ed.], *Der Kanon der Bibel*, 1990, 25–51) makes criticism of Harnack too simple and writes: 'If one understands the New Testament canon as a collection of books to be read out in worship, one can rightly call it a legacy of the apostolic age' (43). But the simple fact that documents were also read out which were not later accepted into the canon already tells against this (e.g. I Clement, Barnabas, Hermas, etc.). So why this anachronism?

658. Cf. above 148–50.

659. On this cf. Andreas Lindemann, 'Die Funktion der Herrenworte in der ethischen Argumentation des Paulus im ersten Korintherbrief', in *The Four Gospels (FS Frans Neyrinck)*, BETL C, 1992, 677–88, though he disputes 'that Paul in any case attaches supreme authority to the instructions of Jesus known to him.'

660. The Jewish Christian Hegesippus, who undertook a journey from Palestine to Rome in the second half of the second century, knows only the

Lord, or the law and the prophets, as the sole criterion. He speaks of the Jerusalem community as though it were the church. James takes this over and is succeeded by his cousin Simeon. Certainly, Hegesippus is aware of the existence of other churches, since his journey takes him through Corinth to Rome, where he was able to convince himself of the right doctrine. That cannot disguise the fact that the Jerusalem church had a special significance for Christianity as a whole. It is not lists of succession to episcopal office in the church centres founded by the apostles, as in Eusebius, which safeguard the orthodoxy of the whole church, but the continuity of those who held office as bishops in Jerusalem in the earliest period. In other words, Hegesippus does not yet know the apostles as bearers of tradition, and thus in the second half of the second century represents an earlier standpoint on the question of the canon (cf. Lüdemann, *Opposition* [n.2], 167).

661. Cf. M. Eugene Boring, 'Christian Prophecy and the Sayings of Jesus. The State of the Question', *NTS* 29, 1983, 104–12 (with bibliography); id., 'The Voice of Jesus in the Apocalypse of John', *NT* 34, 1992, 334–59.

662. Cf. Harnack, *Chronologie* (n.528), 681–700 (the *euaggelion tetramorphon*'); Thornton, *Zeuge* (n.235), 55–7.

663. Against Vielhauer, *Geschichte* (n.10), 738.

664. Thornton, *Zeuge* (n.235), 56.

665. However, it is too much to say 'that Marcion already had the collection of the four canonical Gospels in Rome' (Thornton, *Zeuge*, 62). Cf. Campenhausen, *Formation* (n.497), 173f., and Schneemelcher, 'Bibel' (n.650), 36: Marcion certainly (!) did not have any canon of four Gospels.

666. Gaius in Epiphanius, *Haer* 51 – in the struggle against the Montanists (see n.696 below). It should be noted that Irenaeus already reports a rejection of the Gospel of John by 'orthodox' Christians, cf. *Haer* III 11,9: 'Others again, who reject the gift of the Spirit, which in the latter times has been poured out upon the human race by the good pleasure of the Father, do not admit that aspect presented by John's Gospel in which the Lord promised that he would send the Paraclete, but reject both the Gospel and the prophetic Spirit. They are truly wretched, who wish to be pseudo-prophets, but who set aside the gift of prophecy from the church... By their attitude they basically also reject Paul and his teaching of charisms in I Corinthians and commit the sin against the Holy Spirit.'

667. In addition to *I Apol* 26,1–3, cf. *I Apol* 56,1–4; *Dial* 120,6.

668. On Scheemelcher, 'Bibel' (n.650), 33; there is also a correct observation in ibid., 'The linguistic echoes can only be interpreted as a sign of the general Christian edifying language of this period.' Campenhausen, *Formation* (n.497), 204: 'We do not find any testimony to the Acts of the

Apostles before Irenaeus.' Cf. now the instructive survey by C. K. Barrett, *The Acts of the Apostles* I, ICC, 1994, 30–48 (41–4: Justin).

669. But cf. also Irenaeus, *Haer* III 3,3: 'If then anyone carefully scrutinizes from the Acts of the Apostles the time when he (viz.) Paul went up to Jerusalem on the aforementioned matter (viz. the Apostolic Council), he will find those years mentioned by Paul coinciding with it.' On the use of Acts Harnack comments: 'This book was chosen, not because it was already valid, but because there was no better one and an *acta omnium apostolorum* was needed against Marcion and the Gnostics' (Harnack, *Testament* [n.650], 53). 'Thus Acts is the key to the understanding of the Catholic canon and at the same time shows its "novelty"' (Harnack, *Lehrbuch* I [n.496], 382 n.2 [on 383]). Harnack thinks 'that the placing of this book in the growing canon shows evidence of reflection, of conscious purpose, of a strong hand acting with authority; and that by such conscious action the ideal canon, in outline at least, was realized in the form of the bipartite New Testament both apostolic and catholic' (Harnack, *Origin* [n.650], 69, in italics in Harnack).

670. Cf. Harnack, *Origin* (n.650), 69.

671. Cf. also Col. 4.16; Eph. 3.4; II Cor. 1.13; 3.1.

672. Thus Trobisch, *Entstehung* (n.429); for criticism cf. Andreas Lindemann, *ThLZ* 115, 1990, 682f. On the early copying and circulation of Paul's letters cf. the excellent study by Harry Y. Gamble, *Books and Readers in the Early Church. A History of Early Christian Texts*, 1995, 98f. In contrast to my own view, Gamble thinks that 'Ephesians was intended for broad dissemination from the outset' (98).

673. Schnelle, *Einleitung* (n.10), 407.

674. Cf. Kümmel, *Introduction* (n.368), 487f.

675. Adolf Martin Ritter, 'Die Entstehung des neutestamentlichen Kanons: Selbstdurchsetzung oder autoritative Entscheidung?', in Alaida and Jan Assmann (eds.), *Kanon und Zensur. Archäologie der literarischen Kommunikation* II, 1987, 93–9: 96.

676. Harnack, *Origin* (n.650), 169f.

677. Ibid., 170.

678. Vielhauer, *Geschichte* (n.10), 786.

679. Cf. the following examples from Tertullian, *Praesc* 3; 7; 15; 25; 26. Cf. also 16f. above.

680. Cf. Franz Overbeck, *Über die Auffassung des Streits des Paulus mit Petrus in Antiochien*, 1877 (= 1968), 8.

681. Cf. Noormann, *Irenäus* (n.97), 522, who incomprehensibly underestimates the central place of the passages from the Pastorals mentioned above in the work of Irenaeus. For details of the use of the Pastorals by Irenaeus cf. ibid., 76f. (*Haer* I 10,2/I Tim 2.4); 83f. (*Haer* I 16,3/Titus

3.11,10); 96f. (*Haer* II 20,3/I Tim 1.10); 113f. (*Haer* III 5,3/Titus 2.14); 140f. (*Haer* III 18,7/I Tim 2.5); 337f. (*Haer* V 17,1/I Tim 2.5).

682. For Hebrews and its canonization cf. Overbeck, *Geschichte* (n.60), 1–70.

683. Cf. William Wrede, *Der literarische Rätsel des Hebräerbriefes*, FRLANT 8, 1906, 39–64, who also emphasizes that Hebrews would hardly have been accepted into the New Testament canon without Pauline stylization (85). The 'refutation' by Ohlig, *Begründung* (n.650), 67–75, of the thesis that Hebrews got into the canon only because it was regarded as a letter of Paul is incomplete. Ohlig does not take into account the clear evidence that Hebrews was only later made a letter of Paul.

684. Eusebius, *HE* VI 20, 3: 'And there has reached us also a dialogue of Gaius, a very learned person (which was written in Rome in the time of Zephyrinus), with Proclus the champion of the Phrygian heresy. In this dialogue, in which he curbs the recklessness and audacity of his opponents in composing new scriptures, he mentions only thirteen epistles of the holy apostle, not numbering the Epistle to the Hebrews with the rest; seeing that even to this day among the Romans there are some who do not consider it to be the apostle's.'

685. Eusebius, *HE* V, 26: of Irenaeus is extant 'a certain book of various discourses, in which he mentions the Epistle to the Hebrews and the so-called Wisdom of Solomon, quoting some passages from them'.

686. He regards it as a letter of Barnabas and writes in *Pud* 20: 'And, of course, the Epistle of Barnabas is more generally received among the churches than that apocryphal "Shepherd" (= Hermas) of adulterers.'

687. Cf. Dieter Lührmann, 'Gal 2⁹ und die katholischen Briefe. Bemerkungen zum Kanon und zur *regula fidei*', ZNW 72, 1981, 65–87; Ohlig, *Begründung* (n.650), 75–81.

688. *HE* II 23, 25; VI 14, 1.

689. For the details cf. Lührmann, 'Gal 2' (n.687), and the particularly rich information on the individual letters in Bleek, *Einleitung* (n.650).

690. Cf. already Muratorian Canon 47–50: 'The blessed apostle Paul himself, following the rule of his predecessor John, writes by name to seven churches...'

691. Thus in Andrew of Caesarea in the preface to his commentary on Acts, PG 106, 220 (reprinted in Lindemann/Paulsen, *Die apostolischen Väter*, 1992, 296).

692. On this cf. Schneemelcher -Wilson II (n.243), 620–39.

693. Cf. Norbert Brox, *Der Hirt des Hermas*, KAV 7, 1991.

694. Cf. Harnack, *Origin* (n.650), 83–93 ('Why has only one Apocalypse been able to keep its place in the New Testament? Why not several – or none at all?').

695. Eusebius, *HE* II 25, 6; III 28, 1f.; III 31, 4.

696. Epiphanius, *Haer* 51, 4,5: 'The writings of John do not agree with the other apostles.' 'They accept neither the Gospel of John nor his revelation' (51, 3, 3). Epiphanius polemically calls the defenders of this statement Alogoi, because they are without understanding (51, 3, 3). It follows from Eusebius *HE* III 28, 2, that the Roman presbyter Gaius is an influential member of this group (cf. Hengel, *Question* [n.563], 26–8).

697. Campenhausen, *Formation* (n.497), 327.

698. Hans von Campenhausen, 'Die Entstehung des Neuen Testaments' (1962), in Ernst Käsemann (ed.), *Das Neue Testament als Kanon. Dokumentation und kritische Analyse zur gegenwärtigen Diskussion*, 1970, 109–23: 110.

699. Harnack, *Testament* (n.650), 14.

700. We cannot investigate here the question whether Montanism played a decisive role in the development of the canon. On this cf. Henning Paulsen, 'Die Bedeutung des Montanismus für die Herausbildung des Kanons', *VigChr* 23, 1978, 19–52 (with bibliography).

701. Campenhausen, 'Enstehung' (n.497), 384 (the book ends with these remarks).

702. Unfortunately Adolf Martin Ritter ('Hans von Campenhausen und Adolf von Harnack', *ZThK* 87, 1990, 323–39) does not go into this point. A similar departure from history is to be noted in Campenhausen's endorsement of the physical resurrection of Jesus (cf. Lüdemann, *Resurrection* [n.3],18). Harnack energetically denies this and puts forward the (subjective) vision hypothesis (cf. Lüdemann, *Resurrection*, 221 n.353). Harnack's critical position is certainly to be preferred in both the questions addressed.

703. Schmithals, *Theologiegeschichte* (n.68), 301.

704. Alfred Loisy, *The Gospel and the Church*, 1903, 166.

705. Cf. on this and on Loisy generally the informative account by Gerhard Heinz, *Das Problem der Kirchenentstehung in der deutschen protestantischen Theologie des 20.Jahrhunderts*, TST 4, 1974, 122–39 (122 n.480, examples of misunderstandings of Loisy's concern).

706. Adolf Harnack, *What is Christianity?* (1900), reissued 1957. Loisy's work is a direct answer to Harnack. Cf. Harnack's review of Loisy, *Evangelium*, *ThLZ* 29, 1904, 598f. Harnack acknowledges many of Loisy's statements, 'not as an opposition but as a supplement, the need for which was not first made clear to me by Loisy' (59). Franz Overbeck sees in this review of Harnack's an obligatory silence and an act of wisdom (Franz Overbeck, *Werke und Nachlass*, Vol.4, 1995, 553). However, this is unfair to Harnack, as is most of what Overbeck wrote about him. Nevertheless, a synthesis of Overbeck and Harnack is indicated today in

the framework of a historical retrospect and the new beginning presented by the challenge of the third millennium.

707. Loisy, *Gospel* (n.704), 166.

708. Sanders, *Jesus* (n.148), 330. Cf. also the 'rule' of the Jesus Seminar: 'Beware of finding a Jesus entirely congenial to you' (Funk/Hoover, *Gospels* [n.10], 5).

709. Cf. Matt 18.12–14 with the parallel Luke 15.3–7, which emphasizes at the redactional level (v.7) – in a truly Lukan way – conversion as a condition of salvation.

710. Cf. the crystal-clear acount by Sanders, *Figure* (n.148), 239–48.

711. This is related twice in the New Testament, independently, in Mark 2.1–12; Luke 7.36–50. For the problem cf. Ingo Broer, 'Jesus und das Gesetz. Anmerkungen zur Geschichte des Problems und zur Frage der Sündenvergebung durch den historischen Jesus', in id. (ed.), *Jesus und das jüdische Gesetz*, 1992, 61–104 (with bibliography).

712. Cf. II Cor. 5.31; John 8.46; I John 3.5; I Peter 2.22. Cf. esp. Heb.4.15: Jesus 'was tempted in all things as we are, yet without sinning.' Erich Grässer (*An die Hebräer*, EKK XVII/1,1990) does not want to understand the text 'in the sense of a dogmatically guided picture of the sinlessness of Jesus, but in accordance with contextual exegesis' (256), and emphasizes: '"Without sinning" means that Jesus did not yield to the danger of possible apostasy' (ibid.). But doesn't that amount to the same thing?

713. On Udo Schnelle, *Neutestamentliche Anthropologie. Jesus – Paulus – Johannes*, BThSt 18, 1991, 176: 'Anyone in search of the humanity must look at Jesus. He will recognize that the one man Jesus Christ is wholly God. Jesus' humanity can only be understood in terms of his Godhead, for Jesus did not live from himself, but in a unique bond with the Father ... Anyone who ignore the humanity of Jesus or takes offence at his divinity gets him quite wrong.' These are no longer historical statements. Cf. also the two following notes.

714. One might recall Friedrich Nietzsche, *Beyond Good and Evil* (n.392), no.65a: 'We are most dishonourable towards our God: he is not *permitted* to sin.'

715. The baptism of John took place 'for the forgiveness of sins. It was the... guarantee that in the future final judgment God himself will not impute to those who have been baptized sins committed before baptism' (Stegemann, *Essener* [n.8], 303). However, we can ignore this, since here we are concerned only with Jesus' consciousness of sin.

716. Cf. Theodor Lorenzmeier, 'Wider das Dogma von der Sündlosigkeit Jeus', *EvTh* 31, 1971, 452–71. It is significant that this bold approach immediately had to be commented on by one of the then co-editors of the

journal: Helmut Gollwitzer, 'Zur Frage der "Sündlosigkeit Jesu"', ibid., 496–506. Gollwitzer complains 'that there is no special reflection on the concept of sin in Lorenzmeier. Clearly he takes it for granted that this term is so much a matter of course that it does not need to be clarified' (501). According to Gollwitzer, the doctrine of the sinlessness of Jesus 'relates neither to a self-attestation of the historical man Jesus nor to the observation of others... What is presented here is not empirical evidence but an eschatological verdict' (505). And finally: '(T)he resurrection as the "valid testimony" to the righteousness of this crucified one is the source for the doctrine of the sinlessness of Jesus which the New Testament takes so 'for granted' – not, however, the resurrection as an isolated miracle performed on the individual Jesus but as the revelation of the dawn of the kingdom of God which he announced, as the revelation not only of his but in him also of our new, sinless, obedient, free and fulfilled life' (506). With due respect, Gollwitzer's remarks are a classic example of the way in which the historical is completely unhinged by eschatology. Lorenzmeier and all those who follow him have the New Testament texts on their side; these still betray the fact that Jesus did not claim sinlessness for his own person. That can be said without defining the concept of sin.

717. Walter Bauer, *Das Leben Jesu im Zeitalter der neutestamentlichen Apokryphen*, 1909 (= 1967), 330.

718. Translation follows Schneemelcher -Wilson I (n.489), 133.

719. Cf. the full survey by Bauer, *Leben* (n.717), 329–33. For the baptism of Jesus see ibid., 110–41. In the third-century 'Preaching of Paul' Jesus explicitly confesses his own sin (cf. Bauer, *Leben*, 110f., and Schneemelcher-Wilson II [n.243], 33).

720. Pannenberg, *Creed* (n.624), 60f.

721. As soon as they become doctrines or even dogmas everything goes wrong here. Johannes Müller commented on this in his day: 'Quite spontaneously the idea came to me that God is quite indifferent to what we believe and that the exclusively important thing is that we believe, that faith is alive in us as an element of our beings, as a sense and sensitivity for life in which we encounter God as present. At any rate, God only smiles at orthodox and other doctrines in all the religions and systems of thought, at all grandiose earthly views, and simply shakes his head over the pious way in which importance is attached to them. God has deep compassion for those who have such a yoke of faith hung round their necks, under which they quail with fear and doubt in consciousness and consciences. Before God, doctrines of the divinity of Christ, the Holy Spirit and all the other pieces are similarly childish babbling and the foolish fantasies of human, all-too-human vanities of images of God' (Johannes Müller, *Grüne Blätter. Zeitschrift für persönliche und allgemeine Lebensfragen*,

Vol.XXXVIII, 1936, 119f.).

722. Wrede, 'Paulus', in Rengstorf, *Paulusbild* (n.232), 96.

723. For the relationship between Jesus and Paul see the profound analysis by Jüngel, *Paulus* (n.332).

724. Nigg, *Buch der Ketzer* (n.76), 428.

725. Cf.also the rich study on the history of its exegesis by Walter Bauer, 'Das Gebot der Feindesliebe und die alten Christen' (1917), in id., *Aufsätze und Kleine Schriften*, ed. Georg Strecker, 1967, 235–52.

726. Cf. Käsemann, 'III, Zusammenfassung', in id., *Kanon* (n.698), 399–410: 403; cf. also Wagner, *Lage* (n.17), 80.

727. Therefore there is also no reason to follow Falk Wagner (*Lage*) in regarding only 'maintaining the canonical validity of the Old Testament ... as problematical' (86). Maintaining the canonical validity of the New Testament is equally problematical. But they both derive their real significance from Jesus. Cf. also Fritz Maass, *Was ist Christentum?* , 1982, 95: 'If there is a renewal of Christianity, it can only have as its basis the interpretation of human life through Israel and Jesus.'

728. Cf. Wagner, *Lage*, passim. At last a systematic theologian has found the courage to make clear statements here, especially also on 'a newly imposed biblical theology' (85) which 'is causing what was once the critical and enlightened profile of Protestant exegesis to sink under the mass of a new confusion' (86).

729. Julius Wellhausen, *Skizzen und Vorarbeiten. Sechstes Heft*, 1899, 165.

730. Cf. Wagner, *Lage*, 51–7; for the consequences in the present cf. 54: 'The authoritarian model of the proclamation of the word which maintains the fiction that God himself speaks through the mouth of church officials contributes to the increasing speechlessness on the part of members far and near.'

731. To the possible criticism that the Jesus and his message which I have reconstructed is too narrow a basis for a modern Christianity, I reply with John Hick: '(A) Christian does not have to accept those philosophical and theological theories of the third and fourth centuries. I think that we can base our Christianity upon Jesus' teachings concerning the reality and love and claim of God, and upon the love ethic that has developed out of it. This provides a framework for life regardless of how much or how little detail we know for sure about Jesus' life' ('A Remonstrance in Concluding', in *Jesus in History and Myth*, ed. R. Joseph Hoffmann and Gerald A. Larue, 1986, 211–17:214).

Bibliography

Barnett, Albert E., *Paul Becomes a Literary Influence*, 1941

Bauer, Walter, *Aufsätze und Kleine Schriften*, 1967

—, *Das Leben Jesu im Zeitalter der neutestamentlichen Apokryphen*, 1909 (= 1967)

—, *Orthodoxy and Heresy in Earliest Christianity* (1934), second enlarged edition by Georg Strecker, 1964

Becker, Jürgen, *Paulus. Der Apostel der Volker*, 1989

Berger, Klaus, *Theologiegeschichte des Urchristentums. Theologie des Neuen Testaments*, 1994

Bernoulli, Carl Albrecht, *Die wissenschaftliche und die kirchliche Methode in derTheologie*, 1897

Betz, Hans Dieter, *Galatians*, Hermeneia, 1988

Brox, Norbert, *Offenbarung, Gnosis und gnostischer Mythos bei Irenäus von Lyon*, 1966

— (ed.), *Pseudepigraphie in der heidnischen und jüdisch-christlichen Antike*, WdF CDLXXXIV, 1977

—, *Falsche Verfasserangaben. Zur Erklärung der frühchristlichen Pseudepigraphie*, SBS 79, 1975

Campenhausen, Hans von, *Ecclesiastical Authority and Spiritual Power in the Church of the First Three Centuries*, 1969

—, 'Das Bekenntnis im Urchristentum', ZNW 63, 1972 = id., *Urchristliches und Altkirchliches*, 1979, 217–72

—, *The Formation of the Christian Bible*, 1972

—, 'Irenäus und das Neue Testament', ThLZ 90, 1965, cols. 1–8

—, 'Polycarp von Smyrna und die Pastoralbriefe' (1951), in id., *Aus der Frühzeit des Christentums. Studien zur Kirchengeschichte des ersten und zweiten Jahrhunderts*, 1963, 197–252

—, *The Fathers of the Greek Church*, 1963

—, *The Fathers of the Latin Church*, 1964

—, 'Des Alte Testament als Bibel der Kirche vom Ausgang des Urchristentums bis zur Entstehung des Neuen Testaments', in id., *Aus der Frühzeit des Christentums. Studien zur Kirchengeschichte des ersten und zweiten Jahrhunderts*, 1963, 152–96

Chadwick, Henry, 'Die Absicht des Epheserbriefes' ZNW 51, 1960. 145–53

Colpe, Carsten, *Das Siegel der Propheten. Historische Beziehungen zwischen Judentum, Judenchristentum, Heidentum und frühem Islam*, ANTZ 3, 1990

Conzelmann, Hans, *A History of Primitive Christianity*, 1973

—, *An Outline of the Theology of the New Testament*, 1969

—, *Theologie als Schriftauslegung*, BEvTh 65, 1974

Dassmann, Ernst, *Der Stachel im Fleisch. Paulus in der frühchristlichen Literatur bis Irenäus*, 1979

Dunn, James D.G., *Unity and Diversity in the New Testament. An Enquiry into the Character of Earliest Christianity*, 1990

Elze, Martin, 'Häresie und Einheit der Kirche im 2. Jahrhundert', ZThK 71, 1974, 389–409

Funk, Robert W., Roy W. Hoover, The Jesus Seminar, *The Five Gospels. The Search for the Authentic Words of Jesus*, 1993

Gager, John, 'Das Ende der Zeit und die Entstehung von Gemeinschaften', in Wayne A. Meeks (ed.), *Zur Soziologie des Urchristentums*, ThB 62, 1979, 88–130

Georgi, Dieter, *Der Armen zu gedenken. Die Geschichte der Kollekte des Paulus für Jerusalem*, second revised and enlarged edition, 1994

—, *Die Geschichte der Kollekte des Paulus für Jerusalem*, ThF 38, 1965

Goodspeed, Edgar J, *The Formation of the New Testament*, 1926

—, *The Key to Ephesians*, 1956

—, *The Meaning of Ephesians*, 1933

—, *New Solutions of New Testament Problems*, 1927

Goppelt, Leonhard, *Christentum und Judentum im ersten und zweiten Jahrhundert. Ein Aufriss der Urgeschichte der Kirche*, BFChTh 2/55, 1954

Haenchen, Ernst, *The Acts of the Apostles*, 1974

Harnack, Adolf, *Bible Reading in the Early Church*, 1912

—, *The Origin of the New Testament and the Most Important Consequences of the New Creation* (1914), 1925

—, *Geschichte der altchristlichen Literatur bis Eusebius, Teil II: Die Chronologie, Band 1: Die Chronologie der Literatur bis Irenäus nebst einleitenden Untersuchungen*, 1958

—, *Über den dritten Johannesbrief*, TU 15/3b, 1897

—, *Judentum und Judenchristentum in Justins Dialog mit Trypho*, TU 39. 1, 1913

—, *Lehrbuch der Dogmengeschichte. I. Die Entstehung des kirchlichen Dogmas*, ⁴1909

—, *Marcion. Das Evangelium vom fremden Gott. Neue Studien zu Marcion*, TU 45/1, 1924 (= 1960)

—, 'Die Neuheit des Evangeliums nach Markion' (1929), in id., *Aus der*

323

Werkstatt des Vollendeten, 1930, 128–43

—, 'Das Problem des zweiten Thessalonicherbriefs', *SB* 1910, 560–78
(= id., *Kleine Schriften zur alten Kirche* II, 1980, 560–78)

—, 'Untersuchungen über den apokryphen Briefwechsel der Korinther mit
dem Apostel Paulus' (1905), in *Kleine Schriften zur Alten Kirche,
Berliner Akademieschriften 1890–1907*, 1980, 737–69

—, *What is Christianity?* (1900), reissued 1957

Hengel, Martin, *The Johannine Question*, 1989

—, 'Jakobus der Herrenbruder – der erste "Papst"?', in *Glaube und
Eschatologie. Festschrift für Werner Georg Kümmel zum 80.Geburtstag*
(ed. Erich Grässer and Otto Merk), 1985, 71–104

—, *The Zealots. An Investigation into the Jewish Freedom Movement in
the Period from Herod I until 70 AD*, 1989

Hilgenfeld, Adolf, D*ie Ketzergeschichte der Urchristenthums urkundlich
dargestellt*, 1884 (= 1966)

Holl, Karl, 'Zur Auslegung des 2. Artikels des sog. apostolischen Glaubensbekenntnisses' (1919), in id., *Gesammelte Aufsätze zur Kirchengeschichte II, Der Osten*, 1928, 115–22

—, 'Der Kirchenbegriff des Paulus in seinem Verhältnis zu dem der
Urgemeinde' (1921), in id., *Gesammelte Aufsätze zur Kirchengeschichte
II. Der Osten*, 1928, 44–67

—, 'Tertullian als Schriftsteller' (1897), = id., *Gesammelte Aufsätze zur
Kirchengeschichte* I–II, 1928, 1–12

Holmberg, Bengt, *Paul and Power*, CB.NT 11, 1978

Käsemann, Ernst, 'Ketzer und Zeuge. Zum johanneischen Verfasserproblem', (1951), in id., *Exegetische Versuche und Besinnungen* I, 1960,
168–87

— (ed.), *Das Neue Testament als Kanon. Dokumentation und kritische
Analyse zur gegenwärtigen Diskussion*, 1970

Kelly, J. N. D., *Early Christian Creeds*, 1950

Klauck, Hans-Josef, *Der erste Johannesbrief*, EKK XXIII/1, 1991

—, *Der zweite und dritte Johannesbrief*, EKK XXIII/2, 1992

—, *Die Johannesbriefe*, EdF 276, 1991

Klein, Günter, 'Der Synkretismus als theologisches Problem in der ältesten
christlichen Apologetik', ZThK 64, 1967, 40–82 (= id., *Rekonstruktion
und Interpretation*, BEvTh 50, 1969, 262–301)

Klijn, A. F. J., 'The Apocryphal Correspondence between Paul and the
Corinthians', *VigChr* 17, 1963, 2–23

— and Reinink, G. J., *Patristic Evidence for Jewish Christian Sects*, NT.S
36, 1973

Knox, John, *Marcion and the New Testament*, 1942 (= 1980)

Köster, Helmut, *Einführung in das Neue Testament im Rahmen der*

Religionsgeschichte und Kulturgeschichte der hellenistischen und römischen Zeit, 1980 (= Koester, Helmut, *Introduction to the New Testament*, 1984)

—, *Ancient Christian Gospels. Their History and Development*, 1990

—, 'Häretiker im Urchristentum', *RGG³* 3, 1959, cols. 17–21

— and James M. Robinson, *Trajectories through Early Christianity*, 1971

Koschorke, Klaus, *Die Polemik der Gnostiker gegen das kirchliche Christentum*, Nag Hammadi Studies XII, 1978

—, 'Paulus in den Nag-Hammadi-Texten', *ZThK* 78, 1981, 177–205

Krüger, Gustav, *Das Dogma vom neuen Testament*, 1896

Kümmel, Werner Georg, *Römer 7 und das Bild des Menschen im Neuen Testament. Zwei Studien*, ThB 53, 1974

Lampe, Peter, *Die stadtrömischen Christen in den ersten beiden Jahrhunderten*, WUNT II 18, ²1989

Lietzmann, Hans, *A History of the Early Church. I. The Beginnings of the Early Church* (1932), ³1953; 2. *The Founding of the Church Universal*, 1938

Lindemann, Andreas, 'Zum Abfassungszweck des Zweiten Thessalonicherbriefes', *ZNW* 68, 1977, 35–47

—, 'Der Apostel Paulus im 2. Jahrhundert', in Jean-Marie Sevrin (ed.), *The New Testament in Early Christianity*, BETL LXXXVI, 1989, 39–67

—, *Die Aufhebung der Zeit. Geschichtsverständnis und Eschatologie im Epheserbrief*, StNT 12, 1975

—, 'Bemerkungen zu den Adressaten und zum Anlass des Epheserbriefes', *ZNW* 67, 1976, 235–51

—, 'Paulus und die korinthische Eschatologie. Zur These von einer "Entwicklung" im paulinischen Denken', *NTS* 37, 1991, 373–99

—, *Paulus im ältesten Christentum. Das Bild des Apostels und die Rezeption der paulinischen Theologie in der frühchristlichen Literatur bis Marcion*, BHTh 58, 1979

Loisy, Alfred, *The Gospel and the Church*, 1903

Lona, Horacio E., *Über die Auferstehung der Fleisches*, BZNW 66, 1993

—, *Die Eschatologie im Kolosser- und Epheserbrief*, fzb 48, 1984

Lorenzmeier, Theodor, 'Wider das Dogma von der Sündlosigkeit Jesu', *EvTh* 31, 1971, 452–73

Lüdemann, Gerd, *The Resurrection of Jesus. History, Experience, Theology*, 1994

—, *Earliest Christianity according to the Traditions in the Acts of the Apostles. A Commentary*, 1989

—, *Paul, Apostle to the Gentiles, 1, Studies in Chronology*, 1984

—, *Opposition to Paul in Earliest Jewish Christianiy*, 1989

Marxsen, Willi, *Der Zweite Thessalonicherbrief*, ZBK 11, 2, 1982

Meeks, Wayne A., *The First Urban Christians. The Social World of the Apostle Paul*, 1983

Merklein, Helmut, 'Paulinische Theologie in der Rezeption des Kolosser- und Epheserbriefes', in Karl Kertelge (ed.), *Paulus in den neutestamentlichen Spätschriften*, QD 89, 1981, 25–69

Metzger, Bruce M., *The New Testament Canon*, 1987

Mödritzer, Helmut, *Stigma und Charisma im Neuen Testament und seiner Umwelt. Zur Soziologie des Urchristentums*, NTOA 28, 1994

Müller, Ulrich B., *Zür frühchristlichen Theologiegeschichte*, 1976

Munck, Johannes, *Paul and the Salvation of Mankind*, 1959

Nigg, Walter, *Das Buch der Ketzer*, ⁴1962

—, *Geschichte des religiösen Liberalismus*, 1937

—, *Franz Overbeck. Versuch einer Würdigung*, 1931

Noormann, Rolf, *Irenäus als Paulusinterpret. Zur Rezeption und Wirkung der paulinischen und deuteropaulinischen Briefe im Werk des Irenäus von Lyon*, WUNT II, 66, 1994

Overbeck. Franz, *Über die Auffassung des Streits des Paulus mit Petrus in Antiochien*, 1877 (= 1968)

—, *Zur Geschichte des Kanons*, 1880 (= 1965)

Pagels, Elaine, *The Gnostic Gospels*, 1980

Pannenberg, Wolfhart, *The Apostles' Creed in the Light of Today's Questions*, 1973

—, 'The Crisis of the Scriptural Principle' (1962), in *Basic Questions in Theology* I, 1970, 1–14

Paulsen, Henning, 'Zur Wissenschaft vom Urchristentum und der alten Kirche – ein methodischer Versuch', ZNW 68, 1977, 200–30

Peel, Malcolm Lee, *The Epistle to Rheginos. A Valentinian Letter on the Resurrection*, 1969

Pratscher, Wilhelm, *Der Herrenbruder Jakobus und die Jakobustradition*, FRLANT 139, 1987

Rengstorf, Karl Heinrich (ed.), *Das Paulusbild in der neueren deutschen Forschung*, WdF XXIV, ³1982

Ritter, Adolf Martin, *Charisma und Caritas. Aufsätze zur Geschichte der Alten Kirche*, 1993

—, 'Die Enstehung des neutestamentlichen Kanons: Selbstdurchsetzung oder autoritative Entscheiden?', in Alaida and Jan Assmann (ed.), *Kanon und Zensur. Archäologie der literarischen Kommunikation* II, 1987, 93–9

—, 'Hans von Campenhausen und Adolf von Harnack', ZThK 87, 1990, 323–39

Robinson, James M., 'Die Bedeutung der gnostischen Nag Hammadi Texte für die neutestamentliche Wissenschaft', in *Religious Propaganda and*

Missionary Competition in the New Testament World. Essays Honoring Dieter Georgi, NTS 74, 1994, 23–41

—, 'Jesus – from Easter to Valentinus (or to the Apostles' Creed)', *JBL* 101, 1982, 5–37

Roloff, Jürgen, *Die Kirche im Neuen Testament*, 1993

—, *Der Erste Timotheusbrief*, EKK XV 15, 1988

Sanders, E. P., 'Jewish Association with Gentiles in Galatians 2:11–14', in *The Conversation Continues, Essays on Paul and John. In Honor of J. Louis Martyn* (ed. Robert T. Fortna and Beverly R. Gaventa), 1990, 170–88

—, *The Historical Figure of Jesus*, 1993

—, *Jesus and Judaism*, 1985

—, *Paul and Palestinian Judaism*, 1977

Schmithals, Walter, *Theologiegeschichte des Urchristentums. Ein problemgeschichtliche Darstellung*, 1994

Schnackenburg, Rudolf, *Der Brief an die Epheser*, EKK X, 1982

Schneemelcher, Wilhelm and R. McL.Wilson, *New Testament Apocrypha* I, ²1991; *New Testament Apocrypha* II, ²1992

Schnelle, Udo, *Einleitung in das neue Testament*, UTB 1830, 1994

Schoeps, Hans-Joachim, *Paul. The Theology of the Apostle in the Light of Jewish Religious History*, 1961

—, *Theologie und Geschichte des Judenchristentums*, 1949

Schottroff, Luise, *Lydia's Impatient Sisters. A Feminist Social History of Early Christianity*, 1995

Schüssler-Fiorenza, E., *In Memory of Her. A Feminist Theological Reconstruction of Christian Origins*, 1983

Speyer, Wolfgang, *Die literarische Falschung im heidnischen und christlichen Altertum. Ein Versuch ihrer Deutung*, HKAW I, 2, 1971

Stegemann, Hartmut, *Die Essener, Qumran, Johannes der Täufer und Jesus. Ein Sachbuch*, ⁴1994

Strecker, Georg, 'Chiliasmus und Doketismus in der johanneischen Schule', *KuD* 38, 1992, 30–46

—, *Eschaton und Historie*, 1979

—, *Die Johannesbriefe*, KEK 14, 1989

—, *Das Judenchristentum in den Pseudoklementinen*, TU 70, 1958 (²1981)

—, Appendix to Walter Bauer, *Orthodoxy and Heresy in Earliest Christianity*, 1964, 241–85

Trilling, Wolfgang, *Der zweite Brief an die Thessalonicher*, EKK XIV, 1980

Vallée, Gérard, *A Study in Anti-gnostic Polemics. Irenaeus, Hippolytus and Epiphanius*, 1981

Vielhauer, Philipp, *Geschichte der urchristlichen Literatur. Ein!eitung in* das Neue Testament, die Apokryphen und die Apostolischen Väter, 1975

Vögtle, A., *Die Dynamik des Anfangs. Leben und Fragen der jungen Kirche*, 1988

Vouga, François, *Die Johannesbriefe*, HNT 15/III, 1990

Wagner, Falk, *Zur gegenwärtigen Lage des Protestantismus*, 1995

Weinel, Heinrich, *Paulus. Der Mensch und sein Werk: Die Anfänge des Christentums, der Kirche und des Dogmas*, Lebensfragen, 1904

Weiss, Johannes, *Jesus' Proclamation of the Kingdom of God* (1892); second fully revised edition, *Die Predigt Jesu vom Reich Gottes*, 1900

—, *Earliest Christianity* (1917), reissued 1957

Wengst, Klaus, *Bedrängte Gemeinde und verherrlichter Christus. Ein Versuch über das Johannesevangelium*, 1990

Wenz, Gunther, 'Sola Scriptura? Erwägungen zum reformatorischen Schriftprinzip', in Jan Rohls and id. (ed)., *Vernunft des Glaubens. Wissenschaftliche Theologie und kirchliche Lehre* (FS Wolfhart Pannenberg), 1988

Wolter, Michael, *Die Pastoralbriefe als Paulustradition*, FRLANT 146, 1988

Wrede, William, *Die Echtheit des zweiten Thessalonicherbriefs untersucht*, TU 24.2, 1903

Index of Authors

Lutz, H., 238
Luz, U., 231, 233

Maas, F., 321
MacDonald, D. R., 290
MacDonald, M. Y., 242
Malherbe, A., 308, 309
Markschies, C., 238, 241, 245, 288
Martyn, J. L., 302
Marxsen, W., 114, 280, 281–3
Mason, S., 266
May, G., 295
Meade, D. E., 278
Meeks, W. A., 238, 245, 269, 303
Mehlhausen, J., 232
Meijering, E. P., 240, 299
Meinhold, P., 238
Merk, O., 251, 262
Merkel, H., 285
Merklein, H., 242, 270, 271, 286
Metzger, B. M., 278, 313
Michel, O., 240
Mimouni, S. C., 250
Mitton, C. L., 285
Mödritzer, H., 255
Moeller, B., 238
Mosheim, J. L. v., 6, 238, 241
Mühlenberg, E., 238, 288
Müller, H. M., 235, 237, 269
Müller, J., 320
Müller, K., 242, 251
Müller, U. B., 138, 290
Munck, J., 45, 259
Murphy-O'Connor, J., 269
Mussner, F., 286

Neufeld, K. H., 309, 313
Neusner, J., 255
Niebuhr, K.-W., 274, 276
Nietzsche, F., xvi, 231, 283, 293, 294, 319

Nigg, W., 238–41, 309, 321
Nitzsch, F., 243
Noormann, R., 246, 250, 276, 313
Norris, F. W., 241

Oberlinner, L., 288
Oepke, A., 267
Ohlig, K.-H., 312, 317
Ollrog, W.-H., 273
Osten-Sacken, P. van der, 261, 276
Ott, H., 235
Overbeck, F., 8, 148, 239, 240, 270, 314, 316–18

Pagels, E., 246, 249
Pannenberg, W., 2, 191, 212, 232, 234, 255, 268, 310, 311, 320
Paulsen, H., 231, 280, 317, 318
Pearson, B. A., 242
Peel, M. L., 135, 287, 288
Peter, N., 240
Pfister, O., 73, 237, 268
Pratscher, W., 251
Pritz, R. A., 250

Räisänen, H., 240
Rebell, W., 259, 303
Regull, J., 295
Reinbold, W., 277
Reinink, G. J., 261, 262
Reinmuth, E., 274
Reiser, M., 273
Reitzenstein, R., 275
Renan, E., 267
Rengstorf, K. H., 262, 267
Reventlow, H. Graf, 283
Riesner, R., 263
Rigaux, B., 262
Ringleben, J., 234
Rist, M., 281, 292

Subject Index